6
SIXTH
EDITION

Invitation to Critical Thinking

JOEL RUDINOW

SANTA ROSA JUNIOR COLLEGE

VINCENT E. BARRY

BAKERSFIELD COLLEGE

THOMSON

✦

WADSWORTH

Australia • Brazil • Canada • Mexico • Singapore • Spain • United Kingdom • United States

THOMSON

WADSWORTH ™

Invitation to Critical Thinking, Sixth Edition
Joel Rudinow and Vincent E. Barry

Acquisitions Editor: *Worth Hawes*
Editorial Assistant: *Patrick Stockstill*
Technology Project Manager: *Julie Aguilar*
Marketing Manager: *Christina Shea*
Marketing Assistant: *Mary Anne Payumo*
Marketing Communications Manager: *Stacey Purviance*
Project Manager, Editorial Production: *Samen Iqbal*
Creative Director: *Rob Hugel*
Art Director: *Maria Epes*

Print Buyer: *Linda Hsu*
Permissions Editor: *Roberta Broyer*
Production Service: *Graphic World Publishing Services*
Copy Editor: *Graphic World Publishing Services*
Cover Designer: *Yvo Riezebos*
Cover Printer: *Thomson West*
Compositor: *International Typesetting and Composition*
Printer: *Thomson West*

Library of Congress Control Number: 2006940532

ISBN-13: 978-0-495-10371-4
ISBN-10: 0-495-10371-3

Thomson Higher Education
10 Davis Drive
Belmont, CA 94002-3098
USA

For more information about our products, contact us at:
Thomson Learning Academic Resource Center
1-800-423-0563

For permission to use material from this text or product,
submit a request online at **http://www.thomsonrights.com.**
Any additional questions about permissions can be submitted
by e-mail to **thomsonrights@thomson.com.**

PREFACE

Reflecting on the occasion of this sixth edition of *Invitation to Critical Thinking*, we find it rather sobering to realize that this textbook is as old as many of the students who read it. Much has changed in the world since this book was first published, and so the book itself has had to change to remain in touch with the world inhabited by its students. Many of the examples we used in earlier editions have disappeared from common shared awareness down the memory hole into the dustbin of history. And yet the need in this generation for basic critical thinking skills remains as deep and urgent as ever. And so, although we have had to overhaul the book's contents considerably, the instructional agenda remains the same. We continue to focus on the recognition, analysis, evaluation, and composition of arguments as discursive tools of rational persuasion. New and newly revised topical coverage includes:

- Bloom's taxonomy: the cognitive and affective dimensions of thinking and language yields much clearer exposition of reference, denotation, and connotation in language;
- Revised casting system consistent with prevailing graphic conventions;
- Inclusive and exclusive disjunction;
- Constructive and destructive dilemma;
- Fallacy of illicit disjunctive syllogism;
- Mill's Method of Residues;
- Inference to the best explanation;
- False inference to the best explanation;
- Internet research tools and tips.

The technology of education has been revolutionized in the Information Age. The lecture/discussion approach typical of classroom management a generation ago now seems increasingly quaint and primitive in comparison to the 24-hour global virtual classroom imagined in so many of the educational planning documents we're seeing today. The pace of change is all but overwhelming. One thing it has forced us to do as authors of a textbook is to think rather deeply about *how* we teach critical thinking, and about how we *might* teach critical thinking. And this has in turn brought two perennial challenges into sharp focus. The first challenge shows up in the observation—confirmed in our classroom experience over and over for years—that the critical thinking course seems generally to work best for those students who already think critically. Such students tend to develop and flourish in the course and seem to get a great deal out of it. Conversely, the students who are most desperately in need of instruction in critical thinking tend to find the text and the course so profoundly baffling and disorienting that they easily give up on it before they show or see any progress. Yet these are the students one most wants to reach. A second and related challenge has to do with integrating two essential areas of instructional emphasis that nevertheless seem inevitably at odds with each other. On the one hand, there is a need to break the complexity of critical thinking down into manageable chunks and provide the kind of exercise that moves the student in an orderly way through the material, building skill from the ground up toward greater and more advanced mastery. This is especially important for the student who finds the material most challenging and unfamiliar. On the other hand, there is the need to ground and motivate study by demonstrating the relevance of the material in "real world" applications, where unfortunately you never find things broken down according to the instructional agenda of the course, however that agenda has been laid out. In this new edition you will find introductory analytical overviews of each Unit to orient you to the instructional agenda throughout the book.

We are committed in this book to an approach to teaching and learning that we would call "dialogical." Students learn best when they fully "engage with" the text. We want to do whatever we can think of to get the reader engaged in a dialogue. The text is designed accordingly to engage the student in a variety of intellectual activities and exercises organized by means of "Dialogue Boxes" interspersed throughout each of the chapters. These include:

- Definitions—where crucial terminology is defined and explained;
- Thought Experiments—where scenarios and other exercises in imagination and hypothetical reasoning are woven into expository passages of the text;
- Application Exercises—to support learning transfer;
- Review Exercises—self-testing quizzes to support learning retention;
- And Speaking of—where topics covered in the text are linked to current events;
- Writing Assignments—which also make good topics for class discussion;
- Discussion Topics—which also make good topics for writing assignments;
- The Term Project Series—a series of exercises indicated by this icon 🖎 and running throughout the text to integrate the entire Critical Thinking skill set;
- Answers & Hints Appendix—to reinforce learning; exercises accompanied by this ✳ icon are addressed in the Appendix.

Ancillary to the text itself, a host of supporting tools and materials are available through the book's website: http://www.thomsonedu.com/philosophy/ Rudinow. These include:

- Summaries and study guides—overviews outlining learning objectives for each chapter;
- PowerPoint lecture notes—for both instructors and students;

- Glossaries—reinforced with online flash cards;
- Short discussion exercises—supported by an electronic bulletin board for discussion online;
- An electronic bulletin board—supports critique and peer review of writing assignments;
- Exercises—with interactive online tutorial support;
- Online quizzes—with instant scoring and feedback;
- An online grade book—supports both course management and distance learning.

Our work as educators would not be possible without the support and encouragement of our colleagues. I would especially like to express my gratitude to the members of the Department of Philosophy, to Bill Stone in the CATE lab, and to the rest of the faculty and staff at Santa Rosa Junior College. What a great place to work!

This is dedicated, with all my love, to my family

JOEL RUDINOW
Sonoma, CA
March 1, 2007

CONTENTS

UNIT 2: ARGUMENT: FUNDAMENTAL MEDIUM OF RATIONAL DELIBERATION   83

Chapter 3: Argument   85

Chapter 4: Argument Analysis I: Representing Argument Structure   105

UNIT 4: INDUCTIVE REASONING   227

Chapter 8: Evaluating Inductive Arguments I: Generalization and Analogy   229

Chapter 9: Evaluating Inductive Arguments II: Hypothetical Reasoning and Burden of Proof   257

UNIT 5: EVALUATING WHOLE ARGUMENTS   283

Chapter 10: Evaluating Premises: Self-Evidence, Consistency, and Indirect Proof   285

Chapter 11: Informal Fallacies I: Assumptions, Language, Relevance, and Authority   303

Chapter 12: Informal Fallacies II: Inductive Reasoning   355

Chapter 13: Making Your Case: Argumentative Composition   379

Appendix: Answers & Hints for Selected Exercises   403

Index   407

LIST OF FEATURES

Chapter 2: Language   45

Chapter 6: Evaluating Deductive Arguments I: Categorical Logic   159

Chapter 7: Evaluating Deductive Arguments II: Truth Functional Logic   199

Chapter 8: Evaluating Inductive Arguments I: Generalization and Analogy   229

Chapter 9: Evaluating Inductive Arguments II: Hypothetical Reasoning and Burden of Proof   257

Chapter 10: Evaluating Premises: Self-Evidence, Consistency, and Indirect Proof   285

Chapter 11: Informal Fallacies I: Assumptions, Language, Relevance, and Authority   303

Chapter 12: Informal Fallacies II: Inductive Reasoning   355

Chapter 13: Making Your Case: Argumentative Composition   379

The Basics

What critical thinking is
Why we need it
What makes it so rare
What makes it so "difficult"
What language has to do with it

> If we want to understand something very complex, we must approach it very simply, and therein lies our difficulty—because we always approach our problems with assertions, with assumptions or conclusions, and so we are never free to approach them with the humility they demand.
>
> —JIDDU KRISHNAMURTI

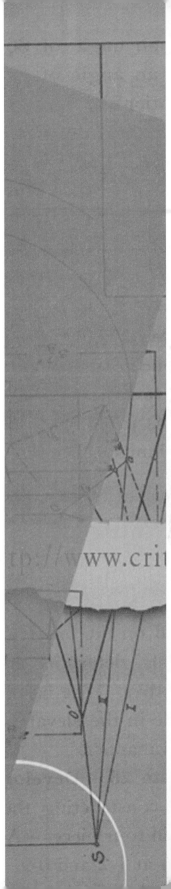

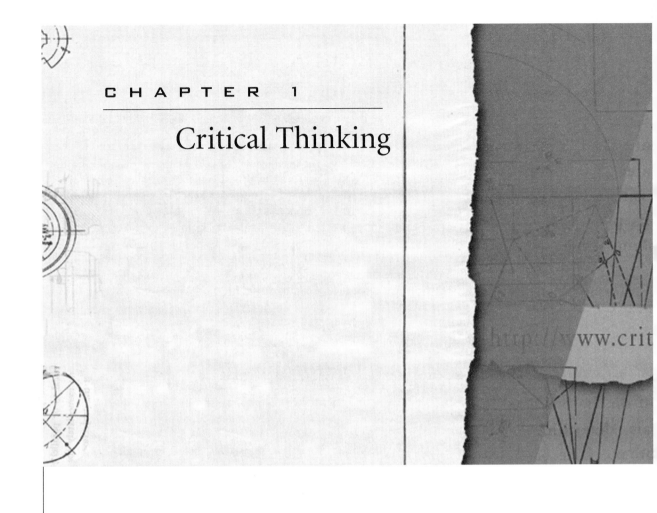

Critical Thinking

■ ne of the biggest surprises of the 2006 summer movie season was a documentary film based on former Vice President Al Gore's traveling slide show about global warming. In the film, the slide show, and a companion book, Gore makes the case that we are presently teetering on the brink of global environmental catastrophe—involving extremes of weather, flooding, drought, wildfire, crop failure, famine, epidemic disease, and so on. And all of this is the result of climate change caused largely by human energy consumption—the burning of fossil fuels. The film (as well as the slide show and the book) is titled *An Inconvenient Truth*. A Google tour of the blogosphere quickly demonstrates that as we write these words the questions of global warming, or climate change, and of its probable causes and possible implications all remain open and controversial in the public mind. The urgency and far-reaching significance of Gore's warnings makes them impossible to ignore. But are Gore's assessments and predictions reliable? Are they based on good science? Or do they amount to environmental hysteria? Should we dismiss warnings like Gore's as unfounded and irrational, or should we heed them and take immediate action? If so what action or actions should we be taking? There are many passionately held and diametrically opposed opinions in circulation—a good place to begin a discussion of Critical Thinking.

But what about that title: *An Inconvenient Truth?* At the beginning of a discussion of Critical Thinking, we find this title suggestive of several crucial questions we must each wrestle with at a deep personal level. Ask yourself, What is my relationship to the truth? Do I seek the truth in my own life? Have I found the truth? How do I know when I've found the truth? Do I speak the truth? Do I ever deny the truth? And when it comes to a matter of public controversy, how do I determine what the truth is? Is it even possible to determine what the truth is in such a situation? Are the systems and processes involved in global climate science, for example, so large and complex that the truth cannot be determined? Or is the truth just so *inconvenient* that people can't face it? Keep these questions in mind. We return to them throughout this chapter.

THE IMPORTANCE OF CRITICAL THINKING

Every so often we hear or read about oppressive communities within which the thinking of individual members, and particularly of young people, is subjected to high levels of destructive influence and control. A BBC reporter writes of a summer school run by the group Islamic Jihad in which Palestinian boys aged 12 to 15 are trained to become suicide bombers.[1] An investigative journalist reports on a highly stratified series of subtle and sophisticated initiation rituals and experiences designed to indoctrinate people into the Church of Scientology.[2] Other recent examples, or should we say, reported examples, include the Branch Davidians, Reverend Jim Jones' Jonestown Massacre, and the Heaven's Gate dooms-day cult, in which one Marshall Herff Applewhite led 38 of his followers in a mass suicide. The members of Heaven's Gate left videotaped statements explaining their actions and beliefs. According to Applewhite and his followers, the appearance of the Hale-Bopp comet was a divine sign of salvation, and a space ship cruising in the tail of the comet was waiting to pick them up and take them to the "next level" beyond this mortal human world. When the story broke in 1997, it immediately became global front-page news. Here in the United States, the three major news weeklies, *Time, Newsweek,* and *U.S. News & World Report,* all ran extensive cover stories, complete with elaborate side bars on UFOs, the Internet, comets, and cults. The *Time* and *Newsweek* covers were nearly identical (Figure 1.1), with captions that read "Inside the Web of Death," and "'Follow Me': Inside the Heaven's Gate Mass Suicide." These headlines seemed to acknowledge how bizarre the whole episode looked from the outside, while appealing to the morbid curiosity of many readers who wanted a closer look, an inside perspective, a glimpse into what makes such people tick. The *U.S. News & World Report* cover caption put it this way: "Lost Souls: How Reasonable People Can Hold Unreasonable Beliefs."

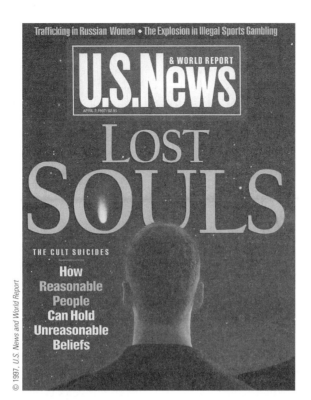

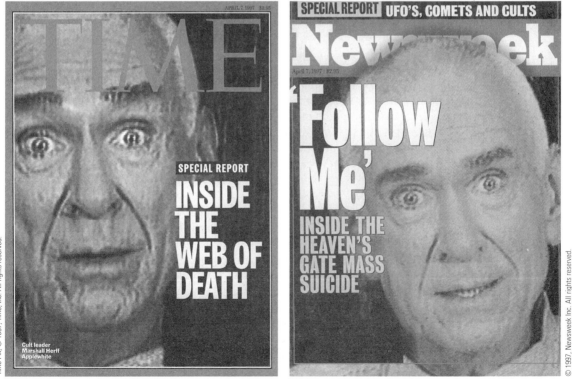

FIGURE 1.1 *Time, Newsweek,* and *U.S. News & World Report* covers

This poses an interesting question: How is it that reasonable people come to hold unreasonable beliefs? Notice how this question involves a special kind of **assumption.** To entertain this question in the context of this story, you must first assume that at least some of the 39 members of the Heaven's Gate cult were reasonable people and that at least some of the beliefs that led them to commit mass suicide were unreasonable beliefs. In Critical Thinking we call this sort of assumption a **presupposition.** Do you think these are reasonable assumptions? We come back to this shortly.

AND SPEAKING OF: | Words in Boldface

You may be wondering why we keep putting boldface on certain words (like **assumption**). These are words that we think we should define clearly to avoid misunderstandings. Words in boldface are listed in the glossary at the end of the chapter.

Whether or not the members of Heaven's Gate were reasonable people, and however reasonable or unreasonable their beliefs may have been, it certainly seems reasonable to suppose that occasionally perfectly reasonable people come to hold unreasonable beliefs about one thing or another. And this too is a pretty good point at which to begin talking about Critical Thinking. Ask yourself, Am I a reasonable person? Do I hold any unreasonable beliefs?

The Heaven's Gate mass suicide is just an extreme case of a common tendency to be misled against our better judgment. You probably know people you consider reasonable who nevertheless hold or have held beliefs that you consider not entirely reasonable and maybe even downright unreasonable, beliefs that maybe lead them into all kinds of avoidable trouble. Tune in to Oprah, Dr. Phil, or Judge Judy any day of the week and you will see a parade of more or less reasonable people tangled up in difficulties of their own and one another's making. How does this happen? Why is it that so many otherwise intelligent people enter patterns of deeply dysfunctional behavior that they can't seem to recognize or understand as such? How do reasonable people become sucked into abusive relationships or taken in by hucksters and confidence artists when just a little Critical Thinking about the situation they are in might protect them from exploitation? One answer is that there are so many interfering urges, pressures, inducements, and distractions that make it hard, even for reasonable people, to reliably differentiate between reasonable and unreasonable beliefs and courses of action. There are, in other words, many obstacles to Critical Thinking. We come back to this topic later in this chapter. But this shows why Critical Thinking is so important for each of us. Critical Thinking is empowering and can improve a person's chances of success in a relationship or career, as a potential consumer of products and services, as a citizen and member of a community, and so on, throughout the variety of social roles each of us may be destined to play. This is because

Critical Thinking is essential to something even more fundamental and basic: personal autonomy. "Autonomy" comes from the Greek words *auto,* for self, and *nomos,* for regulation. An autonomous person is self-regulating or self-directing. Autonomy is empowering because it makes that person less dependent upon—and so less vulnerable to—the dictates, directions, and influence of others. A person who can make up his or her own mind doesn't *need* others to tell her what to think or do and so is less likely to be dominated by others. Ask yourself: How free and independent am I in my search for the truth? Do I make up my own mind, or do I allow others to do this for me?

As important as Critical Thinking is to individual well-being, it is equally important to us collectively as a society. As citizens of a democratic republic, we enjoy a process of government that is now almost universally recognized as ideal and enlightened—in its theoretical conception, at least—one in which political power is held collectively by the entire citizenry and distributed equally among them according to the principle "one person, one vote." But Critical Thinking is essential for such a system to function properly, as one of the chief architects of the system, Thomas Jefferson, pointed out when he said,

> In a republican nation, whose citizens are to be led by reason and persuasion and not by force, the art of reasoning becomes of the first importance.[3]

Sadly, Critical Thinking is not as much in evidence in American political life as Jefferson would have hoped. Examples abound. But we will take just one from several years ago (so as not to provoke an immediate reflexive reaction on the part of any reader). Consider California's notorious turn-of-the-millennium energy crisis. Most Californians were cheerfully oblivious to looming problems in the state's electricity industry until the summer of 2000, when the electricity rates in the San Diego area abruptly tripled. Suddenly, small businesses were being forced into bankruptcy and ratepayers were hysterically calling for boycotts and rate strikes. Elsewhere in the state, business carried on more or less as usual well into the fall, but then in January 2001, again seemingly without warning, the managers of the state's power grid began to announce a series of power shortages and "rolling blackouts" throughout the state. Within weeks, two of the state's largest electric utility companies, Southern California Edison and Pacific Gas and Electric Company, announced that they were on the brink of bankruptcy.

We thought these events presented an opportunity to demonstrate the importance, as well as some of the difficulty, of thinking critically. And so, as this news was breaking, we challenged our students to research the unfolding crisis and invited them to venture opinions about what was going on and what ought to be done about it. We pointed out to our students that each of them was directly affected by the crisis, and there was no shortage of information about it available to them, and that as consumers and citizens they each had both a stake and a voice in the process.

The responses to this challenge, especially in the early stages of the exercise, were telling. Quite a few members of the class were ready to venture opinions right away. Someone would say something like, "Well, I think the problem is that

we Californians are just wasting a lot of electricity." Or "Well, I think the problem is that the environmentalists have kept any new power plants from being
built while the population and the high-tech economy have grown so fast that
demand for electricity is through the roof!" Or "Well, I think the problem is that
the big energy corporations are manipulating the markets so as to drive up prices
and extort rate hikes." Things became interesting when we challenged them—or
when they challenged one another—to defend any of these ideas. Where did they
get these ideas? How did they know that these things were true? Or if they didn't
know that these things were true, what reason did they have for thinking these
things were true? Were they just speculating? These questions led to general con-
versational chaos in the class, because little research had gone into the formation
of any of these opinions. Most of these ideas were in circulation in the media, but
did that make any of them more reasonable than the others? And how reliable
were the sources? As Californians, most of us at this stage, students and instructors alike, were caught flat-footed. We were all sadly ignorant of the actual nature
and origins of California's energy crisis when it broke into the news, although we
might not have wished to admit it.

As we began to look more deeply into the matter, the class soon learned that
in 1996 California had enacted legislation that "deregulated" the electric power
industry. What did "deregulate" mean? Did this mean that there were no longer
any regulations at all governing the electric power industry? Well, what did it say
in the legislation? At this stage, puzzlement and curiosity began to slide down-
ward, through disappointment toward despair. Members of the class began to
throw up their hands and show other signs of being ready to give up, and this
increased when we placed a copy of the legislation[4] on reserve in the campus
library. Some students wondered in exasperation, "Do you really expect me to go
and read a 70-page government document, which refers in its opening paragraph
to some 20 or so distinct sections of the state Civil Code, the Commercial Code,
the Government Code, and the Public Utilities Code, whatever *they* might be?"
We suggested that there might perhaps be someone out there who could digest
the legislation for us and explain it to us. We asked the students to see what was
available on the subject in the library or on the Internet. After a morning's
browse of the Internet and peek into the periodical literature on the crisis, class
morale was falling somewhere between cynical apathy and frustration bordering
on rage. Here are some typical student reactions:

> "All we're finding here is a lot of controversy among 'the experts' whose theo-
> ries and analyses conflict."

> "And they speak in acronyms and technical terms that no regular person can
> begin to understand."

> "And how can you trust any of these sources anyway?! Everybody's got an axe
> to grind. They could *all* be lying!"

> "If you want us to come up with answers to the energy crisis, maybe you could
> show us a better way of going about it, because things *aren't* getting any clearer.
> They are getting more and more confusing. This is like thinking in reverse. If
> we keep up like this, how will we *ever* figure out what is really going on?"

This was an example of what we teachers like to call a "teachable moment" (a moment when there's enough suspense and concentrated frustration built up in the classroom that people are ready to *learn something*). Here was a room full of typical young-adult citizens of California, suddenly realizing that the state's electric energy industry had been operating for almost 5 years under a new set of complex and mysterious rules enacted by their own elected representatives in state government. At the same time, they were discouraged because they could make neither head nor tail of the public controversy surrounding either the legislation or the energy crisis. Can you see how perfectly this exemplifies Jefferson's point about democracy and the "art of reasoning"?

DISCUSSION TOPIC 1.1 | Democracy and the "Art of Reasoning"

Explain how Jefferson's point about democracy and the "art of reasoning" is reflected in the classroom experience reported here.

AND SPEAKING OF: | The Importance and Scarcity of Critical Thinking

Here is an excerpt from an article by Charles J. Hanley published August 13, 2006, by the Associated Press News Service. If you really want to see evidence of the importance and scarcity of Critical Thinking, search the blogosphere for commentary on this story.

Enduring Faith in WMD?
By Charles J. Hanley
Associated Press

Did Saddam Hussein's government have weapons of mass destruction in 2003? Half of America apparently still thinks so, a new poll finds, and experts see a raft of reasons why: a drumbeat of voices from talk radio to die-hard bloggers to the Oval Office, a surprise headline here or there, a rallying around a partisan flag, and a growing need for people, in their own minds, to justify the war in Iraq.

People tend to become "independent of reality" in these circumstances, says opinion analyst Steven Kull.

The reality in this case is that after a 16-month, $900 million-plus investigation, the U.S. weapons hunters known as the Iraq Survey Group declared that Iraq had dismantled its chemical, biological and nuclear arms programs in 1991 under U.N. oversight. That finding in 2004 reaffirmed the work of U.N. inspectors who in 2002–03 found no trace of banned arsenals in Iraq.

Despite this, a Harris Poll released July 21 found a full 50 percent of U.S. respondents—up from 36 percent last year—said they believe Iraq did have the forbidden arms when U.S. troops invaded in March 2003, an attack whose stated purpose was elimination of supposed WMD. Other polls also have found an enduring American faith in the WMD story.

"I'm flabbergasted," said Michael Massing, a media critic whose writings dissected the largely unquestioning U.S. news reporting on the Bush administration's shaky WMD claims in 2002–03.

"This finding just has to cause despair among those of us who hope for an informed public able to draw reasonable conclusions based on evidence," Massing said.

Influence on opinion

Timing may explain some of the poll results. Two weeks before the survey, two Republican lawmakers, Pennsylvania's Sen. Rick Santorum and Michigan's Rep. Peter Hoekstra, released an intelligence report in Washington saying 500 chemical munitions had been collected in Iraq since the 2003 invasion.

"I think the Harris Poll was measuring people's surprise at hearing this after being told for so long there were no WMD in the country," said Hoekstra spokesman Jamal Ware.

But the Pentagon and outside experts stressed that these abandoned shells, many found in ones and twos, were 15 years old or more, their chemical contents were degraded, and they were unusable as artillery ordnance. Since the 1990s, such "orphan" munitions, from among 160,000 made by Iraq and destroyed, have turned up on old battlefields and elsewhere in Iraq, ex-inspectors say. In other words, this was no surprise.

"These are not stockpiles of weapons of mass destruction," said Scott Ritter, the ex-Marine who was a U.N. inspector in the 1990s. "They weren't deliberately withheld from inspectors by the Iraqis."

Conservative commentator Deroy Murdock, who trumpeted Hoekstra's announcement in his syndicated column, complained in an interview that the press "didn't give the story the play it deserved." But in some quarters it was headlined.

"Our top story tonight: The nation abuzz today . . ." was how Fox News led its report on the old, stray shells. Talk-radio hosts and their callers seized on it. Feedback to blogs grew intense.

"Americans are waking up from a distorted reality," read one posting.

Other claims about supposed WMD had preceded this, especially speculation since 2003 that Iraq had secretly shipped WMD abroad. A former Iraqi general's book—at best uncorroborated hearsay—claimed "56 flights" by jetliners had borne such material to Syria.

Sustaining the spin

But Kull, Massing and others see an influence on opinion that's more sustained than the odd headline.

"I think the Santorum-Hoekstra thing is the latest 'factoid,' but the basic dynamic is the insistent repetition by the Bush administration of the original argument," said John Prados, author of the 2004 book *Hoodwinked: The Documents That Reveal How Bush Sold Us a War.*

Administration statements still describe Saddam's Iraq as a threat. Despite the official findings, Secretary of State Condoleezza Rice has allowed only that "perhaps" WMD weren't in Iraq. And Bush himself, since 2003, has repeatedly insisted on one plainly false point: that Saddam rebuffed the U.N. inspectors in 2002, that "he wouldn't let them in," as he said in 2003, and "he chose to deny inspectors," as he said this March.

The facts are that Iraq—after a four-year hiatus in cooperating with inspections—acceded to the U.N. Security Council's demand and allowed scores of experts to conduct more than 700 inspections of potential weapons sites from Nov. 27, 2002, to March 16, 2003. The inspectors said they could wrap up their work within months. Instead, the U.S. invasion aborted that work.

As recently as May 27, Bush told West Point graduates, "When the United Nations Security Council gave him one final chance to disclose and disarm, or face serious consequences, he refused to take that final opportunity."

"Which isn't true," observed Kathleen Hall Jamieson, a scholar of presidential rhetoric at the University of Pennsylvania. But "it doesn't surprise me when presidents reconstruct reality to make their policies defensible." This president may even have convinced himself it's true, she said.

Americans have heard it. A poll by Kull's WorldPublicOpinion.org found that seven in 10 Americans perceive the administration as still saying Iraq had a WMD program. Combine that rhetoric with simplistic headlines about WMD "finds," and people "assume the issue is still in play," Kull said.

"For some it almost becomes independent of reality and becomes very partisan." The WMD believers are heavily Republican, polls show.

A need to believe?

Beyond partisanship, however, people may also feel a need to believe in WMD, the analysts say.

"As perception grows of worsening conditions in Iraq, it may be that Americans are just hoping for more of a solid basis for being in Iraq to begin with," said the Harris Poll's David Krane.

Charles Duelfer, the lead U.S. inspector who announced the negative WMD findings two years ago, has watched uncertainly as TV sound bites, bloggers and politicians try to chip away at "the best factual account," his group's densely detailed, 1,000-page final report.

"It is easy to see what is accepted as truth rapidly morph from one representation to another," he said in an e-mail. "It would be a shame if one effect of the power of the Internet was to undermine any commonly agreed set of facts."

The creative "morphing" goes on.

As Israeli troops and Hezbollah guerrillas battled in Lebanon on July 21, a *Fox News* segment suggested, with no evidence, yet another destination for the supposed doomsday arms.

"ARE SADDAM HUSSEIN'S WMDS NOW IN HEZBOLLAH'S HANDS?"[5] asked the headline, lingering for long minutes on TV screens in a million American homes.

WHAT IS CRITICAL THINKING?

Jefferson spoke of the "art of reasoning." That's what we mean by Critical Thinking. You're about to embark upon a course of study in Critical Thinking, and you have a right to know what you're getting into. We think of Critical Thinking as a set of conceptual tools with associated intellectual skills and strategies useful for making reasonable decisions about what to do or believe. That fancy-sounding formulation can be condensed to this: Critical Thinking is using reason to make up your mind.

DEFINITION 1.1 | **Critical Thinking**

Using reason to make up your mind

There are those words "reason" and "reasonable" again. Maybe now would be a good time for us to define them.

The word "reasonable" derives from the word "reason." So we'll start there. "Reason" comes from the Latin word *ratio,* for calculation or computation, a highly disciplined use of intelligence for problem solving. We think of **reason** as the capacity to use disciplined intelligence to solve problems.

DEFINITION 1.2 | **Reason**

The capacity to use disciplined intelligence to solve problems

---

On this basis, it is fairly easy to explain the meaning of other words in the same family. For example, "reasoning" can be understood as using disciplined intelligence to solve a problem or determine a course of action. A "reasonable decision" can be understood as one arrived at through the use of reason. A "reasonable person" can be understood as someone who (at least ordinarily) uses reason to decide what to do or believe. An "unreasonable person" can be understood as someone who fails or refuses to use reason to decide what to do or believe. And so on.

IS CRITICAL THINKING NEGATIVE?

Lots of people seem to think that the word "critical" involves negativity almost by definition; criticism is faultfinding and a critic is a faultfinder, so anything with the word "critical" in its name must be similarly concerned with finding faults, weaknesses, and other negative things. This myth comes primarily, we think, out of a misunderstanding of the word "critical." The word "critical" and its cognates, "criticism," "critic," "critique," and so on, all derive from the Greek word *kritikos,* for discernment or the ability to judge, which in turn derives from the Greek word *krinein,* for decision making. This is the way we prefer to understand Critical Thinking. It is concerned with decision making—period. So yes, it is interested in finding faults and in negative considerations but not only in these things. It is equally concerned with recognizing strengths and other positives. Critical Thinking is interested in the pros and the cons.

DISCUSSION TOPIC 1.2 | **How Can Reasonable People Hold Unreasonable Beliefs?**

Remember that question we started with about the members of Heaven's Gate: "How is it that reasonable people come to hold unreasonable beliefs?" How would you answer the question we posed in response to it: Is it reasonable to assume that at least some members of the Heaven's Gate cult were reasonable people and that at least some of their beliefs were unreasonable beliefs? We'll come back to this shortly.

Reason is a special and important capacity. Some have held that it is a distinctively human capacity. An old tradition defines humans as the "rational animals," the only species with the capacity to reason. Other animals have intelligence. But, according to this particular tradition, *only humans cultivate and develop their intelligence through discipline so as to solve problems.* There are others who disagree with this and think that there is evidence of reason and reasoning in the behavior of at least some nonhuman animals, too.

DISCUSSION TOPIC 1.3 | Is Reasoning Distinctively Human?

What do you think about this? Do you think reason is a distinctively human capacity, or not? Why? Or why not?

But regardless of whether reason is a distinctively human characteristic or not, and whether it is *confined to* the human species or not, it has certainly proven an important species-survival trait in humans. Without it, we would be severely handicapped in the struggle for survival. It is therefore easy to see how we come to recognize reason as an essentially human trait, one that pertains to humans *as* humans. This does not mean that all members of the species are equally reasonable or are equally reasonable at all times. What it does mean is that we *presume* that all members of the human species have reason. In other words, they all have the capacity to cultivate and develop their intelligence through discipline so as to solve problems. We do not restrict this presumption to exclude any category of humans. This presumption is not gender specific. It is not restricted by age, race, or ethnicity. It applies to all humans as humans.

DISCUSSION TOPIC 1.4 | Is Reasoning Essentially Human?

Do you think reason is an essentially human trait or not? Why?

DISCIPLINE

In this definition of reason, the word "disciplined" is important. Take a moment to reflect on the meaning of **discipline.** There are two things we think we should point out about this crucial concept. First, any discipline will have rules, or at least regularities. To master any discipline, you need to learn the rules and regularities. Second, discipline takes practice. Music is a good example of a discipline. To become a musician, you need to learn some rules and regularities by practicing. The same is true of Critical Thinking. Some people worry that entering into a discipline, with all of its rules and regularities, means submitting to some form of enforced conformity to some rigid orthodoxy—in other words, that all critical thinkers must come out thinking in exactly the same way. This is worrisome because thinking is one of the ways in which we become, manifest, and express ourselves as individuals. But if we think for a minute about the comparison to music as a discipline, this worry can be dismissed. All great musicians throughout history have been highly distinctive individuals. The same is true of writing as a discipline. Practice leads to greater mastery, which opens many avenues for individual self-expression. And so, too, with thinking.

IS THERE ROOM FOR CREATIVITY?

When we said that Critical Thinking involves discipline, we meant that it involves mastering rules and regularities and requires practice. Sometimes people jump from this to the conclusion that Critical Thinking does not involve or encourage creativity. We think this stems in part from the (mistaken) idea that creativity is essentially a matter of *breaking* the rules. On the contrary, it often turns out that creativity is greatly involved in *following* the rules. Sometimes it takes original creative insight to know just how to interpret and apply the rules in a given situation. Such situations are often described as calling for judgment or discretion. We hope and anticipate that you'll occasionally recognize examples of this sort of situation as you work your way through this book.

WRITING ASSIGNMENT 1.1 | Freewrite

Freewriting, like brainstorming, is a technique for liberating creative mental energy. When you freewrite you don't worry about parallel sentence structure, split infinitives, sentence fragments, or any of the other editorial problems your instructors will nag you about when you're working on an essay. When you freewrite you don't worry about anything—even spelling—that might interfere with simply getting your ideas flowing and on paper.

Here's the exercise: Now that you've learned how we define Critical Thinking, what do you think you can gain from studying it? Take out a fresh sheet of paper and freewrite for 15 minutes on the topic of what you hope and expect to get out of a course in Critical Thinking. Don't plan what you're going to write. Just start writing. And don't stop to reconsider, refine, edit, or correct what you've written. Just keep writing. If you can't think of a good way to begin, just complete this sentence: "What I hope and expect to get out of a course in Critical Thinking is . . ."

When you have written for 15 minutes, finish your thought and save what you've written. We'll be coming back to this. Ready? Go.

OBSTACLES TO CRITICAL THINKING

> It is difficult to get a man to understand something when his salary depends upon his not understanding it. —UPTON SINCLAIR

Naturally, what people actually gain from the study of Critical Thinking varies widely and depends on many variable factors. What we hope our students will

come away with in the end boils down to this: Critical Thinking is a natural development of reasoning capacity with many useful applications in daily life. We hope that everyone who studies the concepts, skills, and strategies that we cover in this book will come to understand them as natural refinements of common sense. And we expect that anyone who arrives at this understanding will find many opportunities to apply Critical Thinking in daily life.

This may sound nice, but it gives rise to a bit of a puzzle: We are saying that Critical Thinking is natural for us as humans. However, when we pay attention to the way people actually think and behave, the impression is that a lot of normal people don't think critically. Or they think critically about certain things on certain occasions but not at all about other things (sometimes the things that matter most). And this makes us wonder: Why isn't something as important and natural as Critical Thinking more common? Why do so many people seem unable to tell the difference between thinking critically and thinking in completely uncritical ways? Why do so many people find Critical Thinking so *un*natural—not only so difficult but also so difficult to understand—when they first begin to study it? As we said earlier in this chapter, we think the answer is that there are many obstacles to Critical Thinking—urges, pressures, inducements, and distractions that make it hard, even for reasonable people, to think critically. In addition, we are taught to believe things and understand things in ways that confuse, mislead, and otherwise interfere with the natural refinement of common sense. So, as it unfortunately turns out, many of us need to *unlearn* a fair amount before we begin to appreciate how natural Critical Thinking can be for us. Many people find that they need to radically reorient themselves and their thinking

FIGURE 1.2

processes and to change some deeply engrained thinking habits as they learn what it is like to think critically.

For example, go back and review that class discussion of California's energy crisis. Or take a quick tour of global warming blogs. It seems that people are often ready to make up their minds to one degree or another on the basis of . . . what? Well, often on the basis of little or no particular information from sources whose identity is vague and indeterminate and whose credibility and reliability are simply assumed. Common sense tells us that in a general discussion, where conflicting ideas are being advanced in competition against one another, the question must arise of whether ideas have enough of a basis to hold their own. And so we find that we must look more deeply into the sources of our information and the assumptions underlying our beliefs to think critically about what is at issue. If people have not learned how to do this, it can seem like "thinking in reverse," probably because, at least for a while, it seems to take us further from making up our minds. The search for truth seems long and hard. This can be discouraging—raising obstacles to Critical Thinking Let's start with a common myth, illustrated in Figure 1.2.

RELATIVISM OR SUBJECTIVISM

Sometimes people become so discouraged that they seem to give up searching for the truth altogether. They even say things like, "There's really no such thing as the 'truth,' at least not 'Truth' with a capital 'T.'"

DISCUSSION TOPIC 1.5 | **"No Such Thing as the 'Truth,' at Least Not with a Capital 'T'"**

What do you think about this? First, what do you think that the statement "There's really no such thing as the 'truth,' at least not 'Truth' with a capital 'T'" *means?* Second, do you think it's true? Or not? Third, does it make sense to ask whether it's true?

No doubt there are quite a few things that might be meant by this statement. But they all probably boil down to some version or variation of this: *The so-called truth is always relative to some particular point of view; in other words, what's true for me may not be true for you.* This position is often referred to as **relativism** or **subjectivism.** It is a big obstacle to Critical Thinking. We say it is a "myth," and we propose to refute it with an argument. Here is the argument: It is impossible to say or believe that relativism or subjectivism is true without contradicting yourself. (Try it.) Therefore it is unreasonable to say or believe that relativism or subjectivism is true.

DISCUSSION TOPIC 1.6 | Incoherence of Relativism

What do you think about this? Do you find this argument convincing? Explain. Why? Or why not?

It would not be surprising if the question were to arise in this discussion of what we mean by "truth." This turns out to be a surprisingly deep philosophical question, because there are several competing philosophical theories of truth. If you are interested in learning about and considering these theories in detail, we recommend taking a course in metaphysics, epistemology, or both.[6] For our purposes here, overcoming the obstacle to Critical Thinking posed by relativism or subjectivism, we are going to assume a commonsense understanding of the nature of truth. We are going to assume that **truth** is a relationship between a belief or a statement on the one hand and reality or the world on the other. A belief or statement is true only if it corresponds to something real. For example, if you believe or say that there is a growing hole in the Earth's ozone layer, your belief or statement is true only if there really is a growing hole in the Earth's ozone layer. Suppose that you believe or say that burning fossil fuels builds up carbon dioxide in the atmosphere, which traps solar energy, and that this causes glaciers and polar ice to melt, raises sea levels and ocean temperatures, and thereby increases the frequency and intensity of hurricanes. Your belief or statement is true only if that's what is really going on. On the basis of this conception of truth, what can we say about the search for truth? Well, the search for truth can be long and hard. Scientists have had to work long and hard to find out about the Earth's ozone layer. And to the extent that disagreement persists among scientists who have studied the Earth's ozone layer, or the greenhouse effect, we should recognize that the search for truth may still be ongoing. But long and arduous research programs can eventually arrive at reliable conclusions. And in many instances the search for truth is neither long nor hard. For example, it's not all that difficult to find out how much you weigh, is it?

LIMITED RELATIVISM OR SUBJECTIVISM

Often people will cling to some *limited* version of relativism or subjectivism, even after granting that relativism or subjectivism can't generally be true. A popular version of limited relativism or subjectivism is based on a distinction between matters of fact and matters of opinion that goes something like this: Factual matters are matters that pertain to the facts. The facts, in turn, are those things that are provable or knowable beyond doubt or question. Everything else is a matter of opinion. And, when it comes to matters of opinion, there's really no such thing as the "truth," at least not "Truth" with a capital "T." We return to a discussion of this the distinction between factual matters and matters of opinion in the section on issue classification later in this chapter.

DISCUSSION TOPIC 1.7 | Fact vs. Opinion

Does this view seem any more reasonable than *general* relativism or subjectivism? Explain.

One way in which this limited version of relativism or subjectivism may be stronger and more defensible than the general across-the-board version is that it cannot so easily be refuted by instantly deriving a self-contradiction from it. But it is still a major obstacle to Critical Thinking. One big problem with it is that most everything, even science, turns out to be a matter of opinion, simply because it is so hard to prove or know anything beyond doubt or question. The problem arises when we give up the search for truth just because we recognize room for doubt and disagreement. Critical Thinking doesn't give up the search for truth so easily. To overcome the obstacles to Critical Thinking posed by relativism or subjectivism, whether limited or not, we must cultivate an attitude of *patience and tenacity in pursuit of the truth*. We will be coming back to this shortly.

EGOCENTRISM

Another big obstacle to Critical Thinking—a kind of opposite to relativism or subjectivism—arises out of the tendency to cherish and defend those beliefs most closely associated with an individual's identity. Even in science we can find examples of **egocentrism** standing in the way of Critical Thinking. Galileo's astronomical treatise, the *Dialogue on the Two Chief Systems of the World* (1632), was a thoughtful and devastating attack on the traditional geocentric view of the universe proposed by the ancient Greek Ptolemy (second century A.D.) and accepted by most scholars and scientists of Galileo's time. Galileo's treatise was therefore an attack not only on the views that these authorities held but also on the authoritative status that they were privileged to enjoy and on their self-images. Their reaction was to censor Galileo. Pope Urban, who was persuaded that the character of Simplicio, the butt of the whole dialogue, was intended to represent himself, ordered Galileo to appear before the Inquisition. Although never formally imprisoned, Galileo was threatened with torture and ordered to renounce what he had written. In 1633, he was banished to his country estate. His *Dialogue,* with the works of Kepler and Copernicus, were placed on the Index of Forbidden Books, from which they were not withdrawn until 1835. This tendency to cherish and defend those beliefs most closely associated with individual identity is not *un*natural. We're each naturally inclined to favor and defend our selves and anything with which we identify ourselves. We are naturally egocentric in our thinking, as well as in our interests and concerns. But this natural and understandable tendency, if left unchecked, can, as in the case of Galileo and his contemporaries, close an individual's mind to the possibility that he or she is mistaken. And that would surely stand in the way of thinking critically. To understand how to keep this natural inclination in healthy check, start with a series of thought experiments[7]:

THOUGHT EXPERIMENT 1.1 | **Some of My Beliefs Are False**

Try saying, "Some of my beliefs *are not* true." Do you notice a problem with this? If so, explain. Do you nevertheless find it a reasonable thing to say about yourself? If so, explain.

Some people notice a problem when they say "Some of my beliefs are not true," because they recognize that part of believing something is believing that it *is* true. Some people find this problem manifesting itself at the level of their own particular beliefs: "If I were to do an inventory of my beliefs, wouldn't they all strike me as true?"

THOUGHT EXPERIMENT 1.2 | **A Belief Inventory I**

Try the preceding thought experiment using some of your beliefs. Identify 5–10 beliefs that you have. Do they all strike you as true? Or does it occur to you to wonder whether any of them might not be true? What more general conclusion, if any, do you draw from these results?

What is a belief, anyway? Think of a **belief** as a kind of investment of trust or confidence. A belief, like any other investment, can be difficult to abandon, even when evidence begins to show that it was a bad investment. Realizing and writing off a loss can be so painful that many people will hang on to a bad investment in the hope that it will eventually turn around to become a good one. "Is this evidence really conclusive? Maybe there's something wrong with this evidence." Questioning the evidence against a belief is one thing, but when this reluctance to admit to making a bad investment in a belief rises to the level of *denying* or *refusing to heed* the evidence, then what we have is not Critical Thinking but wishful thinking.

THOUGHT EXPERIMENT 1.3 | **Self-Deception**

What do you think you would do if you became aware of evidence indicating that one or more of your beliefs is not true?

Some people say, "If I found out that something was not true, I would just stop believing it." It would be nice if things were this simple, but we often engage in wishful thinking and we are capable even of profound self-deception. "How can this be?" you might wonder. "How can a person know that something is not true and continue to believe it? How can a person be both the successful deceiver and the victim of the deception at the same time?" These are good questions. There is something deeply puzzling about the phenomena of self-deception. But self-deception is a fact of human life, and we're sure that if you think for a minute or so you'll be able to come up with an example or two from your own experience of the sort of thing we're talking about. You probably know people who have on occasion talked themselves into believing things that they knew weren't true: for example, that they were ready for the midterm exam when they knew at some level that they weren't prepared. If we were *perfectly* rational creatures, we would no doubt recognize the inconsistency involved in self-deception, so self-deception probably would never occur. But there is no doubt that it does occur. We are rational creatures, but not perfectly so. We are also (in some ways and at some times) irrational creatures, and our wishes and desires often overwhelm our good sense. So we often persist in believing what we want to believe or what we wish were true despite what we know or have every good reason to believe.

THOUGHT EXPERIMENT 1.4 | A Belief Inventory II

A moment ago we imagined someone saying, "If I were to do an inventory of my beliefs, wouldn't they all strike me as true?" Try to describe what it would be like to complete an inventory of your beliefs. How long would it take? How would you start? What kind of procedure would you use? How would you keep track? . . . After you've struggled with this for a while, go ahead and begin an inventory of your beliefs, on paper. Give yourself a measured 5 minutes and see what you come up with.

Most people are immediately struck by the realization that they have many more beliefs to keep track of than they ever would have imagined had they not been prompted to consider enumerating them. If people try to organize an inventory of their beliefs by sorting them into categories, a similar realization occurs: beliefs of so many different kinds!

THOUGHT EXPERIMENT 1.5 | Metabeliefs

Do you have any beliefs about how many beliefs you have? For example, do you believe that you have more beliefs than you can count? If so, what category would such a belief fall into? When did you realize that you had beliefs of this sort? For example, were you aware that you had beliefs of this sort before you tried this thought experiment?

By this point, most people are struck by what might be described as a major inventory control problem. This problem arises out of two conditions. First, there is uncertainty about the current inventory of beliefs. How many of these beliefs that I've just noticed have been with me all along? And how many more beliefs do I have yet to notice? Second, there is the dynamic condition of our belief systems. In other words, our belief systems are not static. They are constantly undergoing change and revision as we deal with incoming information. Consider how this process normally works. We live in what has come to be known as the "information age," a label that derives from the awesome volume of information bombarding us daily. Just think of the amount of material contained in the average metropolitan daily newspaper. Multiply that by 7 days a week and then again by the number of metropolitan population centers you can think of in a few short minutes. Add to this weekly, monthly, quarterly, and annual publications; books; radio; and television—literally hundreds of separate stations, channels, and cable services, many of them broadcasting round the clock. Then add the Internet! This should be enough to make the point that there's far too much information to pay attention to, let alone absorb. Consequently, each of us has to be selective about where we direct our attention in this overwhelming flow of information. Actually, this is nothing new or peculiar to our age. It's part of the human condition. There's always more to pay attention to than any of us has attention for. And if you're like most people, even within the narrow range of information you do become aware of, you continue to be selective. Some incoming information is actively incorporated into your belief system, and other information is rejected. What do you suppose are the main factors that govern this process? What do you suppose determines these selections? Among the most important and influential of these factors are the existing contents of our belief systems. The way we deal with incoming information is determined largely by what we already believe. Our belief systems are "self-editing."

DISCUSSION TOPIC 1.8 | Common Sense Skepticism

What do you suppose common sense would suggest at this stage?

Each of us has a large and constantly evolving belief system comprising a huge number of beliefs—so many that trying to count them seems crazy. Most of these beliefs we routinely just assume. In other words, we take them for granted. We regard them as true without questioning them, or determining the adequacy of whatever evidence there may be to support them, or wondering where they came from and whether those sources are reliable or not. So, if you're like most people, a large part of your belief system is probably "subterranean," and functions in a largely unexamined way, as a set of assumptions of which you are probably not even fully aware and that influences its own ongoing evolution. Based on the sheer size of a normal person's belief system, common sense surely suggests the strong probability that some of those beliefs are not true, especially as long as they remain unexamined.

THOUGHT EXPERIMENT 1.6 | A Critical Thinking Koan ❋

Suppose that you were able to complete a thorough inventory of every one of your beliefs. And suppose that you had been able to weed out each false or dubious item from that inventory. Now here you are at the end, considering the last item in the inventory: Belief # 457,986,312 "Some of my beliefs are not true." What do you think you should do with this belief? Would you weed it out, or not? Explain.

To overcome the obstacles to Critical Thinking posed by the pitfalls of ego-centrism, we must cultivate an attitude of "intellectual humility"—in other words, a recognition of our fallibility or liability to error—yet maintain a patient and tenacious commitment to the pursuit of truth. But, as we shall see, even such a healthy attitude as intellectual humility can give rise to another kind of obstacle to Critical Thinking.

INTIMIDATION BY AUTHORITY

An **authority** is an expert source of information outside ourselves. The source can be a single individual (a parent, a teacher, a celebrity, a clergy member, the president), a group of individuals (doctors, educators, a peer group, a national consensus), or even an institution (a religion, a government agency, an educational establishment). Whatever its form, authority can exert considerable influence on our belief systems. And it's easy to see why. Consider how difficult it is to become an expert about *anything*. Nobody can ever hope to become an expert about *everything*. There's almost always going to be someone around who knows more about whatever it is that we're interested in than we do. So a person with a healthy attitude of intellectual humility will likely find it helpful to consult authorities for their expert opinions.

THOUGHT EXPERIMENT 1.7 | Sources of My Beliefs

Reconsider your belief inventory with regard to sources. How many of the things that you believe can you trace back to direct experience? Take as an example some area of interest or concern that is of intimate personal importance to you (like your physical health). How many of the things that you believe about your physical health have you derived from sources other than your direct experience? In such cases, can you identify the precise source of the belief? Explain.

If you're like most of the rest of us, chances are that a lot of the things you believe you've obtained from other sources. Beliefs about world history, the direction of the economy, the events of the day, the existence of God and an after-life, the state of your health, the climate—what are the sources of all of these beliefs? It's likely that you developed many of them by relying on the words of others, sources you are in effect trusting as authorities. Again, all of this is normal and natural. But common sense should warn you that there is a risk inherent in trusting someone other than yourself when you make up your mind. How do you know that the authority you trust is reliable?

Beyond this inherent risk (a risk that can at least be managed) there is a deeper danger. We can rely so much on authority that we stop thinking for our-selves. For a vivid and extreme example, look at what happened to the mem-bers of the Heaven's Gate cult. Inside the cult, a rigid authoritarian regime trained members to "purify" their "vehicles" (bodies) through systematic self-denial and unquestioning obedience to authority. Punishable offenses included "knowingly breaking any instruction or procedure; trusting one's own judg-ment or using one's own mind; having private thoughts; curiosity; criticizing or finding fault with one's teacher or classmates."[8] Such blind acceptance of and obedience to authority is incompatible with intellectual autonomy and Critical Thinking.

But just how likely is it that a normal, intelligent person would be susceptible to such a debilitating abuse of trust? How vulnerable are we to the dictates of authority? How subtle might its negative influence be? Consider a series of experiments conducted by psychologist Stanley Milgram in the 1960s.[9] Milgram's famous experiment consisted of asking subjects to administer strong electrical shocks to people whom the subjects couldn't see. The subjects were told that they could control the shock's intensity by means of a shock generator with 30 clearly marked voltages, ranging from 15 to 450 volts and labeled from "Slight Shock (15)" to "XXX—Danger! Severe Shock (450)." We should point out that the entire experiment was a setup: No one was administering or receiving shocks. The subjects were led to believe that the "victims" were being shocked as part of an experiment to determine the effects of punishment on memory. The "vic-tims," who were confederates of the experimenters, were strapped in their seats with electrodes attached to their wrists "to avoid blistering and burning." They were told to make no noise until a "300-volt shock" was administered, at which point they were to make noise loud enough for the subjects to hear (for example, pounding on the walls as if in pain). The subjects were reassured that the shocks, although extremely painful, would cause no permanent tissue injury. When asked, a number of psychologists predicted that no more than 10% of the sub-jects would follow the instruction to administer a 450-volt shock. In fact, well over half did (26 out of 40). Even after hearing the "victims" pounding, 87.5% of the subjects (35 out of 40) followed instructions to increase the voltage. It seems clear that many normal, intelligent people, when instructed by an authority, will act against their better judgment. To overcome the obstacles to Critical Thinking posed by the intimidating influence of authority, we simply need to maintain our "intellectual independence."

CONFORMISM

Further experiments seem to show that not only people's actions but also their judgment is susceptible to external influence. For example, look at the line segments in Thought Experiment 1.8.

THOUGHT EXPERIMENT 1.8 | Reliability of Perception

Which of the three lines on the left matches the one on the right?

A _____

B _____   _____

C _____

Do your trust your perceptual judgment here? Line segment B is the one that matches the line segment on the right. Do you think you could ever be persuaded to doubt your perceptions and choose A or C? Maybe not, but experiments indicate that many normal, intelligent people can be persuaded to alter their perceptual judgments, even when their judgments are obviously correct. These experiments involved several hundred individuals who were asked to match lines just as you did. In each group, however, only one subject was naive; that is, unaware of the nature of the experiment. The others were instructed to make incorrect judgments in some cases and to exert peer pressure on the naive subject to change his or her correct judgment. The results: When subjects were not exposed to peer pressure, they inevitably judged correctly. But peer pressure produces a measurable and significant tendency toward conformity, with the tendency increasing as the majority increased toward unanimity.[10] What is most interesting about these results is what they show about the power of peer pressure. Psychologically we are all, at some level, aware of our liability to error, even in our perceptual judgments. But it is still remarkable that peer pressure is powerful enough to erode people's confidence in their own perceptual experience and judgment. Consider how much more intimidating peer pressure must be when applied to anything more remote from you than your own perceptual experience and judgment.

What accounts for such intimidating power? Like many other creatures, humans are social animals. Our chances of survival and of flourishing are greatly enhanced by association with others of our kind. We do much better in groups than as individuals. So we are naturally fearful of isolation. At the same time, cooperation among individual members and group loyalty are both essential to the successful organization of any group, to the coordination of any group project, and to the maintenance of the group as a stable entity. So there is a natural tendency in any group toward conformity and orthodoxy. And there arises within any group a hierarchy of authority through which orthodoxy is established and conformity to it is reinforced. All of this is natural and makes sense in terms of its survival value for the individual, for the group, and for the species. However, if this natural and functional tendency is not kept within healthy limits, the fear of isolation can overcome our basic common sense, increasing rather than minimizing our liability to error. To overcome the obstacles to Critical Thinking posed by the intimidating influence of authority, peer pressure, and orthodoxy, we need to cultivate and maintain "intellectual courage."

ETHNOCENTRISM

Another major obstacle to Critical Thinking—a close relative of egocentrism— also arises out of our natural tendency as social animals to gather in groups and to identify ourselves with and in terms of our social groupings. To see how this happens, try the next thought experiment.

THOUGHT EXPERIMENT 1.9 | **Identity and Culture**

How many distinct cultural groups can you identify in 5 minutes by simply describing yourself, as in "I am a(n) _____"? (You could even start with your name, which identifies your family.)

However narrowly or broadly these groupings are defined—from kinship groupings (families) to something as broad as a gender—cultural categories play an important role in the formation of our individual personal identities because we largely identify ourselves in terms of them. Ethnic consciousness, like self-awareness, and ethnic pride, like self-esteem, are important ingredients in a healthy personality and society. But each has corresponding perversions that, when they arise, stand as obstacles to Critical Thinking (and cause lots of other serious grief). The natural human tendency to be egocentric also can affect our attitudes regarding groups with which we identify. So there arises a tendency to believe in the superiority of our family, our circle of friends, our age group, our religion, our nation, our race, our ethnicity, our gender, our sexual orientation, and our culture. Thus egocentricity, the view that mine is better—my ideas, my experience, my values, my agenda—becomes **ethnocentricity,** the view that ours is better—our ideas, our values, our ways. In recent years cultural identity has gained recognition as a matter of political importance. Multiculturalism is high on the agenda of most educational institutions now sensitive to the importance of cultural diversity in the community and the curriculum. Instructors strive to reflect multiple cultural perspectives in their courses (and authors in their textbooks). In Critical Thinking, cultural diversity and an awareness of alternative cultural perspectives are especially useful because of the limitations inherent in any given cultural perspective. An appreciation of cultural diversity contributes to open-mindedness, an essential ingredient of Critical Thinking. To overcome the obstacles to Critical

Thinking posed by ethnocentrism, we must cultivate an attitude of respectful intellectual tolerance and maintain and strengthen our intellectual humility.

UNEXAMINED ASSUMPTIONS

As we were writing the fifth edition of this book, the world was still reeling in shock over the spectacular multiple airliner hijacking and attack on the World Trade Center towers in New York City and the Pentagon in Washington, D.C. At the time, we said that we had no doubt that these stunning events would live on in collective memory, and indeed they have. In the 5 years since, we cannot identify a single day upon which we have not heard a reference to September 11, 2001, in public discourse. As you read these words, we'd like you to try to move yourself imaginatively back in time to September 11, 2001. Perhaps you remember where you were and what you were doing when you first learned that two airliners, apparently hijacked, had flown directly into the two World Trade Center towers in New York City—followed by fires and eventually the collapse of both buildings—and a third airliner had apparently crashed directly into the Pentagon in Washington, D.C. In particular, we'd like you to try to recover a sense of the confusion and of the urgency we all felt to know what was happening and to figure out what to do about it.

To help you conjure the mood, let us remind you that at that time, thousands of people remained missing and unaccounted for; rescue workers were digging through rubble searching for survivors; and the New York Stock Exchange was shut down, as was all commercial air travel to, from, and within the United States. There was considerable speculation about the identities and affiliations of the perpetrators of the attacks. But, as of that moment, only a handful of fragments from the beginnings of the investigation had been made public. The FBI had published passenger lists and boarding passes from the flights. Cell phone calls from passengers aboard one of the hijacked airliners reported that hijackers with knives had taken control of the flight. A car had been impounded at Boston's Logan Airport. A few individuals had been "detained for questioning." There was, again, considerable speculation about the identities and affiliations of the perpetrators of the attacks. But it had already focused on a particular terrorist organization led by one Osama bin Laden, whose base of operations was reported to be in Afghanistan. President George W. Bush, Vice President Dick Cheney, Secretary of State Colin Powell, and other government officials, as well as the television journalists covering the story, were careful to refer to bin Laden only as the "prime suspect." Meanwhile, however, the Bush administration was mobilizing an international coalition, as well as domestic public support, for a "war against terrorism."

THOUGHT EXPERIMENT 1.10 | **Suspending Judgment**

See if you can feel how difficult it is to suspend judgment. If someone asks you, "What do you think is happening?" or "What do you think we should do about it?" you are *suspending your judgment* when you sincerely say "I don't know."

There comes a point for most people at which it is no longer possible to suspend judgment. The urgency of the need we feel to initiate some plan of action makes the suspense unbearable. Although we may not know what has happened to any degree of certainty, we nevertheless feel we must do *something*. So we begin to make assumptions. Do you remember that "assumption" was among the first words we said we needed to define clearly to avoid misunderstanding? Here is what we mean by "assumption." An assumption is a claim that is taken to be true without argument. In this definition we use two terms, "claim" and "argument," which also need to be explained. A **claim** is a statement that claims for itself (whether rightly or wrongly) the value of being true. If someone says, "Hi, how are you?" this would not be a claim—the language is not being used to make a statement that claims to be true. If someone asks you "What time is it?" this would not be a claim. But if someone says something like, "The attack on the World Trade Center towers in New York City was the work of the bin Laden terrorist organization al-Qaeda," a claim is being made. Or if someone were to say, "The attack on the World Trade Center towers was orchestrated by high-level officials of the U.S. government and the buildings were destroyed by controlled demolition to create a pretext for global war," a claim is being made (actually several claims). Argument is a concept that we define and develop in detail in Chapters 3 through 5 of this book. For now, just think of an argument as support for a claim. So an assumption is a statement that claims to be true and is taken to be true without support.

DEFINITION 1.3 | Assumption

A claim taken to be true without support

REVIEW EXERCISE 1.1 | Find the Argument

Argument is a concept we have already put to use in this chapter. Where?

Perhaps you have heard the following cliché: Beware of assumptions; to "assume" makes an "ass" out of "u" and "me." This is part of a widespread myth according to which *all* assumptions are suspect or dangerous, so we should try to avoid making *any* assumptions.

THOUGHT EXPERIMENT 1.11 | Assumption-free Thinking

Pick any topic or subject, and try thinking about it without making any assumptions.

The main problem with this widespread myth is that it is practically impossible to follow as a recommendation for how to conduct reasoning. The more seriously you take it, the more paralyzed you become. All reasoning must start somewhere. When Thomas Jefferson wrote in the Declaration of Independence,

> We hold these truths to be self-evident, that all men are created equal, that they are endowed by their Creator with certain unalienable Rights, that among these are Life, Liberty and the pursuit of Happiness.

these were the starting points of the reasoning. When he said "We hold these truths to be self-evident," he was saying that he thought it reasonable to assert these claims without support, that is, as assumptions.

Of course, there is risk involved in making any assumption: namely the risk that what you are assuming is not true. No doubt we're making some assumptions when we say this, but it seems clear that in practice it is impossible to reason about anything without making at least some assumption or assumptions. Some such risk is inherent and inevitable in reasoning as such. In other words, there is no way to eliminate this risk entirely. But this risk increases—in other words, assumptions are more dangerous—to the extent that they remain **hidden.** As long as assumptions are hidden, they are not open to discussion, to challenge, to debate, and to deliberate consideration (as any serious claim to the truth should be). So the obvious way to keep the risk down would be to *be aware of the assumptions we're making*. Notice that Jefferson's assumptions in the Declaration of Independence are not hidden. Thus we would replace the cliché "beware of assumptions" with the maxim "be aware of assumptions" and posit this as a Critical Thinking rule of thumb.

CRITICAL THINKING TIP 1.1 | **Awareness of Assumptions**

~~BEWARE of Assumptions~~   Be AWARE of Assumptions

There is also an important corollary to this rule of thumb: *Don't forget the assumptions you are making* (don't forget that they *are* assumptions). This is essential to avoiding one of those pitfalls that leads otherwise reasonable people into unreasonable beliefs and ill-advised courses of action. Assumptions in their essential nature—by definition—are taken to be true without support. So, as we just explained, the risk of error increases as soon as we forget about the need to discuss, challenge, debate, and deliberately consider whether what we are assuming is true. And don't forget the point we made earlier about the difficulty this poses for many people. Seriously examining assumptions, on the basis of which you thought you were going to make up your mind, can easily seem like "thinking in reverse."

DISCUSSION TOPIC 1.9 | 9/11 Assumptions

Five years (and counting) past September 11, 2001, do we have any clearer understanding than we had on that day of what occurred? In discussing this question, pay careful attention to and make note of assumptions as they emerge and come into play.

INFERENTIAL ASSUMPTIONS

Where should we look for assumptions? Common sense would suggest that we be especially vigilant in two particular directions. Whenever people are making inferences or drawing conclusions—by which we mean reasoning from one claim to another—we should look for assumptions between the claims in the inference.

REVIEW EXERCISE 1.2 | Identifying Hidden Assumptions (Between the Lines)

Suppose a fellow student says to you, "As a society, we really shouldn't be relying on computers as much as we do." And you wonder why, and she says, "Well, don't forget, computers are designed and built by humans." What is she assuming?

In the example in the preceding exercise, your hypothetical fellow student says, "As a society, we really shouldn't be relying on computers as much as we do." You ask, "Why?" And she says, "Computers are designed and built by humans." Notice how the reasoning here goes from her *answer* back to the claim you challenged. But how does the reasoning move from the claim "computers are designed and built by humans" to the claim you originally challenged "that we shouldn't rely on computers as much as we do"? There is an assumption being made that serves as a missing link in the chain of reasoning. Can you figure out what this assumption is? Assumptions that play this sort of linking role are often called **inferential assumptions.** We return to this concept in Chapters 3 and 4.

PRESUPPOSITIONS

Another important place to look for assumptions is *underneath* the claims being made. Sometimes, to make sense of what is stated or expressed explicitly, we are required to assume additional claims that are not stated explicitly.

REVIEW EXERCISE 1.3 | Identifying Hidden Assumptions (Beneath the Surface)

Go back to the pictures on page 5 in this chapter. Read the caption under the main headline of the magazine *U.S. News & World Report*. What two assumptions do you have to make to understand this caption?

This is the way the *U.S. News & World Report* cover works: The caption under the main headline "Lost Souls" reads "How Reasonable People Can Hold Unreasonable Beliefs." To make sense of this caption, you need to assume that the 39 members of the Heaven's Gate cult (or at least some of them) were reasonable people, and you need to assume that the beliefs that led them to commit mass suicide (or at least some of those beliefs) were unreasonable beliefs. Assumptions of this kind—the kind that must be made for what is explicitly said to make sense—are called presuppositions. We develop this concept in Chapter 3.

DISCUSSION TOPIC 1.10 | UFO Cover-up

On June 24, 1997, the United States Air Force issued its official explanation of the Roswell Incident. The Roswell Incident is probably the most famous incident of an alleged Earth landing of extraterrestrials, long thought by many UFO believers to involve a government cover-up, because the sightings occurred and the debris was collected on and around a government military reservation (Roswell Air Force Base in New Mexico) and because the government maintained an "official silence" about the incident for 50 years. The official explanation: An experimental high-altitude weather balloon and several humanoid crash-test dummies fell to Earth from high altitudes. Conspiracy theorists were not convinced. There was much debate. Here is an opinion we heard on the radio. How many assumptions can you identify?

> There's no government cover-up, and there were no aliens. Look, if you were an alien and you were scoping out the earthly terrain, the last place you'd go would be to one of the most highly fortified and tightly secured military installations in the United States.

From this discussion of obstacles to Critical Thinking, a sort of "portrait of the critical thinker" begins to emerge. A critical thinker is a person who combines an array of "intellectual virtues" and displays these virtues in his or her intellectual life. A critical thinker is patient, tenacious, humble, courageous, tolerant, and respectful of diversity of opinion in pursuit of the truth. The critical thinker sticks with the search for truth. The critical thinker is not in a hurry to finish the search for truth, although it may be long and arduous. The critical thinker is humble in recognizing his or her limitations and liability to error. But the critical thinker is not easily intimidated by authority or by popular opinion or peer pressure. The critical thinker recognizes the value of diverse perspectives and viewpoints and is respectful of the views of others with whom he or she may disagree. With this portrait of the critical thinker in mind, return to a question we raised earlier in this chapter: How is it that reasonable people come to hold unreasonable beliefs? Chances are that this is because people have given up the search for truth, lost their patience and jumped to a hasty conclusion of the search for truth, become intimidated (lost their courage and independence), or become arrogant (lost their humility) in pursuit of the truth.

REVIEW EXERCISE 1.4   A Critical Thinking Self-Assessment

Assess your own habits of mind in terms of the intellectual virtues found in the preceding portrait of the critical thinker.

I am a truth seeker

- ☐ always
- ☐ most of the time
- ☐ some of the time
- ☐ seldom
- ☐ never

In seeking the truth, I would describe myself as

- ☐ extremely patient
- ☐ relatively patient
- ☐ about average
- ☐ somewhat impatient
- ☐ very impatient

In seeking the truth, I would describe myself as

- ☐ very tenacious (I refuse to give up)
- ☐ relatively tenacious (I don't give up easily)
- ☐ about average
- ☐ someone who will give up
- ☐ easily defeated

In seeking the truth, I would describe myself as

- ☐ very aware of my limitations and liability to error
- ☐ sometimes aware of my limitations and liability to error
- ☐ about average
- ☐ when I'm right, I'm right
- ☐ I'm always right

In seeking the truth, I would describe myself as

- ☐ extremely skeptical of authority
- ☐ skeptical of authority
- ☐ about average
- ☐ susceptible to persuasion by authority
- ☐ easily swayed by authority

In seeking the truth, I would describe myself as

- ☐ a contrarian (I tend to go against the conventional wisdom)
- ☐ indifferent to popular opinion or peer pressure
- ☐ about average

☐ mindful of the views of my peers and the public

☐ easily intimidated by peer pressure and popular opinion

In seeking the truth I, would describe myself as

☐ eager to learn about views and understandings that conflict with my own

☐ interested in views and understandings that conflict with my own

☐ about average

☐ not much interested in views and understandings that conflict with my own

☐ annoyed by views and understandings that conflict with my own

I speak the truth

☐ always

☐ most of the time

☐ some of the time

☐ rarely

☐ never

The truth about the things that matter most to me is knowable.

☐ I strongly agree with this statement.

☐ I agree with this statement.

☐ I don't know.

☐ I disagree with this statement.

☐ I strongly disagree with this statement.

The truth about the things I care about is simple.

☐ I strongly agree with this statement.

☐ I agree with this statement.

☐ I don't know.

☐ I disagree with this statement.

☐ I strongly disagree with this statement.

The truth about the things I care about is complex and difficult to capture in words.

☐ I strongly agree with this statement.

☐ I agree with this statement.

☐ I don't know.

☐ I disagree with this statement.

☐ I strongly disagree with this statement.

WRITING ASSIGNMENT 1.2 | A Critical Thinking Role Model

Based on your understanding of Critical Thinking as defined and explained so far in this chapter, identify the person or people you think best exemplify it. Explain your selection.

LOOKING AHEAD: ISSUES AND DISPUTES

You may have heard the expression "Reasonable people may differ." An **issue** is what we call a topic about which reasonable people may differ. Should there be a law against abortion? Should animals be used in medical experimentation? Does intelligent extraterrestrial life exist? What is the average temperature of the water in Lake Tahoe? Is there a global environmental crisis? What drives people to commit acts of terrorism? Does the Federal Reserve Board's move to raise interest rates indicate that its members think the recession is over? These are all questions to which a number of significant and conflicting alternative responses are both genuinely open and defensible. These are all good examples of our concept of an issue.

DEFINITION 1.4 | **Issue**

A topic about which reasonable people are likely to disagree

Sometimes it seems as though reasonable people may differ about anything, everything, even nothing. It would help if we could dispense with disputes over nothing. So before we begin to discuss issues, let us explain more deeply what we mean by "*genuinely* disputable" by pointing out and setting aside another kind of thing that often *passes for* an issue.

MERE VERBAL DISPUTES

Philosopher William James tells the story about how on a camping trip everyone entered a dispute over the following puzzle:

> The corpus of the dispute was a squirrel—a live squirrel supposed to be clinging to one side of a tree-trunk; while over against the tree's opposite side a human being was imagined to stand. This human witness tries to get sight of the squirrel by moving rapidly round the tree, but no matter how fast he goes, the squirrel moves as fast in the opposite direction, and always keeps the tree between himself and the man, so that never a glimpse of him is caught. The resultant metaphysical problem now is this: Does the man go round the squirrel or not? He goes round the tree, sure enough, and the squirrel is on the tree; but does he go round the squirrel?[11]

James's idea was that although you can easily imagine people going round and round in an endless dispute over such a puzzle, you can just as easily dissolve the puzzle by drawing a simple terminological distinction: it all depends upon what you mean by "going round" the squirrel.

> If you mean passing from the north of him to the east, then to the south, then to the west, then to the north again, obviously the man does go round him, for he occupies these

successive positions. But if on the contrary you mean being first in front of him, then on the right of him, then behind him, then on the left, and finally in front again, it is quite as obvious that the man fails to go round him, for by the compensating movements the squirrel makes, he keeps his belly turned towards the man all the time, and his back turned away.[12]

Because it hardly matters to which meaning of "going round" the squirrel applies, this could be called a merely verbal dispute. To put it another way, there's no real issue here; the dispute arises out of a simple ambiguity (for an explanation of this concept, see the section on ambiguity and vagueness in Chapter 2) in the way the puzzle is worded. A similar example is the old dispute that results from the question, "If a tree falls in the forest and nobody is there to hear it, is there a sound?" Clarifying the meaning of "sound" dissolves the dispute. If you're talking about sound *waves,* then presumably there are sounds whether or not anyone is there to hear the tree fall. But if you mean sound *sensations*—the experience of sound—then the falling tree makes no sound, because no one is there to experience the sound sensations.

Perhaps it would be nice if all issues were as trivial as these. Perhaps it would be nice if all disputes arose out of simple ambiguities and could be dismissed as mere matters of semantics. On the other hand, perhaps it would be boring if all disputes were idle and there were no real, serious, and urgent issues to argue about. Reasonable people may differ about this, possibly leading to another kind of idle dispute. In any case, most genuinely important disputes are concerned with genuine issues. The rest of this book will be devoted to developing and refining strategies and procedures for resolving serious disputes about real and important issues, which are as varied as all of human interest and concern.

ISSUE ANALYSIS

Because they inherently involve conflict, all issues present a certain amount of psychological discomfort. They all seem to cry out for resolution. But a critical thinker must discipline himself or herself to be patient in pursuit of the truth. Thus another aspect of thinking critically that often gives the impression of "thinking in reverse" has to do with issues and their analysis. Before we begin to make up our minds about how to resolve a given issue, it is useful to do some analysis of the issue.

REVIEW EXERCISE 1.5 | Epigram

Reread the epigram at the beginning of this chapter by Jiddu Krishnamurti. Reflect on how his insight might apply at this stage of your reading.

Among the immediate challenges that most issues present is their inherent complexity. Take the first of the issues we mentioned in the section "Looking Ahead: Issues and Disputes" as an example. The question of whether there should be law against abortion, even though it is worded as a simple yes-or-no question, is hardly a simple issue. The minute you look at it closely and begin to confront it seriously, you will see that it is not just one issue but more like a whole nest of them, resembling a can of worms. This is because there are so many things under the umbrella heading of "abortion" that reasonable people can disagree about. For example, reasonable people will disagree over whether abortion belongs in the same moral category as murder, homicide, elective surgery, birth control, or all of these. Reasonable people will disagree over whether a woman's reproductive processes are private and over whether the government may legitimately interfere with her choices. Reasonable people will disagree over whether the fetus is a person or only a potential person. Reasonable people will disagree over whether potential people have rights. Reasonable people will disagree over whether the right to life overrides other rights that may come into conflict with it and over whether the right to life includes the right to use another person's body as a life support system. Even among those who agree that the law *should* restrict abortion, reasonable people will disagree, for example, over whether the restriction should be total or partial, rigid or flexible and, if partial and flexible, over what the exceptions should be, and so on. So much complexity! It seems even that there might be too many dimensions of complexity to count. The challenge this poses for human intelligence is confusion: another one of those things that make it difficult—even for reasonable people, and even when they're not distracted by external pressures or internal longings and fears—to discriminate between reasonable and unreasonable beliefs. Most interesting issues are deep and complex enough to present this sort of challenge. So the first step of issue analysis is to take the issue apart and see what subsidiary issues are contained within it.

THOUGHT EXPERIMENT 1.12 | Issue Analysis I

Set the egg timer for 3 minutes. Then brainstorm for subsidiary issues. See how many distinct issues you can see arising out of one of the following issues:

- Was the war on Iraq justified?
- Were the presidential elections in 2000 and 2004 "stolen"?
- Are humans changing global climate patterns?
- What is the average temperature of the water in Lake Tahoe?
- What drives people to commit acts of terrorism?
- Should animals be used in medical experimentation?

The next step is to find an approach to the issue that will help us bring its complexity under intellectual control rather than allowing its complexity to confuse and overwhelm us. One approach that immediately occurs to many people is to narrow the focus of the inquiry. For example, rather than try to resolve the whole nest of issues we can see arising out of the abortion debate, we might confine ourselves to the issue over whether the fetus is a person or only a potential person. This approach is a reasonable one and is often useful. But, it never disposes of the problem. Suppose we do narrow our focus to the issue over the status of the fetus. Is the fetus a person or just a potential person? But here again, the minute you look closely at this issue and begin to confront it seriously, what you will see is not just one issue. What are the biological changes that take place during fetal development? How do the criteria for personhood relate to the biology of fetal development? Is personhood simply a biological matter? Or is it an essentially political matter? Or a spiritual matter? What precisely is meant by this word "person"? What are the criteria for being a person? And so on.

LOGICAL PRIORITY

With any such complex inquiry, what we really need is to be able to develop an orderly **agenda of inquiry.** An agenda is a list of things to do. The function of an agenda is to monitor progress, especially when there are a lot of things to keep track of. An agenda of inquiry would be a list of issues to resolve. Its function would be to let you know whether you are making progress toward resolving the main issue (the issue you started with) in which the others are embedded, rather than going in circles or wandering aimlessly and becoming lost in it all. To develop an agenda, we must **prioritize,** which simply means putting things into some kind of serial order. In any agenda, something has to come first, something has to come next, and so on. There may often be several reasonable orders to follow in an agenda of inquiry. And an agenda of inquiry probably ought to be always open to revision. Nevertheless, some ways of ordering an agenda of inquiry are more logical than others. Suppose we start by trying to resolve the issue of what to do about global warming. Shortly, we should notice that any resolution to this issue that we might consider presupposes some resolution to the subsidiary issue of what the *causes* of global warming are. And similarly, we should notice that *this* presupposes a specific resolution (in the affirmative) to the issue about whether global warming is occurring. This would indicate that the issue as to the reality of global warming comes logically before the issue as to its causes, which in turn comes logically before the issue as to the remedies. Similarly, any resolution to the issue of whether the fetus is a person will presuppose some resolution to the issue of what the criteria for personhood are. In other words, the issue as to the criteria for personhood comes logically before the issue of whether the fetus is a person. Whenever we notice this sort of relationship, it makes sense to address issues in order of their **logical priority.**

THOUGHT EXPERIMENT 1.13 | **Issue Analysis II**

Take the list of subsidiary issues you brainstormed in the preceding exercise and prioritize it.

ISSUE CLASSIFICATION

The next step of issue analysis comes from recognizing that there are different types of issues and that strategies and procedures appropriate for issues of one type may not be appropriate for issues of other types. For example, the procedures for determining the average temperature of the water in Lake Tahoe will not be of much use in resolving the question of whether animals should be used in medical experimentation. We propose that you sort issues into the following three categories: factual issues, evaluative issues, and interpretive issues.

In this connection, we use the terms "factual," "evaluative," and "interpretive" in a way that departs slightly but significantly from what we believe is current popular usage. Our impression is that people generally draw a sharp distinction between factual matters and evaluative and interpretive matters but also that people generally do not draw any sharp and clear distinction between evaluative and interpretive matters. We touched upon this in the section on limited relativism or subjectivism. Again, popular usage seems to go something like this: Factual matters pertain to the facts. The facts are everything that is proven or known beyond doubt or question. Everything else (values, interpretations, whatever) is a matter of opinion and as such can never be proven or established as true.

If you agree with any of this, we're going to try to talk you out of it (remember our earlier discussion about limited relativism and how it constitutes an obstacle to Critical Thinking). First, this way of talking and thinking fails to recognize the need for strategies and procedures to resolve issues about what the facts are. Second, it doesn't open up any useful strategic or procedural options for resolving evaluative or interpretive issues. We are therefore going to stipulate meanings with somewhat greater precision and utility than popular conventional usage has for the words "factual," "evaluative," and "interpretive." We will use **factual** to refer to matters that can be investigated by the methods either of empirical science or of documentary research. We will use **evaluative** to refer to matters that concern the merits of things. And we will use **interpretive** to refer to matters that concern the meanings of things.

These categories are neither mutually exclusive nor exhaustive. This means that a given issue may have aspects that belong to more than one of these categories or may fall outside all of them. Bear in mind that the purpose of this categorical scheme has little to do with labeling issues or sorting them "correctly." It's more about clarifying the agenda of inquiry. Recognizing a given issue as belonging to a particular type is potentially valuable in determining what strategies and procedures will be most likely to lead to a resolution of the issue. To approach an issue as a factual issue is to raise questions of *evidence*. What sort of evidence would be relevant and decisive? What evidence is already available that bears on the issue? What additional evidence is required? What sorts of experiment or research would be needed to obtain that additional evidence? To approach an issue as an evaluative issue is to raise questions of *standards*. To approach an issue as an interpretive issue is to raise the question of interpretive *hypotheses*.

FACTUAL ISSUES

In modern Olympic history, which nation has won the most medals in weight lifting? What city is the world's coldest national capital? What is the average temperature of the water in Lake Tahoe? All of these are factual questions. They illustrate what we mean by saying that factual matters can be investigated by doing empirical science or documentary research. If a dispute were to arise about any of these questions, say, during a game of *Jeopardy* or *Trivial Pursuit,* there are already well-established procedures available for settling it. We might look the information up in a reliable source (documentary research). If the information is not already recorded, we could easily imagine the sort of scientific investigation by which the information could be gathered.

Having said that, we should also note that not all factual issues are equally simple. Suppose that we needed to figure out how many feral cats are living in the city of San Francisco. In this case, the question is not theoretically difficult to answer. It's a simple factual matter of counting the cats. But in practice, how is anyone going to count all feral (wild) cats in the city of San Francisco? They run away. They hide. They breed like, uh, feral cats. So we would need to estimate the number in some way. Things might not be simple even with the simple-sounding examples we mentioned earlier. Suppose we were asked to determine the average temperature of the water in the Pacific Ocean. You can begin to appreciate the difficulty of determining at least some matters of fact.

Doing good science involves both evaluation and interpretation, as does doing good documentary research. The question of whether or not there is a global environmental crisis is an excellent example. Suppose we approach it initially as a factual question. What sort of evidence would be relevant? Well, suppose there were hard, empirical evidence of significant changes in weather patterns on a global scale. That would be relevant evidence. Notice that evaluation (of the evidence) is already involved. *Hard* evidence has merit, and *significant* changes merit attention. Supposing for the moment that we do have hard evidence of significant global weather anomalies, we would still need some understanding of their causes to answer the original question. This will involve interpreting the evidence we already have, as well as additional evidence that we may seek, concerning, for example, extraordinary fluctuations in the average temperature in the Pacific Ocean. We discuss all of this further in Chapters 8 and 9.

EVALUATIVE ISSUES

Reconsider the first two issues we mentioned earlier: Should there be a law against abortion? Should animals be used in medical experimentation? One thing should be clear right away: neither of these issues can be resolved simply as a matter of fact. We could not possibly hope to settle a dispute over the right and proper legal status of abortion by doing documentary research alone. Nor could we hope to settle a dispute over the use of animals in experimental medicine on the basis of empirical science alone. Not that documentation and empirical evidence are irrelevant to these issues. Just as evaluation and interpretation are important parts of any good factual inquiry, so good science and good documentary research often play a crucial role in evaluation and interpretation. But no amount of empirical evidence, documentation, or both could be *by itself* decisive in either of these issues. So it would make sense to approach them initially not as factual issues. The word "should" in each question is a clue that each issue is fundamentally evaluative, which raises the question of standards. What standards of evaluation are we concerned with? In each issue, it is apparent that moral or ethical standards are central. So they will need to be clarified in the course of the inquiry. Interpretive and factual questions will take their place in the agenda of inquiry as they arise in the process of clarifying and applying these moral or ethical standards. We discuss this further in Chapter 10.

INTERPRETIVE ISSUES

Suppose that in her first speech before the United Nations General Assembly the newly appointed U.S. ambassador makes five explicit references to human rights, free trade, opium, democracy, and Hong Kong. Is the United States "sending a message" to Beijing? And if so, what is the message? Or take this example from our earlier list of issues: does the Federal Reserve Board's move to raise interest rates indicate that its members think the recession is over? These questions indicate issues concerning what things mean or how they should be understood. Such issues often arise in our attempts to understand things whose meanings may be flexible, complicated, multilayered, obscure, or even deliberately veiled. Issues of this sort are probably the most complex and difficult issues procedurally that we are likely to encounter in everyday discourse. Yet they are also fundamental to the process of communication because they have to do with the discernment of meaning. Indeed, perhaps most of the activities you will be performing throughout this book involve interpretation. Deciding whether or not a particular passage is an argument involves interpretation. Deciding whether a passage is intended to serve an expressive, persuasive, or informative function involves interpretation. There is no single simple procedure for resolving interpretive issues or settling interpretive disputes. Rather, there are many kinds of information relevant to interpretation, some of which have already been mentioned and some of which we discuss further in Chapters 2, 9, and 10.

For example, the conventions governing the use of a term or expression are relevant to its interpretation. Similarly, there are diplomatic conventions, which would be relevant to the interpretation of communications between one government, for example, through its U.N. ambassador, and another. In addition to conventions, information about the context surrounding a passage is relevant to its interpretation. Knowing that a particular speech was delivered before the U.N. General Assembly, rather than, for example, by confidential communiqué to the Chinese ambassador, is an important piece of information that can guide us closer to an accurate understanding of what was meant. Contextual information in the case of oral communication, as well as in film and video, includes facial expression, vocal inflection, bodily posture, and timing.

It should be apparent already that gathering and sifting evidence of such variety, especially in living contexts where time is of the essence, is a process of considerable complexity and subtlety. And there is a good deal of disagreement among theorists about what the proper procedures are for doing interpretive work and how they should be applied in different sorts of interpretive controversy. Nevertheless, interpretation is something you are probably good at by now. You no doubt already recognize that some interpretive issues can be resolved relatively firmly and easily whereas others are more difficult and may be quite resistant to resolution. In disputed cases, perhaps the most useful procedural strategy is the use of hypothetical reasoning. This involves formulating and testing interpretive hypotheses. A **hypothesis** is a particular sort of conscious assumption. It is an idea we *assume* to be true for the purpose of exploring or testing it. This procedure also has important applications in dealing with factual issues. We discuss it in greater detail in Chapter 9.

REVIEW EXERCISE 1.6 | **Issue Analysis III**

Logically prioritize each of the following sets of related issues or questions—and explain your decisions:

- ☐ Should there be a law against hate speech on the Internet?   ✱
- ☐ What is hate speech?
- ☐ Should the service provider or the government be responsible for the enforcement of regulations prohibiting hate speech over the Internet?
- ☐ What kinds of penalties should be imposed on people who post hate speech on the Internet?

- ☐ Is time travel possible?
- ☐ Is time travel technically feasible?
- ☐ Is the technical feasibility of time travel worth investigating?
- ☐ What is meant by "time travel"?

- ☐ What are the defining criteria for being a person?
- ☐ Should abortion be prohibited under criminal law as a form of homicide?
- ☐ Is abortion a form of homicide?
- ☐ Is the human fetus a person?

- ☐ Should same-sex couples be allowed to join in legally sanctioned marriages?
- ☐ Will the recognition of same-sex marriages undermine the purposes of the institution of legally sanctioned marriage?
- ☐ What purpose or purposes are served by the institution of legally sanctioned marriage?
- ☐ Could civilization survive the collapse of an institution as important as legally sanctioned marriage as a result of the recognition of same-sex marriages?

COMPOSING AN ISSUE STATEMENT   An **issue statement** is a composition whose purpose is to clearly communicate an interest in a topic, a topic about which we anticipate disagreement among reasonable people.

An issue statement can be composed briefly, for example, as a single short sentence, or at greater length, for example, as the opening chapter of a book. The ability to compose issue statements is essential both to successfully communicating our opinions and to understanding the viewpoints of others (as we explain in Chapter 5). Either way, composing an issue statement can and should involve careful and appropriate use of the techniques of issue analysis discussed earlier in this chapter. Eventually, when you compose a complete argumentative essay, a well-crafted issue statement will be an important part of your essay's introduction. We work on this in greater detail in Chapter 13.

WRITING ASSIGNMENT 1.3 | Issue Statement

Compose a 250-word issue statement (one-page standard double-spaced) incorporating your results from Thought Experiments 1.12 and 1.13. In your issue statement, try not to take sides.

WRITING ASSIGNMENT 1.4 | Term Project

Compose a 250-word issue statement (one-page standard double-spaced) presenting an issue of your choice. In your issue statement, try not to take sides.

GLOSSARY

agenda of inquiry   an organized list of issues to resolve
assumption   an unsupported claim
assumption, hidden   an unstated or implied assumption
assumption, inferential   a hidden assumption that functions as added support, linking a stated premise with a conclusion
authority   an expert or source of information outside oneself
belief   an idea in which one has invested one's confidence
claim   a statement that is either true or false
critical thinking   using reason to make up your mind
discipline   the cultivation of mastery through practice
egocentrism   favoritism for oneself and the beliefs, values, traditions, and groups with which one identifies
ethnocentricity   favoritism for the beliefs, values, and traditions of one's ethnic group
hypothesis   An idea assumed to be true for the purpose of exploring or testing it
issue   a topic about which reasonable people may disagree
issue, factual   an issue to be resolved by either methods of empirical science or documentary research
issue, evaluative   an issue concerning the merits of things

issue, interpretive   an issue concerning the meanings of things

issue statement   a composition whose purpose is to communicate interest in a topic about which reasonable people may disagree

logical priority   a kind of order among issues, where one issue presupposes a resolution of a second issue; the second comes logically before the first

presupposition   an assumption required to make sense of what is explicitly stated

prioritize   to place in order as a series

reason   1. the human capacity to use disciplined intelligence to solve problems
       2. a claim used as a premise
       3. a claim used as an explanation

relativism   the view that the truth is relative and varies

subjectivism   the view that the truth is relative or varies from individual to individual

truth   the agreement of an idea with reality

worldview   the self-regulating system of assumptions and other beliefs through which one receives and interprets new information

ADDITIONAL EXERCISES

As you work through the exercises throughout this book, keep in mind what we said earlier about relativism and the search for truth. There are some questions for which there's no such thing as *the* correct answer, yet even in such cases most likely some answers will be better than others. What matters most is how you reason your way to your answer and whether your reasoning holds up under scrutiny. When you discuss these exercises, don't be afraid to challenge answers that may be offered by your instructors. But you should also try to understand and appreciate the reasoning your instructors may have to offer in support of their preferred answers.

■ **THOUGHT EXPERIMENT 1.14 WORLDVIEW**   We will use the term **worldview** to refer to the self-regulating system of assumptions and other beliefs according to which a person views the world or deals with incoming information. One of the most valuable things about the diversity of cultures you will find on most contemporary college campuses is what you can learn from cultures other than your own about the limitations of your worldview. Here is an exercise in self-awareness and appreciation of cultural diversity: Try to identify three items in your worldview that are not shared by or that conflict with the worldview of a typical member of some identifiable culture other than your own. You may find it useful, perhaps even necessary, to approach one or more of your fellow students whose cultural heritage or heritages differ from your own and learn a bit from them about the distinctive characteristics of their culture or cultures.

■ **THOUGHT EXPERIMENT 1.15 CULTURAL AWARENESS**   Another valuable thing about cultural diversity is what you can learn about common or shared humanity. Here is a follow-up exercise in cultural awareness: Try to identify three items in your worldview that are or would be shared by a typical member of some identifiable culture other than your own.

▦ **DISCUSSION TOPIC 1.11 SELF-DECEPTION REVISITED**   From your experience, give an example of self-deception in which you or someone you know persisted in maintaining a belief in the face of powerful contradictory evidence. As best you can, explain how this was possible for the person.

▦ **THOUGHT EXPERIMENT 1.16 AUTHORITATIVE SOURCES**   Identify 10 beliefs that you hold on the basis of some external authority. As best you can, identify the authoritative source of the belief in each case. Then evaluate the authority. Is the authority generally reliable? Is the authority an appropriate one for the belief in question?

▦ **RESEARCH ASSIGNMENT 1.1 WEB SOURCES**   Google "critical thinking" and log the first 10 citations. How does the information from these sources compare with what you've learned so far in this book?

Internet Address	Site Name	Brief Description

▦ **WRITING ASSIGNMENT 1.5 FREEWRITE REWRITE**   With this introductory chapter under your belt, review what you wrote earlier in Writing Assignment 1.1, your freewrite on what you hope and expect to get out of a course of Critical Thinking. Have your hopes and expectations changed as a result of your reading and experiences in the course so far? With the benefit of these experiences, edit your earlier thoughts into a short essay of one or two pages on the topic of what you hope and expect to get out of a course in Critical Thinking.

NOTES

[1] Jeremy Cooke, "School Trains Suicide Bombers," *BBC News,* July 18, 2001.

[2] Janet Reitman, "Inside Scientology: The Church of Scientology." *Rolling Stone* 995 (March 9, 2006): 55–65.

[3] Thomas Jefferson, Declaration of Independence.

[4] California State Assembly Bill #1890.

[5] Charles J. Hanley, AP News Service, August 13, 2006.

[6] Metaphysics is the branch of philosophy concerned with the nature of reality; epistemology is the branch of philosophy concerned with belief and knowledge.

[7] This series of thought experiments is derived from Jonathan Bennett's unpublished lectures on Descartes, given at the University of British Columbia, 1970–1972.

[8] *Newsweek,* August 7, 1997.

[9] Stanley Milgram, *Obedience to Authority: An Experimental View* (New York: Harper & Row, 1974).

[10] See S. E. Asch, "Effects of Group Pressure Upon the Modification and Distortion of Judgment," in M. H. Guetskow (ed.), *Groups, Leadership and Men* (Pittsburgh: Carnegie Press, 1951); S. E. Asch, "Opinions and Social Pressure," *Scientific American* (September 1955): 31–35; S. E. Asch, "Studies of Individual and Conformity: A Minority of One Against a Unanimous Majority," *Psychological Monographs* 70 (1956): 9.

[11] William James, *Pragmatism, Lecture II* (Cambridge, MA: Harvard University Press, 1975).

[12] Ibid.

CHAPTER 2

Language

"Some people have a way with words.

Some no have way." —STEVE MARTIN

Sometimes people wonder why there is a chapter on language in a book about thinking. Try to imagine what thinking would be like without language. Hard to imagine, isn't it? The harder you try, the more you notice language creeping into the effort. The more you notice yourself trying to "put the ideas into words," so to speak. The more it seems clear that thinking, as we know it, can't be separated from language. Language is a fundamental medium of our thinking—a basic environment and material within which our thoughts take form and gain expression. There are other ways, perhaps, in which our thinking takes shape and comes out. Language (narrowly conceived, as words) is not the only thing you pay attention to in finding out what and how people think. Posture, gesture, vocal inflection, timing, context, and so on, are all meaningful dimensions of human communication, and they often guide our interpretations of people's words. But no dimension is more important than language itself. It is language that is most central and basic. Indeed, to say

that the other dimensions of human communication are meaningful is almost as good as saying that they are linguistic dimensions of human communication—either part of language (more broadly conceived) or at least language-like. In any case, when you boil it all down, the most important and best way of finding out what and how people think is by attending to what they *say*.

WHAT IS LANGUAGE?

This is one of those questions you hope your children don't ask you when they're little and persistent in their curiosity. But here is a powerful way to approach a question like this: think in terms of *function*.[1] For example, try to imagine having never seen a corkscrew before and coming across one at a garage sale. What is *this*? What *is* this? Answer: What it does is what it is, and what it *is,* is what it *does.* Or, more precisely, what it is designed to be used for is essential to its nature. So think about language in the same way.

THOUGHT EXPERIMENT 2.1 | Uses of Language

Use your imagination. How many distinct uses of language can you think of in 5 minutes?

Use or Function	Example

We imagine that you will have noticed that language has a variety of actual and potential uses. Marvel for just a moment at the flexibility, utility, and power of language as a set of tools. Language can be used to describe the world or some part of it, pose problems, suggest solutions, issue orders, make agreements, tell stories, tell jokes, sing songs, exchange greetings, buy things, sell things, make friends, insult enemies, and so on. Can language be said to serve any specific *single, essential* function amid all this variety? Remember these points from chapter 1: Humans are social animals. Our chances of survival and of flourishing are greatly enhanced by association with others of our kind. We do much better in groups than as individuals. This places a high premium on *cooperation* and *coordination with others*. Thus the essential function, as well as the functional essence, of language would seem to be communication. What exactly is communication? **Communication** is what we do to achieve common understanding—essential to cooperation and coordination—among two or more sentient beings.

FUNCTIONS OF LANGUAGE

Consider the variety of actual and possible uses of language from the point of view of critical thinking. Given our understanding of critical thinking as a discipline for making reasonable decisions about what to do or believe, it makes sense to single out several general uses or functions of language for special attention.

THE INFORMATIVE FUNCTION OF LANGUAGE

Begin with a concept we introduced in Chapter 1: "A claim is a statement that claims for itself (whether rightly or wrongly) the value of being true." Writing in 370 B.C., Hippocrates, the father of Western medicine, wrote,

> Speaking generally, all parts of the body which have a function, if used in moderation and exercised in labors to which each is accustomed, become healthy and age slowly. But if unused and left idle, they come liable to disease, defective in growth, and age quickly.

Hippocrates was reporting the results of empirical observation and making general claims about how physical exercise and health are related, claims he clearly thought to be true and wanted others to accept as true. *When we use language in this way for making claims, language is performing its* **informative** *function.* A few more typical examples:

Washington, D.C., is the capital of the United States of America.

The number of category 4 and 5 hurricanes has almost doubled in the last 30 years.

U.S. presidential elections are held every 4 years.

Business administration is currently the most popular college major.

One out of 10 Americans has herpes.

The Democrats have never controlled the U.S. House of Representatives.

Notice that the last statement is false. "Informative," as we are using it here, includes *misinformation*. Not just true statements but also false statements, statements whose truth is not yet determined, and statements whose truth may be in doubt, such as "Extraterrestrial life exists" and "The next U.S. president will be a Republican," all count as examples of the informative function of language.

THE EXPRESSIVE FUNCTION OF LANGUAGE

In addition to its utility for making claims and conveying information, language has important and powerful capacities to express and arouse emotion. A bumper sticker we used to see quite a lot reads:

"Mean people suck!"

Quite possibly the authors of this statement, as well as some of those who drive around with it on their cars, are making a claim they think is true. But the main thing that such a bumper sticker accomplishes is to express an "attitude"— to vent and to arouse emotional energy. *Whenever language is used to vent or arouse feelings, it is said to perform its* **expressive** *function.* Poetry furnishes some of the best examples of the expressive function of language, such as the following poem by William Wordsworth:

So fair, so sweet, withal so sensitive,
Would that the Little Flowers were to live,
Conscious of half the pleasures which they give . . .

Here again, although the poet *may* be making a claim he thinks is true and worth communicating about the aesthetic value of flowers, the poetry more powerfully expresses emotion and evokes an emotional mood in the reader. The importance of the expressive function of language for critical thinking has to do with the role of emotion in decision making. Emotional energy is powerful, easily capable of overwhelming common sense.

This is not to say that emotions should play *no role* in decision making. Emotional energy can and sometimes does reinforce and enhance a process of rational deliberation. But again, given our understanding of critical thinking as a discipline for making reasonable decisions about what to do or believe, it is generally advisable to be aware of the expressive function and use of language insofar as it may interfere with rational decision making. Again, we stress that *awareness* is not the same as *wariness*. If someone says, "*Beware* of emotional language," he or she is, in effect, engaging in a mild form of fear mongering—itself an instance of emotional language. Fear can and often does cloud judgment, but we cannot think of a single example or situation in which awareness would cloud judgment. (We come back to this topic at the end of this chapter.)

CRITICAL THINKING TIP 2.1 | **Awareness of Emotion in Language**

~~BEWARE of Emotion~~   Be AWARE of Emotional Language

REVIEW EXERCISE 2.1 | **Emotional Language Awareness I**

To highlight the emotional dimension of language, British philosopher Bertrand Russell once proposed a word game: Write a single action or description so that the first person (I or we) comes out sounding emotionally positive, the second person (you) neutral, and the third person (he, she, or they) negative. Like this: I have reconsidered my position, you changed your mind, and he went back on his word.

1. I am tidy, you _____, and she is fussy.
2. I _____, you _____, and he is a tightwad.
3. I have high self-esteem, you _____, and she _____.
4. I _____, you're easily amused, and she's frivolous.
5. I take pride in my appearance, you _____, and he's so vain.
6. We _____, you support a capitalist economic system, and they _____.

THE DIRECTIVE FUNCTION OF LANGUAGE

Refocus again on the functional essence of language and the survival value of coordination and cooperation for us all as humans. Any interest in coordination or cooperation quickly translates into an interest in other people's behavior and ways of influencing it. How do we convince other people to cooperate with us? How do we make them to do what we want? We say things like,

"Please pass the butter."
"Caution: Keep hands and feet away while machine is in use."

Language serves a **directive** *function when it is used in an attempt to influence the behavior of another person.* If someone is in a position of power or authority, then perhaps he or she can issue commands and give orders, but ordinarily, when we are with our peers, our directive uses of the language take the form of requests and suggestions. When we make requests and offer suggestions, we generally are counting on at least a willingness to cooperate in the other party. But what do we do when we can neither command nor presuppose a willingness to cooperate? Generally, under these circumstances we need to be **persuasive.** We try to influence the beliefs and motivations behind the behavior we want. Language is flexible and powerful enough to lend itself well to this purpose. Critical thinking is especially interested in this particular kind of directive use of language—what we will call "persuasive language." This is where the directive function of the language comes to incorporate the informative and expressive functions of language, because to influence people's beliefs and motivations, it is often necessary to convince people to accept certain claims as true and it often proves useful to arouse emotional energy. For example, remember the quotation from Hippocrates we used earlier to illustrate the informative function of language:

> Speaking generally, all parts of the body which have a function, if used in moderation and exercised in labors to which each is accustomed, become healthy and age slowly. But if unused and left idle, they come liable to disease, defective in growth, and age quickly.

We encountered this quotation posted on the wall of a health club in the gymnasium near the mirror wall that people face when they are on the exercise machinery. Next to the quotation is a life-sized photo-poster showing a young woman athlete in peak physical condition about to serve a volleyball. She looks great! In this context, the quotation is clearly being used persuasively as a motivator.

REVIEW EXERCISE 2.2 | Functions of Language   ✳

For each of the following examples, determine the *primary* language function. (Occasionally there is more than one primary language function.) Be prepared to explain the reasoning behind your answer.

Informative	The suspect left the scene driving a green convertible with out-of-state plates.	Explain your answer:
Expressive		
Directive		
Persuasive		

Informative	Follow highway 12 west to Madrone Road, take Madrone to Arnold Drive, then turn left and drive 2 miles 'till you see the golf course.	Explain your answer:
Expressive		
Directive		
Persuasive		

Informative	"We must all hang together or assuredly we shall all hang separately." —Ben Franklin (to other signers of the Declaration of Independence)	Explain your answer:
Expressive		
Directive		
Persuasive		

	Informative	Teenage moviegoer after seeing *Spiderman:* "Awesome!"	Explain your answer:
	Expressive		
	Directive		
	Persuasive		

	Informative	Combine 2 cups water and 1 tablespoon butter and bring to a boil. Stir in rice and spice mix, reduce heat, and simmer for 10 minutes.	Explain your answer:
	Expressive		
	Directive		
	Persuasive		

	Informative	How 'bout those Dallas Cowboys cheerleaders, ya know what I'm sayin'?!	Explain your answer:
	Expressive		
	Directive		
	Persuasive		

	Informative	Noticing that it was 5 minutes past bedtime, Mrs. Cleaver said, "Okay Beaver, let's close the book now and go to bed."	Explain your answer:
	Expressive		
	Directive		
	Persuasive		

	Informative	"If we don't do something, Saddam might attack us. And he might attack us with a more serious weapon." —George W. Bush	Explain your answer:
	Expressive		
	Directive		
	Persuasive		

	Informative	"Yemeni and American officials said five other people, described as lower-level al-Qaeda operatives, were in the car with Mr. Harthi when it was destroyed by the missile as the vehicle drove in a remote region of Yemen." —*New York Times*, November 8, 2002	Explain your answer:
	Expressive		
	Directive		
	Persuasive		

	Informative	"20 of the 21 hottest years measured have occurred within the last 25 years." —Al Gore, *An Inconvenient Truth*	Explain your answer:
	Expressive		
	Directive		
	Persuasive		

MEANING IN LANGUAGE

How do words get to mean what they mean? (Another one of those questions you hope your children don't ask you.) Let's start by briefly examining a primitive theory: that words are essentially labels for things. For example, the word "cat" functions as a label. It stands for and points to the animal. We can use it not only to identify an individual animal, distinguishing it from other things, but also to categorize the animal (grouping things together—in this case, to refer to feline creatures). A moment's reflection and you can readily see how useful labels are. Just imagine how hard it would be to talk about people, as a group, if we didn't have labels like "humanity" or "people." Imagine how hard it would be to talk about the functions of language if we didn't have the word "function"—or some other word with the same function. Labels also help us point things out or refer specifically to a particular part of a complex situation, as in "Please pass the *butter.*" Labels help us orient ourselves in new and unfamiliar surroundings, as in "Where's the *restroom?*" Labels are like verbal handles, enabling us to mentally come to grips with our world and our experience. In Arabic, there are more than 5,000 words that pinpoint differences of age, sex, and bodily structure among camels. Consider how much more it must be possible to say—and to think—about camels in Arabic than in English. From this, we can appreciate how tempting it may be to generalize from labels to the whole of language.

Next, how do labels come to mean what they mean? How does the word "cat" come to stand for the animal and the category? Speakers of English use "cat," speakers of French use *chat,* speakers of Spanish use *gato,* and speakers of German use *katze.* These are similar enough to make us wonder if there isn't a natural connection between the label and what it is a label for. Some labels, like "hiccup" and "splash," do seem to have an identifiable natural connection to the things they stand for. A label that *sounds like* what it is a label for is called an "onomatopoeia." But most labels don't have this sort of obvious and straightforward connection with their jobs: for example, "onomatopoeia"—or for that matter, *any* of the words in this sentence. Some of them—"for," "any," "the," "in"—don't even seem to function as labels.

For a more comprehensive and deeply explanatory theory of meaning, we might do well to return to the notion of language's essential function, or functional

B.C.   by johnny hart

essence, as a set of tools for achieving common understanding and look at things this way: Words are noises that humans have assigned meanings to. Speakers of English use "cat" to refer to feline creatures, speakers of French use *chat,* and so on. There is nothing required or natural about such assignments of meaning to noises. Any other sound *could* have been made to stand for what "cat" stands for in English, and likewise in the other language communities. These assignments of meaning are merely conventional; that is, they are based on human conventions. Other words, like "the," "and," "so," and "on," have meanings in accordance with their conventional uses, with the roles they conventionally play in putting words together into meaningful sentences. Much the same can be said of syntax as of word meaning. **Syntax** refers to the structural regularities in the ways words are put together to communicate thoughts and ideas. In English, we put adjectives before nouns, as in "white house." In Spanish, the adjective typically follows the noun: *casa blanca.* The difference is a matter of convention.

What is a convention? A **convention** is simply a behavioral regularity that we maintain and follow to solve problems of coordination. Suppose that you and your friend are cut off in the middle of a cell phone conversation. You have what we might call a "coordination problem." What each of you should do depends on what the other person does. If you both dial each other's cell phone number, you both hear a busy signal. If you both hang up and wait, well, . . . you wait. You resume contact if, and only if, one of you dials while the other waits. What should you do? Suppose that in the past when this sort of thing has happened you have always been the one to dial, that this has worked, that you know it has worked, that your friend knows it has worked, that you know that your friend knows it has worked, that you know that your friend knows that you know this, and so on. If you pick up the phone and dial while your friend waits, and if you do these things because you are both thinking that this will solve the coordination problem, because both of you know that it has worked in the past, you are following a convention.[2] The basic problems of communication, understanding one another and making yourself understood, are coordination problems. Language can usefully be understood as a vast system of conventions that we learn to follow to solve such problems.

A number of interesting and important consequences follow from this way of viewing language. First, linguistic conventions are, in one sense, arbitrary. This means that they *could have been* other than they are. Indeed, linguistic conventions evolve, sometimes quite rapidly and dramatically. But although linguistic conventions could have been other than they are and may change over time, they nevertheless regulate meaningful discourse. Linguistic conventions are thus a lot like the rules in a game.

Think of the rules governing organized sports like American football or basketball and you'll see what we mean. One rule in American football states that the length of the playing field between the end zones is 100 yards; another prescribes exactly 11 players on the field per team. These rules are arbitrary; they could be other than what they are. For example, Canadian football is played on a 110-yard field with 12 players on the field from each side. And the rules of a game can be changed by common consent. For example, the 3-point field goal in professional and collegiate basketball is a relatively late addition to the game. But the rules, whatever they are, regulate the game. If you choose to play American football, then you must play by its rules. If you play Canadian football, you must observe its rules.

Similarly, in playing the language game, we must generally abide by the conventions of the particular language in which we are attempting to communicate. And we can rightly expect others to do the same. Conventions in language are more flexible and informal than rules are in games. For one thing, you aren't thrown out of the game for committing five unconventional speech acts. Furthermore, sometimes violating a linguistic convention can be a creative and effective way of communicating something unique and special. Nevertheless, meaningful departures from the conventions of our language presuppose those conventions as generally binding. If this were not the case, departing from our language's conventions would lead to hopeless confusion.

In *Through the Looking Glass,* Alice and Humpty Dumpty have the following conversation:

> "There are 364 days when you might get un-birthday presents."
> "Certainly," said Alice.
> "And only *one* for birthday presents, you know. There's glory for you!"
> "I don't know what you mean by 'glory,'" Alice said.
> Humpty Dumpty smiled contemptuously. "Of course you don't—till I tell you. I meant, 'there's a nice knock-down argument for you!'"
> "But 'glory' doesn't mean 'a nice knock-down argument,'" Alice objected.
> "When I use a word," Humpty Dumpty said, in a rather scornful tone, "it means just what I choose it to mean—neither more nor less."[3]

Just imagine the confusion that would reign if, like Humpty Dumpty, each of us used words to mean exactly what we wanted them to mean, "neither more nor less." To avoid such chaos and inconvenience, we generally presuppose a conventional interpretation of what someone says. If a writer or speaker doesn't indicate a departure from conventional usage, we normally assume that the person is following conventional usage. This works both ways, which is why it's generally best to *follow conventional usage* when we try to communicate. When we do use words in an unconventional way, we need to give our audience extra guidance to our meaning. If we don't, we're likely to lose them. It should be obvious what happens when you and your audience are not coordinated regarding what you mean: communication breaks down.

AND SPEAKING OF: | **Communication Breakdown**

Neighbors chop down redwood: Claim to have had permission

By William Wetmore
Index-Tribune staff writer

An East Napa Street front yard is now barren, following a misunderstanding between neighbors.

When Rene Alonzo returned to Sonoma in early December, he drove straight past his East Napa Street home. Realizing his mistake, he backed up, parked and slowly got out of his car. Seeing his lawn, he gasped and fell back against the vehicle. The house was the same as always, but his prized old-growth trees were gone.

Alonzo had been away for six weeks, caring for his wife who is in the hospital. He hoped to bring her back to the Sonoma house that she has owned for 35 years since before their marriage. But after seeing the property, Alonzo wanted to spare her the shock.

Three trees had been removed, along with hedges on the side of the house. Alonzo couldn't believe what he was seeing. "These trees are 150 years old," he said.

Alonzo said that a caretaker at the house had contacted him while he was away and said that the new neighbors had asked permission to remove a single overhanging branch from one of the trees. Alonzo agreed but said that he had no idea they were going to take out the entire trees. "We don't even know the neighbors. We've never even met them," Alonzo said.

Mona Couchman has lived at 351 East Napa Street with her husband and 3-year-old daughter since September. She said that her family decided to have the trees removed on the Monday after Thanksgiving because they were top heavy and could possibly fall and hurt people. "Our neighbors are very upset about it, but it seems that this is an issue of dangerous trees," Couchman said.

Couchman said that she wanted to contact Alonzo, but the caretaker would not give her his number. She said that the caretaker understood that they were going to remove the trees and was surprised when Alonzo was shocked. "We're very reasonable people. We wouldn't do it if we knew how irate he would be," Couchman said. According to Couchman there was no mention of only removing one branch. "We never, ever said that," she said.

Alonzo claims that his property is worth half a million dollars less now that the trees are gone. "It would have been better if they knocked down part of the house. At least you could rebuild it," he said.

The incident was reported to the Sonoma Police Department, but Capt. Robert Wedell said that it is no longer being investigated as a crime because "there was no intent to do harm. It's now up to the parties to resolve it," Wedell said.[4]

DISCUSSION TOPIC 2.1 | Communication Breakdown

What factors can you identify to account for the breakdown in communication between the neighbors in the preceding story?

DIMENSIONS OF MEANING: PRECISION AND CLARITY

The story you just read discusses a pair of next-door neighbors who have never spoken to each other face to face, and probably never will. Their only communications so far have been through intermediaries, first the caretaker, then the police, and now the lawyers. No doubt there are several important lessons to be drawn from this unfortunate tale. You can see, for instance, what people mean when they say, "Get it in writing." And you can see the importance of two dimensions of communication in particular, precision and clarity.

AMBIGUITY AND VAGUENESS

Let us now distinguish and define two important concepts that have to do with precision and clarity in communication and that will prove increasingly useful as we proceed: ambiguity and vagueness. Each of these can be a source of confusion in communication (which may help explain why they are so often confused with each other). To say that a term or expression is **ambiguous** is to say that it has more than one conventional meaning. In other words, it can be conventionally understood in more than one way. For example, the word "bank" can be conventionally understood as

- a noun for any piled up mass, such as snow or clouds
- a noun for the slope of land adjoining a body of water
- a noun for the cushion of a billiard or pool table
- a verb for the action of directing a shot at an angle off a surface (such as a billiard cushion or a backboard)
- a verb for the action of tilting an aircraft in flight
- a noun for a business establishment authorized to receive and safeguard money and to lend money at interest
- a verb for the action of putting something of value away in safekeeping

Saying that a term is **vague** means that it is not entirely clear what it does and doesn't apply to. In technical terms, a vague term or expression is one that has an indefinite "extension" (this term is discussed in more detail later in this chapter). For example, the term "bald" clearly applies to actor Jason Alexander or basketball commentator Dick Vitale. It clearly does not apply to former President Bill Clinton or actor Brad Pitt. But there is an indefinite area between where it isn't clear whether a person is bald or not. Vagueness itself admits of degrees according to how big the "gray area" is. Thus "bald" is less vague than "happy," and "vague" is itself vague (which is a vague thing to say).

DEFINITION 2.1 | Ambiguous

A term or expression with more than one distinct conventional meaning

---

DEFINITION 2.2 | Vague

A term or expression with an indefinite extension, that is, fuzzy boundaries

---

Vagueness and ambiguity are both singled out as the focus of criticism, for example, in the margins of student essays. Indeed, in such essays they often undermine the clarity and precision of communication. But it is important also to be aware that both vagueness and ambiguity are useful features of the language. They each contribute to language's inherent *flexibility*. Ambiguity gives language the flexibility to handle multiple meanings at once. Without ambiguity, many jokes, plays on words, and puns and much of the richness of poetry and literature in general would be impossible. Vagueness gives language the flexibility it needs to adapt to unforeseen and unforeseeable situations, by leaving questions of definition and judgment open to deliberation in context.

By permission of Johnny Hart and Creators Syndicate, Inc.

REVIEW EXERCISE 2.3 | Ambiguity and Vagueness

In each of the following examples, highlight in one color any terms or expressions that are used in an ambiguous way and highlight in another color any terms or expressions that are vague. Supply a key for your color choices and explain your answers.

	Explain your answers:
Rappers continue to get a bad rap in the press.	
How do reasonable people come to hold unreasonable beliefs?	
Headline: Drunk Gets Nine Months in Violin Case	
The streets are perfectly safe here in New York City. It's the muggers you have to watch out for.	
Random urinalysis for drugs in safety-sensitive job categories does not constitute an unreasonable search.	
A man walks up to the Zen Buddhist hot dog vendor and says, "Make me one with everything."	
Nuclear energy is just as natural as any other fuel and cleaner than many already in use.	
Let me reassure the public that your government is doing everything within its power to make sure that the traveling public is as secure against the threat of terrorism as it can possibly be.	
According to the Supreme Court, flag burning is protected under the First Amendment as an instance of political speech.	

DEFINITIONS

A definition is an explanation of the meaning of a term. The word "definition" and its close relatives "define," "definite," "definitive," and so on, all come from the Latin *definire,* for setting boundaries or limits. The most basic use that we have for definitions is in teaching people a language. One simple definition often used for teaching a language consists in pointing out examples of the term being defined. For example, if someone didn't know what "reptile" meant, you could help that person by pointing out snakes, lizards, turtles, crocodiles, and so on. This kind of definition is called an **ostensive definition**—from the Latin word for show, as in "*show* me what it means." Another basic strategy of definition, also useful for the purpose of teaching new or unfamiliar vocabulary, is through synonyms. From the Greek for same name, **synonyms** are words or expressions that have the same meaning. For example, suppose we run across the word "poltroon" in a line of verse about pirates (rhymes with "doubloon"). If we didn't know that "poltroon" is a synonym for "coward," we might easily wind up thinking that the line was about a parrot or a drunken sailor. Knowing where a word comes from can tell you a lot about what it means, and many words have fascinating histories—or **etymologies.** For example, the word "etymology" comes through Middle English and old French from the Medieval Latin *ethimologia,* which is derived from the Latin *etymologia,* which came from the Greek *etumologia,* which is based on the Greek word *etumon,* which means true sense of the word. Even fluent speakers of

any language regularly need help in understanding a new or unfamiliar term (like "burka" or "gigabyte"), because language is dynamic and evolving constantly. This is why we have dictionaries—and why they need to be updated periodically.

REVIEW EXERCISE 2.4 | Definition Scavenger Hunt

- Make up one example of definition by synonymy.
- Find an example of definition by synonymy in a dictionary.
- Find two examples of stipulated definition (explained later) in this chapter.
- Find four examples of etymology in the paragraph immediately preceding this exercise.

WHAT DICTIONARIES DON'T DO

In a good dictionary, in addition to the spelling and the pronunciation key, we are likely to find examples, synonyms, etymologies, and other information helpful in understanding the conventional meanings of words. But a dictionary generally won't tell you the meaning of a word being used in an unconventional way—although knowing what the word conventionally means is often helpful and may even be essential for figuring out the unconventional meaning.

Suppose a writer or speaker wants to communicate an idea for which no conventionally understood term is exactly right. This could happen when there's an invention or new category to deal with (like "gigabyte"). But it can also happen with well-established vocabulary that needs to depart from conventional usage so that we can get our meanings across. Typically, this will be to achieve *greater precision* than is generally needed for conventional purposes of communication. In a specialized or technical discipline like geometry, words like "point," "line," and "plane" are given meanings that are more precise than their conventional ones. In legal and other policy contexts, it is often necessary to make distinctions and classifications more precisely than conventional vocabulary will express. For example, "In this contract, for purposes of determining benefit eligibility, a 'full-time employee' shall be defined as an 'employee working 25 hours or more per week.'" For these purposes definitions are often **stipulated.** The word "stipulate," which comes from the Latin word for bargaining, means to specify as in an agreement. In effect, when we stipulate a definition, we lay down the terms of an agreement about how a word is to be used and understood in the context of a discourse in which conventional usage and understanding are inadequate or unsuitable.

The next three thought experiments reveal something else dictionaries don't generally do, or at least don't generally do well or reliably.

THOUGHT EXPERIMENT 2.2 | Essential Definitions I

Read the following list of words and check the ones you're confident that you know and understand:

☐ art	☐ entertainment	☐ love	☐ pornography
☐ beauty	☐ freedom	☐ music	☐ religion
☐ communication	☐ information	☐ news	☐ sign
☐ drugs	☐ jazz	☐ obscenity	☐ terrorism

> We'd be willing to bet that you know and understand every word on this list. We'd be willing to bet that if you ran across any of these words in a sentence, you wouldn't need to look the word up in a dictionary. And we think you'd be able to use any of these words quite comfortably and correctly in your conversation and writing, because you are already familiar with the conventional meanings of all of these words. Right?

THOUGHT EXPERIMENT 2.3 | Essential Definitions II

Go through the preceding list and see how many of these words you'd be able to teach to another person ostensively. Remember, this means being able to point out examples to indicate what the word means.

Still no problem, right? Maybe a little problem here and there with one or two of the more "abstract" ones. But in general, manageable, yes? Now pay close attention: here comes something a bit more challenging. What does the word "bridge" mean? In one sense, as a label, the word means what it refers or "points" to—in this case, a group of objects called bridges. This relationship between a label and the things it points to is called **reference.** And the set of things referred to by a term is called the term's **referential extension.** For example, the referential extension of the word "bridge" includes the Golden Gate Bridge; the referential extension of the word "building" includes the Empire State Building. Suppose that part of what the word "bridge" means as a label is the set of things it refers to (that is, its referential extension)—including the Golden Gate Bridge. And part of what the word "building" means as a label is its referential extension, including the Empire State Building. OK?

A word like "building" has a large and diverse referential extension. This is the case because there are lots of buildings and lots of *different kinds of* buildings in the world—including the Empire State Building, the Sydney Opera House, the Pentagon, the lighthouse at Point Reyes, my house, and your house, and the outhouse behind the barn (and the barn). They're all buildings. But *not everything* is a building. This book is not a building. Nor is every structure a building; nor is everything that has ever been built a building. The Golden Gate Bridge is a structure, and it was built, but it is *not* a "building." Why is this and how do we know? In this and most cases, we know because there are *criteria* that determine the referential extension of the term. Bridges and buildings are bridges or buildings because they satisfy criteria that qualify them as bridges or buildings rather than, say, tunnels or microchips. These criteria, which define the refer-ential extension of a term, we will call its **referential criteria**. And let's say that part of what the word "bridge" means as a label is the set of referential criteria that define its referential extension. Add the two together, the label's referential extension and its referential criteria, and you have the label's *literal* meaning.

THOUGHT EXPERIMENT 2.4 | Essential Definitions III

Here's a real challenge: Take any of the words on the list in Thought Experiment 2.2 and explain its referential criteria. The referential criteria of a word form the set of criteria that define the word's referential extension, which is the set of things it refers to.

"Criteria," the plural form of "criterion," derives from the same Greek root as "critical," which, as you should remember from Chapter 1, is about decision making. Criteria are rules or standards for decision making. So the criteria that define a word's extension would be the rules or standards according to which we decide whether the word applies or not. We expect that you will find this surprisingly hard. Take "music," for example. Remember, this is a word you know well. It's in your working vocabulary. You don't need a dictionary to help you understand a question like, "Would you like to listen to some music?" And you can easily identify examples of music. Now try to state the criteria according to which you decide whether some-thing is music or not. This is not as easy as you might think. What you're trying to state here is a kind of definition that we're going to refer to as an **essential defini-tion.** People have often described what we're challenging you to try to do here as stating the *essence*—or essential nature—of (in this case) music. Another way to describe what you're trying to do is this: Think of the referential extension of the word "music" as though it were a bounded territory. The things that the word "music" refers to are inside the boundaries of the territory; things that the word "music" does not refer to are outside the boundaries. What you're trying to do is produce a verbal map of the territory, or describe its boundaries in words. (Remember that the word "definition" comes from the Latin for setting boundaries or limits.)

AND SPEAKING OF: | Definitions and Classifications

Pluto Is Demoted to "Dwarf Planet"

Dennis Overbye
New York Times

After years of wrangling and a week of bitter debate, astronomers voted on a sweep-ing reclassification of the solar system. In what many of them described as a triumph of science over sentiment, Pluto was demoted to the status of a "dwarf planet."

In the new solar system, there are eight planets, at least three dwarf planets and tens of thousands of so-called "smaller solar system bodies," like comets and asteroids.

For now, the dwarf planets include, besides Pluto, Ceres, the largest asteroid, and an object known as UB 313, nicknamed Xena, that is larger than Pluto and, like it, orbits out beyond Neptune in a zone of icy debris known as the Kuiper Belt. But there are dozens more potential dwarf planets known in that zone, planetary scientists say, and the number in that category could quickly swell.

The vote completed a stunning turnaround from only a week ago when the assembled astronomers had been presented with a proposal that would [have] included 12 planets, including Pluto, Ceres, Xena and even Pluto's moon Charon.

It has long been clear that Pluto, discovered in 1930, stood apart from the previously discovered planets. Not only was it much smaller than them, only about 1,600 miles in diameter, smaller than the Moon, but its elongated orbit is tilted with respect to the other planets and it goes inside the orbit of Neptune part of its 248-year journey around the Sun.

Two years ago, the International Astronomical Union appointed a working group of astronomers to come up with a definition that would resolve this tension. The group, led by Iwan Williams of Queen Mary University in London, deadlocked. This year a new group with broader roots, led by Owen Gingerich of Harvard, took up the problem.

According to the new rules a planet must meet three criteria: it must orbit the Sun, it must be big enough for gravity to squash it into a round ball, and it must have cleared other things out of the way in its orbital neighborhood. The latter measure knocks out Pluto and Xena, which orbit among the icy wrecks of the Kuiper Belt, and Ceres, which is in the asteroid belt. Dwarf planets only have to be round.

In the aftermath, some astronomers pointed out that the new definition only applies to our own solar system and that there was so far no such thing as an extra-solar planet.[5]

You might wonder what special purpose or purposes essential definitions serve. Assuming that people are familiar with the word we're defining, there's no need to teach it as a new vocabulary item. And in that case, why would we need *any* definition? Sometimes the way things are classified is a matter of great importance.

Suppose the local city government has just passed a new city ordinance regulating the sale and distribution of "obscene" and "pornographic" materials to minors. Now suppose the local purveyor of recorded entertainment (CDs, tapes, videos) is brought up on charges of violating the ordinance in connection with the sale of a Britney Spears music video to a 16-year-old. The case turns partly on whether or not the Britney Spears video is obscene, pornographic, or both, and that turns on the criteria for "obscenity" and "pornography." These would presumably be stipulated in the city ordinance. But suppose you are on the city council and you have to *draft* the ordinance. You have the challenge of coming up with the wording of the criteria according to which it will be decided whether something is obscene or pornographic. There you are, back at the challenge of formulating the essential definitions. But couldn't you just look these up in a dictionary?

THOUGHT EXPERIMENT 2.5 | **Essential Definitions IV**

Go ahead and try it: Go through the list and see how many satisfactory essential definitions you can find in a good dictionary. Try "terrorism."

Occasionally you may find a satisfactory essential definition in a dictionary. But it is better to approach this as a "figure it out" kind of a challenge rather than a "look it up" kind of a challenge. Why is that so? Take the last word on the list as an example. Here is the definition of "terrorism" supplied by the *American Heritage*

Dictionary of the English Language, "The use of terror, violence, and intimidation to achieve an end."[6] According to this definition, any act of war, indeed, any deliberate use of violence or intimidation, down to the actions of a schoolyard bully or the enforcer on a hockey team, would qualify as terrorism. Do we really want to define this category so broadly? Or do we want a definition that makes finer distinctions possible? Conventional usage of the term "terrorism" is, we think, slightly more selective, like this: "Terrorism is when 'the bad guys' (the enemy) use terror, violence, and intimidation to achieve an end." But this implies a double standard and is therefore clearly useless for any serious discussion of international political conflict. Sometimes, as in connection with international politics, we are not in a position of authority that allows us to just stipulate a meaning that departs from general conventional usage. Such definitions truly need to be negotiated.

AND SPEAKING OF: | Defining Terrorism

The Faces of Hezbollah

Tom Foreman
CNN correspondent

What makes a terrorist?

I don't mean why do people start bombing, and shooting and fighting from the shadows. I mean what should the definition be?

The United States and others clearly call Hezbollah a terrorist group: the source of countless raids, bombings and attacks on Israel; the bombing of the U.S. Marine barracks in Beirut in 1983, which left 241 people dead; and the architects of all those displays in which young men cover their faces, strap mock bombs to their chests, and parade before the cameras pledging to kill any and all soldiers and civilians alike who oppose their cause.

All this makes Hezbollah, especially for many Westerners, the very definition of a terrorist group.

But some people describe another part of Hezbollah. They talk about a group that is beloved in southern Lebanon for running schools, hospitals, social services, even clearing snow in the winter for some communities that the official government of Lebanon does not serve. They say these things make Hezbollah something other than a terrorist group: A quasi-government; a nation within a nation.

All of this is done for Shiite Muslim families. The Shiites in Lebanon have long felt economically and politically deprived, and Hezbollah clearly gives many of them a feeling of both military and social strength.

So for one side, Hezbollah is a killing machine bent on seizing by terror what it wants from the world; for the other side, Hezbollah is a brave force, fighting for the rights of its people.

So what should the standard be? If you ran a newsroom, how would you define who is called a terrorist and who is not? What, for you, is Hezbollah?[7]

In the obscenity and pornography example, we need a ruling as to whether the Britney Spears video is obscene or not. An essential definition of "obscenity" should tell us what to look for in the video to see if it satisfies or fails to satisfy the criteria for obscenity. In the case of terrorism, we need a set of criteria that will help us distinguish acts of terrorism from other kinds of behavior that may or may not involve the use or threat of violence. We are now going to present concepts and strategies for figuring out this sort of definition when just looking it up isn't a satisfactory option.

NECESSARY AND SUFFICIENT CONDITIONS

First, let us stipulate the definitions of two important ingredients of essential definitions: necessary conditions and sufficient conditions. To fulfill its function, an essential definition must allow you to do two things: rule things in and rule things out. Necessary and sufficient conditions are the parts of an essential definition that enable you to rule things in and rule things out.

A **necessary condition** is a characteristic or set of characteristics required for membership in the word's extension. To illustrate, we will use an example that's easier to define essentially than any of the words on the preceding list. We will define the word "square" as used in plane geometry. The essential definition can be stated in two words: equilateral rectangle. In this definition, both "equilateral" and "rectangle" indicate necessary conditions. In other words, something must be both equilateral and rectangular to be included in the extension of the word "square." If you find out that the shape is not equilateral or is not rectangular, you don't need to know anything more about it. You already know enough to rule it out.

DEFINITION 2.3 | **Necessary Condition**

A characteristic required for membership in a word's extension

---

A **sufficient condition** is a characteristic or set of characteristics that is by itself adequate for membership in the word's extension. Again, in the essential definition of "square" as an equilateral rectangle, the set of characteristics, equilateral and rectangle, together constitute a sufficient condition. In other words, if you find out that the shape is both equilateral and rectangular, you don't need to know anything more about it. You don't have to know its size, age, color, value, or molecular structure. You already know enough to rule it in.

DEFINITION 2.4 | **Sufficient Condition**

A characteristic that is by itself adequate for membership in a word's extension

---

A DIALOGICAL APPROACH TO ESSENTIAL DEFINITIONS

As we said in the preceding section, providing an essential definition of a word like "square" is relatively simple and straightforward. "Obscenity" is harder to define.

"Music" is much harder to define. Words like "music," "art," "information," "jazz," and "love," and others like "justice," "liberty," "equality," "racism," and "terrorism," are so hard to define in this way that many people give up. People who persist in the attempt to formulate essential definitions of words like these are often called philosophers, and their attempted essential definitions are often called philosophies or theories and take a whole book to present and explain, as in Immanuel Kant's philosophy of art or John Rawls's *A Theory of Justice.* This involves thinking in a careful and disciplined way about the examples and the precise wording of the definition. We call the following approach "dialogical," because it goes back and forth in dialogue form. To illustrate it, we'll continue with the simple example we used earlier to explain necessary and sufficient conditions.

STEP 1   Formulate a definition. Just go for it. Write it down (so that it stays put and doesn't start changing and evolving before you reach step 2). When we gave the essential definition of "square" earlier, we were able to do it in two words and we reached it in one step, without any of this back and forth business. Squareness is a simple essence to capture in words, but that's rare. We can't often expect to find the essence in one step of two words. In most interesting cases, we're likely going to need to try something and then tinker with it, refine it, and adjust it. This dialogical approach is designed to help the tinkering process stay on a productive track. For purposes of illustration, imagine that we had initially defined the word "square" as an equilateral shape.

CRITICAL THINKING TIP 2.2: | **Three Things to Avoid**

Circularity: A definition is circular if it defines a word in terms of itself. The problem with circularity is that it defeats the purposes of definitions. Once, when we were learning Spanish, we ran across a conjugated form of the verb *fructificar.* Having no idea what this meant, we referred to the Spanish/English dictionary in the back of the book, where we learned that *fructificar* is Spanish for to fructify. But what we really needed to know was what "to fructify" means ("to fructify" is to bear fruit). The rest we had already figured out. The purposes of the definition will be defeated by circularity whether you are trying to teach the conventional meaning of a new or unfamiliar word, to stipulate an unconventional meaning, or to give an essential definition.

Obscurity: A similar problem results from obscurity. If the terminology in which the definition is formulated is even less familiar than the word being defined, or is more difficult to grasp and understand, then the definition will be harder to understand than the word whose meaning it is supposed to explain. It's not always possible to avoid obscurity, especially in formulating an essential definition, because people are not all familiar with the same words. What is obscure to one reader may be quite familiar to another. Even more important, sometimes the ideas you need to capture in words are themselves out of the ordinary and only relatively obscure words will do the trick. Basically, you should try to keep the words as simple and familiar as the ideas you're working with will permit.

Negativity: A definition should explain what a word means, not what the word doesn't mean. Some words defy affirmative definition. "Orphan" means a child whose parents are not living; "bald" means the state of not having hair on one's head. Unless negativity is an essential element in the meaning of the word, try to formulate the definition in the affirmative.

STEP 2 Critique step 1 by example. In our example, and using what we know about shapes, we can see that something's not entirely right about the definition of "square" as an equilateral shape. And we can demonstrate this using an example:

The example does two important things. First, it exposes a flaw in the definition as formulated in step 1, because the example fits all criteria specified in the definition but is not a legitimate member of the extension of the word "square." In other words, the example *refutes* the definition. An example used for this purpose, or to accomplish this purpose, we will call a **counterexample.** There are two kinds of counterexample: those that show that the definition is too broad or overly inclusive or that it lets in too much (this is how the preceding triangle example works), and those that show that the definition is too narrow or overly restrictive or that it leaves out too much. An example that *is* a legitimate member of the extension of a word but does not satisfy all criteria specified in a proposed definition would show that definition to be too narrow. The second thing the counterexample does is point the way in step 3.

STEP 3 Revise the original definition. Look at our example: what was wrong with the definition of "square" as an equilateral shape? The first definition was too broad, as demonstrated by the counterexample in step 2, so we know we need to make the definition more restrictive. That means adding another necessary condition. How shall we formulate it? The counterexample in step 2 gives good guidance here: not enough sides. That's what we want to add to the definition in step 3. So we would revise the definition to say that "square" means equilateral quadrilateral. ("Quadrilateral" means four-sided figure).

STEP 4 Repeat step 2 (critique step 3 by example). Once again, using what we know about shapes we can see that something's still not entirely right about the definition of "square" as an equilateral quadrilateral. And we can demonstrate this by example:

STEP 5 Repeat step 3 (revise the revised definition). Look at our example: what was wrong with the definition of "square" as an equilateral quadrilateral? Once again our definition was too broad, as demonstrated by our counterexample in step 4, so we know we need to make the definition even more restrictive. That means adding another necessary condition. How shall we formulate it? The counterexample in step 4 again gives good guidance: the angles are not 90-degree

angles. That's what we want to add to the definition at this point. And so we arrive at "square" means equilateral rectangle. ("Rectangle" means four-sided figure with 90-degree angles).

STEP 6   Keep going as needed. At this point, the process is complete for the essential definition of the word "square," because it isn't possible to refute the current definition by example. Anything that fits all criteria specified in the current definition will be a legitimate member of the extension of the word, and vice versa: any member of the extension will satisfy all the criteria in the definition. The word and the definition are "coextensive," which means they have the same extension. That's how we know we're done.

REVIEW EXERCISE 2.5 | Essential Definitions V

Critique the following formulations as though they were intended to function as essential definitions. Explain your criticisms. Use examples where appropriate.

	Too broad	A "dinosaur" is an extinct animal.	Explain your answer:
	Too narrow		
	Circular		
	Unclear or figurative		

	Too broad	"Rape" is forcing a woman to have sex against her will.	Explain your answer:
	Too narrow		
	Circular		
	Unclear or figurative		

	Too broad	"Faith is the substance of things hoped for, the evidence of things not seen." —Hebrews 11:1	Explain your answer:
	Too narrow		
	Circular		
	Unclear or figurative		

	Too broad	"Economics is the science which treats of the phenomena arising out of the economic activities of men in society." —J. M. Keynes	Explain your answer:
	Too narrow		
	Circular		
	Unclear or figurative		

	Too broad	A "circle" is a closed plane curve.	Explain your answer:
	Too narrow		
	Circular		
	Unclear or figurative		

Too Broad	Explain your answer:
Too Narrow	
Circular	
Unclear or figurative	

Something is "circular" if it is of or pertains to a circle or is the property of circularity.

Too broad	Explain your answer:
Too narrow	
Circular	
Unclear or figurative	

"Pornography" is any pictorial display of human sexuality or nudity.

Too broad	Explain your answer:
Too narrow	
Circular	
Unclear or figurative	

A "definition" is an explanation of the meaning of a term.

Too broad	Explain your answer:
Too narrow	
Circular	
Unclear or figurative	

"Alimony" occurs when two people make a mistake and one of them continues to pay for it.

AND SPEAKING OF: | Essential Definitions

Here is an excerpt from an interview of George H. W. Bush, conducted by Robert I. Sherman, reporter for the *American Atheist News Journal*, during the elder Bush's campaign for the presidency in 1987.

> Sherman: What will you do to win the votes of the Americans who are atheists?
> Bush: I guess I'm pretty weak in the atheist community. Faith in God is important to me.
> Sherman: Surely you recognize the equal citizenship and patriotism of Americans who are atheists?
> Bush: No, I don't know that atheists should be considered as citizens, nor should they be considered patriots. This is one nation under God.

It seems Bush is saying that if you're an atheist, you can't be a citizen, which makes believing in God a necessary condition of citizenship.

GENUS AND DIFFERENTIA

A related strategic approach involves a two-step procedure and the concept of categories:

STEP 1 Locate the referential extension of the term you are defining within a larger category (called the **genus**). For example, squares are part of the larger category of plane geometric figures.

STEP 2   Specify the feature or set of features (called the **differentia**) that distinguishes the extension you are defining from the rest of the larger category. In this case, you want to specify the feature or set of features that distinguishes squares from the rest of the plane geometric figures:

Term	Larger Category	Distinguishing Characteristics
Square	Plane geometric figure	With four equal sides and 90-degree angles

Similarly:

Term	Larger Category	Distinguishing Characteristics
Spoon	Utensil	Consisting of a small, shallow bowl with a handle, used in eating or stirring
Watch	Machine	Portable or wearable for telling time
Ethics	Branch of philosophy	Concerned with morality

Notice that the definition of "square," which we arrived at by using the dialectical approach, is worded differently than the one we arrived at by using genus and differentia. But the two definitions, "equilateral rectangle" and "plane geometric figure with four equal sides and 90-degree angles" are synonymous. They express the same criteria. The necessary and sufficient conditions for being in the extension of "square" are the same in either case. These two strategic approaches can also be effectively combined. If you're stuck, you can use the genus-and-differentia approach to formulate an initial definition and you can use the dialectical approach to critique and refine a definition by genus and differentia.

REVIEW EXERCISE 2.6 | Essential Definitions VI

Here's that list again. Apply the techniques and strategies just discussed and see if you can give a clear and concise essential definition (statement of the referential criteria) for one or more of the items on this list. Use both the dialectical method and the genus-and-differentia approach.

1. art
2. beauty
3. communication
4. drugs
5. entertainment
6. freedom
7. information
8. jazz
9. love
10. music
11. news
12. obscenity
13. pornography
14. religion
15. sign
16. terrorism

DIMENSIONS OF MEANING: COGNITIVE AND AFFECTIVE

CONNOTATIONS

The American educational psychologist Benjamin Bloom developed a now-famous approach to organizing educational objectives. Known as Bloom's Taxonomy, it divides domains and levels of critical thinking and learning generally into three major categories—the **cognitive** (or intellectual, having to do with analysis, inference, and knowledge), the **affective** (or emotional, having to do with attitude), and the **psychomotor** (having to do with physical skills). The previous section on essential definitions focused on what we call the literal meaning of a label, and as such it pertains to the cognitive dimensions of meaning in language. But equally important to meaning and communication in language and hence to critical thinking are the affective dimensions of language, those that account for the emotional energy of language and animate it in its expressive applications. In addition to their literal meanings, most words also come loaded with a penumbra of additional dimensions of (nonliteral) meaning that arise out of their conventional associations and conventionally understood further implications. We call these nonliteral added dimensions of meaning the word's **connotations.** For example, the literal meaning of "prima donna" is its set of referential criteria, the principal female singer in an opera company, plus its referential extension, which would be all principal female singers in opera companies. But, probably because some of the most notorious principal female opera singers have been vain and temperamental, the term has come by conventional association to carry the added meaning of a vain, temperamental person. Consequently, using the term "prima donna," especially outside of the specialized context of opera, is an effective put-down. Similarly, the word "tabloid" literally means a newspaper formatted at half the size of a standard-size newspaper page and with no horizontal fold. But because many newspapers in tabloid format have tended toward journalistic sensationalism, the word "tabloid" conventionally carries an additional negative or pejorative connotation of disreputable journalism. Connotations need not be derogatory. Many are complimentary. "Statesman" sounds more honorable than "politician." "Moderate" sounds more thoughtful than "wishy washy" or "middle of the road." Here you can see the importance of language's expressive function to what we might call the "artistry" of persuasion. It becomes possible, through the careful selection of terminology (choosing a word such as "artistry," for example), to color a statement in a reassuring way, in an ironic way that undermines the otherwise reassuring tone, in an alarming way, or in any number of other emotionally potent ways.

Earlier in this chapter, when we introduced the expressive function of language, we encouraged greater awareness of the emotional power of language. Do you remember the exercise in which you "conjugated" action words or descriptions so that in the first person they sound emotionally positive, in the second person they sound emotionally neutral, and in the third person emotionally negative? Return to that exercise and look at it a little more deeply—and a little more critically.

THOUGHT EXPERIMENT 2.6 | **Emotional Language Awareness II**

Try these again:

1. I am tidy, you _____, are she is fussy.
2. I'm thrifty, you _____, and he is a tightwad.
3. I have high self-esteem, you _____, and she's on a major ego trip.

Did you have any trouble filling in the blanks in the exercise with appropriate language? For example, if "He is a *tightwad*" (obviously negative), and "I am *thrifty*" (positive), what's the *neutral* description? "You are *frugal*"? *Budget conscious?* These, too, sound kind of positive, don't they? We think that although the exercise is instructive and contains a large and important kernel of truth, it is potentially misleading in several ways. The instructions we gave you presuppose, or at least invite you to assume, that the emotional content of language ranges across a continuum from positive to negative with a neutral zone in the middle. That's an oversimplification. First, the emotional capacity and content of language is richer and more varied than can be captured or fairly represented along a simple linear continuum. It's more like a spectrum or palette of color than a line. Second, we must be careful not to encourage the assumption that a given word or phrase carries its emotional baggage wherever it goes or has the same emotional tone *regardless of context.* Following the career of an emotionally potent word (for example, the word "liberal" or the word "pimp"—as in "pimp my ride") can be an eye-opener into the amazing *flexibility and malleability* of language in its expressive employment. Finally, we think that as you raise your level of awareness of the emotional content and power of language and as your sensitivity to all of its colorful nuances grows, you'll find it increasingly difficult to identify emotionally neutral substitutes for language that strikes you as emotionally tinged. Maybe not impossible—but harder and harder in more and more instances. In other words, you will increasingly appreciate the *pervasiveness* of language's emotional energy and the *subtlety* of its influence on the affective dimensions of our thinking.

Nevertheless, as we hinted a moment ago, there is a large and important insight contained in the positive–neutral–negative way of understanding things, and here it is: When it comes to attitude, particularly in the context of persuasive discourse, the categories that matter most are the simple ones: positive and negative. Does the language engender a positive attitude or a negative one? Does the language draw you toward the object or repel you from it? Does it make you more or less enthusiastic? More or less reluctant? More or less committed? That's what matters most. Remember that the persuasive use of language is a subcategory of the directive use of language. When language is used persuasively, someone is trying to influence your beliefs, motivations, and ultimately behavior. They want you to *believe* this (positive) or *disbelieve* that (negative). They want to motivate you to *do* this (positive) or *refrain* from doing that (negative). So pay close attention to how words are selected and deployed to shape and determine attitude.

THOUGHT EXPERIMENT 2.7 | Favorable vs. Unfavorable

In traffic, have you ever noticed how anyone going slower than you is an "idiot," and anyone going faster than you is a "maniac"? The same thing can be called by different names, depending on whether you're for it or against it. For example, if you're for a proposal to outlaw retail discounts on certain merchandise, you might call it the "fair trade practices act"; if you're against it you might call it a "price-fixing law." Take any current issue on your local, the state, or the national legislative agenda and name it, first favorably and then unfavorably.

Probably the two most important areas in which this recommendation would be helpful would be in relation to advertising (and/or sales promotion) and political rhetoric. Each of these areas constitutes a vast and complex topic and is of increasingly urgent interest as the deeply deceptive techniques of advertising move farther into the center of political discourse. Canadian humorist Stephen Leacock once described advertising as "the science of arresting human intelligence long enough to get money from it." We delve into the subject of advertising and its deceptive strategies more deeply in Chapter 11. But let us dwell here for a moment on the subject of political rhetoric. In politics, it often matters what you call something as much or more than what it is. George Orwell, in his famous essay "Politics and the English Language," said, "Political language . . . is designed to make lies sound truthful and murder respectable." And linguist Geoffrey Nunberg observes the following:

> A large part of the Republicans' successes over the past 30 years or so is attributable to their ability to change the political subject—diverting resentments that have their roots in economic inequalities to debates over "values," making programs that chiefly benefit the wealthy sound like they're aimed at benefiting the middle class, turning *government* into a term of abuse, and making reservations about the direction of American foreign policy sound like signs of weakness of purpose or questionable loyalty. The right couldn't have achieved all of that except by bending the meanings of words to their purposes and by getting Americans to accept those new meanings.[8]

For example, in response to generally negative public attitudes toward Republican environmental policy, Republican consultant Frank Luntz offered suggestions for a makeover, which are listed in the next exercise.

DISCUSSION TOPIC 2.2 | Assessing Political Rhetoric

For each part of the Republican environmental policy makeover listed here, first determine what the term or expression refers to then explain the emotional content, its intended effect on attitude, and the extent to which the term's emotional force is misleading:

1. Use "common-sense solutions" or "balanced approaches" in place of "rollbacks" and "deregulation."

2. Use "climate change" in place of "global warming."

3. Stress the need for "sound science."

4. Make frequent use of words like "healthy," "clean," and "safe" (for example, in naming legislation such as President George W. Bush's Healthy Forests Initiative).

This is not simply a partisan matter, as though the political right wing or the Republican party alone wants to control public attitudes through the effective use of emotionally potent catchphrases. A generation ago, in the 1960s and 1970s, the language was moving substantially toward the left in its emotional tone, with terminology like "affirmative action" and "gender equity" and slogans like "equal pay for equal work" and "give peace a chance." Indeed, there is always a dynamic struggle going on between rival political constituencies over the emotional content of language. So, as a critical thinker, you need to become more deeply aware of this struggle as it plays out in your life and times. On the other hand, this does not mean, nor should you assume, that all political discourse is *equally* deceptive. That's again too simplistic. The way to approach this is on a case-by-case basis, asking the following questions: Precisely where is the language deceptive in its emotional tone? Where and in what way or ways does it distort reality?

DISCUSSION TOPIC 2.3 | **Emotional Language Awareness III**

Here are a few more examples. For each example, first determine what the term or expression refers to, then explain the emotional content and its actual or intended effect on attitude and the extent to which the term's emotional force is misleading:

1. Liberal media
2. Privatization of Social Security
3. The ownership society
4. The estate tax
5. The death tax
6. Affirmative action
7. Reverse discrimination

The same considerations apply to what is often described as the "framing of issues" in political discourse. The terminology in which issues are presented for discussion is typically a contentious matter. Because any issue involves conflict and controversy, typically the parties in the discussion have a persuasive agenda and want to "frame" the issue persuasively, by carefully choosing terminology that encourages positive attitudes toward their own position and engenders negative attitudes toward their opponents' positions.

AND SPEAKING OF: | **Emotionally Loaded Political Rhetoric**

Here's an example from a group that calls itself the Center for the Study of Carbon Dioxide and Global Change:

> Is carbon dioxide a harmful air pollutant, or is it an amazingly effective aerial fertilizer? Explore the *positive* side of this issue in the new half-hour documentary, *The Greening of Planet Earth: The Promise for the 21st Century & Beyond.*[9]

Notice how the issue statement presents a choice between an alarming idea, which if true would give cause for grave concern, and a more hopeful alternative idea, puffed up with the word "amazingly." And just in case the reader doesn't see the message, the "positive" side of the issue is explicitly labeled as such in italics. This is not what we'd call a well-balanced issue statement. Its bias is all too obvious—to the point of being clumsy.

WRITING ASSIGNMENT 2.1 | Emotional Language Awareness IV

Critique the issue statement presented earlier in the quotation from the Center for the Study of Carbon Dioxide and Global Change. Do this in terms of the emotional connotations of particular instances of the language used in its presentation. See if you can formulate at a less biased presentation of the issue in 50 words or less. Then try 25 words or less.

WORDS AND PICTURES

They say a picture is worth a thousand words. How much more powerful, then, is material composed out of words *and* pictures? A great deal of the material that circulates in the mass media is composed of carefully selected words and phrases, carefully coordinated with carefully chosen and composed images. The effect on our attitudes as consumers of these carefully crafted compositions (please note the careful choice of words in this paragraph, by the way) is often more profound than we are aware of when we receive such messages. We may manifest an attitude, experience a shift in attitude, or find ourselves expressing an attitude in response to some such message without looking deeply into the mechanisms bringing about these very attitudes. To conclude this discussion, we urge you to pay the same close and well-focused attention to the imagery that accompanies the verbal content of the messages that animate public discourse.

CRITICAL THINKING TIP 2.3 | Words and Pictures Together

Be AWARE of the Persuasive Power of Words and Pictures Together

DISCUSSION TOPIC 2.4 | Words and Pictures

What is the meaning of this magazine cover (Figure 2.1)? What do you guess the lead story might be? What agenda do you imagine is being advanced here? Discuss the affective dimensions of this display, paying attention to the interaction between word and picture.

FIGURE 2.1 Words and Pictures

WRITING ASSIGNMENT 2.2 | Term Project

At the end of Chapter 1 (Writing Assignment 1.4), your instructions were to compose a one-page issue statement. Review and revise that composition. Identify the key terms and concepts in your first draft that are essential to understanding what the issue is. Make sure that these terms are clearly defined. Check to see that you are using terminology in ways consistent with conventional usage or that where you depart from conventional usage your intended meaning is clear. Check your draft for emotionally loaded descriptions or labels. Where there is a detectable bias, try to reformulate the wording to eliminate it. Remember the distinction between the informative and the persuasive uses of language. An issue statement should not be a persuasive composition.

GLOSSARY

affective   emotional—having to do with attitude

ambiguous   a term or expression with more than one conventional meaning

cognitive   intellectual—having to do with analysis, inference, and knowledge

communication   interaction aimed at common understanding

connotation   the emotional effect of a term

convention   a behavioral regularity followed to solve interpersonal coordination problems

counterexample   an example used to refute a general claim, as in a definition

definition   an explanation of the meaning of a term or expression

definition, essential   an explanation that gives the criteria that define the extension of a term

definition, ostensive   a meaning shown by example

definition, stipulated   an explanation that specifies an unconventional meaning of a term for use in a specific context of discourse

differentia   characteristics that distinguish the extension of a term from the genus

directive   language used to influence behavior

etymology   the history of a word

expressive   language used to vent or to arouse emotional energy

extension   the set of objects denoted by a term

genus   a larger category within which the extension of a term is located

informative   language used to make claims

necessary condition   a characteristic or set of characteristics required for membership in the word's extension

persuasive   language used to influence behavior indirectly by influencing beliefs and motivations

psychomotor   having to do with physical skills

reference   the relationship between a word and the objects it "points to"

referential criteria   criteria defining referential extension of a term

referential extension   set of things referred to by a term

sufficient condition   a characteristic or set of characteristics that is by itself adequate qualification for membership in the word's extension

synonyms   words or expressions that have the same meaning ("synonymy" is the sameness of meaning)

syntax   conventional structural regularities for combining words meaningfully

vague   a term or expression with an indefinite extension

ADDITIONAL EXERCISES

■ **WRITING ASSIGNMENT 2.3 WRITING STYLES**   Spend a few (5–10) minutes observing what happens in an open public area, like a busy intersection, the campus quadrangle, or a shopping mall. Write a paragraph that contains a strictly factual descriptive account of what you observed. Next write a paragraph that, besides being informative, is entertaining. Then write a paragraph that uses the information in a persuasive way.

Informative

Entertaining

Persuasive

■ REVIEW EXERCISE 2.7 LOCATING AND EXPLAINING AMBIGUITY AND/OR VAGUENESS

In each of the following examples, highlight in one color any terms or expressions that are used in an ambiguous way, and highlight in another color any terms or expressions that are vague. Supply a key for your color choices and explain your answers.

	Explain your answers:
Asked why he robbed banks, notorious bank robber Willy Sutton replied, "That's where the money is."	
He was thrown from the car as it left the road. Later he was found in the ditch by some stray cows.	
As the great escape artist Harry Houdini drove south along Jefferson Boulevard, he suddenly turned into a side street.	
Baseball pitcher Tug McGraw, asked if he preferred Astroturf to grass, said, "I don't know. I never smoked Astroturf."	
Sexual harassment is defined as unwelcome sexual advances, requests for sexual favors, and other verbal or physical conduct of a sexual nature when • submission to such conduct is made either explicitly or implicitly a term or condition of an individual's employment, admission, or academic evaluation; submission to such conduct is used as a basis for evaluation in personnel decisions or academic evaluations affecting an individual; • such conduct has the purpose or effect of unreasonably interfering with an individual's performance or of creating an intimidating, hostile, offensive, or otherwise adverse working or educational environment; • or the conduct has the purpose or effect of interfering with a student's academic performance; creating an intimidating, hostile, offensive, or otherwise adverse learning environment; or adversely affecting any student.	

■ REVIEW EXERCISE 2.8 DEFINITION SCAVENGER HUNT REVISITED

How many definitions can you find in the first two chapters of this book? List them in the chart given here, and continue onto a new page if necessary.

Page #	Term Defined	Definition

Page #	Term Defined	Definition

REVIEW EXERCISE 2.9 MISINFORMATION   In the following examples, highlight any terms or expressions that are either undefined and should be defined or are defined in an incorrect or inadequate way and should be redefined. Explain your answers.

Explain your answers:

I don't know why some people get so mad about companies like Enron that deceive, or even victimize, the public. Such practices are part of the meaning of free enterprise, which everyone knows is the foundation of our political, social, and economic institutions. Free enterprise means that all of us should do what we think is best for ourselves. That's all business is doing—looking out for itself. If consumers are deceived or damaged, then that's their fault. Let them take a page from the book of free enterprise and look out for themselves. Rather than condemning business for being ambitious, aggressive, shrewd, and resourceful, we should praise it for acting in accordance with the doctrine of free enterprise, which is the American way.	
Murder is whatever prevents a life from coming into existence. By this account, abortion is murder. All societies have proscriptions against murder, and rightly so. There is no more heinous act than to take the innocent life of another. A society that does not stand up to murderers cannot call itself truly civilized. It's obvious, then, that if the United States is worthy of the term "civilized," it must prohibit abortion and deal harshly with those who have committed or commit abortions, because these people are murderers.	

■ **REVIEW EXERCISE 2.10 CONVENTION VS. EMOTION**   Explain both the conventional meaning and the current emotional connotations of the following terms:

Term	Conventional Meaning	Emotional Connotations
adult entertainment		
blogger		
drug-free zone		
extremist		
family entertainment		
free market		
free trade		
free world		
fundamentalist		
hardliner		
Islamofascist		

Term	Conventional Meaning	Emotional Connotations
ivory tower		
neoconservative		
neoliberal		
reality television		
suicide bomber		
the troops		

REVIEW EXERCISE 2.11 CATCHPHRASES Imagine yourself as the creator of a successful national consulting firm specializing in political slogans. Your clients cover the spectrum of issues and interest groups. This month a dozen of your clients have scheduled rallies in major cities for the causes listed here. Your job is to come up with a set of five catchy slogans for each group to successfully communicate its message. You'll be briefing and coaching spokespeople for each group on how to "stay on message." You're also scheduled to address a national radio audience at the end of the month on the topic of "Successful Strategies for Political Communication." You plan to use your work for your current roster of clients to explain the secrets of your success. Below is your client list. Good luck!

1. Friends of the Earth: lobbying for higher fuel-economy standards, tighter federal limits on industrial greenhouse-gas emissions, and subsidies for solar and wind electricity generation
2. The Competitive Enterprise Institute: counterdemonstration lobbying for the elimination of federal regulation of automobile fuel efficiency and subsidies for nuclear power
3. People for the Ethical Treatment of Animals (PETA): opposing the use of animal subjects in AIDS research at the State University Medical Center
4. AIDS Coalition to Unleash Power (ACT UP): counterdemonstration in support of accelerating the pace of AIDS research
5. National Organization for the Reform of Marijuana Laws (NORML): supporting national legislation to permit medical use of marijuana
6. Drug Abuse Resistance Education (DARE): counterdemonstration to keep marijuana classified as an illegal substance
7. EarthFirst: supporting a moratorium on logging in old-growth redwood forests
8. National Wise Use Coalition: counterdemonstration supporting the rights of private interests to harvest timber resources on private lands
9. American Family Association (AFA): opposing a permit for a Eminem concert
10. American Civil Liberties Union (ACLU): counterdemonstration against censorship
11. San Francisco Historical Preservation Society: supporting a citywide ordinance banning skateboarding on all sidewalks and public spaces
12. *Thrasher* magazine: counterdemonstration in support of skateboard right-of-way

NOTES

[1] The Greek philosopher Aristotle was an early developer of this approach. For a more recent treatment of this concept as a general strategy, see David N. Perkins, *Knowledge as Design* (Hillsdale, NJ: Erlbaum, 1986).

[2] This account of linguistic convention is derived from Jonathan Bennett, *Linguistic Behavior* (London: Cambridge University Press, 1976), and David Lewis, *Convention* (Cambridge, MA: Harvard University Press, 1969).

[3] Lewis Carroll, *Through the Looking Glass,* in *The Complete Works of Lewis Carroll* (New York: Random House, 1936), p. 214.

[4] William Wetmore, "Neighbors Chop Down Redwood, Claim to Have Had Permission," *Sonoma Index-Tribune,* Tuesday, December 25, 2001, p. 1.

[5] Dennis Overbye, "Pluto Is Demoted to 'Dwarf Planet,'" *New York Times,* August 24, 2006.

[6] *American Heritage Dictionary of the English Language* (New York: Houghton Mifflin, 1979), p. 1,330.

[7] CNN correspondent Tom Foreman, "The Faces of Hezbollah," *Anderson Cooper's 360 Blog,* July 25, 2006.

[8] Geoffrey Nunberg, *Talking Right: How Conservatives Turned Liberalism into a Tax-Raising, Latte-Drinking, Sushi-Eating, Volvo-Driving, New York Times-Reading, Body-Piercing, Hollywood-Loving, Left-Wing Freak Show* (New York: PublicAffairs, 2006).

[9] www.co2science.org.

UNIT 2

Argument: Fundamental Medium of Rational Deliberation

Defined functionally and structurally
  Argument identification
  ──Argument analysis

Is this the right room for an argument?
I told you once.
No, you haven't.
Yes I have.
When?
Just now.
No you didn't.
I did.
Didn't!
Did!
You did not!
Yes, I did!
No you didn't!
Yes I DID!
No, you DIDN'T!
DID!
Oh now look. This isn't an argument.
Yes it is.
No it isn't. It's just a contradiction.
No it isn't.
It IS!
It is NOT!
Look. You just contradicted me.

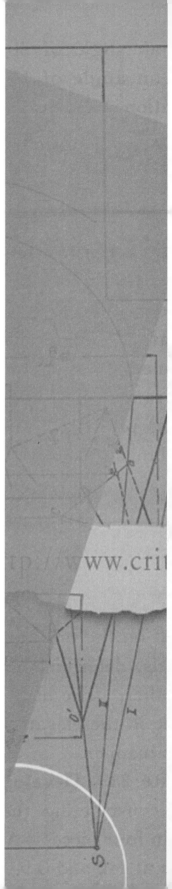

I did not.

Oh, you did.

Nonsense.

Oh, this is futile . . .

No it isn't.

I came here for a good argument.

No, you didn't. No, you came here for an argument.

Well, an argument isn't just a contradiction.

Can be.

No it can't. An argument is a connected series of statements intended to establish a proposition.

No it isn't.

Yes it is. It's not just contradiction.

Look, if I'm going to argue with you I must take up a contrary position.

Yes, but that's not just saying "No it isn't."

Yes it is.

No it ISN'T![1]

—MONTY PYTHON'S FLYING CIRCUS

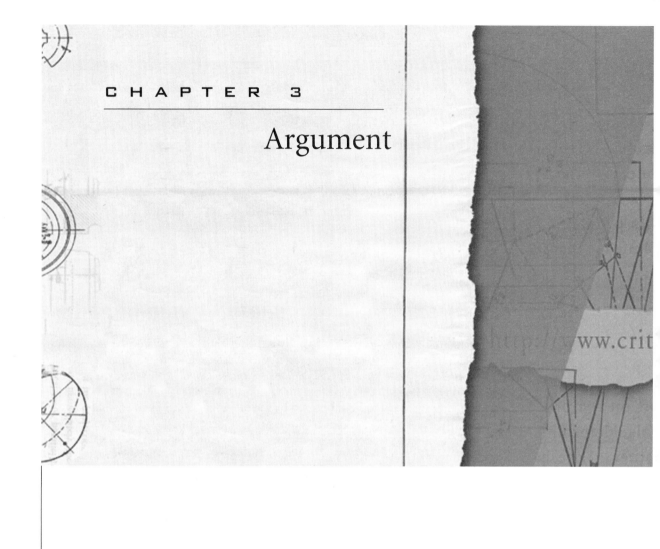

CHAPTER 3

Argument

Suppose that you and some other reasonable person find yourselves divided over an issue, say what rules should apply to trials of people accused of international terrorism. One of you is of the opinion that such cases should be tried under international law, and the other person thinks that such cases should be tried under the laws of the nation that has suffered a terrorist attack. What do reasonable people do when they recognize they are divided over an issue? They argue. In this chapter, we introduce and develop the concept of an argument as at once a product of critical thinking and an object to which critical thinking is applied.

The word "argument" is ambiguous. For clarity, we center on one of its conventional meanings and set aside the other as outside our focus of primary concern. In this book, we are primarily concerned not with the sense of the word "argument" in which two people *have* an argument, but rather with the sense in which an individual person *makes* or *offers* an argument. In this sense, an **argument** can

"This is where your mother and I had our first argument."

be defined as a composition primarily intended to persuade by appealing to a person's reasoning capacity. This gives the referential criteria of the word "argument" (in the sense of making an argument) by reference to function. We can also define this concept by reference to compositional structure, as follows: An argument is a composition consisting of a set of claims, one of which is understood or intended to be supported by the other or others. The two definitions fit together nicely because the structure suits the function. If you want to persuade by appealing to someone's reasoning capacity, compose a series of claims, with the one you want the person to believe supported by the others. So we can combine the two definitions as shown in Definition 3.1.

DEFINITION 3.1 │ Argument

A composition primarily intended to persuade by appealing to a person's reasoning capacity and consisting of a set of claims, one of which is understood or intended to be supported by the other or others

---

In what follows, we use both parts of this definition. The functional part of the definition serves as a basis for argument identification. The structural part of the definition serves as a basis for argument analysis.

Our study of argument can be divided into four main skill areas: identification, analysis, evaluation, and design and construction. Argument identification is about recognizing arguments and telling them apart from other sorts of material. Argument **analysis** is about taking arguments apart to understand how they are put together and designed to work. Argument evaluation involves appraising their strengths and weaknesses. And argument design and construction is about generating original arguments of our own.

Here is a simple example of an argument: International legal institutions cannot be relied upon to bring international terrorists to justice. And international terrorists are not entitled to the protection of the U.S. Constitution or Bill of Rights. Therefore international terrorists should be tried in secret by U.S. military tribunals. "International terrorists should be tried in secret U.S. military tribunals" is the claim the other claims are intended to support and establish. For the purposes of our study of critical thinking, the relationships of support are the ones that matter. We want to focus on the argumentative structure of the composition—rather than its grammatical structure. If we wanted to, we could combine all three claims in the preceding argument into a single sentence. "Since we can't rely on international legal institutions to bring international terrorists to justice, and the U.S. Constitution and Bill of Rights don't apply to international terrorists, they should be tried in secret by U.S. military tribunals." So here is a point to bear in mind as you proceed: although the grammatical structure of a passage is *sometimes* a good guide to its argumentative structure, it's the argumentative structure (*regardless of* its grammatical structure) that we want to get at.

ARGUMENT IDENTIFICATION

Arguments are compositions in language, which as you know is an immensely flexible medium of expression. Open any magazine or daily newspaper and you will find a variety of material composed in language, including some arguments. Listen in on any conversation and you will hear many things going on, quite possibly including argumentation. It is not difficult to identify cases of verbal conflict, especially when you are involved. But identifying arguments, in the sense relevant to our purposes, can be more difficult, especially when they are embedded in larger, more complex contexts. This is partly because recognizing arguments involves recognizing the speaker's or the writer's intentions, and speakers and writers can have complex intentions that they do not always make clear in what they write and say.

Distinguishing arguments from explanations, jokes, greetings, narratives, or instructions is a matter of discerning the author's intentions to persuade by appealing to reason. Sometimes it is clear that the author is trying to persuade in this way. In that case, the author has unmistakably put forward an argument. Sometimes it is clear that the author is trying to do something other than persuade by appealing to reason. In that case, what the author has put forward is not an argument. Sometimes an author may be trying to do two or more things at once, say, persuade by appealing to reason and amuse the reader. Sometimes it's just not clear what the author is trying to do.

We often make claims without arguing for them: Baseball is a popular sport in the United States. Football is generally played in the winter. Hockey is a popular sport in Canada. Basketball can be played inside or outside. Soccer is played throughout the world. Taken individually, these claims are nonargumentative. They just say what they say. Taken as a group, these claims are still nonargumentative. None of them is intended to support or establish any of the others, so they do not constitute an argument.

We also make claims when we are trying to explain things: The class on the history of music has been canceled for lack of enrollment. The horse was frightened by a snake in the grass. Last night's rain made the streets wet. These are explanatory claims. They help explain something: the cancellation of the class, the spooking of the horse, the wet pavement. They are, in other words, presumably intended to help someone understand something better.

The basic difference between such nonargumentative passages and arguments is one of intent or purpose. If people are interested in establishing the truth of a claim and offer evidence intended to do that, then they are making an argument. But if they regard the truth of a claim as nonproblematic, or as already having been established, and are trying to help us understand *why* it is the case (rather than *establish that it is* the case), then they are explaining. Thus, when we say, "The streets are wet because it rained last night," ordinarily we would not be trying to establish that the streets are wet. Presumably that fact is already apparent to any observer, so we would more likely be offering an explanation of how they got that way. But if we say, "You should take your umbrella today, because the weather forecast calls for rain," we would not understand the statement "you should take your umbrella" as an established truth, because advice like this ordinarily isn't offered to people we think are already convinced. In this case, we are more likely setting forth an argument.

In deciding whether a given passage is or is not presenting an argument, take care not to let your evaluative judgments, especially your immediate and negative ones, determine your decision. We have often seen students excluding passages from the category of arguments simply on the grounds that they find the passages unconvincing. "It sure doesn't appeal to *my* reasoning capacity, so I don't even recognize it as an argument." Remember that argument identification comes before argument analysis, which comes before argument evaluation. And remember that even a *bad* argument is an argument.

REVIEW EXERCISE 3.1 | Argument Identification   ✳

Which of the following passages express or contain arguments? You can use either the functional or the structural parts of the definition of "argument" or both to make your determination.

Argument	"A principle I established for myself early in the game: I wanted to get paid for my work, but I didn't want to work for pay." —Poet Leonard Cohen	Explain your answer:	
Explanation			
Other			

Argument	I object to lotteries, because they're biased in favor of lucky people.	Explain your answer:	
Explanation			
Other			

Argument	The most serious issue facing journalism education today is the blurring of the distinctions between advertising, public relations, and journalism itself.	Explain your answer:	
Explanation			
Other			

Argument	"Even the most productive writers are expert dawdlers, doers of unnecessary errands, seekers of interruptions—trials to their wives and husbands, associates, and themselves. They sharpen well-pointed pencils and go out to buy more blank paper, rearrange their office, wander through libraries and bookstores, change words, walk, drive, make unnecessary calls, nap, day dream, and try not 'consciously' to think about what they are going to write so they can think subconsciously about it."
Explanation	
Other	

Explain your answer:

—Donald M. Murray, "Write before Writing"

Argument	"Gentlemen of the jury, surely you will not send to his death a decent, hard-working young man, because for one tragic moment he lost his self-control? Is he not sufficiently punished by the lifelong remorse that is to be his lot? I confidently await your verdict, the only verdict possible: that of homicide with extenuating circumstances."
Explanation	
Other	

Explain your answer:

—Albert Camus, *The Stranger*

Argument	"It seems that mercy cannot be attributed to God. For mercy is a kind of sorrow, as Damascene says. But there is no sorrow in God; and therefore there is no mercy in him."
Explanation	
Other	

Explain your answer:

—Thomas Aquinas

Argument	I knew a guy once who was so influenced by statistics, numbers ruled his entire life! One time he found out that over 80% of all automobile accidents happen within 5 miles of the driver's home. So he moved!
Explanation	
Other	

Explain your answer:

Argument	"Willy Loman never made a lot of money. His name was never in the paper. He's not the finest character that ever lived. But he's a human being, and a terrible thing is happening to him. So attention must be paid. He's not to be allowed to fall into his grave like an old dog. Attention, attention must be paid to such a person."
Explanation	
Other	

Explain your answer:

—Arthur Miller, *Death of a Salesman*

ARGUMENT ANALYSIS

As we indicated earlier, argument analysis involves taking arguments apart into their structural elements so as to better understand how they are designed and intended to work. Argument analysis is a natural extension of argument identification, because argument identification already involves recognizing a set of claims as composed for a certain intended purpose.

PREMISES AND CONCLUSIONS

If an argument is a set of claims, some of which are understood or intended to support the other or others, then we may proceed to define two important basic concepts for both argument identification and argument analysis: the concepts of premise and conclusion. The **premises** of arguments are the claims offered in support of the conclusion. The **conclusion,** or **thesis,** is the claim that the premises are offered to support.

Thus far we have considered two simple arguments:

We can't rely on international legal institutions to bring international terrorists to justice, and the U.S. Constitution and Bill of Rights don't apply to international terrorists.

International terrorists should be tried in secret by U.S. military tribunals.

The weather forecast calls for rain.

You should take your umbrella today.

The solid line indicates the transition from supporting material to what the material supports, or from premise or premises to conclusion. Statements above the line are the premises; statements below the line are conclusions. We will call this line the **inference line.** The word **inference** refers to the step we take in our minds from the premise or premises to the conclusion. As soon as you recognize something as an argument, you are in position to take a positive first step in argument analysis: identify the conclusion. Make this a rule of thumb for argument analysis.

CRITICAL THINKING TIP 3.1 | **Find the Conclusion**

First Find the Conclusion

SIGNAL WORDS

As mentioned earlier, identifying arguments can be difficult, especially when they are embedded in larger contexts, because recognizing arguments involves recognizing the author's intentions. Similarly, identifying the premises and conclusion of an argument can be difficult, especially when we find them embedded in longer passages. If you read and listen carefully, however, you can pick up clues to the presence of arguments and to the identity of premises and conclusions in written or spoken discourse. One

TABLE 3.1   Conclusion Signals

- so
- therefore
- thus
- consequently
- it follows that
- as a result
- hence
- in conclusion
- shows that
- this entails
- this implies
- we may infer that

of the most important clues is the **signal word,** or signal expression. Speakers and writers can and often do signal their intentions by using a word or expression to indicate the presence of a premise or conclusion or relationship of support. Table 3.1 lists some of the words and phrases that conventionally indicate conclusions.

On first reading a passage, it is often useful to circle such signals when you run across them, especially if the passage you are reading is long and complex. Doing so alerts you to the crucial relationships of support within the passage and thus gives you "landmarks" to its argumentative structure.

> International legal institutions cannot be relied upon to bring international terrorists to justice. And international terrorists are not entitled to the protection of the U.S. Constitution or Bill of Rights. (Therefore,) international terrorists should be tried in secret by U.S. military tribunals.

Noticing the word "therefore" in the last sentence helps us locate the argument's conclusion, "International terrorists should be tried in secret by U.S. military tribunals." It also helps us recognize that the first two claims are offered as reasons or premises in support of that conclusion.

Just as "therefore" is conventionally used to signal a conclusion, there are several conventional ways to signal premises. Table 3.2 lists some of the words and phrases that conventionally indicate premises.

TABLE 3.2   Premise Signals

- since
- because
- for
- follows from
- after all
- due to
- inasmuch as
- insofar as

Again, in reading a passage, it can be quite useful to circle such expressions so as to locate and keep track of premises.

> (Since) we can't rely on international legal institutions to bring international terrorists to justice, and (because) the U.S. Constitution and Bill of Rights don't apply to international terrorists, they should be tried in secret by U.S. military tribunals.

In this passage, the words "since" and "because" introduce the premises that support the arguer's position in favor of secret military trials in cases of terrorism.

Having said this, we need to add two words of caution: first, a reminder about ambiguity. Many of the words conventionally used to signal arguments have other conventional applications. So you can't simply rely on the presence of the signal words listed here as a foolproof indication of the presence of an argument. For example, if we compare

> You should take your umbrella today, because the weather forecast calls for rain.

with

> The streets are wet because it rained last night.

we see that the first is an argument in which the word "because" introduces a premise but the second is an explanation. In the second, the word "because" introduces a claim whose intended function is not to *prove* or *establish* but rather to *explain* the wetness of the streets. "Because" and other such terms (like "since" and "for") are ambiguous in this way. Sometimes they indicate the presence of an argument, and sometimes they do not. Like most interpretive work, identifying arguments—and even recognizing an expression as an argument signal—is largely context dependent.

Second, many of the arguments you will encounter contain no signals. Sometimes you're just supposed to understand that an argument is being presented.

> Look, if we can't trust international law to convict terrorists, who don't deserve the protection of our Constitution or Bill of Rights anyway, why shouldn't they be tried in secret by the U.S. military?

This passage, in one sentence, still makes three claims. And evidently the passage is an argument, because one of the claims made in it is supported by the others. How can we tell this? Start by taking the sentence as a whole and ask yourself, What is its *point*?

REVIEW EXERCISE 3.2 | **Find the Conclusion**

Highlight the point of the passage:

Look, if we can't trust international law to convict terrorists, who don't deserve the protection of our Constitution or Bill of Rights anyway, why shouldn't they be tried in secret by the U.S. military?

We expect that you will have zeroed in on the question at the end, "why shouldn't they [the terrorists] be tried in secret by the U.S. military?" Even though it is expressed in the grammatical form of a question, there is a claim being made here: The terrorists *might as well* be tried in secret by the U.S. military. Now ask the natural next question, *Why* should we accept this claim? As soon as you ask this "why" question, you can see that the rest of the sentence is responding to your question with two additional claims: "We can't trust international law to convict terrorists," and "terrorists don't deserve the protections of our Constitution or Bill of Rights." In effect, the author has anticipated a challenge—naturally arising in the mind of any reasoning being—that a controversial claim be given some rational support and has tried to meet this challenge. These two additional supporting claims are therefore the argument's premises. Notice again that it is the argumentative structure, not the grammatical structure, that matters for our purposes in critical thinking. Notice also that in any passage of argumentative material, argument analysis boils down to simply figuring out what supports what.

REVIEW EXERCISE 3.3 | Argument Signals

Circle the signals and highlight the conclusions in the following passages:

1. Our whole class has to stay after school for an hour. So I'm going to need a ride home, because the bus leaves right after school.

2. Humans and many higher animals have similar neurophysiological structures. Humans and animals exhibit many of the same behavioral responses to stimuli. It is reasonable to suppose that animals feel pain and pleasure as we humans do.

3. "And he went from there, and entered their synagogue. And behold, there was a man with a withered hand. And they asked him, 'is it lawful to heal on the Sabbath?' so that they might accuse him. He said to them, 'what man of you, if he has one sheep, and it falls into a pit on the Sabbath, will not lay hold of it and lift it out? Of how much more value is a man than a sheep? So it is lawful to do good on the Sabbath'" (Matthew 12:9–12).

4. Two out of three people interviewed preferred Zest to another soap. Therefore Zest is the best soap available.

5. In the next century, more and more people will turn to solar energy to heat their homes because the price of gas and oil will become prohibitive for most consumers and the price of installing solar panels will decline.

6. People who smoke cigarettes should be forced to pay for their own health insurance since they know smoking is bad for their health; and they have no right to expect others to pay for their addictions.

7. It's no wonder that government aid to the poor fails. Poor people can't manage their money.

8. Even though spanking has immediate punitive and (for the parent) anger-releasing effects, parents should not spank their children, for spanking gives children the message that inflicting pain on others is an appropriate means of changing their behavior. Furthermore, spanking trains children to submit to the arbitrary rules of authority figures who have the power to harm them. We ought not to give our children those messages. Rather, we should train them to either make appropriate behavioral choices or to expect to deal with the related natural and logical consequences of their behavior.

9. Public schools generally avoid investigation of debatable issues and instead stress rote recall of isolated facts, which teaches students to unquestioningly absorb given information on demand so that they can regurgitate it in its entirety during testing situations. Although students are generally not

allowed to question it, much of what is presented as accurate information is indeed controversial. But citizens need to develop decision-making skills regarding debatable issues to truly participate in a democracy. It follows then that public schools ought to change their educational priorities to better prepare students to become informed responsible members of our democracy.

10. Ever since the injury to Jerry Rice, the Raider running game has been under pressure to produce. But since their win–loss record is best in the AFC West, we must conclude that the loss of Rice, while damaging to their overall offense, has not been devastating.

11. Late-night radio talk show host: I've heard more heart attacks happen on Monday than on any other day of the week, probably because Mondays mark a return to those stressful work situations for so many of you. So let's all call in sick this Monday, OK, folks, because we don't want any of you to check out on us.

12. Since capital punishment is a form of homicide, it requires a strong justification. Simple vengeance is not an adequate justification for homicide. Therefore, since there is no conclusive evidence that capital punishment deters violent crime, capital punishment is not justified.

DEEPER ANALYSIS

Recognizing that people generally require reasons to persuade them to accept a controversial claim, we set forth an argument. In the argument, additional claims are made in support of the claim we are trying to persuade people to accept. But these additional claims may be challenged as well. Recognizing this, authors often anticipate the need to supply further support for the premises of their arguments—in other words, to build in arguments for the premises of their arguments. Therefore arguments often call for analysis in depth, as layer upon layer of support may be required.

International legal institutions, (because) they are fragile and poorly established, cannot be relied upon to bring international terrorists to justice. And international terrorists are not entitled to the protection of the U.S. Constitution or Bill of Rights, (because) these documents pertain only to U.S. citizens. (Therefore) international terrorists should be tried in secret by U.S. military tribunals.

Circling the signal words in the preceding passage helps us recognize several important features of this argument's structure. It enables us to notice first that the premise "international legal institutions cannot be relied upon to bring international terrorists to justice," has embedded in it an additional claim "they [international legal institutions] are fragile and poorly established." Once we see this, we can also recognize that this claim is intended to support the one it is embedded in. Similarly, we notice that the premise "international terrorists are not entitled to the protection of the U.S. Constitution or Bill of Rights" is now followed by a further supporting claim: "these documents [the U.S. Constitution and Bill of Rights] pertain only to U.S. citizens."

From this relatively brief example, you can already see that a great deal of complexity can be packed into a few words. So you can easily imagine what challenge might be involved in taking apart a large and complex argument and keeping track of all relationships of support among its many claims. In chapter 4 we give you a few tools for coping with this kind of challenge.

REVIEW EXERCISE 3.4 | **Layers of Support**   ❊

Circle the signals, and then highlight the conclusions in the following passages. Next highlight the premises. Use a second color for premises that support the conclusion directly, and a third color for premises that support other premises. Supply a key for your color choices.

1. The mother-in-law can't be the murderer. The victim, a vigorous 200-pound athlete, was strangled by the murderer's bare hands. The murderer must have well-developed upper body strength. The mother-in-law is a frail 80-year-old woman.

2. Part of believing something is believing that it's true. So if I were to do an inventory of my beliefs, they'd all seem true to me. Or, to put it another way, if I knew something was false, I wouldn't believe it. So it doesn't really make sense for me to say that some of my beliefs are false.

3. I've been mistaken in the past. I've learned on numerous occasions, and pretty much throughout my life, that things that I believed to be true were really false. Why should it be any different now? So if I were to do an inventory of my beliefs, I probably wouldn't notice the false ones, but I'd still bet there are some in there somewhere.

4. "Nor is there anything smart about smoking. A woman who smokes is far more likely than her nonsmoking counterpart to suffer from a host of disabling conditions, any of which can interfere with her ability to perform at home or on the job. . . . Women who smoke have more spontaneous abortions, stillbirths, and premature babies than do nonsmokers, and their children's later health may be affected."[2]

5. "Since the mid-'50s, for example, scientists have observed the same characteristics in what they thought were different cancer cells and concluded that these traits must be common to all cancers. All cancer cells had certain nutritional needs, all could grow in soft agar cultures, all could seed new solid tumors when transplanted into experimental animals, and all contained drastically abnormal chromosomes—the 'mark of cancer.'"[3]

HIDDEN DEPTHS

In Chapter 1 we explained how important it is to be aware of the assumptions that may be involved in the reasoning being analyzed and that one important place to look for hidden assumptions is "underneath" the claims being made in the argument. We defined "presuppositions" as the kind of assumption that must be made for what is explicitly said to make sense. In this example, from one of the exercises at the end of Chapter 1, an argument is being made against the claim that extraterrestrials crash-landed at the United States Air Force Base at Roswell, New Mexico:

> If you were an alien and you were scoping out earthly terrain, the last place you'd go would be to one of the most highly fortified and tightly secured military installations in the United States.

Notice that this argument presupposes alien reasoning as essentially similar to human reasoning, in particular that aliens would be able to recognize a military installation as such if they saw one and that they would recognize such a place as dangerous and to be avoided.

REVIEW EXERCISE 3.5 | Hidden Presuppositions

What presuppositions can you identify in the argument from Review Exercise 3.2:

> Look, if we can't trust international law to convict terrorists, who don't deserve the protection of our Constitution or Bill of Rights anyway, why shouldn't they be tried in secret by the U.S. military?*

Presuppositions:

_____

_____

_____

*This presupposes that we know who the terrorists are before they have been tried and before their guilt has been established in court.

Just as people sometimes put forward arguments without signals, leaving it up to the listener or reader to recognize the argument as such, so people often put forward arguments that aren't completely stated. Sometimes what's hidden is the part of the argument we want to find first. Sometimes it's the argument's point, or conclusion, that you're just supposed to understand. Suppose that you are standing in line at the polling place on Election Day, waiting to have your registration verified and receive your official ballot, and you overhear the official say to the person in front of you:

> "I'm sorry sir, but only those citizens whose names appear on my roster are eligible to vote, and your name does not appear."

Clearly there is something further implied here. The implied conclusion, which is evidently intended to follow from the two claims explicitly made, is that the person in front of you is not eligible to vote. This example, then, expresses an argument. And recognizing it as such depends upon recognizing that the two explicitly stated claims "point to" the unstated conclusion.

REVIEW EXERCISE 3.6 | Unstated Conclusions

Each of the following arguments has an unstated conclusion. Formulate the conclusion.

1. I'm sorry, but you may stay in the country only if you have a current visa, and your visa has expired.

   Therefore

   _____

2. God has all the virtues, and benevolence is certainly a virtue.

   Therefore

   _____

3. Either the battery in the remote control is dead or the set's unplugged; but the set is plugged in.

   Therefore

---

4. All mammals suckle their young, all primates are mammals, and orangutans are primates.

   Therefore

---

5. Software is written by humans, and humans make mistakes.

   Therefore

---

6. Legislation that can't be enforced is useless, and there's no way to enforce censorship over the Internet.

   Therefore

In chapter 1 we explained that another important place to look for hidden assumptions is *between* the claims being made in the argument. We defined "inferential assumptions" as the kind of assumptions that play the role of "missing link in the chain of reasoning." Suppose once more that you are standing in line at the polling place on Election Day and you overhear the official say to the person in front of you:

> "I'm sorry sir, but only those citizens whose names appear on my roster are eligible to vote."

Again, the context makes clear that the official is offering support for the claim that the person in front of you is not eligible to vote. But in addition to the unstated conclusion, there is an unstated premise:

> "Your name does not appear on my roster."

Implied conclusions and premises are important parts of the logical structure of the arguments in which they occur, and they need to be taken into account in our analyses and evaluations of such arguments. How do we tell that there is an unstated claim (that the person's name does not appear on the roster of eligible voters) in the last example? Look between the premise and the conclusion:

Only those citizens whose names appear on my roster are eligible to vote.

Therefore you are not eligible to vote.

The missing premise, "your name does not appear on my roster," is clearly implied, because it would seem to be the only way to get from the explicitly stated premise to the conclusion.

REVIEW EXERCISE 3.7 | Hidden Inferential Assumptions   ✳

What is the hidden inferential assumption in the following example?

> International terrorists are not entitled to the protection of the U.S. Constitution or Bill of Rights, because these documents pertain only to U.S. citizens.

Answer: This depends on the additional inferential assumption that international terrorists are not U.S. citizens.

Each of the following arguments has an unstated premise. Formulate the missing premise.

1. All propaganda is dangerous. Therefore Fox network news is dangerous

because

2. UCLA will play in the Rose Bowl because the Pac-10 champion always plays in the Rose Bowl,

and

3. Everything with commercial potential eventually becomes absorbed into the corporate world, so the Internet will eventually be absorbed into the corporate world

because

4. Hip-hop is a fad, so it will surely fade

because

This is the most challenging kind of argument analysis, for the obvious reason that some of the things we are trying to account for are hidden. In Chapter 5 we give you a few additional tools for coping with this kind of challenge.

GLOSSARY

analysis   the process of breaking complex things down into their constituent elements

argument   (defined functionally) a composition primarily intended to persuade by appealing to a person's reasoning capacity; (defined structurally) a composition consisting of a set of claims, the thesis or conclusion of which is supported by the premise or premises

conclusion   the claim in an argument supported by the premise

inference   mental step in reasoning from premise(s) to conclusion

inference line   line used in representing arguments to separate premise(s) from conclusion

premise   the claim in an argument that supports the conclusion; there can be more than one premise to an argument
signal word   the word indicating the presence of an argument or argument part
thesis   the conclusion, especially in an extended argument

ADDITIONAL EXERCISES

The following additional exercises should help you determine your readiness to move on to Chapters 4 and 5.

■ **REVIEW EXERCISE 3.8 ARGUMENT IDENTIFICATION**   In each of the following examples, check all issue categories that apply. Most important, explain each classification you make.

Argument	The game has been delayed because of rain.	Explain your answer:
Explanation		
Other		

Argument	"While taking my noon walk today, I had more morbid thoughts. What is it about death that bothers me so much? Probably the hours. Melnick says the soul is immortal and lives on after the body drops away, but if my soul exists without my body I am convinced all my clothes will be loose fitting." —Woody Allen	Explain your answer:
Explanation		
Other		

Argument	I've heard more heart attacks happen on Monday than on any other day of the week, probably because Mondays mark a return to stressful work situations for so many.	Explain your answer:
Explanation		
Other		

Argument	"Gentlemen of the jury, surely you will not send to his death a decent, hard-working young man, because for one tragic moment he lost his self-control? Is he not sufficiently punished by the lifelong remorse that is to be his lot? I confidently await your verdict, the only verdict possible: that of homicide with extenuating circumstances." —Albert Camus, *The Stranger*	Explain your answer:
Explanation		
Other		

Argument	"One woman told me that brown spots, a bugaboo to older women, were twice as numerous on the left side of her face and arm due to daily use of her car. The right, or interior, side of her face and right arm showed far fewer brown spots. Since these unattractive marks seem to be promoted by exposure to the sun, either cover up or use a good sunscreen."[4]	Explain your answer:
Explanation		
Both		
Other		

Argument	"In bureaucratic logic, bad judgment is any decision that can lead to embarrassing questions, even if the decision was itself right. Therefore no man with an eye on a career can afford to be right when he can manage to be safe."[5]	Explain your answer:
Explanation		
Both		
Other		

REVIEW EXERCISE 3.9 ARGUMENT STRUCTURE   Using the punctuation and signals as clues to missing elements, fill in the blanks of the following "argument skeletons" with the letter *P* (for premise), *PS* (for premise support), or *C* (for conclusion). Then flesh out each argument skeleton with claims.

1. _____ and _____ . So, _____ .

2. _____ , because _____ , since _____ .

3. Inasmuch as _____ , _____ , for _____ .

4. _____ . Therefore, since _____ , _____ .

5. _____ . Therefore _____ , because _____ .

6. _____ . This follows from _____ , and _____ .

7. _____ , because _____ and _____ .

8. Since _____ , as _____ , _____ , for _____ .

9. _____ for the reasons that _____ and _____ .
   Thus, because _____ , _____ .

REVIEW EXERCISE 3.10 ARGUMENT CONSTRUCTION   Assume that each of the following passages is an argument. Fit the claims in each passage into the argument skeleton provided.

1. College education affects earning potential. Research shows that college graduates make more money over a lifetime than noncollege graduates do. _____ , for _____ .

2. This new diet won't help me lose weight. No diet I've ever tried has worked. _____. So _____.

3. Bill must be a poor student. Bill spends most of his time watching ESPN. _____, since _____.

4. Students come to school to learn. Students should have no say in curriculum decisions. Because _____, _____.

5. Pornography doesn't contribute to sex crimes. Pornography shouldn't be restricted. Since _____, _____.

6. Sexually promiscuous people have a greater chance of getting AIDS than people who aren't sexually promiscuous. AIDS is a sexually transmitted disease. People who use condoms run less risk of getting AIDS than people who don't. _____ because _____ and _____.

7. It's no business of government if a person wants to commit suicide. Laws prohibiting suicide are indefensible. Whether or not people should be able to harm themselves is strictly their own affair. _____ because_____, since _____.

8. Parents need to be careful about imposing punishment and bestowing rewards on children. Giving rewards too quickly can set up the parent for blackmail. Deferring punishment can be a sign of weakness. _____, for _____ and _____.

9. There are no natural rights. Social anthropologists report that the rights accorded people vary from society to society and even within a society over time. Since _____, as _____, it follows that _____.

10. When the civil-rights movement began in the early 1950s, the South had a lock on leadership positions in the U.S. Senate. That made congressional leadership in the assault on racial discrimination highly unlikely. Whatever progress blacks, and women for that matter, have made in attaining equal rights with white males, they can thank the Supreme Court for. Without the resolute backing of the Supreme Court, there could have been no civil-rights revolution. _____, because _____, since _____, for _____.

▨ **REVIEW EXERCISE 3.11 ARGUMENT ANALYSIS I**   For each of the following passages, either highlight or state the conclusion:

1. "Yond Cassius has a lean and hungry look. . . . Such men are dangerous" (William Shakespeare, *Julius Caesar*).

2. "Only demonstrative proof should be able to make you abandon the theory of Creation; but such a proof does not exist in nature" (Moses Maimonides, *The Guide for the Perplexed*).

3. "When we regard a man as morally responsible for an act, we regard him as a legitimate object of moral praise or blame in respect of it. But it seems plain that a man cannot be a legitimate object of moral praise or blame for an act unless in willing the act he is in some important sense a 'free' agent."[6]

4. "There is . . . strong evidence, based on a review of thousands of military documents and hundreds of interviews with military personnel, that the U.S. approach to pacifying Iraq in the months after the collapse of [Saddam] Hussein helped spur the insurgency and made it bigger and stronger than it might have been."[7]

5. "It is worth saying something about the social position of beggars, for when one has consorted with them, and found that they are ordinary human beings, one cannot help being struck by the curious attitude that society takes toward them."[8]

6. "In bureaucratic logic, bad judgment is any decision that can lead to embarrassing questions, even if the decision was itself right . . . no man with an eye on a career can afford to be right when he can manage to be safe"[9]

7. "You and I are far from that stage of mastery [of the exacting writer], but we are none the less obliged to do some rewriting beyond the intensive correcting of bad spots. For in the act of revising on the small scale one comes upon gaps in thought and—what is as bad—real or apparent repetitions or intrusions, sometimes called 'backstitching.'"[10]

REVIEW EXERCISE 3.12 ARGUMENT ANALYSIS II The following examples can be understood as arguments with layers of support—conclusions, supported by premises, with further support for premises. Identify conclusion, premises, and premise support in each case.

1. The longer elected officials hold office, the more likely it is they will become corrupt. The reason is that power corrupts and over time officeholders become more powerful. Therefore, there should be a limit to the number of years any elected officials may serve.

2. The wise person doesn't smoke. Smoking kills, but it's also expensive and offensive. Statistics show that nonsmokers increasingly object to the smoker's violation of their right to breathe smoke-free air.

3. Humans are fallible, so they'll make mistakes. Because mistakes are unintentional, it's clear that human fallibility often mocks our best laid plans.

4. None of us left to ourselves can attain all we desire. That's why societies are necessary. But societies cannot survive without compromise and cooperation. Hence, each of us must strive to see things from the other person's viewpoint.

5. In a democracy, the people exercise government in person. But in a republic, they express their will through representatives. Obviously, then, the United States is a republic. The only way to reserve and enrich democratic freedoms in a republic is for the people to be educated enough to select representatives wisely. Therefore, Americans should take education seriously.

REVIEW EXERCISE 3.13 ARGUMENT RECONSTRUCTION The following eight sentences were extracted from an op-ed column titled "Television, More Vast Than Ever, Turns Toxic," by Newton H. Minow, former chairman of the Federal

Communications Commission (FCC). Can you reassemble them into a logically coherent argument?

If a broadcaster won't provide public service aimed at improving the lot of children and the democratic process, Congress and the FCC should find someone who will—or make the broadcaster pay for using the channel.

Second, the democratic process is what enables us to choose our leaders.

Beyond this, we are one of the only three countries that do not provide public-service time to political candidates; the others are Sri Lanka and Taiwan.

Dinner-hour sitcoms and teen-oriented dramas show indiscriminate and consequenceless sex, and cable and video make available to children in their own homes movies they would not be permitted to see in a theater.

An estimated $1 billion went to TV stations last year to buy campaign commercials, while TV news about campaigns dramatically declined.

Quality TV for children will never be lucrative enough to earn its way onto the schedule.

As former Democratic senator and presidential candidate Bill Bradley summarized it, "Today political campaigns function as collection agencies for broadcasters. You simply transfer money from contributors to television stations."

So it must be the price of admission to the airwaves.[11]

RESEARCH ASSIGNMENT 3.1 TERM PROJECT   At the end of Chapter 1 (Writing Assignment 1.4), the instructions were to draft a one-page issue statement, which you revised at the end of Chapter 2 (Writing Assignment 2.2). Now try a little research. Research essentially means finding out something we don't already know. In researching an issue, we need to gain access to reliable information relevant to our topic, and most important, because our topic is the subject of debate and disagreement among reasonable people, we need to gain access to arguments of a reasonably high standard representing the diversity of opinion on our topic. Go to InfoTrac and research the issue articulated in your issue statement. Your goal is to identify at least three extended arguments representing at least two distinct positions on your issue. We recommend looking ahead to the section in Chapter 13 on research and the media, pp. 383–392.

NOTES

[1] "The Argument Clinic," in Roger Wilmut (ed.), *Monty Python's Flying Circus—Just the Words*, vol. 2 (New York: Random House, 1989), p. 86.

[2] Jane E. Brody and Richard Engquist, "Women and Smoking," in *Public Affairs Pamphlet 475* (New York: Public Affairs Committee, 1972), p. 2.

[3] Michael Gold, "The Cells That Would Not Die" in "This World," *San Francisco Chronicle*, May 17, 1981, p. 9.

[4] Virginia Castleton, "Bring Out Your Beauty," *Prevention* (September 1981): 108.

[5] John Ciardi, "Bureaucracy and Frank Ellis," in *Manner of Speaking* (New Brunswick, NJ: Rutgers University Press, 1972), p. 250.

[6] C. Arthur Campbell, "Is 'Freewill' a Pseudo-Problem?" *Mind* LX, No. 240 (1951): 447.

UNIT 2   Argument

104

7 Thomas E. Ricks, "Military Forgot Lessons of Vietnam," *Washington Post,* July 23, 2006, p. A1.

8 George Orwell, *Down and Out in Paris and London* (New York: Berkley, 197), 1959, p. 125.

9 Ciardi, "Bureaucracy and Frank Ellis," p. 250.

10 Jacques Barzun, "All Good Writing Is Rewriting," in *Simple and Direct* (New York: Harper & Row, 1976), p. 184.

11 Adapted from Newton N. Minow, "Television, More Vast Than Ever, Turns Toxic," *USA Today,* May 9, 2001, p. 15A.

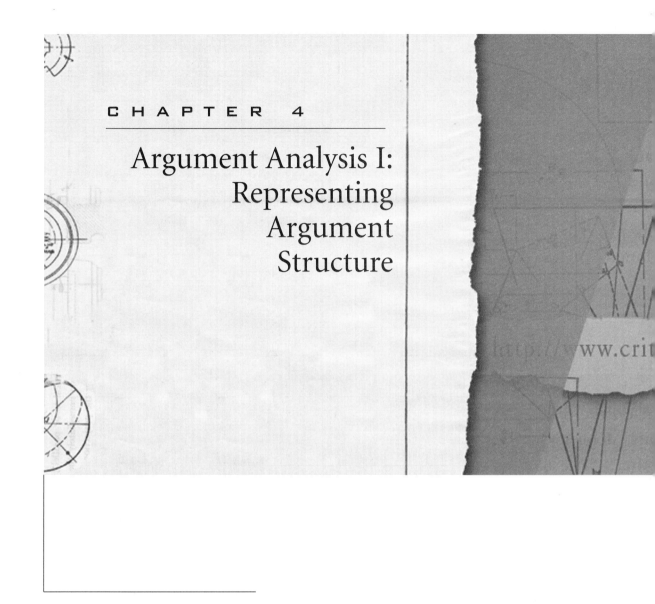

CHAPTER 4

Argument Analysis I: Representing Argument Structure

THE GOAL OF ARGUMENT ANALYSIS

The basic purpose of analysis—the intellectual process of taking complex things apart into their more basic elements—is to help us understand complex things. In Chapter 1 we applied analysis to issues. Here we apply analysis to arguments. Argument analysis is important in critical thinking as a crucial first step toward argument evaluation. In this connection, it is worth bearing in mind what we said in chapter 1 about being patient in pursuit of the truth. When we're "involved" in an issue, and especially in the heat of discussion, as soon as we recognize that an argument is being presented, we may feel ready to endorse or reject it, often

"But I see you're having difficulty following my argument."

simply on the basis of whether we agree with its point or not. However, before we pass judgment as to the merits of an argument, we need to make sure that we have understood the argument accurately, fairly, and in detail. That is the goal of argument analysis. The main reason it comes *before* argument evaluation is that it makes no sense to pass judgment on something we don't adequately understand.

In Chapter 3 we defined an "argument" as (a) a composition primarily intended to persuade by appealing to a person's reasoning capacity and (b) a composition consisting of a set of claims, one of which is understood or intended to be supported by the other or others. Just as the functional part of the definition (a) is a good basis for argument identification, the structural part of the definition (b) will now serve as a basis for argument analysis. Breaking an argument down into its constituent elements is a matter of taking it apart structurally. The crucial structural relationships in arguments, as you can see clearly in the structural definition, are relationships of support. So argument analysis boils down to figuring out what supports what. With short and simple arguments, this can be a relatively easy thing to do, especially if the argument is fully expressed, with signal words clearly indicating which claim is the conclusion and which claim or claims support it. But many of the arguments you will encounter in real life are more challenging and difficult to deal with. An argument may be long and complex. It may be less than fully expressed. Parts of the argument may be veiled or implied, or perhaps just not worded clearly. Material extraneous to the argument may surround or be mixed in with the claims that make up the argument. In this chapter, we offer you strategies and suggestions for analyzing arguments that present these challenges.

A good place to begin would be with the goal of argument analysis: a fair and accurate understanding of the argument in detail. How could we know if we had achieved this goal? How could we tell whether our understanding of someone else's argument is fair and accurate? One way to proceed would be to compare our understanding of the argument to the author's understanding of it. If we could talk directly to the author of the argument, we might say something like:

> If I understand you're argument correctly, your point is . . .

or

> Are you saying, . . .

Then we would restate the argument to the author in our own words. The author could then tell us whether we understood or whether we misunderstood in any way.

We can't always do this. We can't expect to be able to check the accuracy of our grasp of every argument directly with its author. Nevertheless, this is good way to understand the goal of argument analysis. Can we take the argument apart and reassemble it in our own words without changing what it means or how it is designed to work as a tool of rational persuasion? In a word, can we **paraphrase** the argument? This is a good test—indeed, probably the best test—of the adequacy of our grasp of another person's argument. In the end, it's the paraphrase that matters. The paraphrase is the measure of the degree to which we have succeeded in achieving the goal of argument analysis. We will return to paraphrasing in Chapter 5.

ELEMENTARY PROCEDURES

People who have a great deal of practice and experience with arguments and argumentation can often go straight to paraphrasing and can do so accurately and "intuitively"—that is, without resort to other procedures. But when you are just beginning the study of arguments and your intuitions are not grounded in extensive experience and practice, additional techniques and procedures may be not only useful but essential in establishing a firm footing in argument analysis.

CIRCLING AND HIGHLIGHTING

Begin with two simple procedures introduced in Chapter 3. When we recognize that an argument is being presented, a useful first step would be to scan the passage for signal words, and circle any found. Thus, for example, words would be circled as shown in the following passage:

> International legal institutions, (because) they are fragile and poorly established, cannot be relied upon to bring international terrorists to justice. And international terrorists are not entitled to the protection of the U.S. Constitution or Bill of Rights, (because) these documents pertain only to U.S. citizens. (Therefore) international terrorists should be tried in secret by U.S. military tribunals.

A second step would be to identify the argument's conclusion and highlight it.

APPLICATION EXERCISE 4.1 | Highlighting I

You do the highlighting. We'll show you WHERE.

International legal institutions, (because) they are fragile and poorly established, cannot be relied upon to bring international terrorists to justice. And such terrorists are not entitled to the protection of the U.S. Constitution or Bill of Rights, (because) these documents pertain only to U.S. citizens. (Therefore) INTERNATIONAL TERRORISTS SHOULD BE TRIED IN SECRET BY U.S. MILITARY TRIBUNALS.

A third step would be to challenge the argument's conclusion, in effect asking *why* we should accept it as true. We will then find that wherever the passage is responding directly to this question there are premises, which we could highlight in a new color, so as to distinguish these premises clearly from the argument's conclusion.

APPLICATION EXERCISE 4.2 | Highlighting II

You do the highlighting. We'll show you **where.**

International legal institutions, (because) they are fragile and poorly established, **cannot be relied upon to bring international terrorists to justice.** And **international terrorists are not entitled to the protection of the U.S. Constitution or Bill of Rights,** (because) these documents pertain only to U.S. citizens. (Therefore) INTERNATIONAL TERRORISTS SHOULD BE TRIED IN SECRET BY U.S. MILITARY TRIBUNALS.

Deeper layers of support may be discovered by repeating the third step. We now challenge the argument's premises highlighted in the preceding exercise, in effect asking why we should accept them as true. We will find that wherever the passage is responding directly to *this* question there are further premises, which we could highlight in a new color, so as to distinguish them clearly from the claims that they support.

APPLICATION EXERCISE 4.3 | **Highlighting III**

You do the highlighting. We'll show you *where*.

International legal institutions, (because) *they are fragile and poorly established,* **cannot be relied upon to bring international terrorists to justice. And international terrorists are not entitled to the protection of the U.S. Constitution or Bill of Rights,** (because) *these documents pertain only to U.S. citizens.* (Therefore) INTERNATIONAL TERRORISTS SHOULD BE TRIED IN SECRET BY U.S. MILITARY TRIBUNALS.

REVIEW EXERCISE 4.1 | **Circling and Highlighting**

Circle the argument indicators and highlight the following examples:

1. (Since) it is only a matter of time before space-based missile defense technology becomes obsolete, and (since) the funds that would be used to develop this technology are sorely needed to rebuild the economy, now is not the time to invest in a missile defense shield.

2. The history of technology shows that all technology eventually becomes surpassed and outmoded. Therefore it is only a matter of time before space-based missile defense technology becomes obsolete, and since the funds that would be used to develop this technology are sorely needed to rebuild the economy, now is not the time to invest in a missile defense shield.

3. A space-based missile defense shield is our only realistic option for national defense in the nuclear age. After all, any defense program that relies on nuclear deterrence raises the risk of nuclear war, and that is not a realistic option for national defense. The Star Wars program is the only option yet proposed that does not rely on nuclear deterrence.

MAPPING

Many people find it helpful to visualize argument structure. One of the simplest ways of visualizing argument structure would be in terms of spatial relationships. Using only two dimensions (easiest to handle on a sheet of paper) and the preceding example, we can arrange the claims in the argument to reflect the hierarchy and structure of the relationships of support (Figure 4.1).

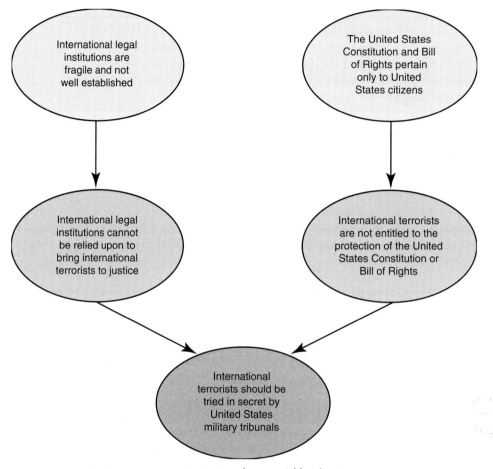

FIGURE 4.1 Argument Map I

The support flows from the top of the diagram to the conclusion at the bottom with the two **main premises** in the middle, each of which is supported in turn by a further premise.

A system like this could be easily expanded to represent deeper and more elaborate argument analysis. In this same example in Chapter 3, we noted that there were additional claims presupposed and implied within the argument. The claim that international terrorists are not entitled to the protection of the U.S. Constitution and Bill of Rights presupposes that we know who the terrorists are before trial. And the inference from the claim that the U.S. Constitution and Bill of Rights pertain only to U.S. citizens to the claim that international terrorists are not entitled to the protection of the Constitution and Bill of Rights depends on the additional assumption that the terrorists are not U.S. citizens. These hidden elements might be represented in another diagram (Figure 4.2).

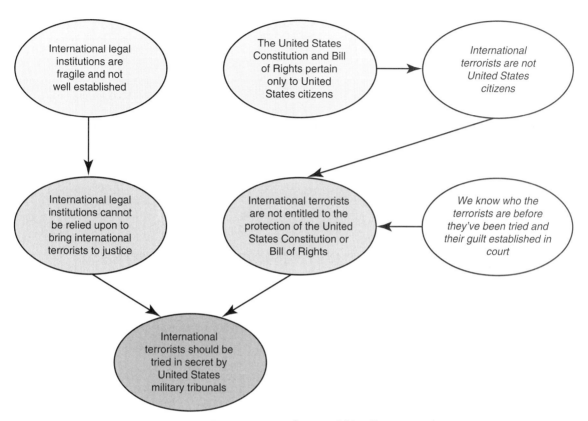

FIGURE 4.2 Argument Map II

The new shade and the use of *italics* sets these new elements apart as implied or hidden in the original passage. Also notice that the inference from the claim that the U.S. Constitution and Bill of Rights pertain only to U.S. citizens to the claim that international terrorists are not entitled to the protection of the Constitution and Bill of Rights now goes *through* the additional hidden inferential assumption that the terrorists are not U.S. citizens.[1] Looking ahead to the evaluation of arguments, we can already see from the diagram that attention is drawn to the second of the two main premises as a possibly vulnerable point in the argument;

CASTING

A graphic system for representing argument structure should do what an organizational flowchart does for understanding any complex system. Ideally, it should be capable of representing an indefinitely large number of elements (in the case of arguments, claims) and an indefinitely large number of **relevant** relationships among them. Notice in the two preceding diagrams how the complexity of the graphic system of representation grows with the complexity of the

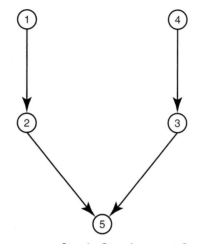

FIGURE 4.3 Step-by-Step Argument Casting I

analysis. A great deal can be done with colors, shapes, typefaces, symbols, arrows, and two spatial dimensions. But we also want a system that is simple enough to learn, remember, and apply to the kind of material we're likely to encounter in our everyday lives—material like newspaper stories and magazine articles. To that end, we now present a simplified variation on the preceding mapping system—a system we will call **casting.** The casting system follows essentially the same steps as used earlier in mapping the argument (see Figure 4.3). The claims that constitute the argument are isolated and marked for identification and then arranged in two-dimensional space so as to reflect the relationships of support among them.

1. Put brackets at the beginning and end of each claim.
2. Number the claims consecutively in their order of appearance in the passage.
3. Arrange the numbers spatially on the page according to relationships of support among the claims they stand for.

Using the preceding example, the casting system works as follows (see Figure 4.3 and compare Figure 4.1):

[International legal institutions, (because) {they are fragile and poorly established ①}, cannot be relied upon to bring international terrorists to justice. ②] And [international terrorists are not entitled to the protection of the U.S. Constitution or Bill of Rights ③], (because) [these documents pertain only to U.S. citizens. ④] (Therefore,) [international terrorists should be tried in secret by U.S. military tribunals. ⑤]

Notice the special brackets { } used to isolate claim 1 as the support for claim 2, in which it is embedded.

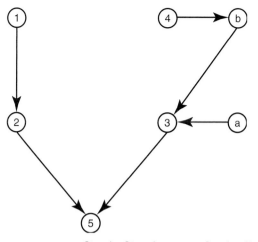

FIGURE 4.4 Step-by-Step Argument Casting II

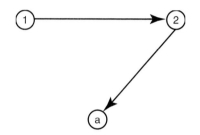

FIGURE 4.5 Step-by-Step Argument Casting III

The system can be extended to represent hidden or unstated elements within the argument. To keep this distinction clear (the one between explicit and implicit claims of the argument), we will use letters instead of numbers to represent hidden or unstated elements. Using the same example, the casting would look as shown in Figure 4.4 (compare Figure 4.2).

Here the letter (a) represents the claim that we know already who the terrorists are and the letter (b) represents the claim that the terrorists are not U.S. citizens, as explained earlier. Implied but unstated conclusions can be handled like in a similar way. For example, consider this argument from *Julius Caesar:*

[Yond Cassius has a lean and hungry look (1)]. [Such men are dangerous (2)].

This leads to the unstated conclusion: Cassius is dangerous. We may represent it as a crucial element in the argument by assigning it the letter a (see Figure 4.5).

REVIEW EXERCISE 4.2 | Basic Casting

Complete the castings of the following arguments.

Since {it is only a matter of time before space-based missile defense technology becomes obsolete ①}, and since {the funds that would be used to develop this technology are sorely needed to rebuild the economy ②}, {now is not the time to invest in a missile defense shield ③}.

{The history of technology shows that all technology eventually becomes surpassed and outmoded ①}. Therefore, {it is only a matter of time before space-based missile defense technology becomes obsolete ②}. Because {the funds that would be used to develop this technology are sorely needed to rebuild the economy ③}, {now is not the time to invest in a missile defense shield ④}.

{A space-based missile defense shield is our only realistic option for national defense in the nuclear age ①}. After all, {any defense program that relies on nuclear deterrence raises the risk of nuclear war ②}, and {that is not a realistic option for national defense ③}. {The Star Wars program is the only option yet proposed that does not rely on nuclear deterrence ④}.

Although the complexity and variety of arguments you may encounter is practically endless, you can do quite a bit to orient yourself to the argument using just the few simple tools outlined earlier (also, see Figure 4.6). It is important not to confuse the grammatical structure of a passage in a composition with the structure of the argument it conveys. In some cases, with carefully and clearly written passages of argumentation, the grammar and the structure of the argument may coincide. The author may construct the passage so that the grammar can be used as a guide to the argument. But in many cases this is not possible. What matters most for argument analysis is not the grammar of the composition but what supports what. A general rule of thumb is as follows: Break a grammatical unit down only when different parts of the grammatical unit play separate and distinct roles in the argument in terms of support relationships. By the same token, disregard grammatically distinct repetitions of the same claim. Finally, remember to stay focused on the argument. In many cases, the composition that you're analyzing will contain material extraneous to the argument: tangential asides, background information, entertaining embellishments, rhetorical flourishes, and so on. Occasionally, we encounter passages in which the author draws and defends a conclusion while

1. Circle argument indicators.
2. Use highlighters to identify conclusion, main premises, and further supporting premises.
3. Put brackets at the beginning and end of each claim.
4. Number the claims consecutively in their order of appearance in the passage.
5. Arrange the numbers spatially on the page according to relationships of support among the claims they stand for.

FIGURE 4.6 Summary of Highlighting + Casting System

conceding a point to the opposition. Such "concession claims" may be germane to the discussion, and they may make a diplomatic contribution to the reception of the author's thesis, although they do not by themselves lend support to it. A general rule of thumb is to *be thorough but stay relevant.* If you think you understand and can explain the distinct contribution a given claim makes to the argument, include it in your analysis. Otherwise, leave it out.

REVIEW EXERCISE 4.3 | Highlighting and Basic Casting

There is no better way to build and hone skills in this area than practice. Use the highlighting and casting system outlined earlier on the following examples.

1. That cell phone we looked at yesterday stores a half-hour's worth of messages, as opposed to this one, which stores 20 minutes. It also has better automated dialing features than this one; and this one's $30 more expensive. I think we should buy that other one.

2. A college education makes you aware of interests you didn't know you had. This helps you choose a satisfying job. Job satisfaction is your best assurance of personal well-being. Certainly, personal well-being is a goal worth pursuing. Therefore a college education is a worthy goal.

3. Capital punishment should not be permitted because it consists of killing humans, and killing humans should never be permitted by society.

4. Because killing humans should never be permitted by society, capital punishment should not be permitted; for it consists of killing humans.

5. Most marriages between people under 20 end in divorce. This should be enough to discourage teenage marriages. In addition, marrying young reduces life options. Married teenagers must forget about adventure and play. They can't afford to spend time "finding themselves." They must concentrate almost exclusively on earning a living. What's more, early marriages can make parents out of young people, who can hardly take care of themselves, let alone an infant.

6. "Suicide no longer repels us. The suicide rate is climbing, especially among blacks and young people. What's more, suicide has been appearing in an increasingly favorable light in the nation's press. When we surveyed all articles on suicide indexed over the past 50 years in the *Readers' Guide to Periodical Literature,* we found that voluntary deaths . . . generally appear in a neutral light. Some recent articles even present suicide as a good thing to do. . . . They are written in a manner that might encourage the reader to take his own life under certain circumstances."[2]

7. We must stop treating juveniles differently from adult offenders. Justice demands it. Justice implies that people should be treated equally. Besides, the social effects of pampering juvenile offenders have sinister social consequences. The record shows that juveniles who have been treated leniently for offenses have subsequently committed serious crimes.

8. "More and more silent evidence is being turned into loudly damning testimony. Over the past ten years, no area has developed faster than the examination of blood stains. Before we used to be satisfied with identifying a blood sample as type A, B, AB, or O. Now we have three or more different antigen and enzyme systems. The probability that any two people will share the same assessment of their blood variables is 0.1% or less. The size, shape, and distribution of blood spatters tells much about the location and position of a person involved in a crime. The use of bite-mark evidence has skyrocketed. Even anthropology is making a courtroom contribution. Some anthropologists can identify barefoot prints as well as match a shoe to its wearer."[3]

9. Capital punishment does ensure that a killer can never strike again. But it consists of killing humans, and killing humans should never be allowed. Therefore capital punishment should not be permitted.

10. A college education increases your earning potential. In addition, it makes you aware of interests you didn't know you had. Most important, it teaches the inherent value of knowledge. It is true that a college education is expensive. Nevertheless, a college education will be worth every penny it costs.

INTERMEDIATE CHALLENGES

From the beginning of this book, we have pointed out that there are often hidden claims to account for in argument analysis. Critical Thinking Tip 1.1 was to be aware of assumptions, especially "between" and "underneath" claims presented persuasively in arguments. We have used several examples involving hidden claims to illustrate the tools of argument analysis presented in this chapter. In dealing with such hidden elements, the hard part is not the diagramming. It is not difficult to handle hidden claims in the mapping or casting systems presented here (just use letters instead of numbers). The hard part is figuring out *where* and *what* the hidden elements are.

Not that this is always hard. Sometimes it's quite obvious. Suppose someone says, "Do you trust your textbooks? I don't. I'm convinced they contain mistakes because they're written by humans." Now look at the argument in the last sentence:[4]

[I'm convinced they (textbooks) contain mistakes (1)] *because* [they're written by humans (2)].

It's obvious (isn't it?) that there's a hidden premise in here, namely, "Humans make mistakes," or something like that, represented by the letter (a) in Figure 4.7.

In an obvious case like this one, the question of just how we figure this out doesn't arise any more than the questions of where and what the hidden premise is. All of this is clear. The problem is that it's not always clear. As you might expect, typically it's not obvious where or what the hidden claims in an argument might be, for the simple—and obvious—reason that they're hidden.

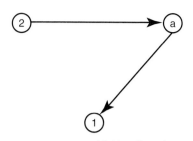

FIGURE 4.7 Hidden Premise

Suppose you and a friend are solving a puzzle in which you are supposed to match the names and brief biographies of 20 people from a set of clues, and your friend says, "Pat must be a man because here in the fifth clue it says that Pat is Jason's father." You can see from the claim that Pat is Jason's father that Pat must be a man. But this conclusion does not follow from the claim that Pat is Jason's father *alone*. It also depends on the definition of a father as a male parent, the claim that a parent is presumably an adult, and the definition) of a man as an adult human male. Ordinarily it would not be necessary to spell out these three claims explicitly as premises to fully appreciate the reasoning any more than it was necessary to spell them out in the original presentation of the reasoning. In general, we go to the trouble of spelling out these hidden elements in the reasoning when the hidden or missing elements are both *crucial* and *controversial* and when they *bear on the evaluation of the argument*. It is important to go to this trouble especially when there seems to be something wrong with a particular argument, for example: "You say textbooks don't contain mistakes? Here, I'll prove to you that they do. My science book says that whales are mammals. But everybody knows that whales live in the sea. And that's what a fish is, an animal that lives in the sea."[5] We will reconstruct this argument fragment shortly. For now, it is sufficient to note that the reasoning evidently has *some* weaknesses in it *somewhere*. Spelling out all of its elements, even the ones that are obvious, becomes useful when we attempt to pinpoint those weaknesses.

In the real world of public discourse, arguments are often presented as sketches or fragments—what logicians traditionally refer to as **enthymemes.** This means that parts of the reasoning are left for readers or members of the audience to recognize on their own, guided by the context and the logic of the argument. And this is something that happens with great frequency in the media and in everyday conversation. Why is this? This happens for several reasons, some good, some not so good. Here is a good reason. Sometimes, as in the "humans make mistakes" example, things are *so* obvious that spelling them out completely and explicitly would be unnecessary, needlessly time consuming, or even insulting to the intelligence of the audience. So people often leave things out of their presentation of the argument as a matter of economy or common courtesy. On the other hand, sometimes people leave things out because they aren't completely aware of all of the assumptions that their reasoning depends on. And sometimes there is even an attempt gloss over elements that the argument's maker

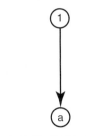

FIGURE 4.8 Finding a Hidden Premise I

would prefer the audience did not notice or consider carefully. In any case, because this is something that happens with great frequency in the real world of public discourse, it is worth focusing on the question of how we figure out where and what the hidden claims may be in an argument.

It is worth reminding ourselves what we are up to in all of this. When we reconstruct argument fragments, we are trying to make sense of what people say (and don't say). Imagine that you are waiting to be seated at a busy beachfront restaurant immediately behind an attractive couple who happen to be barefoot. The hostess looks at the barefoot couple, says not one word, but points to a sign that reads "No shirt, no shoes, no service." In this context, it is reasonable to understand the hostess's gesture as a justification for refusing to seat the couple; in other words, it functions as an argument in support of her refusal to seat them. If we were casting the argument, we might represent her refusal to seat the bare-foot couple by assigning it the letter (a). So far, the argument looks as shown in Figure 4.8.

Here, (1) stands for "If you are not wearing a shirt and shoes, you will be refused service" (what the sign means) and (a) stands for "you are being refused service" (addressed to the barefoot couple). There is also an unstated premise, namely, that the customers are not wearing shoes. And you can easily understand why it's not stated: again, because it's obvious—especially, we may presume, to the couple. If we want our casting to reflect this as a part of the justification for the refusal of service (which it certainly is), we assign it the letter (b). So the fully analyzed argument looks as shown in Figure 4.9.

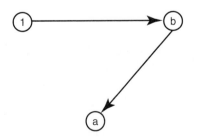

FIGURE 4.9 Finding a Hidden Premise II

Here, (b) stands for "you are not wearing shoes" (addressed to the barefoot couple). The hostess does not say a word, but the *context and the inner logic of the argument help us make sense* of her gesture as a meaningful one and grasp its meaning as an argument. So return to the obvious example. How do we know that the hidden claim is "Humans make mistakes" and not something different, like "Elephants make mistakes" or, something completely different, "Cycling is a great way to meet other single people"? Well, you could say, "We know that 'Humans make mistakes' is the hidden claim because it's the one that makes the most sense of what the arguer *did* say."

REVIEW EXERCISE 4.4 | Casting Hidden Claims

Formulate the missing elements and complete the casting for each of the following arguments. Pay close attention to your reasoning as you work out each of these examples. See if you can feel the force of logic at work.

{I'm sorry, but you may stay in the country only if you have a current visa (1)}; {your visa has expired (2)}. Hidden Claim(s):	Casting:
{God has all the virtues (1)}, (SO) {God must have benevolence (2)}. Hidden Claim(s):	Casting:
{Either the battery in the remote control is dead or the set's unplugged (1)}; but {the set is plugged in (2)}. Hidden Claim(s):	Casting:
{All species of mammal suckle their young (1)}, {all primates are mammals (2)}, and {orangutans are primates (3)}. Hidden Claim(s):	Casting:

So far the examples are all relatively obvious. But many cases are more difficult. There are often *several ways* of making sense of what someone says. Then, too, sometimes what people say doesn't make much sense. It won't always be possible to know, with certainty, which of several statements should be cast in the role of missing premise or whether we should be bothering to look for missing premises. The bad news is that there is no simple algorithm for making sense of what people say. Rather, it involves the application of multiple criteria that sometimes conflict with one another. Hence it tends to yield multiple solutions, each with competing advantages and liabilities. The most we can expect by way of systematic guidance to this sort of process is a set of guidelines—rules of thumb we will continue to present here as tips. The good news is that you already know how to do this sort of interpretive work, at least in obvious cases like those discussed already. And as you work with these guidelines, building experience, cultivating sensitivity and judgment, and keeping in mind that you may expect to find exceptions to any rule of thumb, you will become even better at it.

Our interest in making sense of what people say by reconstructing their arguments from fragments has to do with assessing the merits of these arguments as reasoning. What we want to know is how good or bad the argument is. This is because we are trying to determine how much sway to give the argument in our deliberations and decision making. What this means in common sense terms is that we want as complete and as fair a rendition of the argument as we can arrive at.

COMPLETENESS

Back we go again to the obvious example (Figure 4.7). The argument as originally stated was, "I'm convinced they [textbooks] contain mistakes because they're written by humans." Consider how we know there is an unstated premise in it. In other words, how do we know that the original statement of the argument is not complete? Just focus on the premise for a moment: "Textbooks are written by humans." True enough. But *from this claim alone* the conclusion "Textbooks contain mistakes" doesn't follow. If it is clear that the conclusion doesn't follow from the premise (or, more precisely, from the totality of the premises) explicitly presented in the argument, then we should be on the lookout for hidden premises. When we say "doesn't follow" we are using an important and fundamental concept of logic—the concept of deductive validity (which we discuss more thoroughly in Chapter 6). For now, understand this concept to mean simply that even if the premise is true the conclusion could still be false.

REVIEW EXERCISE 4.5 | **Does It Follow?**   ✳

For each pair of claims, suppose that the first claim is true then determine whether the second one "follows."

	Follows	Prisons do not rehabilitate anyone.
	Does not follow	Prisons are ineffective as punishment for criminal behavior.

	Follows	No weapons of mass destruction were found.
	Does not follow	No weapons of mass destruction were there to be found.

	Follows	The United States must become energy independent.
	Does not follow	The United States should develop widespread collection and use of solar energy.

	Follows	Abortion involves the taking of a human life.
	Does not follow	Abortion should never be encouraged.

	Follows	There are 35 students registered in this class.
	Does not follow	There are at least 30 students registered in this class.

	Follows	God is perfect.
	Does not follow	Therefore God is good.

	Follows	Everything with commercial potential eventually becomes absorbed into the corporate world, so
	Does not follow	the Internet will eventually be absorbed into the corporate world.

	Follows	People born at exactly the same time often have vastly different life histories and
	Does not follow	personalities. Therefore astrology is not a reliable predictive system.

	Follows	The right to life is irrevocable.
	Does not follow	Therefore there should be laws guaranteeing it.

	Follows	It has rained because if it hadn't the streets would be dry, and they are not so.
	Does not follow	

	Follows	Oxygen must have been present in the building because the building burned.
	Does not follow	

	Follows	Professor Barry isn't in class, so he must be in his office.
	Does not follow	

When we identify an argument as an enthymeme—when we determine, in other words, that its conclusion doesn't follow from its explicitly stated premises alone—we in effect sense a gap or hole in it. But we can be more specific than this. The hole has a shape that we can discern, to some extent at least, by paying close attention to what surrounds it—to the argument's conclusion and explicit premise or premises. Think of this as similar to searching for a missing piece in a jigsaw puzzle. You study closely the shapes and colors of the pieces that surround the one you're searching for. This helps you find the missing piece. When the puzzle is an incompletely stated argument and what you're searching for is a missing premise, you can guide yourself by paying close attention to what the conclusion and explicit premise or premises of the argument are about. This helps you gain a better sense of the shape of the hole or gap you're trying to fill, and so of the missing premise that can fill it. In the example we've been discussing, the conclusion is about textbooks and things that contain mistakes, and the premise is about textbooks and things written by humans. What we are looking for is something that will complete this circle of relationships, as it were. What we should be looking for then, is a claim that makes some connection between things written by humans and things that contain mistakes.

REVIEW EXERCISE 4.6 | **Completing the Argument**   ✳

Complete the following arguments, using all and only the words from the following list:

benevolence, depends, develop, effective, fails, homicide, never, unless, virtues, why

1. God has all the virtues. And _____ is one of the _____. So God must have benevolence.

2. Abortion involves the taking of a human life. That's _____, and you would _____ encourage homicide, would you? So abortion should not ever be encouraged.

3. Prisons do not rehabilitate anyone. No criminal penalty that _____ to rehabilitate can be _____. That's _____ prisons are ineffective as punishment for criminal behavior.

4. The United States must become energy independent. _____ we develop widespread collection and use of solar energy, our survival _____ on increasingly scarce petrochemical energy. That's why the United States should _____ widespread collection and use of solar energy.

FAIRNESS

We assume that anyone reading this book has a "sense of fairness." However, if we all have an intuitive sense of fairness, we also all know how easy it is to fall into dispute over—and how difficult it can be to resolve—*issues* of fairness. A common sense rule of thumb in applying the concept of fairness in pursuit of the truth would be "when in doubt, don't be *un*fair."

CRITICAL THINKING TIP 4.1 | Fairness

When in doubt, don't be *un*fair

What does the rule of thumb in critical thinking tip 4.1 mean in practice? Remember that argument analysis is a means to the end of determining how good or bad the argument is. In practice then, the general rule of thumb, "When in doubt, don't be unfair," means that in analyzing a given argument, we should *try to avoid discrediting* the argument. Of two otherwise equally reasonable competing interpretations, we should subscribe to the one that does the argument the most credit. In other words, as indicated earlier, we should favor the interpretation that *makes the most sense of* what the arguer did say.

As applied to argument analysis, the first consideration regarding fairness would be *accuracy.* Analysis is a form of interpretation. Whenever we complete an argument by attributing an unstated claim to it, we are interpreting the text of the argument and going beyond what the text of the argument says. **Text** means the retrievable record of what was said. With written arguments we don't generally have the convenient opportunity to question an argument's creator if we think there are hidden elements in the argument. We have only—or primarily—the text of the argument to consult. In oral contexts, when we are listening to someone present an argument, the opportunity for questioning that person is often available. But even so, as we already pointed out, people are not always fully aware of all assumptions they are making, and there may even be an unwillingness to learn or to admit that some particular claim is assumed or implied within a given argument or position. So again, we fall back on the text. In assessing the accuracy of the analysis of an argument, remember, from Chapter 2, that we are entitled to assume a conventional understanding of the words in the text of an argument. We may also use logic (as we explain further in Chapter 6) as a guide to our analysis. All of this is governed by the general rule of thumb "when in doubt, don't be unfair."

PLAUSIBILITY

When formulating a hidden claim, we should favor the most plausible of the available alternative formulations. Plausibility is a concept we will develop and apply more deeply and extensively in Chapter 7. The word "plausibility" literally means deserving of applause. But it has a more precise technical meaning relating to credibility or believability. In technical terms, **plausibility** is an estimate of a claim's capacity to survive close critical examination. If we were to devise strenuous tests designed to *falsify* a claim, how well would the claim survive such tests? A claim is plausible to the extent that we think it likely the claim would survive such tests. A claim is implausible to the extent that we think it unlikely the claim would survive such tests. Plausibility, in other words, is a *preliminary estimate* of a claim's truth value. Consider this example:

Since Smith is a police officer, he's probably in favor of gun-control legislation.

Here the conclusion, "Smith is probably in favor of gun-control legislation," does not follow from the premise "Smith is a police officer" alone. To complete the inference, we are looking for a claim that makes some connection between being a police officer and favoring gun-control legislation. There are a number of distinct alternatives we might consider casting in the role of missing premise. Take, for example, these two:

1. All police officers favor gun-control legislation.
2. Most police officers favor gun-control legislation.

The first formulation is less plausible than the second one. This is because the first formulation makes a stronger claim than the second one. The stronger a claim is, the harder it is to prove (and the more vulnerable it is to refutation). All it would take to refute the claim made in the first formulation is to find one police officer opposed to gun-control legislation. But this would not be enough to refute the claim made in the second formulation. So we should favor the second alternative in reconstructing this argument.

REVIEW EXERCISE 4.7 | Plausibility

Rank the following sets of claims in terms of plausibility. Compare your rankings with those of someone else in the class. Wherever your rankings conflict, explain your initial ranking. Compare notes and see whether your ranking is affected.

1. a. Some produce sold in the major supermarkets is irradiated.
   b. A lot of the produce sold in the major supermarkets is irradiated.
   c. Most produce sold in the major supermarkets is irradiated.

2. a. Tax evasion is a common practice.
   b. Everybody cheats on their taxes.

3. a. Cell phone usage is on the rise.
   b. The cell phone industry is growing at the rate of 65.89% a month.

4. a. It is probable that the al-Qaeda terrorist network is still actively planning attacks.
   b. It is possible that the al-Qaeda terrorist network is still actively planning attacks.
   c. The al-Qaeda terrorist network is certainly still actively planning attacks.

5. a. There is intelligent life in outer space.
   b. Some nonhuman animals have the capacity for language.

6. a. The use of computer technology in weapons systems increases the risk of a nuclear accident.
   b. The perfection of a space-based missile defense system is feasible.

7. a. Some assassins of President John F. Kennedy are still alive.
   b. Some assassins of President John F. Kennedy presently hold high office in the U. S. government.

8. a. Human adults generally use less than 10% of the capacity of their minds.
   b. The universe is finite.

Put this all together and apply it to the following example, which we've already been discussing:

> You say textbooks don't contain mistakes? Here, I'll prove to you that they do. My science book says that whales are mammals. But everybody knows that whales live in the sea. And that's what a fish is, an animal that lives in the sea.

Begin by numbering the claims for casting:

> [You say textbooks don't contain mistakes? Here, I'll prove to you that they do. (1)] [My science book says that whales are mammals. (2)] But everybody knows that [whales live in the sea. (3)] And that's what [a fish is an animal that lives in the sea. (4)]

Notice that we have bracketed the first two sentences as claim 1. This is an example of grammatical structure and logical structure diverging from each other. Claim 1 is evidently the conclusion, and we can easily capture it in a single sentence: "Textbooks contain mistakes." You may also have noticed that we ignored the (bad) grammar of the sentence in bracketing claim 4. But claim 4 really needs to be reworded to accurately reflect the argument. The arguer evidently is trying to say, "Any animal that lives in the sea is a fish." This, at any rate, is how we would paraphrase claim 4. Claim 2 is offered as direct support for the conclusion. But what about claims 3 and 4? They both seem intended to contribute support for the conclusion, but the support is not direct. And there seem to be some missing links involved. Nevertheless, a preliminary casting of these relationships might be helpful at this stage (see Figure 4.10).

Suppose it's true that the arguer's science book says that whales are mammals (claim 2). The conclusion would not follow from that alone that textbooks contain mistakes. What claim would complete the inference from this premise to the conclusion? One additional implied claim is that the arguer's science book is a textbook. A second additional implied claim is that the statement that whales are mammals is mistaken, or simply, "Whales aren't mammals." The first of these claims is obvious— and obviously part of the arguer's position. The second is implausible—indeed,

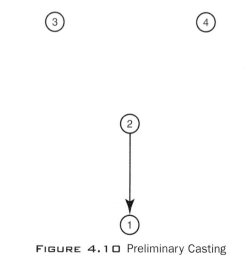

FIGURE 4.10 Preliminary Casting

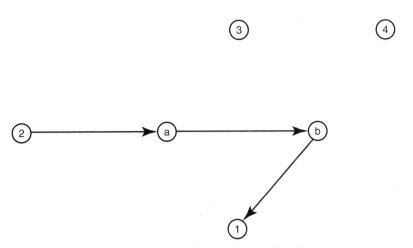

FIGURE 4.11 More Advanced Casting

false—but it must be part of the arguer's position, as we can see quite clearly from claims 3 and 4, which are offered in support of it. Therefore, despite the falsity of the claim that whales are not mammals, it is not unfair to attribute it to the argument. So assign the letter ⓐ to the first and the letter ⓑ to the second of these hidden claims.

ⓐ   "My science book is a textbook."

ⓑ   "Whales aren't mammals."

Then cast the result as shown in Figure 4.11. The inference from claim 2 to the conclusion (claim 1) now goes *through* the hidden claims a and b.

Now consider the relationship between claims 3 and 4 and unstated claim b. Suppose it is true that whales live in the sea (claim 3) and that any animal that lives in the sea is a fish (claim 4). It would not follow from these two claims alone that whales are not mammals. What would follow from these two claims alone is the claim that whales are fish. But from this claim alone, the claim that whales are not mammals still would not follow. If we add the claim that no fish are mammals, which is true by definition—and again obviously part of the arguer's position—then the argument is complete. So assign the letter ⓒ to the claim that whales are fish and the letter ⓓ to the claim that no fish are mammals.

ⓒ   "Whales are fish."

ⓓ   "No fish are mammals."

And now we can complete the casting (Figure 4.12): The inference goes from claim 3 through claim 4 to the unstated claim c, and from there through unstated claim d to unstated claim b.

In this case, the analysis of the argument enables us to precisely pinpoint the argument's weakness: claim 4. Everything else in the argument is true, presumably true, or logically derived from what is offered in its support.

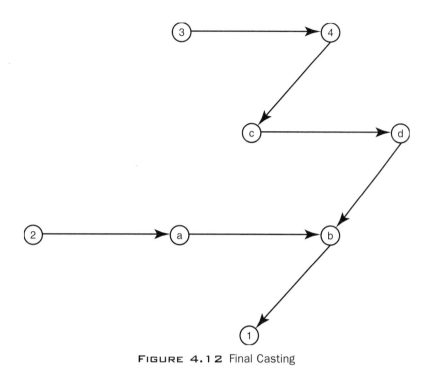

FIGURE 4.12 Final Casting

| **Reconstructing Missing Premises**   ✳

Select the best reconstruction of the missing premise from the alternatives offered for each of the following enthymemes.

Everything with commercial potential eventually becomes absorbed into the corporate world, so the Internet will eventually be absorbed into the corporate world.	Corporations have the power to absorb any business assets they want to.
	Corporations are inherently profit oriented and so are naturally drawn to anything with commercial potential.
	The Internet has commercial potential.

Some of these people can't be golfers. They're not carrying clubs.	Some golfers are carrying clubs.
	Everyone carrying clubs is a golfer.
	All golfers carry clubs.

Constitutionally, only the House of Representatives may initiate a money-raising bill. Thus, when the Senate drafted the recent tax bill, it acted unconstitutionally. Therefore the proposed tax bill should not be made law.		Any bill the Senate drafts should not be made law.
		Any bill that originates unconstitutionally should not be made law.
		Any tax bill originating in the Senate should not be made law.

If capital punishment isn't a deterrent to crime, then why has the rate of violent crime increased since capital punishment was outlawed?		Because the rate of violent crime has increased since capital punishment was outlawed, it must be a deterrent.
		An increase in the rate of crime following the abolition of a punishment proves that the punishment is a deterrent.
		An increase in the rate of crime following the abolition of a punishment is evidence that the punishment is a deterrent.

"I feel that since we are doing a science fiction show, morals don't enter into it—because none of it is true." —X-Files director Kim Manners		All science fiction is immoral.
		All science fiction is false.
		Morals enter only into the real world.

Add naught to MacNaughton—because you don't dilute a great Canadian whisky.		MacNaughton is a great Canadian whisky.
		Adding something to a great Canadian whisky would dilute it.
		MacNaughton is a great Canadian whisky, and adding something would dilute it.

"Murphy's law of [computer] programming states that no nontrivial program is free of bugs. A corollary states that any program with more than 10 lines is by definition nontrivial. The bottom line—your program will have bugs."[6]		Any computer program with 10 lines or less is trivial.
		Your computer program is nontrivial.
		Your computer program has more than 10 lines.

People born at exactly the same time often have vastly different life histories and personalities. Therefore astrology is not a reliable predictive system.		People who believe in astrology are superstitious.
		If astrology were a reliable predictive system, people born at exactly the same time would not have vastly different life histories and personalities.
		No two people are born at exactly the same time.

Because no human system of justice is infallible and capital punishment imposes an irreversible penalty, capital punishment is an unacceptable form of punishment.	If we could perfect our system of justice so that all and only guilty people were convicted, then capital punishment would be acceptable.
	No irreversible penalty is acceptable as a form of punishment in a fallible system of justice.
	You can let a person out of prison if they turn out to be innocent, but you can't bring a person back to life.

Just as we did with Chapter 3, we close this chapter on basic tools and techniques of argument analysis with a few more examples to practice on. Do your best to analyze the arguments contained in the passages assembled here, using any technique of argument analysis presented in Chapters 3 and 4.

APPLICATION EXERCISE 4.4 | **An Intermediate Challenge**

We consider the following example to be an "intermediate level" challenge. The argument is relatively complex in its structure but is clearly and carefully presented so that the average reader can grasp and follow it.

What Is Global Warming?

Carbon dioxide and other gases warm the surface of the planet naturally by trapping solar heat in the atmosphere. This is a good thing because it keeps our planet habitable. However, by burning fossil fuels such as coal, gas and oil and clearing forests we have dramatically increased the amount of carbon dioxide in the Earth's atmosphere and temperatures are rising.

The vast majority of scientists agree that global warming is real, it's already happening and that it is the result of our activities and not a natural occurrence. The evidence is overwhelming and undeniable.

We're already seeing changes. Glaciers are melting, plants and animals are being forced from their habitat, and the number of severe storms and droughts is increasing.

- The number of Category 4 and 5 hurricanes has almost doubled in the last 30 years.
- Malaria has spread to higher altitudes in places like the Colombian Andes, 7,000 feet above sea level.
- The flow of ice from glaciers in Greenland has more than doubled over the past decade.
- At least 279 species of plants and animals are already responding to global warming, moving closer to the poles.

If the warming continues, we can expect catastrophic consequences.

- Deaths from global warming will double in just 25 years—to 300,000 people a year.
- Global sea levels could rise by more than 20 feet with the loss of shelf ice in Greenland and Antarctica, devastating coastal areas worldwide.
- Heat waves will be more frequent and more intense.

- Droughts and wildfires will occur more often.
- The Arctic Ocean could be ice free in summer by 2050.
- More than a million species worldwide could be driven to extinction by 2050.

There is no doubt we can solve this problem. In fact, we have a moral obligation to do so. Small changes to your daily routine can add up to big differences in helping to stop global warming. The time to come together to solve this problem is now—TAKE ACTION.[7]

As you work, especially with the lengthier and more complex passages, do not be surprised or discouraged if you find that the casting becomes as hard to construct and grasp as the passage itself. Keep the goal of argument analysis in mind—a fair and accurate understanding of the argument in detail. Also bear in mind that the best measure of success in achieving this goal is what we work on in the next chapter—the paraphrase of the argument.

APPLICATION EXERCISE 4.5 | Term Project

At the end of chapter 3 (Research Assignment 3.1), the instructions were to research the issue articulated in your issue statement and to identify at least three extended arguments representing at least two distinct positions on that issue. Now in one of these three extended arguments, locate and highlight the thesis (or conclusion). Then locate and highlight the premises that support the thesis directly. Then locate and highlight the premises that support these main premises. Finally, construct a casting of these elements of the argument.

GLOSSARY

casting   a graphic system for representing the structural relationships within an argument, or a graphic representation of a particular argument

enthymeme   an argument containing an inferential assumption

main premises   the premises offered as direct support for the thesis

paraphrase   a reformulation intended to capture the same meaning

plausibility   the credibility or believability of an idea that one estimates as likely to survive critical scrutiny

relevant   related to the topic under discussion

text   a retrievable record of what was said

ADDITIONAL EXERCISES

Do your best to analyze the arguments contained in the following passages, using any technique of argument analysis presented in chapters 3 and 4. Take note of any areas of difficulty you encounter. Then go on to Chapter 5.

■ **APPLICATION EXERCISE 4.6 EVOLUTION**   "Evolution is a scientific fairy-tale just as the 'flat earth theory' was in the 12th century. Evolution directly contradicts the Second Law of Thermodynamics, which states that unless an intelligent planner is directing a system, it will always go in the direction of disorder and deterioration. Evolution requires a faith that is incomprehensible!"[8]

■ **APPLICATION EXERCISE 4.7 TERRORISM**   " 'We shall make no distinction,' the President proclaimed, 'between terrorists and countries that harbor terrorists.' So now we are bombing Afghanistan and inevitably killing innocent people because it is in the nature of bombing (and I say this as a former Air Force bombardier) to be indiscriminate, to 'make no distinction.' We are committing terrorism in order to 'send a message' to terrorists. . . . War is terrorism, magnified a hundred times. Yes, let's find the perpetrators of the awful acts of September 11. We must find the guilty parties and prosecute them. But we shouldn't engage in indiscriminate retaliation. When a crime is committed by someone in a certain neighborhood, you don't destroy the neighborhood."[9]

■ **APPLICATION EXERCISE 4.8 SEXUAL RELATIONS**   "A scientific colleague of mine, who holds a professorial post in the department of sociology and anthropology at one of our leading universities, recently asked me about my stand on the question of human beings having sex relations without love. Although I have taken something of a position on this issue in my book, *The American Sexual Tragedy,* I have never quite considered the problem in sufficient detail. So here goes. In general, I feel that affectional, as against non-affectional, sex relations are desirable. It is usually desirable that an association between coitus and affection exist—particularly in marriage, because it is often difficult for two individuals to keep finely tuned to each other over a period of years."[10]

■ **APPLICATION EXERCISE 4.9 MANAGED COMPETITION IN HEALTH CARE**   "It isn't likely that managed competition [Bill Clinton's health care reform concept] can be counted on to save money. For one thing, at least two managed-care setups must be present in a community if there is to be competition, and each of them needs a potential market of roughly 250,000 people to achieve economies of scale. Only about half of all Americans, it turns out, live in places densely populated enough to support two or more such programs. What's more, insurers would constantly hustle to win and retain business, because employers would constantly be shopping for better deals, just as they do now. The sales staff, recruiters, advertising personnel, and clerical staff that such 'marketing' entails contribute nothing to the provision of health care. And the physicians, nurses, and others whom insurers and HMOs [health maintenance organizations] hire to oversee—that is, second-guess—the decisions individual doctors make with individual patients—an essential feature of managed care—have to be paid too, adding to the overhead cost. Administrative costs already soak up about $225 billion a year—25 cents of every dollar spent on health care in this country. Under managed competition, such costs would, at best, stay the same. More probably, they would increase."[11]

APPLICATION EXERCISE 4.10 ROLE OF THE PRESS   "To the extent that it is working at all, the press is always a participant in, rather than a pure observer of, the events it reports. Our decisions on where (and where not) to be and what (and what not) to report have enormous impact on the political and governmental life we cover. We are obliged to be selective. We cannot publish the Daily Everything. And so long as this is true—so long as we are making choices that (1) affect what people see concerning their leaders and (2) inevitably cause those leaders to behave in particular ways—we cannot pretend we are not participants."[12]

APPLICATION EXERCISE 4.11 POLITICS AND SCIENCE   "Scientists are human beings with their full complement of emotions and prejudices, and their emotions and prejudices often influence the way they do their science. This was first clearly brought out in a study by Professor Nicholas Pastore in 1949. In this study Professor Pastore showed that the scientist's political beliefs were highly correlated with what he believed about the roles played by nature and nurture in the development of the person. Those holding conservative political views strongly tended to believe in the power of genes over environment. Those subscribing to more liberal views tended to believe in the power of environment over genes. One distinguished scientist (who happened to be a teacher of mine) when young was a socialist an environmentalist, but toward middle age he became politically conservative and a firm believer in the supremacy of genes!"[13]

APPLICATION EXERCISE 4.12 FROM INDIVIDUAL TO SOCIAL PSYCHOLOGY "Many a reader will raise the question whether findings won by the observation of individuals can be applied to the psychological understanding of groups. Our answer to this question is an emphatic affirmation. Any group consists of individuals and nothing but individuals, and psychological mechanisms which we find operating in a group can therefore only be mechanisms that operate in individuals. In studying individual psychology as a basis for the understanding of social psychology, we do something which might be compared with studying an object under the microscope. This enables us to discover the very details of psychological mechanisms which we find operating on a large scale in the social process. If our analysis of socio-psychological phenomena is not based on the detailed study of human behavior, it lacks empirical character and, therefore, validity."[14]

■ **APPLICATION EXERCISE 4.13 FLEXTIME**   "Flextime [flexible working hours] often makes workers more productive because being treated as responsible adults gives them greater commitment to their jobs. As a result it decreases absenteeism, sick leave, tardiness and overtime, and generally produces significant increases in productivity for the work group as a whole. For example, in trial periods in three different departments, the U.S. Social Security Administration measured productivity increases averaging about 20% has reported a decline."[15]

■ **APPLICATION EXERCISE 4.14 CENSORSHIP**   "Government control of ideas or personal preferences is alien to a democracy. And the yearning to use governmental censorship of any kind is infectious. It may spread insidiously. Commencing with suppression of books as obscene, it is not unlikely to develop into official lust for the power of thought-control in the areas of religion, politics, and elsewhere. [John] Milton observed that 'licensing of books . . . necessarily pulls along with it so many other kinds of licensing.' [John Stuart] Mill notes that the 'bounds of what may be called moral police' may easily extend 'until it encroaches on the most unquestionably legitimate liberty of the individual.' We should beware of a recrudescence of the undemocratic doctrine uttered in the seventeenth century by [William] Berkeley, Governor of Virginia: 'Thank God there are no free schools or preaching, for learning has brought disobedience into the world, and printing has divulged them. God keep us from both.'"[16]

■ **APPLICATION EXERCISE 4.15 OBLIGATION**   "What, after all, is the foundation of the nurse's obligation to follow the physician's orders? Presumably, the nurse's obligation to act in the medical interest of the patient. The point is that the nurse has an obligation to follow physician's orders because, ordinarily, patient welfare (interest) thereby is ensured. Thus when a nurse's obligation to follow a physician's order comes into direct conflict with the nurse's obligation to act in the medical interest of the patient, it would seem to follow that the patient's interests should always take precedence."[17]

■ **APPLICATION EXERCISE 4.16 PUBLIC NEEDS VS. INDIVIDUAL RIGHTS**
"American institutions were fashioned in an era of vast unoccupied spaces and pre-industrial technology. In those days, collisions between public needs and individual rights may have been minimal. But increased density, scarcity of resources, and interlocking technologies have now heightened the concern for 'public goods,' which belong to no one in particular but to all of us jointly. Polluting a lake or river or the air may not directly damage any one person's private property or living space. But it destroys a good that all of us—including future generations—benefit from and have a title to. Our public goods are entitled to a measure of protection."[18]

■ **APPLICATION EXERCISE 4.17 DIGITAL MUSIC REVOLUTION**   "These days music is truly global in sweep. The genie's out of the bottle, never to return, with MP3, Napster/Scour, and Freenet and Gnutella rendering all previous lines of demarcation meaningless. There's a revolution in progress, leveling everything in its path. Copyrights, masters, negatives, books, records, and films; it's all the same to a binary number, or a carbon atom and hydrogen qubit. Legislation, global police monitoring by knocking on two million doors—I don't think so. All I know is, you can't afford to make the customer your enemy. They no longer want to purchase a CD with ten or twelve songs on it to get the two they really want. They are also hip enough to know about artists' earnings and no longer want to pay the price for all the people in the middle of the distribution chain. These technological changes have provided an unexpected and highly efficient platform for rebellion for the current generation. We better get together and figure it out—and quickly!"[19]

■ **APPLICATION EXERCISE 4.18 A MISTAKEN COMPARISON**   "In policy debates one party sometimes charges that his or her opponents are embracing a Nazi-like position. . . . Meanwhile, sympathizers nod in agreement with the charge, seeing it as the ultimate blow to their opponents. . . . The problem with using the Nazi analogy in public policy debates is that in the Western world there is a form of anti-Nazi 'bigotry' that sees Nazis as almost mythically evil beings. . . . Firsthand knowledge of our own culture makes it virtually impossible to equate Nazi society with our own. The official racism of Germany, its military mentality, the stresses of war, and the presence of a dictator instead of a democratic system make Nazi Germany in the 1940s obviously different from America in the 1980s."[20]

■ **APPLICATION EXERCISE 4.19 POPULARITY VS. ELITISM**   "There is no other story in rock & roll like the story of Led Zeppelin because the story is an argument—about music, who makes it, who hears it and who judges its meanings. Mainly, though, it's a argument about the work, merits and life of a band that has been both treasured and scorned now for more than thirty-five years. The arguments started as soon as the band did, rooted in . . . a rift between the hard fought values of the 1960s and the real-life pleasures and recklessness of the 1970s. Zeppelin forced a revival of the distinction between popularity and quality. As long as the bands most admired aesthetically were also the bands most successful commercially (Cream, for instance), the distinction was irrelevant. But Zeppelin's enormous commercial success, in spite of critical opposition, revealed the deep division in what was once thought to be a homogeneous audience. That division has now evolved into a clearly defined mass taste and a clearly defined elitist taste."[21]

■ **APPLICATION EXERCISE 4.20 MARKET-MODEL UNIVERSITIES**   "Most of us place enormous faith in our universities. We trust that they are autonomous, independent institutions committed to education, scholarship, academic freedom and the production of knowledge free from the influence of special interest groups. Right?

"Wrong. In the last 25 years, the United States has given birth to a market-model university, one where professors increasingly work 'for hire.' Just last week, the *Wall Street Journal* reported that a major academic study—which found that antidepressants were safe and effective for pregnant women—was tainted by undisclosed conflicts of interest."[22]

■ **APPLICATION EXERCISE 4.21 SEPARATION OF CHURCH AND STATE**   "The treaty [of Tripoli], written by George Washington, has Article Eleven, which begins, 'As the government of the United Sates is not in any sense founded on the Christian religion . . .'

The treaty was ratified by the Senate in 1797 without a single objection and signed by then President John Adams. Article Six of the U.S. Constitution made this treaty doubly binding by saying, 'All treaties made under the authority of the United States shall be bound thereby, anything in the laws of any state to the contrary notwithstanding.'

It should be treasured today as the supreme document for the American doctrine of the absolute separation of church and state."[23]

■ **APPLICATION EXERCISE 4.22 "ONLY THE DEAD HAVE SEEN THE END OF WAR"**   "At the beginning of this millennium, the Cold War was over, the prosperous United States was the sole remaining superpower and global opinion was largely sympathetic to U.S. aims. . . . Only six years later, things couldn't be more different. The Bush administration's tunnel-vision approach to foreign policy has pushed the U.S. and the world into a devastating tailspin of conflict without end. In Afghanistan, this year [2006] is shaping up to be the deadliest yet for U.S. troops. In Iraq, which President Bush promised would be 'a source of true stability in the region' the carnage has been mind-boggling, and by September the fighting will have dragged on for 3 1/2 years—the same length of time it took us to defeat Germany in World War II. The total implosion of the Middle East highlights the continuing decline of U.S. prestige and influence. . . . Engraved on a wall at the British Imperial War Museum is a phrase attributed to Plato: 'Only the dead have seen the end of war.' It was meant as a warning about the perils of arrogance and empire—and the Bush administration seems determined to prove the aphorism's truth.[24]

NOTES

[1] Note to instructors: Many textbooks about critical thinking and informal logic explain the relationship between what we are calling "hidden inferential assumptions" and the explicit elements of the arguments in which they occur as a relationship of "interdependence" with another premise or other premises. They often diagram these relationships using horizontal braces and a plus (+) sign.

[2] Elizabeth Hall and Paul Cameron, "Our Failing Reverence for Life," *Psychology Today* (April 1976): 108.

[3] Bennett H. Beach, "Mr. Wizard Comes to Court," *Time,* (March 1, 1982, p. 90.

[4] When I first began teaching critical thinking in 1984, I adopted Howard Kahane's *Logic and Contemporary Rhetoric* as the textbook for my course. I found this and another related example, which I use later in this chapter, at the end of the first exercise in his chapter 1. I still find these examples useful. This is my humble tribute to the late Kahane, whose textbook is still available and widely used.

[5] Howard Kahane, *Logic and Contemporary Rhetoric,* 5th edition (Belmont, CA: Wadsworth,

[6] Daniel Appleman, *How Computer Programming Works* (Emeryville, CA: Ziff-Davis Press, 1994).

[7] www.climatecrisis.net/thescience.

[8] Edward Blic, *21 Scientists Who Believe in Creation* (Harrisonburg, VA: Christian Light Publications, 1977).

[9] Howard Zinn, "The Odd Way of Thinking," *The Progressive* (November 2001): 8.

[10] Albert Ellis, *Sex Without Guilt* (New York: Lyle Stuart, 1966).

[11] Judith Randal, "Wrong Prescription: Why Managed Competition is No Cure," *The Progressive* (May 1993): 23–24.

[12] Meg Greenfield, "When the Press Becomes a Participant," *The Washington Post Company, Annual Report,* 1984, p. 21.

[13] Ashley Montagu, *Sociobiology Examined* (Oxford: Oxford University Press, 1980), p. 4.

[14] Eric Fromm, *Escape from Freedom* (New York: Avon Books, 1965), p. 158.

[15] Barry Stein et al., "Flextime," *Psychology Today* (June 1976): 43.

[16] Jerome Frank, dissenting opinion in *United States v. Roth,* 354 U.S. 476, 1957.

[17] E. Joy Kroeger Mappes, "Ethical Dilemmas for Nurses: Physicians' Orders versus Patients' Rights," in T. A. Mappes and J. S. Zembatty (eds.), *Biomedical Ethics* (New York: McGraw-Hill, 1981), p. 100.

[18] Amitai Etzioni, "When Rights Collide," *Psychology Today* (October 1977).

[19] Quincy Jones, *Q: The Autobiography of Quincy Jones* (New York: Doubleday, 2000), p. 299.

[20] Gary E. Crum, "Disputed Territory," *Hastings Center Report* (August/September 1988): 31.

[21] Mikal Gilmore (quoting Jon Landau), "The Long Shadow of Led Zeppelin: (savaged by critics, adored by fans, the biggest band of the 70s took sex, drugs, and rock & roll to epic heights before collapsing under the weight of its own heaviness)," *Rolling Stone Magazine* #1006, August 10, 2006, pp. 59–ff.

[22] Jennifer Washburn, "The Best Minds Money Can Buy," *Los Angeles Times,* July 21, 2006, p. B13.

[23] William Edelen, "Thomas Jefferson and the Tyranny of Religion," *Santa Barbara News-Press,* July 2, 2006, p. G3.

[24] Rosa Parks, "Bush's Burned Bridges," *Los Angeles Times,* July 21, 2006, p. B13.

Argument Analysis II: Paraphrasing Arguments

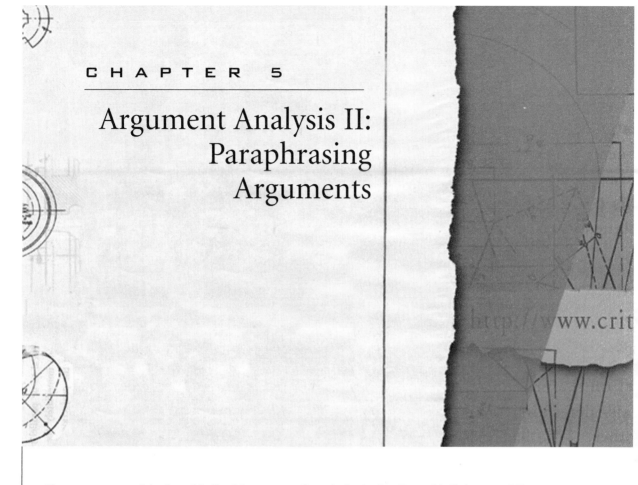

If you want to complain about Marilyn Manson, start from the beginning. Start with Shakespeare. What was *Romeo and Juliet about?* Suicide![1] —OZZY OSBOURNE

In Chapter 4, we introduced the concept of paraphrasing as the best test of your understanding of an argument. Paraphrasing means taking apart and then reassembling a text in your own words. This is both easier and harder than it sounds. We hope and expect that the simple tools, procedures, and guidance presented in Chapter 4 will prove useful in paraphrasing arguments, but you will soon see that paraphrasing arguments goes way beyond the simple and mechanical application of those tools and procedures. We begin by looking at paraphrasing in general and explaining that mysterious remark we just made about its being both easier and harder than it sounds. Try an exercise.

"To paraphrase the great Vince Lombardi, packaging isn't everything, it's the <u>only</u> thing."

THOUGHT EXPERIMENT 5.1 | Joke Headlines I

Look at the text that follows. Imagine that it's a newspaper headline—the joke kind that Jay Leno sometimes uses on *The Tonight Show*. Write out in a grammatically correct sentence what you think the accompanying news story might be.

Iraqi Head Seeks Arms

Complete this sentence: The real story is that . . .

_____

_____

We imagine that most of you will have come up with something like this: The real story is that the leader of Iraq is trying to obtain weapons. See how easy this is? That's paraphrasing. The hard part is explaining how you did it.

Jokes of this type depend on ambiguity. There are two meanings here: the one about the leader of Iraq and one about body parts. Understanding the joke depends on recognizing both. In effect, getting a joke of this type depends on paraphrasing the same text twice. And again, this is both easy (to do) and hard (to explain). We know this is easy to do because people understand jokes like this pretty routinely. Whole batches of these "Believe It or Not . . . Real Headlines from Actual Newspapers" jokes circulate widely on the Internet. Here is a short list of them.

DISCUSSION TOPIC 5.1 | Joke Headlines II

Pay close attention to your reasoning processes as you read the following "Believe It or Not . . . Real Headlines from Actual Newspapers." See if you can figure out precisely how you get these jokes. Are you following any rules?

Police Campaign to Run Down Jaywalkers

Safety Experts Say School Bus Passengers Should Be Belted

Drunk Gets Nine Months in Violin Case

Survivor of Siamese Twins Joins Parents

Farmer Bill Dies in House

Stud Tires Out

Prostitutes Appeal to Pope

Panda Mating Fails; Veterinarian Takes Over

Soviet Virgin Lands Short of Goal Again

British Left Waffles on Falkland Islands

Eye Drops Off Shelf

Teacher Strikes Idle Kids

Bush Wins on Budget, But More Lies Ahead

K9 Squad Helps Dog Bite Victim

Stolen Painting Found by Tree

Two Soviet Ships Collide, One Dies

Red Tape Holds Up New Bridge

Typhoon Rips through Cemetery; Hundreds Dead

Astronaut Takes Blame for Gas in Spacecraft

Kids Make Nutritious Snacks

Air Head Fired

We think that you're following lots of rules. For example paraphrasing the real story meaning of "Teacher Strikes Idle Kids" seems to depend on figuring out that "idle" is the verb and "strikes" is a noun. Here you are applying a rule of syntax or grammar. But distinguishing the "parts of speech" isn't much help when you read "Stolen Painting Found by Tree." In this case, distinguishing the real story meaning from the joke meaning depends on making a "semantic" distinction. In the real story, the preposition "by" means "next to"; in the joke, it means "through the action or agency of." There are more rules than you can shake a stick at. How do you know when to apply which rule?

Here is something even more fascinating. We would not be surprised if you were baffled to one degree or another by what we have just said about syntax and semantics—and maybe even by our explanations of the two jokes—but still *you get the jokes.* The point here is that understanding the joke, which involves paraphrasing the text twice, *does not seem to depend on being able to explain—or even being able to state—the rules you are following* as a speaker of the language when you paraphrase. Easy to do, hard to explain.

This is an example of a larger phenomenon: the awesome complexity of human intelligence. What we each do routinely as fluent speakers of a language—and understanding jokes is a good measure of fluency—is so complex and subtle that to reduce it to a set of calculations and mechanical procedures is a huge undertaking, (called "linguistics"). So this process is so hard to explain not because there are no rules involved or calculations being made, or because the calculations made in a given case can't be traced or the general rules and procedures being followed can't be spelled out. But it *would take a large book* to account for it within a comprehensive system. And it would take a huge amount of computer power even to approximate it mechanically in practice. This, by the way, captures the challenge of artificial intelligence as applied to conversation. The moral of this story is that following the steps and procedures presented in Chapter 4, especially in a mechanical way, will not *by itself* do the trick of argument analysis if we understand argument analysis as a particular variety or application of paraphrasing. At the start of Chapter 4, we indicated that, in the end, it's your paraphrase of the argument—your grasp of the meaning of the text, expressed in your own words—that counts. Underlining, highlighting, mapping, casting—these are all merely means to that end. As useful as these tools may be in many cases, they are to making a full-fledged argument analysis what training wheels are to riding a bike.

For example, now look at the quotation from rock musician Ozzy Osbourne used as the opening epigram for this chapter:

> If you want to complain about Marilyn Manson, start from the beginning. Start with Shakespeare. What was *Romeo and Juliet* about? Suicide!

There is clearly an argument being presented here. But unless you can paraphrase it, you won't get anywhere trying to cast it. So how *do* we go about paraphrasing an argument like this?

DISCUSSION TOPIC 5.2 | **Paraphrasing an Argument I**

Start with this question: What do we need to *know* to *understand* the argument? Go through the argument and list the things that a person would need to know or be familiar with to understand what Ozzy Osbourne is saying.

What do you need to know or be familiar with to understand what Osbourne is saying? Here's our list: You need to know who Marilyn Manson is. You need to know what the complaints about Marilyn Manson were. You need to know who Shakespeare was. It helps to know the plot of *Romeo and Juliet*. It also helps to know who Ozzy Osbourne is. Just for fun (and for a good exercise), *before* you move beyond the next exercise, find this stuff out. Look it up.

RESEARCH ASSIGNMENT 5.1 | Paraphrasing an Argument II

Who is Marilyn Manson? What were the complaints made about him? Who was Shakespeare? What is the plot of *Romeo and Juliet?* Who is Ozzy Osbourne? When you have all of this information, see if you can paraphrase the argument in the space provided here.

Marilyn Manson is the stage name of a 1990s gothic rock act whose lead singer took on the persona Antichrist Superstar. Once you know who Marilyn Manson is, it's easy to figure out what the complaints have been. His work was controversial. Concerts were banned, boycotts were organized against the sale of merchandise, and so on, because of concern that Marilyn Manson's music, music videos, and stage show might exert a satanic influence on teenagers and lead them into depravity. William Shakespeare is the great Elizabethan playwright, whose most famous tragedy, *Romeo and Juliet,* tells the story of the double suicide of two young lovers kept apart by their feuding families. Ozzy Osbourne rose to prominence in the 1970s as lead singer of the British heavy metal band Black Sabbath. He was the subject of much controversy, like that provoked by Marilyn Manson, including a landmark legal battle over the 1981 song "Suicide Solution," allegedly the cause of a teenage gunshot suicide. Now, with this information, go back to paraphrasing Osbourne's argument, starting with the conclusion.

APPLICATION EXERCISE 5.1 | Paraphrasing an Argument III

What is Osbourne's main point in the preceding argument?

What is Osbourne's basis of support for this main point?

With the preceding information, it's not difficult to see that Osbourne's point is to defend Manson (as well as Osbourne's own work) against censorship, based on a comparison with Shakespeare. There you have it: a paraphrase of Osbourne's argument. This was accomplished essentially by *situating the text we're trying to paraphrase in a meaningful context.* This is important enough to qualify as a rule of thumb: whenever we want to paraphrase an argument, we should pause to orient ourselves to the context in which the argument appears. We should begin with a question: what does a person need to know to understand this argument? And we should therefore make sure that we *do* know all that is necessary to understand the argument.

CRITICAL THINKING TIP 5.1 | **Awareness of Assumptions**

When Paraphrasing, Orient Yourself to the Context

It is time to apply what we've learned to some more advanced examples. Let us briefly review. Table 5.1 provides the important guidelines to argument analysis.

TABLE 5.1   Guidelines for Paraphrasing

The goal	To establish a fair, accurate, and detailed understanding of the argument—as a preliminary to rendering a judgment of its quality.
The measure	The paraphrase of the argument—your grasp of the meaning of the text, expressed in your own words—is what counts most.
Rules of thumb	Orient yourself to the argument's context.
	Find the conclusion first.
	When in doubt, don't be unfair—make the argument out to be as reasonable as possible.

ADVANCED APPLICATIONS

So far, the arguments we have used for purposes of illustration have been quite short. Many of the arguments you will encounter are longer. Arguments are often presented in the form of letters, speeches, essays, even whole books. Analyzing short arguments is, as you already know, challenging in several ways. The results of the analysis of short arguments, or more precisely, short presentations of arguments, can easily be longer and more complex than the texts analyzed. This was the case, for example, with the argument analyzed at the end of Chapter 4 about textbooks, mistakes, whales, mammals, and fish. Longer arguments present an additional and "opposite" challenge: the challenge of compressing, or distilling, a lengthy presentation into something that can be grasped more quickly than the original. Fortunately, however, this challenge can be met by approaching it with the guidelines discussed earlier. The goal and the measure of success remain the same. And the rules of thumb still apply. We propose now to illustrate all of this with an example. We suggest that you try your hand at paraphrasing the next argument *before* you read what we have to say about it. So try the following exercise before reading the rest of this chapter.

APPLICATION EXERCISE 5.2 | Paraphrasing an Argument IV

The following is an excerpt of an essay published in the aftermath of the September 11 terrorist attacks. The essay is by the late syndicated columnist Molly Ivins. After reading the passage, follow the guidelines given earlier and paraphrase the argument in 50 words or less.

Destroying Freedoms in Order to Save Them

By Molly Ivins

Fort Worth *Star-Telegram*

December 6, 2001

With all due respect, of course, and God Bless America too, has anyone considered the possibility that the attorney general is becoming unhinged?

Poor John Ashcroft is under a lot of strain here. Is it possible that his mind has started to give under the weight of responsibility, what with having to stop terrorism between innings against doctors trying to help the dying in Oregon and California? Why not take a Valium, sir, and go track down some nice domestic nut with access to anthrax, OK?

Not content with the noxious USA PATRIOT bill (for "Uniting and Strengthening America by Providing Appropriate Tools Required to Intercept and Obstruct Terrorism" Act—urp), which was bad enough, Ashcroft has steadily moved from bad to worse. Now he wants to bring back FBI surveillance of domestic religious and political groups.

For those who remember COINTELPRO, this is glorious news. Back in the day, Fearless Fibbies, cleverly disguised in their wingtips and burr haircuts, used to infiltrate such dangerous groups as the Southern Christian Leadership Conference and Business Executives Against the War in Vietnam. This had the usual comedic fallout and was so berserk that there was a standing rule on the left: Anyone who proposed breaking any law was automatically assumed to be an FBI agent.

Let's see, who might the Federal Fosdicks spy upon today? Columnist Tom Friedman of *The New York Times* recently reported from Pakistan that hateful Taliban types are teaching in the religious schools, "The faithful shall enter paradise, and the unbelievers shall be condemned to eternal hellfire." Frightful! Put the Baptists on the list. Those who agitate against the government, constantly denigrating and opposing it? Add Tom DeLay, Dick Armey and Rush Limbaugh to the list . . .

Paraphrase:

_____

_____

_____

_____

_____

Now that you have paraphrased Ivins's argument, it will be instructive to compare both your process and your results to our own. We'll take you through it step by step. We begin with an orientation to the context of the argument. One of the key contextual dimensions where arguments are concerned is the *issue* to which the argument is addressed. The issue is probably the most important contextual landmark you will be able to find in most cases. Having a clear and solid grasp of the issue will make identifying and formulating the thesis of the argument easier than it would otherwise be. So the first thing we would do is to formulate a brief issue statement.

APPLICATION EXERCISE 5.3 | Issue Statement

We highly recommend reviewing the sections of Chapter 1 on issues, issue analysis, and composing issue statements. When you have done that, answer the following question: "What is the issue Molly Ivins is addressing in her column?" Try to compose your answer in one sentence.

Ivins's argument addresses the issue of the U.S. government's official response to the September 11 terrorist attacks. This is a complex issue. So it might be advisable to do a little issue analysis and focus more precisely: We could start by making a distinction between U.S. *domestic* and *foreign* policy. Ivins's argument is concerned particularly with the government's response in the area of *domestic* security and law enforcement. In general terms, this issue might be expressed in the form of the question, "Is the U.S. government doing what it should be doing with regard to domestic security and law enforcement in response to the September 11 terrorist attacks?"

Besides the issue, what do we need to know to understand Ivins's argument? As in the case of the shorter argument discussed earlier, this research agenda can be derived by carefully scanning or reading through the argument. Go ahead and try it. Then carry out the research. Look the information up (see Discussion Topic 5.2 and Research Assignment 5.1).

RESEARCH ASSIGNMENT 5.2 | Paraphrasing an Argument V

Develop and carry out a contextual research agenda for Molly Ivins's argument. Follow the instructions given in Discussion Topic 5.2 and Research Assignment 5.1.

(blank ruled note-taking lines)

Here are our results: In this case, you need to know that John Ashcroft was the U.S. attorney general in the first term of the George W. Bush administration. You need to know that serious acts of terrorism involving the distribution of deadly anthrax through the mail remained unsolved at the time Ivins's column was written. You need to know at least a little bit about the USA PATRIOT Act—an antiterrorism measure rushed through the Congress and signed into law in October 2001, just six weeks after September 11. It gives sweeping new surveillance powers to U.S. international intelligence and domestic law enforcement agencies, and it eliminates checks and balances that were put into place after previous misuse of surveillance authority by these agencies. You need to know that COINTELPRO is an acronym for covert domestic counterintelligence programs run by the FBI from 1956–1971, in which FBI agents infiltrated domestic political organizations in an attempt to neutralize domestic political dissent and combat the "threat of communism." You need to know that the Southern Christian Leadership Conference was the civil rights organization founded in 1957 by Dr. Martin Luther King. You need to know that revelations of COINTELPRO covert surveillance on law-abiding U.S. citizens, including Dr. King, were what led to the checks and balances now eliminated under the USA PATRIOT Act. You need to know that the Taliban was the repressive theocratic regime that ruled most of Afghanistan and gave safe haven to Osama bin Laden since 1996 and that the events of September 11 turned the Taliban into an "official enemy" of the United States. You need to know that Tom DeLay and Dick Armey are both Texas Republicans and that, as majority whip and majority leader in the House of Representatives, they were two of the most powerful politicians in the United States at the time Ivins published her column. And everybody presumably recognizes Rush Limbaugh as the host of a right-wing radio talk show.

We could go further than this. The more you know about the context, the more deeply you can appreciate the details and nuances of the argument. For example, it also helps to know that Fearless Fosdick was a cartoon character created by cartoonist Al Capp (in the comic strip *Li'l Abner*) as a parody of *Dick Tracy* (Dick Tracy did endless battle with horrible villains and, although occasionally wounded in battle, always got his man). Fosdick is a farce. Gullible and in awe of corrupt authority, he is forever getting shot full of bullet holes like Swiss cheese. It helps to know that COINTELPRO operations often weren't as "covert" as the operatives seemed to think they were. It also helps to recognize the reference in Ivins's title to a notorious Vietnam-era piece of Orwellian doublespeak, in which Pentagon officials explained that it was necessary to "destroy certain villages in order to save them."

But we have enough of a context already to enable us to take the next step and identify Ivins's main point, or thesis. Remember, Ivins's thesis will be her answer to the question in which we formulated the issue in a one-sentence issue statement earlier:

> Is the U.S. government doing what it should be doing with regard to domestic security and law enforcement in response to the September 11 terrorist attacks?

Ivins's answer to this question is evident: She does *not* think that the U.S. government (personified here by Attorney General Ashcroft) is doing what it should be doing in terms of domestic security and law enforcement in response to the terrorist attacks. In particular, Ivins is arguing that the USA PATRIOT Act and Ashcroft's call to reauthorize FBI surveillance of domestic religious and political groups are not what the U.S. government should be doing. Why not?

Asking the question "Why not?" at this point directs attention to the support Ivins offers for her thesis. Rereading the text of her argument against the backdrop of the contextual information assembled earlier, we can now boil that support down to this: The measures Ashcroft has taken and called for will not enhance security against terrorist attacks, but they *will* destroy our freedoms. And if they are applied consistently to those on the domestic scene whose political

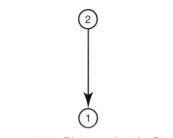

FIGURE 5.1 Diagramming the Paraphrase I

actions and agendas are like those of our "official enemies," the results will be a farce. Although serious acts of terrorism, quite possibly of domestic origin, remain to be solved, we'll wind up spying on Baptists, the Republican congressional leadership, and right-wing talk-radio hosts.

So our paraphrase: Ivins is arguing that the USA PATRIOT Act and reauthorizing FBI surveillance of domestic religious and political groups are not what our government should be doing, because these things will result only in the farcical destruction of our own freedoms (40 words).

Using Chapter 4 tools, we might now underline, highlight, and cast our paraphrase as follows (see Figure 5.1):

[THE USA PATRIOT ACT AND REAUTHORIZING FBI SURVEILLANCE OF DOMESTIC RELIGIOUS AND POLITICAL GROUPS ARE NOT WHAT OUR GOVERNMENT SHOULD BE DOING ①], (because) [**these things will result only in the farcical destruction of our own freedoms ②**].

The conclusion (claim 1) does not follow from the premise (claim 2) alone. There is an additional implied premise—a claim so obvious that it goes without saying: Engaging in the farcical destruction of our own freedoms is not what our government should be doing. Thus, assigning it the letter ⓐ, we might add to the casting as follows (Figure 5.2).

So far, we have arrived at a short paraphrase of a much longer text. In effect, our paraphrase compresses Ivins's entire argument into a single sentence of 40 words, consisting of just two claims: her thesis and one supporting premise (not counting the additional implied premise). In addition, and more important, as a

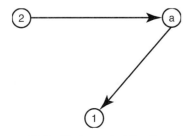

FIGURE 5.2 Diagramming the Paraphrase II

result of the process we used to get this far, we are in a good position to explain the argument in greater depth and detail should that be necessary or desirable. The support for the main premise (claim 2) may be found in the two paragraphs of contextual information we assembled earlier. Indeed, you might have noticed that along the way to our 40-word paraphrase we passed through an intermediate-length paraphrase of Ivins's premises.

PRACTICE, PRACTICE, AND MORE PRACTICE

Practice is the only way to get good at this. And the good news is, the better *you* get, the easier *it* gets. So we conclude this chapter with an array of arguments for you to practice on.

APPLICATION EXERCISE 5.4 | A "Bite-Sized" Editorial

In May, researchers reported in the journal *Nature* that ozone levels in the atmosphere have stabilized—and even increased slightly—in some regions in the past 10 years. The news comes after many previous years of ozone degradation caused by chlorofluorocarbons (CFCs) and other ozone-depleting substances in the atmosphere. Thankfully, more than 180 countries, including the United States and the European Union, have signed the Montreal Protocol, the international ban on CFCs and ozone-depleting substances, since it was ratified in 1987. But these chemicals aren't completely out of the picture; the ban doesn't go into effect until 2010 in developing nations such as China, Mexico, India, and Russia, and there's still a thriving black market for CFC-based substances such as refrigerants. Scientists also say that restoring the full health of the ozone layer will take decades and that it may never return to its pre-CFC levels. The facts here speak loud and clear—these international bans work. Do we need any further proof that a similar pact to curb global warming is a good idea?[2]

APPLICATION EXERCISE 5.5 | A Matched Pair of Opposed Opinion Pieces

The two compositions that follow present opposing positions on another part of the September 11 debate. Paraphrase each of the two arguments using the procedures illustrated earlier. Target length for each paraphrase: 250 words (the rough equivalent of one standard page of double-spaced text).

An Open Letter to President Bush and the U.S. Congress
October 2001

The events of the past few days have made everyone understand how vulnerable a free and open society is to mass destruction and terror. But this terrible vulnerability is part of the strength of such a society, not a hallmark of its weakness. It takes courage to allow the free movement of people and ideas. That courage is predicated on voluntary acceptance of great risk, and not upon ignorance of its likelihood. The immediate response to such a catastrophe is anger and hatred. But the system of laws that supports the U.S. and its allies has been designed by generations of great people to ensure that anger and hatred are never given the final word. Justice, truth, and respect for individual differences are principles whose power far outweighs the thoughtless desire for revenge. More importantly, revenge breeds revenge. It seems terribly dangerous to provide individuals motivated precisely by the desire to increase pain and suffering the luxury of the war they so much desire. Such a war turns them from rigid, totalitarian cowards to soldiers; from failures who are willing to prey upon the innocent to heroic exemplars of the fight against overwhelming external oppression. The craven acts of terrorism perpetrated in New York and Washington are dignified intolerably by their classification as acts of war. The individuals who perpetrated these appalling events must be regarded and treated as criminals, as international pariahs, who have committed crimes against humanity, and who must be brought publicly and rationally to justice. Our great technological power makes us increasingly vulnerable to the rigid madness of the ideologically committed and resentful. To turn against such madness with indiscriminate revenge seeking is merely to react in the same primitive and deadly manner. To risk the slaughter of innocent people in the hunt for such revenge is to absolutely ensure that constant episodes of international terror will come to be the hallmark of 21st-century existence. The entire world stands behind the U.S., in the hope that the commission of crimes against civilization can be exterminated. Such solidarity was absolutely unthinkable even fifteen years ago. The U.S. therefore has an unparalleled opportunity to demonstrate its unshakeable commitment to its own principles, particularly under such conditions of extreme duress, and to provide the world with the hope that democracy and freedom can truly rise above the parochial ideological madness of the past. Such a demonstration would truly lift the American state above all past national institutions, and would continue the tradition of great spirit that allowed for the rehabilitation of Germany and Japan after the Second World War. Perhaps the events of September 11 might therefore be regarded as the last war of the second Christian millennium, instead of the first war of the third. In consequence, we implore you to react with discrimination, to target only those truly responsible, and to avoid the cruel and thoughtless errors characterizing humanity's blind and ethnocentric past. Please punish only the guilty, and not the innocent. Otherwise the cycle of terror that seems an ineradicable part of human existence will never come to an end.

Sincerely,

1. Jordan B. Peterson, Professor, Department of Psychology, University of Toronto, peterson@psych.utoronto.ca.
2. Daniel C. Dennett, University Professor, Director, Center for Cognitive Studies, Tufts University, ddennett@tufts.edu.
3. Steven Pinker, Professor, Department of Brain and Cognitive Sciences, Massachusetts Institute of Technology (MIT), spinker@mediaone.net.
4. Hilary Putnam, Professor Emeritus, Department of Philosophy, Harvard University, hputnam@fas.harvard.edu.

Et al.

War, not "Crimes": Time for a Paradigm Shift

By Daniel Pipes
National Review

October 1, 2001

"Make no mistake: The United States will hunt down and punish those responsible for these cowardly acts." So spoke President Bush in his address to the nation soon after the catastrophic events of September 11.

I agree with the president's sentiments but disagree with two specifics in this statement. First, there was nothing cowardly about the attacks, which were deeds of incredible—albeit perverted—bravery. Second, to "hunt down and punish" the perpetrators is deeply to misunderstand the problem. It implies that we view the plane crashes as criminal deeds rather than what they truly are—acts of war. They are part of a campaign of terrorism that began in a sustained way with the bombing of the U.S. embassy in Beirut in 1983, a campaign that has never since relented. Occurring with almost predictable regularity a few times a year, assaults on Americans have included explosions on airliners, at commercial buildings, and at a variety of U.S. governmental installations. Before last week, the total death toll was about 600 American lives.

To me, this sustained record of violence looks awfully much like war, but Washington in its wisdom has insisted otherwise. Official policy has viewed the attacks as a sequence of discrete criminal incidents. Seeing terrorism primarily as a problem of law enforcement is a mistake, because it means:

- Focusing on the arrest and trial of the dispensable characters who actually carry out violent acts, leaving the funders, planners, organizers, and commanders of terrorism to continue their work unscathed, prepared to carry out more attacks.
- Relying primarily on such defensive measures as metal detectors, security guards, bunkers, police arrests, and prosecutorial eloquence—rather than on such offensive tools as soldiers, aircraft, and ships.
- Misunderstanding the terrorist's motivations as criminal, whereas they are usually based on extremist ideologies.
- Missing the fact that terrorist groups (and the states that support them) have declared war on the United States (sometimes publicly).
- Requiring that the U.S. government have unrealistically high levels of proof before deploying military force. If it lacks evidence that can stand up in a U.S. court of justice, as is usually the case, no action is taken. The legalistic mindset thus ensures that, in the vast majority of cases, the U.S. government does not respond, and killers of Americans pay little or no price.

The time has come for a paradigm shift, toward viewing terrorism as a form of warfare. Such a change will have many implications. It means targeting not just those foot soldiers who actually carry out the violence but the organizations and governments that stand behind them. It means relying on the armed forces, not policemen, to protect Americans. It means defense overseas rather than in American courtrooms. It means that organizations and governments that sponsor terrorism—not just the foot soldiers who carry it out—will pay the price.

It means dispensing with the unrealistically high expectations of proof so that when reasonable evidence points to a regime's or an organization's having harmed Americans, U.S. military force can be deployed. It means that, as in conventional war, Washington need not know the names and specific actions of enemy soldiers before fighting them.

It means retaliating every single time terrorism harms an American. There is no need to know the precise identity of a perpetrator; in war, there are times when one strikes first and asks questions later. When an attack takes place, it could be reason to target any of those known to harbor terrorists. If the perpetrator is not precisely known, then punish those who are known to harbor terrorists. Go after the governments and organizations that support terrorism.

It means using force so that the punishment is disproportionately greater than the attack. The U.S. has a military force far more powerful than any other in the world: Why spend hundreds of billions of dollars a year on it and not deploy it to defend Americans?

I give fair warning: The military approach demands more from Americans than does the legal one. It requires a readiness to spend money and to lose lives. Force works only if it is part of a sustained policy, not a one-time event. Throwing a few bombs (as was done against the Libyan regime in 1986, and against sites in Afghanistan and Sudan in 1998) does not amount to a serious policy. Going the military route requires a long-term commitment that will demand much from Americans over many years.

But it will be worth it, for the safety of Americans depends ultimately not on defense but on offense; on victories not in the courtroom but on the battlefield. The U.S. government needs to establish a newly fearsome reputation, so that anyone who harms Americans knows that retribution will be certain and nasty. Nothing can replace the destruction of any organization or government that harms so much as a single American citizen.

To those who say this approach would start a cycle of violence, the answer is obvious: That cycle already exists, as Americans are constantly murdered in acts of terrorism. Further, by baring their teeth, Americans are far more likely to intimidate their enemies than to instigate further violence. Retaliation will reduce violence, not further increase it, providing Americans with a safety they presently do not enjoy.

ADDITIONAL EXERCISES

At the end of Chapter 4, we supplied 14 examples of argumentation taken from a variety of sources in public discourse for analysis using basic tools and techniques covered in Chapters 3 and 4. Now try these examples again, with the additional tools and techniques of paraphrasing covered in this chapter. See if these don't help you over the rough spots. Keep the goal of argument analysis in mind—a fair and accurate understanding of the argument in detail, expressed in your own words.

■ **APPLICATION EXERCISE 5.6 EVOLUTION**   "Evolution is a scientific fairy-tale just as the 'flat earth theory' was in the 12th century. Evolution directly contradicts the Second Law of Thermodynamics, which states that unless an intelligent planner is directing a system, it will always go in the direction of disorder and deterioration. Evolution requires a faith that is incomprehensible!"[3]

■ **APPLICATION EXERCISE 5.7 TERRORISM**   "'We shall make no distinction,' the President proclaimed, 'between terrorists and countries that harbor terrorists.' So now we are bombing Afghanistan and inevitably killing innocent people because it is in the nature of bombing (and I say this as a former Air Force bombardier) to be indiscriminate, to 'make no distinction.' We are committing terrorism in order to 'send a message' to terrorists. . . . War is terrorism, magnified a hundred times. Yes, let's find the perpetrators of the awful acts of September 11. We must find the guilty parties and prosecute them. But we shouldn't engage in indiscriminate retaliation. When a crime is committed by someone in a certain neighborhood, you don't destroy the neighborhood."[4]

■ **APPLICATION EXERCISE 5.8 SEXUAL RELATIONS**   "A scientific colleague of mine, who holds a professorial post in the department of sociology and anthropology at one of our leading universities, recently asked me about my stand on the question of human beings having sex relations without love. Although I have taken something of a position on this issue in my book, *The American Sexual Tragedy,* I have never quite considered the problem in sufficient detail. So here goes. In general, I feel that affectional, as against non-affectional, sex relations are desirable. It is usually desirable that an association between coitus and affection exist—particularly in marriage, because it is often difficult for two individuals to keep finely tuned to each other over a period of years."[5]

■ **APPLICATION EXERCISE 5.9 MANAGED COMPETITION IN HEALTH CARE**   "It isn't likely that managed competition [Bill Clinton's health care reform concept] can be counted on to save money. For one thing, at least two managed-care setups must be present in a community if there is to be competition, and each of them needs a potential market of roughly 250,000 people to achieve economies of scale. Only about half of all Americans, it turns out, live in places densely populated enough to support two or more such programs. What's more, insurers would constantly hustle to win and retain business, because employers would constantly be shopping for better deals, just as they do now. The sales staff, recruiters, advertising personnel, and clerical staff that such 'marketing' entails contribute nothing to the provision of health care. And the physicians, nurses, and others whom insurers and HMOs [health maintenance organizations] hire to oversee—that is, second-guess—the decisions individual doctors make with individual patients— an essential feature of managed care—have to be paid too, adding to the overhead cost. Administrative costs already soak up about $225 billion a year—25 cents of every dollar spent on health care in this country. Under managed competition, such costs would, at best, stay the same. More probably, they would increase."[6]

■ **APPLICATION EXERCISE 5.10 ROLE OF THE PRESS**   "To the extent that it is working at all, the press is always a participant in, rather than a pure observer of, the events it reports. Our decisions on where (and where not) to be and what (and what not) to report have enormous impact on the political and governmental life we cover. We are obliged to be selective. We cannot publish the Daily Everything. And so long as this is true—so long as we are making choices that (1) affect what people see concerning their leaders and (2) inevitably cause those leaders to behave in particular ways—we cannot pretend we are not participants."[7]

■ **APPLICATION EXERCISE 5.11 POLITICS AND SCIENCE**   "Scientists are human beings with their full complement of emotions and prejudices, and their emotions and prejudices often influence the way they do their science. This was first clearly brought out in a study by Professor Nicholas Pastore in 1949. In this study Professor Pastore showed that the scientist's political beliefs were highly correlated with what he believed about the roles played by nature and nurture in the development of the person. Those holding conservative political views strongly tended to believe in the power of genes over environment. Those subscribing to more liberal views tended to believe in the power of environment over genes. One distinguished scientist (who happened to be a teacher of mine) when young was a socialist an environmentalist, but toward middle age he became politically conservative and a firm believer in the supremacy of genes!"[8]

APPLICATION EXERCISE 5.12 FROM INDIVIDUAL TO SOCIAL PSYCHOLOGY
"Many a reader will raise the question whether findings won by the observation of individuals can be applied to the psychological understanding of groups. Our answer to this question is an emphatic affirmation. Any group consists of individuals and nothing but individuals, and psychological mechanisms which we find operating in a group can therefore only be mechanisms that operate in individuals. In studying individual psychology as a basis for the understanding of social psychology, we do something which might be compared with studying an object under the microscope. This enables us to discover the very details of psychological mechanisms which we find operating on a large scale in the social process. If our analysis of socio-psychological phenomena is not based on the detailed study of human behavior, it lacks empirical character and, therefore, validity."[9]

APPLICATION EXERCISE 5.13 FLEXTIME   "Flextime [flexible working hours] often makes workers more productive because being treated as responsible adults gives them greater commitment to their jobs. As a result it decreases absenteeism, sick leave, tardiness and overtime, and generally produces significant increases in productivity for the work group as a whole. For example, in trial periods in three different departments, the U.S. Social Security Administration measured productivity increases averaging about 20%. None has reported a decline."[10]

APPLICATION EXERCISE 5.14 CENSORSHIP   "Government control of ideas or personal preferences is alien to a democracy. And the yearning to use governmental censorship of any kind is infectious. It may spread insidiously. Commencing with suppression of books as obscene, it is not unlikely to develop into official lust for the power of thought-control in the areas of religion, politics, and elsewhere. [John] Milton observed that 'licensing of books . . . necessarily pulls along with it so many other kinds of licensing.' [John Stuart] Mill notes that the 'bounds of what may be called moral police' may easily extend 'until it encroaches on the most unquestionably legitimate liberty of the individual.' We should beware of a recrudescence of the undemocratic doctrine uttered in the seventeenth century by [William] Berkeley, Governor of Virginia: 'Thank God there are no free schools or preaching, for learning has brought disobedience into the world, and printing has divulged them. God keep us from both.'"[11]

APPLICATION EXERCISE 5.15 OBLIGATION   "What, after all, is the foundation of the nurse's obligation to follow the physician's orders? Presumably, the nurse's obligation to act in the medical interest of the patient. The point is that the nurse has an obligation to follow physician's orders because, ordinarily, patient welfare (interest) thereby is ensured. Thus when a nurse's obligation to follow a physician's order comes into direct conflict with the nurse's obligation to act in the medical interest of the patient, it would seem to follow that the patient's interests should always take precedence."[12]

▓ APPLICATION EXERCISE 5.16 PUBLIC NEEDS VS. INDIVIDUAL RIGHTS

"American institutions were fashioned in an era of vast unoccupied spaces and pre-industrial technology. In those days, collisions between public needs and individual rights may have been minimal. But increased density, scarcity of resources, and interlocking technologies have now heightened the concern for 'public goods,' which belong to no one in particular but to all of us jointly. Polluting a lake or river or the air may not directly damage any one person's private property or living space. But it destroys a good that all of us—including future generations—benefit from and have a title to. Our public goods are entitled to a measure of protection."[13]

▓ APPLICATION EXERCISE 5.17 DIGITAL MUSIC REVOLUTION

"These days music is truly global in sweep. The genie's out of the bottle, never to return, with MP3, Napster/Scour, and Freenet and Gnutella rendering all previous lines of demarcation meaningless. There's a revolution in progress, leveling everything in its path. Copyrights, masters, negatives, books, records, and films; it's all the same to a binary number, or a carbon atom and hydrogen qubit. Legislation, global police monitoring by knocking on two million doors—I don't think so. All I know is, you can't afford to make the customer your enemy. They no longer want to purchase a CD with ten or twelve songs on it to get the two they really want. They are also hip enough to know about artists' earnings and no longer want to pay the price for all the people in the middle of the distribution chain. These technological changes have provided an unexpected and highly efficient platform for rebellion for the current generation. We better get together and figure it out—and quickly!"[14]

▓ APPLICATION EXERCISE 5.18 A MISTAKEN COMPARISON

"In policy debates one party sometimes charges that his or her opponents are embracing a Nazi-like position. . . . Meanwhile, sympathizers nod in agreement with the charge, seeing it as the ultimate blow to their opponents. . . . The problem with using the Nazi analogy in public policy debates is that in the Western world there is a form of anti-Nazi 'bigotry' that sees Nazis as almost mythically evil beings. . . . Firsthand knowledge of our own culture makes it virtually impossible to equate Nazi society with our own. The official racism of Germany, its military mentality, the stresses of war, and the presence of a dictator instead of a democratic system make Nazi Germany in the 1940s obviously different from America in the 1980s."[15]

▓ APPLICATION EXERCISE 5.19 POPULARITY VS. ELITISM

"There is no other story in rock & roll like the story of Led Zeppelin because the story is an argument—about music, who makes it, who hears it and who judges its meanings. Mainly, though, it's a argument about the work, merits and life of a band that has been both treasured and scorned now for more than thirty-five years. The arguments started as soon as the band did, rooted in . . . a rift between the hard fought values of the 1960s and the real-life pleasures and recklessness of the 1970s. Zeppelin forced a revival of the distinction between popularity and quality. As long as the bands most admired aesthetically were also the bands most successful commercially (Cream, for instance), the distinction was irrelevant. But Zeppelin's enormous commercial success, in spite of critical opposition, revealed the deep division in what was once thought to be a homogeneous audience. That division has now evolved into a clearly defined mass taste and a clearly defined elitist taste.[16]

APPLICATION EXERCISE 5.20 TERM PROJECT At the end of chapter 3 (research assignment 3.1), the instructions were to research the issue articulated in your issue statement and to identify at least three extended arguments representing at least two distinct positions on that issue. Now apply all that you have learned about argument analysis to the results of your research. Try to paraphrase each argument you found in your research in 100 words or less.

NOTES

[1] *Rolling Stone* 763, June 26, 1997, p. 28.

[2] Deborah Snoonian, "Ozone Makes a Comeback," *Plenty* (August/September 2006): 16.

[3] Dr. Edward Blic, *21 Scientists Who Believe in Creation* (Harrisonburg, VA: Christian Light Publications, 1977).

[4] Howard Zinn, "The Odd Way of Thinking," *The Progressive* (November 2001): 8.

[5] Albert Ellis, *Sex Without Guilt* (New York: Lyle Stuart, 1966).

[6] Judith Randal, "Wrong Prescription: Why Managed Competition is No Cure," *The Progressive* (May 1993): 23–24.

[7] Meg Greenfield, "When the Press Becomes a Participant," *The Washington Post Company, Annual Report,* 1984, p. 21.

[8] Ashley Montagu, *Sociobiology Examined* (Oxford: Oxford University Press, 1980), p. 4.

[9] Eric Fromm, *Escape from Freedom* (New York: Avon Books, 1965), p. 158.

[10] Barry Stein et al., "Flextime," *Psychology Today* (June 1976): 43.

[11] Jerome Frank, dissenting opinion in *United States v. Roth*, 354 U.S. 476, 1957.

[12] E. Joy Kroeger Mappes, "Ethical Dilemmas for Nurses: Physicians' Orders versus Patients' Rights," in T. A. Mappes and J. S. Zembatty (eds.), *Biomedical Ethics* (New York: McGraw-Hill, 1981), p. 100.

[13] Amitai Etzioni, "When Rights Collide," *Psychology Today* (October 1977).

[14] Quincy Jones, *Q: The Autobiography of Quincy Jones* (New York: Doubleday, 2000), p. 299.

[15] Gary E. Crum, "Disputed Territory," *Hastings Center Report* (August/September 1988): 31.

[16] Mikal Gilmore (quoting Jon Landau), "The Long Shadow of Led Zeppelin: (savaged by critics, adored by fans, the biggest band of the 70s took sex, drugs, and rock & roll to epic heights before collapsing under the weight of its own heaviness)", *Rolling Stone Magazine* #1006, August 10, 2006, pp. 59–ff.

Deductive Reasoning

Why Philosophers
don't appear on
TV commercials

...But if you actually believe
what the label says, you will
conclude that the product is
both good and not good, healthy
and not healthy, and you will
be mired in contradictions...

© Gerald Grow, 1993

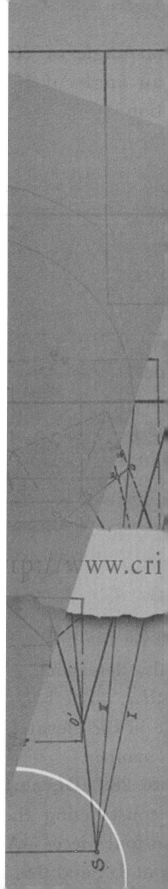

CHAPTER 6

Evaluating Deductive Arguments I: Categorical Logic

Now that we have covered argument identification and analysis, we are ready to address the evaluation of arguments. Most of us intuitively recognize qualitative differences between arguments, especially where the differences are relatively great. That is to say, we have little difficulty in intuitively recognizing the superiority of an excellent argument to one that is extremely weak. But our intuitions may fail to guide us where competing arguments are more closely matched. Different people often have conflicting intuitions about which of two closely matched competing arguments is superior, and we may even experience conflicting intuitions individually. Nor do our intuitions help us explain our evaluative judgments. So we need a bit of theory to support, to guide, and to explain our evaluative intuitions. For theoretical purposes, we'll make a basic distinction between the structural features of an argument and the materials used in its construction. One way to understand this distinction is to think of an argument as a building. Suppose we are evaluating buildings; for example, suppose we're buying a house. Some houses are obviously and intuitively better built than others. We can tell intuitively that the White House is a stronger building than the outhouse. But we need a more systematic set of criteria to make reasonable decisions when houses are more closely matched. Buildings are complicated, so there are many criteria relevant to evaluating buildings. That's why we would want to make the set of criteria systematic. The system gives us organization. One way to organize is to divide. And with buildings, a reasonable and powerful first distinction for purposes of evaluation would be between materials and how those materials are put together—the design and construction. So in evaluating arguments, we could look at materials factors and design factors. In this comparison (or analogy) the "materials" are the premises of the argument and the "design" is the plan according to which the premises are assembled in support of the conclusion. We will begin in this chapter with design factors, returning to materials factors in Chapter 10.

DEDUCTIVE AND INDUCTIVE REASONING

The first consideration in design is always function. In reasoning and its evaluation, an important functional design consideration is inferential security. In Chapter 3 we introduced the term "inference" as the mental step we take in reasoning from a premise or premises to the conclusion. In taking this step, we want to know how secure we are against falling into error. Thus **inferential security** refers to the degree to which an inference is safe. In terms of function we can sort arguments into two design categories: deductive and inductive. **Deductive** inferences are designed to achieve absolute security in the inference. **Inductive** inferences are designed to manage risk of error where absolute security is unattainable.

Consider the following two examples:

1. Your neighbor, Jones, is a member of the American Association of University Professors. Only members of the faculties of accredited colleges and universities are eligible for membership in this association. Therefore your neighbor, Jones, is a college professor.

2. Your neighbor, Jones, wears a tweed sport coat with patches on the elbows; he carries a battered briefcase; and he rides his bicycle to the college campus every day. Therefore your neighbor, Jones, is a college professor.

Notice how much stronger the connection is between the premises and the conclusion in the first example as compared with those in the second example. In the first example, we could say that anyone who fully understands what the sentences in the argument mean must recognize that the premises cannot both be true without the conclusion also being true. But that is not the case with the second argument. In the second example, we could say at most that the premises, if true, make the conclusion reasonable or likely. As we'll go on to explain more fully in the next two chapters, deductive reasoning, when it is well designed and constructed (valid), eliminates all risk of error in the inferential move from the premises to the conclusion. In inductive reasoning, the truth of the premises makes the conclusion reasonable, probable, or likely but not certain. This difference between deduction and induction will be reflected in different sets of evaluative criteria. Accordingly, an early step in the process of evaluating arguments is deciding which set of criteria should be applied—in other words, whether the argument should be evaluated as a deduction or as an induction.

Before we address this question, we'd better clear up an old and widespread misunderstanding about the essential difference between induction and deduction. It is often said that deduction moves from general premises to particular conclusions, and induction moves in the opposite direction from particular premises to general conclusions. It is true of *some* deductive inferences that they move from general premises to particular conclusions. But it's not an essential distinguishing feature of all deductions. For example,

> Ford Motor Company has reported record losses for last year. General Motors has reported record losses for last year. And Chrysler has reported record losses for last year. Therefore all major U.S. auto manufacturers lost money last year.

is a deductive argument with particular premises and a general conclusion. Similarly, it is true of *some* inductive inferences that they move from particular premises to general conclusions. But it's not an essential distinguishing feature of all inductive inferences. For example,

> All U.S. presidents have so far been men. Therefore it is likely that the next U.S. president will be a man.

is an inductive argument with a general premise and a particular conclusion.

DEDUCTIVE AND INDUCTIVE SIGNALS

Just as the presence of arguments, premises, and conclusions are often indicated by signal words, so the "modality" of the inference, that is, whether it should be evaluated as a deductive or an inductive one, is often indicated by signal words. Deductive signals include the following:

- certainly
- necessarily
- must

For example:

> Your neighbor, Jones, is a member of the American Association of University Professors. Only members of the faculties of accredited colleges and universities are eligible for membership in this association. Therefore your neighbor, Jones, *must* be a college professor.

Inductive signals include the following:

- probably
- in all likelihood
- chances are
- it is reasonable to suppose that
- it's a good bet that

For example:

> Your neighbor, Jones, wears a tweed sport coat with patches on the elbows; he carries a battered briefcase; and he rides his bicycle to the college campus every day. *I'd be willing to bet* your neighbor, Jones, is a college professor.

But just as with argument indicator words discussed so far, we need to be aware of the ambiguities and other nuances of meaning in context to avoid overly mechanical readings of things. And, as in all instances of argument analysis, we are guided by the rule of thumb that we should try to make the argument out to be as reasonable as possible. For example, even if someone said,

> Your neighbor, Jones, wears a tweed sport coat with patches on the elbows; he carries a battered briefcase; and he rides his bicycle to the college campus every day. Therefore your neighbor, Jones, *must* be a college professor.

it would still be appropriate to evaluate the argument as an induction. A reasonable and charitable reading would interpret the speaker as having overstated the certainty of the conclusion relative to the premises. And similarly, if someone were to say,

> Your neighbor, Jones, is a member of the American Association of University Professors. Only members of the faculties of accredited colleges and universities are eligible for membership in this association. *I'd be willing to bet* your neighbor, Jones, is a college professor.

it would be appropriate to evaluate the argument as a deduction. A reasonable and charitable reading would interpret the speaker as having understated the certainty of the conclusion relative to the premises.

REVIEW EXERCISE 6.1 | Deductive vs. Inductive ✻

For each of the following passages, indicate whether the argument presented should be considered a deductive argument or an inductive argument.

	Deductive	Because tests proved that it took at least 2.3 seconds to operate the bolt of the rifle, Lee Harvey Oswald could not have fired three times—hitting U.S. President John F. Kennedy twice and Texas Governor John Connally once—in 5.6 seconds or less.
	Inductive	

	Deductive	"At bottom I did not believe I had touched that man. The law of probabilities decreed me guiltless of his blood. For in all my small experience with guns I had never hit anything I had tried to hit, and I knew I had done my best to hit him."
	Inductive	—Mark Twain

	Deductive	All of the leading economic indicators point toward further improvement in the economy. You can bet on an improved third quarter.
	Inductive	

	Deductive	During an interview with the school paper, Coach Danforth was quoted as saying, "I think it's safe to assume that Jason Israel will be our starting point guard next year. Both of our starting guards are graduating this spring and no one else on the team has Jason's speed and ball-handling skills."
	Inductive	

ARGUMENT FORM

For the rest of this chapter and Chapter 7, we concentrate on the first of these two argument design categories, deductive inferences. Chapters 8 and 9 focus on inductive inferences. As a first step, we must introduce the important notion of argument form. Consider the following argument:

(Because) [all humans are mortals ①] and [all Americans are humans ②],
(it follows that) [all Americans are mortals ③].

Casting the argument shows that the premises, ① and ②, together support the conclusion, ③. But we want to look more closely at the *way* in which the premises relate to the conclusion. Let us first represent the argument according to a conventional format:

(1) All humans are mortals.

(2) All Americans are humans.
_____
∴ (3) All Americans are mortals.

In this format, the premises are listed in order of their appearance above the solid line and the conclusion is listed below it. The symbol (∴) can be read as shorthand for "therefore." Notice that in this particular argument there appears to be a strong connection between the conclusion and the premises: it is impossible to deny the conclusion without also denying at least one of the premises (or contradicting yourself). Try it. Consider a second example:

[All corundum has a high refractive index ①]. And [all rubies are corundum ②]. (So)
[all rubies have a high refractive index ③].

Represented in the same conventional format, the argument looks like this:

(1) All corundum has a high refractive index.

(2) All rubies are corundum.
_____
∴ (3) All rubies have a high refractive index.

Notice that here, too, the same strong connection appears to exist between the conclusion and the premises. You might be less well acquainted with the optical properties and gemological classification of precious stones, but if you found out that all corundum has a high refractive index and all rubies are corundum, you would then *know* that all rubies have a high refractive index. (So if a particular stone has a low refractive index it can't be a ruby.) It would be impossible to deny this conclusion without also denying at least one of the premises (or contradicting yourself). Try it. Consider the following two claims:

[All mammals suckle their young ①]. [All primates are mammals ②].

Suppose these two claims are true. What conclusion could you draw from these two claims as premises?

(1)   All mammals suckle their young.

(2)   All primates are mammals.

∴ (3)   ?

If you said, "All primates suckle their young," then notice again that the same strong connection appears to exist between your conclusion and the two premises. Finally, suppose someone argues as follows:

[All propaganda is dangerous ①]. (That's why) [all Fox network news is dangerous ②].

From what you learned in previous chapters, you can see that this argument depends on a missing premise, ⓐ.

(1)   All propaganda is dangerous.

(a)   ?

∴ (2)   All Fox network news is dangerous.

What is missing premise ⓐ? No doubt you can see that the missing premise is the following: "All Fox network news is propaganda." Notice again the strong connection between the conclusion and the two premises. If you suppose that both premises are true, you cannot deny the conclusion without contradicting yourself. Try it. You may have some doubt about the conclusion in this case. But if you doubt the truth of the conclusion, you must also doubt the truth of at least one of the premises. Reconsider the four examples we have just examined.

The four examples in Figure 6.1 have something important in common. It is a single and simple common feature. It explains not only how we can arrive at the conclusion in the third example that "All primates suckle their young" and how we can fill in the missing premise in the fourth example that "All network news is propaganda" but most important, it explains the strong connection that holds between the conclusion of each of the four arguments and its premises. All four arguments follow the same pattern or form. Here is what the form looks like schematically (Figure 6.2).

(1) All humans are mortal.

(2) All Americans are humans.

∴ (3) All Americans are mortal.

(1) All corundum has a high refractive index.

(2) All rubies are corundum.

∴ (3) All rubies have a high refractive index.

(1) All mammals suckle their young.

(2) All primates are mammals.

∴ (a) ?

(1) All propaganda is dangerous.

(a) ?

∴ (2) All Fox network news is dangerous.

FIGURE 6.1 Premise Diagram Quartet

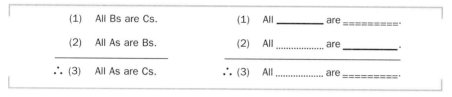

(1) All Bs are Cs.

(2) All As are Bs.

∴ (3) All As are Cs.

(1) All _____ are _____.

(2) All .... are _____.

∴ (3) All .... are _____.

FIGURE 6.2 Argument Pattern I

DEDUCTIVE VALIDITY

Deductive **validity** is another name for the kind of connection that holds between the conclusion and the premises of arguments that follow this (or any other deductively valid) form. The essential property of a deductively valid argument form is this: If the premises of an argument that follows the form are taken to be true, then the conclusion of the argument must also be true. Because this is a feature of the form (or pattern) that an argument follows rather than of the argument's specific content, deductive validity is sometimes referred to as "formal validity."

There are many forms that arguments can follow. Some of them are so commonly used and well known that they have been given names. You just met a variation of Barbara. Barbara is a deductively valid form. This means that for any argument, as long as it follows the form, accepting the premises forces you to accept the conclusion. Try it. Make some up. Even something as absurd as this:

(1) All fish can fly.

(2) All snakes are fish.

∴ (3) All snakes can fly.

REVIEW EXERCISE 6.2 | Deductive Validity ✳

True ✓	A deductively valid argument can have a false conclusion.	Explanation or example:	
False			

True ✓	A deductively valid argument can have false premises.	Explanation or example:	
False			

True ✓	We cannot tell whether a deductive argument is valid without knowing whether its premises are true.	Explanation or example:	
False			

True ✓	A deductively valid argument can have false premises and a true conclusion.	Explanation or example:	
False			

True ✓	A deductively valid argument can have true premises and a false conclusion.	Explanation or example:	
False			

INVALIDITY

Deductively valid argument forms are important because they provide a guarantee that if the premises of the argument are true the conclusion must be as well. But not every form or pattern is deductively valid. Consider the following example:

(1) All Americans are humans.

(2) All Californians are humans.

∴ (3) All Californians are Americans.

Many people initially see nothing deficient in this as a piece of reasoning. This is probably because (1) they can see that the claims are in some way related to each other and (2) they think that all three claims are true. But notice what happens if you ask whether the truth of the premises *guarantees* that the conclusion is true? Suppose the premises are true. Could the conclusion still be false? For example, suppose some Californians are not Americans. This possibility conflicts with neither premise 1 nor premise 2. So accepting both premises does not *force* you to accept the conclusion. If this is difficult to take in, consider this next example:

(1) All men are human.

(2) All women are human.

∴ (3) All women are men.

(1)	All Cs are Bs.		(1)	All ====== are _____.
(2)	All As are Bs.	or	(2)	All .... are _____.
∴ (3)	All As are Cs.		∴ (3)	All .... are =======.

FIGURE 6.3 Argument Pattern II

The falsity of this conclusion is obviously compatible with the truth of these two premises. But this argument follows the same form as the argument about Californians. Here is what the form looks like schematically (Figure 6.3).

Because it is possible for an argument following this form to move from true premises to a false conclusion, it is easy to see that this form is unreliable, or **invalid**. The general name for an unreliable inference is **fallacy.** An inference that is unreliable because it follows an invalid form or pattern is said to be "formally fallacious" or to commit a **formal fallacy.**

TESTING FOR DEDUCTIVE VALIDITY

The two argument forms we've been studying resemble each other closely, yet one is deductively valid and the other is formally fallacious. This is a crucial difference for the purposes of argument evaluation. It is therefore important to be able to reliably distinguish between deductively valid arguments and formally fallacious ones, even though they may look much alike. One way to do this would be to memorize argument forms. But this proves to be an endless and unmanageable undertaking. Fortunately, there is a relatively simple and reliable intuitive procedure for determining whether a particular argument is deductively valid, which derives from the essential property of deductively valid forms mentioned earlier. The procedure consists of asking: "Can we assert the premises and deny the conclusion without contradicting ourselves?" If we *cannot*—that is, if asserting the premises and denying the conclusion results in a contradiction—then the inference *is deductively valid.* If we *can* assert the premises and deny the conclusion without contradiction, the inference is *deductively invalid.*

CRITICAL THINKING TIP 6.1 | Testing for Deductive Validity I

Can I Assert the Premises and Deny the Conclusion without Contradicting Myself?

REVIEW EXERCISE 6.3 | Testing for Deductive Validity II   ✳

Which of the following arguments are deductively valid? Which are invalid?

	Valid	God is perfect. Therefore God is good.	Explanation or example:
	Invalid		

	Valid	Some entertainers are drug users, and all comedians are entertainers, so it stands to reason that some comedians are drug users.	Explanation or example:
	Invalid		

	Valid	Some college professors support the idea of a faculty union, an idea supported by many socialists. So at least some college professors must be socialists.	Explanation or example:
	Invalid		

	Valid	Everyone knows that whales live in the sea, and anything that lives in the sea is a fish. Therefore whales must be fish.	Explanation or example:
	Invalid		

	Valid	All artists are creative people. Some artists live in poverty. Therefore some creative people live in poverty.	Explanation example:
	Invalid		

	Valid	All justices on the Supreme Court are lawyers, and all members of the prestigious Washington Law Club are lawyers, so at least some of the Supreme Court justices are members of the Washington Law Club.	Explanation or example:
	Invalid		

Some people find the validity testing method just described difficult to conceptualize and tricky to keep straight. Here is a variation that may be easier to grasp intuitively. Try to imagine a scenario in which the premises are all true and the conclusion is false. If you can imagine such a scenario, then the inference is not deductively valid. For example, we can imagine a scenario in which the conclusion of the argument about Americans, Californians, and humans is false. Simply imagine that there are some Californians who are not also Americans. Imagine for example that there are some legal residents of the state of California who are not American citizens, say because they are foreigners married to Americans. Notice that both premises would still be true. Thus this scenario test shows that the argument is invalid. But be careful. If you can't imagine such a scenario, it doesn't necessarily mean that the inference is deductively valid. It may simply mean that you haven't been imaginative enough.

REVIEW EXERCISE 6.4 | Using Scenarios to Test for Deductive Validity

Use scenarios to test the validity of the six arguments in the preceding exercise.

Valid	God is perfect. Therefore God is good.	Scenario:
Invalid		

Valid	Some entertainers are drug users, and all comedians are entertainers, so it stands to reason that some comedians are drug users.	Scenario:
Invalid		

Valid	Some college professors support the idea of a faculty union, an idea supported by many socialists. So at least some college professors must be socialists.	Scenario:
Invalid		

Valid	Everyone knows that whales live in the sea, and anything that lives in the sea is a fish. Therefore whales must be fish.	Scenario:
Invalid		

Valid	All artists are creative people. Some artists live in poverty. Therefore some creative people live in poverty.	Scenario:
Invalid		

Valid	All justices on the Supreme Court are lawyers, and all members of the prestigious Washington Law Club are lawyers, so at least some of the Supreme Court justices are members of the Washington Law Club.	Scenario:
Invalid		

CONSTRUCTING FORMAL ANALOGIES

One of the best procedures for demonstrating that an inference is unreliable, or fallacious, is to compose an inference that is analogous to it and that moves from premises that are obviously true to a conclusion that is obviously false. In the case of the last two examples, the second argument is formally analogous to, or follows the same pattern as, the first (Figure 6.3), but it moves from two premises, each of which is obviously true, to a conclusion, which is just as obviously false. Using this analogy, we prove that the original argument—indeed, any argument following this pattern—is fallacious. Try these procedures on a couple of additional examples:

(1)   Some entertainers abuse drugs.

(2)   All comedians are entertainers.

∴ (3)   Some comedians are drug abusers.

Is this a deductively valid argument? In other words, if we assert both of the premises and deny the conclusion, does a contradiction result? It may be true that some comedians abuse drugs, but does it follow from these two premises? No. It is possible for both premises to be true and the conclusion false. Try to imagine a scenario in which both premises are true and the conclusion is false. Suppose it's true that some entertainers abuse drugs and that all comedians are entertainers. What kind of situation would be compatible with these two assumptions and yet incompatible with the conclusion? Well, suppose all drug-abusing entertainers just happen to be accordion players and the rest of the entertainment industry is clean and sober. This may be hard to imagine because it is so at odds with what you may have heard. But it is possible to imagine it. Try it. Notice that what you are imagining is at odds with the conclusion but perfectly compatible with each of the premises. This shows that the conclusion does not follow from the premises.

We now demonstrate that this inference is fallacious by producing a formally analogous inference that moves from obviously true premises to an obviously false conclusion. Step one is to reveal the form of the argument. Using the letter C (or ========) to represent the category of comedians, the letter A (or ....) to represent the category of drug abusers, and the letter E (or _____) to represent the category of entertainers, we go from

(1)   Some entertainers abuse drugs.

(2)   All comedians are entertainers.

∴ (3)   Some comedians are drug abusers.

to

(1) Some Es are As.		(1) Some _____ are ....
(2) All Cs are Es.	or	(2) All ====== are _____ .
∴ (3) Some Cs are As.		∴ (3) Some ====== are ....

Starting with the conclusion, we substitute terms for the abstract placeholders in the formula. We want to pick terms that result in an obviously false conclusion. For example, let C (or ========) now stand for the category of husbands who cheat and let A (or ....) now stand for the category of absolutely faithful wives. That results in the obviously false conclusion that some cheating husbands are absolutely faithful wives. Simply substitute the same terms wherever the abstract placeholders C (or =========) and A (or ....) occur in the formula. This gives us

(1)   Some Es are absolutely faithful wives.

(2)   All cheating husbands are Es.

∴ (3)   Some cheating husbands are absolutely faithful wives.

or

(1)   Some _____ are absolutely faithful wives.

(2)   All cheating husbands are _____.

∴ (3)   Some cheating husbands are absolutely faithful wives.

All we need is a value for E (or _____) that would make both premises 1 and 2 true. Suppose we let E stand for the category of spouses, humans, or married people. That would give us

(1)   Some married people are absolutely faithful wives.

(2)   All cheating husbands are married people.

∴ (3)   Some cheating husbands are absolutely faithful wives.

Here's another example:

(1)   Some mysteries are entertaining.

(2)   Some books are mysteries.

∴ (3)   Some books are entertaining.

Is this a deductively valid argument? In other words, if we assert both of the premises and deny the conclusion does a contradiction result? No, it is possible for both premises to be true and the conclusion to be false. This may be hard to appreciate, especially if you think just about the conclusion and your actual experience. The conclusion is no doubt true as a matter of fact. But it does not follow from these two premises. It is possible to imagine a scenario in which both premises are true and the conclusion is false. Imagine, for example, that no books are entertaining (in other words, imagine that the conclusion is false). This does not conflict with the first premise. It could easily be the case that some books are mysteries and that no books are entertaining. Nor does it conflict with the second premise. Suppose all of the entertaining mysteries are movies.

We demonstrate that this inference is fallacious by producing a formally analogous inference that moves from obviously true premises to an obviously false conclusion. First, we reveal the form of the argument. Using the letter B (or ....) to represent the category of books, the letter M (or =======) to represent the category of mysteries, and the letter E (or _____) to represent the category of things that are entertaining, we go from

    (1)   Some mysteries are entertaining.

    (2)   Some books are mysteries.

∴ (3)   Some books are entertaining.

to

(1) Some Ms are Es.		(1) Some ======= are _____.
(2) Some Bs are Ms.	or	(2) Some .... are =======.
∴ (3) Some Bs are Es.		∴ (3) Some .... are _____.

Again, starting with the conclusion, we substitute terms for the abstract placeholders in the formula. We want to pick terms that result in an obviously false conclusion. For example, let B (or ....) now stand for the category of boys, and let E (or _____) now stand for the category of elderly women. That results in the obviously false conclusion that some boys are elderly women. Simply substitute the same terms wherever the abstract placeholders B (or ....) and E (or _____) occur in the formula. This gives us the following:

(1) Some Ms are elderly women.	(1) Some ======= are elderly women.
(2) Some boys are Ms.	(2) Some boys are =======.
∴ (3) Some boys are elderly women.	∴ (3) Some boys are elderly women.

All we need is a value for M (or==========) that would make both premises true. Again, suppose we let the remaining term M stand for the category of Methodists, Muslims, Minnesotans, Mexican Americans, mammals, or just people. That would give us (for example) the following:

    (1)   Some Methodists are elderly women.

    (2)   Some boys are Methodists.

∴ (3)   Some boys are elderly women.

REVIEW EXERCISE 6.5 | Constructing Formal Analogies

For each of the invalid arguments in Review Exercises 6.3 and 6.4, construct a formally analogous argument that moves from obviously true premises to an obviously false conclusion.

	Invalid Argument	Formally Analogous Argument
Premise		
Premise		
Conclusion		

	Invalid Argument	Formally Analogous Argument
Premise		
Premise		
Conclusion		

	Invalid Argument	Formally Analogous Argument
Premise		
Premise		
Conclusion		

	Invalid Argument	Formally Analogous Argument
Premise		
Premise		
Conclusion		

CATEGORICAL LOGIC

A **syllogism** is defined as a deductive inference from two premises. The argument forms we have been studying so far in this chapter are called **categorical syllogisms** because they are made up of **categorical statements** (claims about relationships between categories of things). The Greek philosopher Aristotle developed a relatively simple but powerful system of logic based on categorical syllogisms. One of his insights was that anything we might want to say about the relationships between any two categories can be said in one of the following four ways. In other words, all categorical statements can be reduced to one of four standard forms (Figure 6.4).

These forms are arranged in Figure 6.4 in a matrix that reflects two major distinctions cutting across each other. The categorical statements in the left-hand column *affirm* an *inclusive* relationship between two categories. The categorical statements in the right-hand column each *deny* such a relationship between the two categories; the relationships they indicate are *exclusive*. This is traditionally

Affirmative		Negative	
A:	Universal Affirmative	**E:**	Universal Negative
e.g.	All mothers are female.	e.g.	No fathers are female.
I:	Particular Affirmative	**O:**	Particular Negative
e.g.	Some women are mothers.	e.g.	Some women are not mothers.

FIGURE 6.4 Categorical Statement Form I

understood as a qualitative distinction and is designated by the terms "affirmative" and "negative." The conventional designation of these statement forms by the letters *A, E, I,* and *O* derives from this *qualitative* distinction shown in the Latin words *affirmo* (I affirm) and *nego* (I deny).

The statements on the top line of the matrix assert the *total* inclusion or exclusion of an entire category in or from another. The statements on the bottom line of the matrix assert the *partial* inclusion or exclusion of one category in or from another. This is traditionally understood as a *quantitative* distinction and is designated by the terms "universal" and "particular."

One way to measure the theoretical power of a system would be to divide the number of cases that the system effectively covers by the size of the theoretical apparatus. By this measure, Aristotle's system of categorical logic is extremely powerful. Look at how simple and elemental the theoretical apparatus is: two major distinctions—universal (all or none) versus nonuniversal (some); and affirmative versus negative—yields four statement forms, which together cover the entire range of claims about category relationships. This is bound to score high on the scale of theoretical power.

TRANSLATING CATEGORICAL STATEMENTS INTO STANDARD FORM

However, there is a catch. Understandably, the power of the system depends heavily on being able to translate into one or another of the four standard forms the variety of things that people say about categories in their actual arguments. However, because language is so flexible and rich in possibilities, and because people are so imaginative and innovative in their use of language, translation into standard form is a matter of some complexity and uncertainty. There are a few general rules, with exceptions, and an indefinitely large set of interpretive guidelines, of which we shall give you the short starter kit.

The general rules are as follows:

- Categorical statements begin with a quantity indicator ("all," "some," or "no").

- There is a verb in the middle ("are" or "are not") to indicate the quality of the statement (whether it is affirmative or negative).

- There are two terms, each denoting a category. The term before the verb is called the subject term, and the term after the verb is called the predicate term.

- Subject and predicate terms must be nouns or noun phrases. For convenience, we use angle brackets < > in the examples that follow to set off the subject and predicate terms from the quantity and quality indicators in standard formulations of categorical statements.

The exceptions to the general rules are as follows:

- You can't say "All <x's> are not <y's>," as in "All the <computers on campus> are not <IBM compatible>." This formulation is disallowed because it is ambiguous. It could mean "Not all the <computers on campus> are <IBM compatible>" (which would be the same as saying, "*Some* of the <computers on campus> are *not* <IBM compatible>"), or it could mean, "None of the <computers on campus> are ." You have to decide whether the statement is supposed to say "Not *all* <x's> are <y's>" or "Not *any* <x's> are <y's>." If the meaning is "Not all <x's> are <y's>," use the O form: "Some <y's> are not <x's>." If the meaning is "Not any <x's> are <y's>," use the E form: "No <x's> are <y's>."
- There are categorical statements about individuals—for example, "David Letterman is a talk show host," "The Artist Formerly Known as 'Prince' is a musician," or "The World Series is an annual event." For all practical purposes (and especially because we are at the beginning of the study of formal logic), it will work best for now to treat any statement like these as though it were a universal affirmative (or *A*) categorical statement, even though there is only one real "category" involved. Categorical logic can handle such statements quite effectively if we pretend that we're talking, for example, about all members of the category <The Artist Formerly Known as 'Prince'> (a category of which there is only one member) when we say that he's in the category <musicians>.

Some interpretive guidelines are as follows:

- Turn adjectives into nouns or noun phrases. In some cases this is straightforward and intuitive. For example, "Bill Gates is wealthy" becomes "<Bill Gates> is a <wealthy man>."
- Use the context to help determine how to formulate the noun phrase. For example, consider the argument "Wealthy individuals enjoy disproportionate access to power. Bill Gates is wealthy. So he must have disproportionate access to power." In the context of this argument, the premise expressed in the second sentence makes the most sense if we interpret it to mean that Bill Gates is in *precisely* the category indicated by the subject term in the first sentence, <wealthy individuals>. This makes the logic of the inference easier to see. Here, "Bill Gates is wealthy" becomes "<Bill Gates> is <a wealthy individual>."
- Turn verbs into nouns or noun phrases. Again, in some cases this is straightforward and intuitive. For example, "Deciduous plants shed their leaves" becomes "All <deciduous plants> are <things that shed their leaves>."
- Use the context to help determine how to formulate the noun phrase. For example, consider this context: "All dancing bears are performing animals. Smokey the Bear is dancing the tango. Therefore Smokey the Bear is a performing animal." Here, the logic of the premise expressed in the second

sentence only makes sense if we render it thus: "<Smokey the Bear> is <a dancing bear>."

- Use the grammar as a guide, but bear in mind that grammatical structure and logical structure often diverge. For example, in the sentence, "Happy is the man who finds work doing what he loves," the subject term, <the man who finds work doing what he loves>, is contained in the grammatical predicate. Also notice that although the subject term is grammatically singular, the meaning for the purposes of categorical logic is plural; "the man who finds work doing what he loves" is meant to stand for the whole category of people who find work doing what they love. So the standard formulation of this statement would be "All <people who find work doing what they love> are <happy people>."

TABLE 6.1   General Rules for Translating into Standard Form

- Categorical statements begin with a quantity indicator.
- There is a verb in the middle to indicate whether the statement is affirmative or negative.
- There are two terms, the "subject term" before and the "predicate term" after the verb, each of which denotes a category.
- Subject and predicate terms must be nouns or noun phrases.

TABLE 6.2   Exceptions to the General Rules

- This formulation "All <x's> are not <y's>," as in "All the <computers on campus> are not <IBM compatible>," is disallowed because it is ambiguous. If the meaning is "Not all <x's> are <y's>," use the *O* form: "Some <y's> are not <x's>." If the meaning is "Not any <x's> are <y's>," use the *E* form: "No <x's> are <y's>."
- There are categorical statements about individuals. Treat proper names of individuals as names of categories.

TABLE 6.3   Interpretive Guidelines

- Turn adjectives and verbs into nouns or noun phrases.
- Use the grammar as a guide, but, most important, use the *context* to determine how to formulate the noun phrases.

REVIEW EXERCISE 6.6 | **Translating Categorical Statements into Standard Form**   ✻

Translate each of the following categorical statements into standard form.

All computer hardware has a short shelf life.	*C* = computer hardware *S* = things with short shelf life	Standard form:
Some of my beliefs are false.	*B* = my beliefs *F* = things which are false	Standard form:

One major corporation is Microsoft.	C = major corporations M = Microsoft	Standard form:

Some of the members of Heaven's Gate were reasonable people.	M = members of Heaven's Gate R = reasonable people	Standard form:

Any discipline has rules, or at least regularities of some kind.	D = disciplines R = things with rules or regularities	Standard form:

El Niño is the cause of some of these abnormal weather patterns.	A = these abnormal weather patterns N = things caused by El Niño	Standard form:

I like action movies.	A = action movies L = things I like	Standard form:

San Francisco is a city in California.	S = San Francisco C = cities in California	Standard form:

My favorite actress is a Gemini.	F = my favorite actress G = Geminis	Standard form:

Dogs love trucks.	D = dogs L = lovers of trucks	Standard form:

THE SQUARE OF OPPOSITION

Return to the matrix we used earlier to introduce the four standard forms of categorical statements. This time we use the same subject and predicate terms in all four examples to highlight differences in quality and quantity. Traditionally, in categorical logic, two categorical statements that differ from each other in quality or in quantity or both but that are otherwise the same are said to stand in opposition to each other. There are several kinds of opposition, depending on whether the difference is one of quality or quantity or both. Start with what might be described as the "strongest" form of opposition. Look at the *A* statement and the *O* statement together (Figure 6.5).

Affirmative	Negative
A: Universal Affirmative e.g. All <bonds> are <secure investments>.	**E:** Universal Negative e.g. No <bonds> are <secure investments>.
I: Particular Affirmative e.g. Some <bonds> are <secure investments>.	**O:** Particular Negative e.g. Some <bonds> are not <secure investments>.

FIGURE 6.5 Categorical Statement Form II

Notice that they can't both be true *and* they can't both be false. This kind of opposition is traditionally called **contradiction.** Look at the *E* and *I* statements together. Like the *A* and *O* statement pair, if either the *E* or the *I* statement is true, the other one must be false; they also contradict each other.

Look at the *A* statement and the *E* statement together (Figure 6.6).

Affirmative	Negative
A: Universal Affirmative e.g. All <bonds> are <secure investments>.	**E:** Universal Negative e.g. No <bonds> are <secure investments>.
I: Particular Affirmative e.g. Some <bonds> are <secure investments>.	**O:** Particular Negative e.g. Some <bonds> are not <secure investments>.

FIGURE 6.6 Categorical Statement Form III

Notice that they can't both be true, but they *might* both be false. This is a somewhat weaker form of opposition than contradiction. This kind of opposition is traditionally called **contrariety.** Two categorical statements that stand in this kind of opposition to each other are called contraries.

Look at the *I* statement and the *O* statement together (Figure 6.7).

Affirmative	Negative
A: Universal Affirmative e.g. All <bonds> are <secure investments>.	**E:** Universal Negative e.g. No <bonds> are <secure investments>.
I: Particular Affirmative e.g. Some <bonds> are <secure investments>.	**O:** Particular Negative e.g. Some <bonds> are not <secure investments>.

FIGURE 6.7 Categorical Statement Form IV

Notice that they *could* both be true but they *can't* both be false. This kind of opposition is traditionally called **subcontrariety.** Two categorical statements which stand in this kind of opposition to each other are called subcontraries.

	Affirmative		Negative
A: e.g.	Universal Affirmative All <bonds> are <secure investments>.	**E:** e.g.	Universal Negative No <bonds> are <secure investments>.
I: e.g.	Particular Affirmative Some <bonds> are <secure investments>.	**O:** e.g.	Particular Negative Some <bonds> are not <secure investments>.

FIGURE 6.8 Categorical Statement Form V

There is something peculiar about the technical way in which logicians use the word "opposition." So far, all the kinds of opposition we have discussed seem to involve some sort of disagreement. But if you look at the *A* and the *I* statements together, you'll see that they seem to agree with each other (Figure 6.8).

It seems reasonable to say that if the *A* statement is true, the *I* statement must also be true, by implication. For example, if it *is* true that all bonds are secure investments, it must surely be true that *some* bonds are secure investments. The same relationship also holds between the *E* and the *O* statements. For example, if it is true that no bonds are secure investments, it must surely be true that some bonds are *not* secure investments. Traditionally, this kind of opposition is called **subalternation.** If two categorical statements with the same subject and predicate terms agree in quality (are both affirmative or both negative) but differ in quality, the universal statement implies its subalternate particular statement. Notice that this is a one-way relationship. The particular statement does not imply the universal statement. Even if it is true that some bonds are secure investments, that does not, by itself, imply that *all* bonds are secure investments. Similarly, even if it is true that some bonds are *not* secure investments, that doesn't, by itself, imply that *no* bonds are secure investments. We can summarize the preceding relationships in what is traditionally called the **square of opposition** (Figure 6.9).

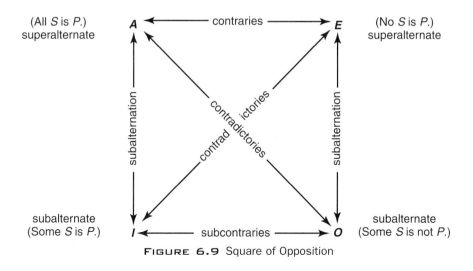

FIGURE 6.9 Square of Opposition

IMMEDIATE INFERENCES AND SYLLOGISMS

Based on the relationships described earlier and represented in the square of opposition, logic traditionally recognizes certain immediate inferences as deductively valid. Inferences such as these are traditionally referred to as **immediate inferences,** meaning that they proceed directly from one single categorical statement as a premise to another as the conclusion.

- Assuming that a given *A* statement is true, its contradictory *O* statement is false, its contrary *E* statement is false, and its subalternate *I* statement is true.
- Assuming that a given *E* statement is true, its contradictory *I* statement is false, its contrary *A* statement is false, and its subalternate *O* statement is true.
- Assuming that a given *I* statement is true, its contradictory *E* statement is false.
- Assuming that a given *O* statement is true, its contradictory *A* statement is false.

Beyond these immediate inferences, there is larger category of inferences, the syllogisms, based on combining two categorical statements as premises. The examples we used earlier to introduce and illustrate the concept of deductive validity were all syllogisms.

REVIEW EXERCISE 6.7 | Immediate Inferences   ✳

In each of the following sets of claims, assume that the first (in **bold**) is true, then highlight the claim or claims from the rest of the set that may be validly inferred from it.

All U.S. Treasury bonds are safe investments.

No U.S. Treasury bonds are safe investments.

Some U.S. Treasury bonds are safe investments.

Some U.S. Treasury bonds are not safe investments.

No U.S. Treasury bonds are safe investments.

Some U.S. Treasury bonds are safe investments.

Some U.S. Treasury bonds are not safe investments.

All U.S. Treasury bonds are safe investments.

Some U.S. Treasury bonds are safe investments.

Some U.S. Treasury bonds are not safe investments.

All U.S. Treasury bonds are safe investments.

No U.S. Treasury bonds are safe investments.

Some U.S. Treasury bonds are not safe investments.

All U.S. Treasury bonds are safe investments.

No U.S. Treasury bonds are safe investments.

Some U.S. Treasury bonds are safe investments.

An immediate inference involves only two categories. A syllogism always involves three. The three categories, and their corresponding terms, have special names. We can demonstrate this terminology using one of the earlier examples:

All <humans> are <mortals>.

All <Americans> are <humans>.
_____

∴ All <Americans> are <mortals>.

Notice that two of the three terms appear in the conclusion but the third does not. The term that appears in the predicate position in the conclusion is called the **major term;** the term that appears in the subject position in the conclusion is called the **minor term.** The term that does not appear in the conclusion is called the **middle term**—the term that "mediates" the inference. It appears once in each of the premises. The premise in which the major term appears is called the **major premise**; the premise in which the minor term appears is called the **minor premise.** Syllogisms in standard form always follow in this order: major premise, minor premise, conclusion.

REVIEW EXERCISE 6.8 | Standard Form   ✳

Put each of the following syllogisms into standard form: major premise first, followed by minor premise, then conclusion.

All Americans are humans.

All humans are mortals.
_____

∴ All Americans are mortals.

All men are human.

All women are human.
_____

∴ All women are men.

Some books are mysteries.

Some mysteries are entertaining.
_____

∴ Some books are entertaining.

MOOD AND FIGURE

Remember, there are only four types of categorical statement: *A, E, I,* and *O,* as arrayed in the square of opposition shown earlier. And three claims in any syllogism: major premise, minor premise, conclusion. Each of these claims may be of any one of the four types. This yields 64 possible combinations (by the formula: 4^3); logicians refer to these combinations as **moods.** The mood of a syllogism is determined by which of the four statement types appear as the major premise, the minor premise, and the conclusion when the syllogism is in standard form. The mood is indicated by a series of three letters, representing the three statement types in the inference in standard order (*AAA, EAE, EIO, AOO,* and so on).

REVIEW EXERCISE 6.9 | **Mood**

1. Using the square of opposition, identify the statement type of the major premise, minor premise, and conclusion in each of the following syllogisms.

2. Test each syllogism for deductive validity using the procedures outlined earlier (see Critical Thinking Tip 6.1).

All humans are mortals.

All Americans are humans.

∴ All Americans are mortals.

All men are human.

All women are human.

∴ All women are men.

Some mysteries are entertaining.

Some books are mysteries.

∴ Some books are entertaining.

Some mysteries are not entertaining.

Some books are not mysteries.

∴ Some books are entertaining.

All mysteries are suspenseful.

Some books are not mysteries.

∴ Some books are not suspenseful.

All **<humans>** are mortals.	All men are **<human>**.
All Americans are **<humans>**.	All women are **<human>**.
∴ All Americans are mortals.	∴ All women are men.

FIGURE 6.1 0 Position of Terms

Look closely at the first two inferences in Review Exercise 6.9. The mood of each of these syllogisms is *AAA*. But, as we have seen since the beginning of this chapter, the first inference is valid and the second one is invalid. What is the difference? The difference has to do with what logicians call the **figure** of each syllogism, which is determined by the *position of the middle term*. Notice that in the first inference (the valid one), the middle term appears in the subject position in the major premise but in the predicate position in the minor premise. In the second inference (the invalid one), the middle term appears in the predicate position in both premises (see Figure 6.10).

In a standard form syllogism, the middle term appears once in each premise, but that can be in either the subject or the predicate position. Because there are two premises, and each premise has both a subject and a predicate, this gives rise to four possible combinations, or figures. Using the letter *S* to indicate the minor term (subject of the conclusion), the letter *P* to indicate the major term (predicate of the conclusion), and the letter *M* to indicate the middle term, the four figures can be depicted as shown Figure 6.11.

1st Figure	2nd Figure	3rd Figure	4th Figure
M-P	P-M	M-P	P-M
S-M	S-M	M-S	M-S
S-P	S-P	S-P	S-P

FIGURE 6.1 1 Quartet of Figures

With 64 moods and four figures, the total number of possible syllogistic forms comes to 256 (64 × 4). Of these, 15 turn out to be deductively valid. The remaining 241 are invalid. Once a syllogism has been translated into and arranged in standard form, its formal structure (its mood and figure) determine whether it is deductively valid or not in accordance with the following set of rules:

• The syllogism must contain exactly three terms, each used consistently throughout the inference (no ambiguity allowed).

• The middle term of the syllogism must be distributed in at least one premise. (A term is **distributed** when the claim in which it appears says something about *every member of the category* to which the term refers. For example, in the premise "All bonds are safe investments," the term "bonds" is distributed but the term "safe investments" is not.)

- If either term is distributed in the conclusion, it must be distributed in the premises.
- A valid syllogism may have at most one negative premise.
- If either premise of the syllogism is negative, the conclusion must be negative.
- If the conclusion of the syllogism is negative, one premise must be negative.

REVIEW EXERCISE 6.10 | Invalid Syllogisms I   ✳

In Review Exercise 6.9, the first syllogism was valid but rest were invalid. Here again are the invalid syllogisms. Which of the preceding rules is violated in each case?

All men are human.

All women are human.
_____

∴ All women are men.

Some mysteries are entertaining.

Some books are mysteries.
_____

∴ Some books are entertaining.

Some mysteries are not entertaining.

Some books are not mysteries.
_____

∴ Some books are entertaining.

All mysteries are suspenseful.

Some books are not mysteries.
_____

∴ Some books are not suspenseful.

VENN DIAGRAMS

As you can plainly see, there's quite a bit to keep track of in categorical logic. Just as with argument analysis, many people find graphics and visualization helpful in grasping this material. For this purpose, British logician John Venn invented a graphic system for representing categorical statements and testing the validity of categorical syllogisms. The system consists of intersecting circles. Each circle represents a category. A shaded area is "vacant"—an area where there are no examples or members. An *X* is used to indicate a "populated" area—an area where there is at least one member. Using two intersecting circles and these simple symbols, we can represent any of the four standard forms of categorical statements (*A, E, I,*

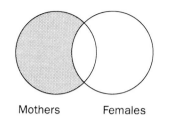

Mothers   Females

FIGURE 6.12 Mothers and Females

and *O*). In Figure 6.12, the circle on the left represents the category of mothers and the circle on the right represents the category of females. The shaded area indicates that there are no members of the category mothers who are not also members of the category females. Thus Figure 6.12 diagrams the statement that all mothers are female.

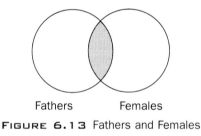

Fathers   Females

FIGURE 6.13 Fathers and Females

In Figure 6.13, the circle on the left represents the category of fathers and the circle on the right represents the category of females. The shaded area indicates that there are no members of the category fathers who are also members of the category females. Thus Figure 6.13 diagrams the statement that no fathers are female.

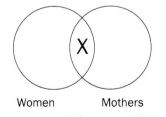

Women   Mothers

FIGURE 6.14 Women and Mothers I

In Figures 6.14 and 6.15, the circle on the left represents the category of women and the circle on the right represents the category of mothers. In Figure 6.14, the *X* indicates that there are some members of the category women who are also members of the category mothers. Thus Figure 6.14 diagrams the statement that some women are mothers. In Figure 6.15, the *X* indicates that there are some members of the category women who are not also members of the category mothers. Thus Figure 6.15 diagrams the statement that some women are not mothers.

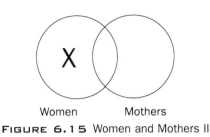

FIGURE 6.15 Women and Mothers II

In a categorical syllogism, there are three terms, corresponding to three categories, two of which appear in the conclusion. In a categorical syllogism, each of the premises states a relationship between one of these two categories, which appear in the conclusion and a third (or "middle") category. Thus to diagram a categorical syllogism, we need three intersecting circles, one for each of the categories in the conclusion and a third for the middle category (Figure 6.16).

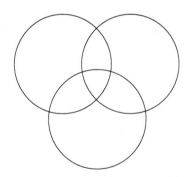

FIGURE 6.16 Three-Circle Venn Diagram

TESTING FOR VALIDITY USING VENN DIAGRAMS

In using the diagram to test for the validity of categorical syllogisms, we should remember what the essential characteristic of deductively valid arguments is: if the premises of an argument that follows the form are taken to be true, then the conclusion of the argument must also be true. In a certain important sense, the conclusion of a deductively valid inference is already contained in its premises. Thus if we represent the information contained in the two premises in the diagram, the conclusion should automatically be represented, *if* the argument is a valid one. Try this with the first of the examples we considered in this chapter:

(1) All Americans are humans.

(2) All humans are mortals.

∴ (3) All Americans are mortals.

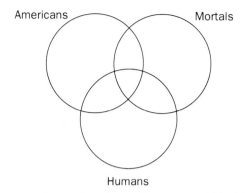

FIGURE 6.17 Americans, Humans, and Mortals I

In Figure 6.17, the circle on the left will represent the category of Americans, the circle on the right will represent the category of mortals, and the lower circle will represent the middle category of humans.

To represent premise 1 in the diagram, we shade all of the Americans circle except where it intersects with the humans circle (Figure 6.18).

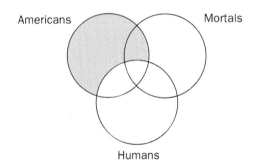

FIGURE 6.18 Americans, Humans, and Mortals II

This indicates that there are no members of the category "Americans" who are not also members of the category "humans." Similarly, we represent premise 2 in the diagram by shading in all of the humans circle except where it intersects with the mortals circle (Figure 6.19).

This indicates that there are no members of the category humans who are not also members of the category mortals. Lo and behold, Figure 6.19 already represents the conclusion because the area inside the Americans circle but outside its intersection with the mortals circle is shaded, indicating that there are no members of the category Americans who are not also members of the category mortals. Thus the diagram demonstrates the validity of the inference.

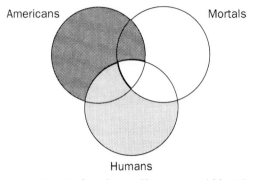

FIGURE 6.19 Americans, Humans, and Mortals III

Try the same procedure with the first formally fallacious example we considered:

    (1)   All Americans are humans.

    (2)   All Californians are humans.
    _____

∴ (3)   All Californians are Americans.

In Figure 6.20, let the circle on the left represent the category of Californians, the circle on the right represent the category of Americans, and the lower circle represent the middle category of humans.

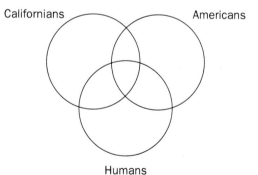

FIGURE 6.20 Californians, Americans, and Humans I

To represent premise 1, we shade the entire Americans circle except where it intersects with the circle of humans (Figure 6.21), indicating that there are no members of the category Americans who are not also members of the category humans.

To represent premise 2, we shade the entire Californians circle except where it intersects with the circle of humans (Figure 6.22), indicating that there are no members of the category Californians who are not also members of the category humans.

Does Figure 6.22 represent the conclusion that all Californians are Americans? It would if the entire area within the California circle were shaded except where

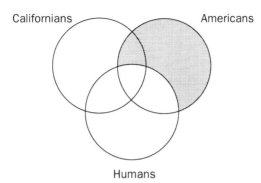

FIGURE 6.21 Californians, Americans, and Humans II

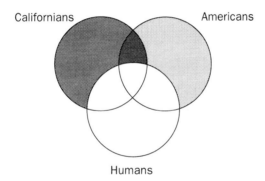

FIGURE 6.22 Californians, Americans, and Humans III

it intersects with the Americans circle. But there remains an unshaded area inside the California circle but outside the Americans circle, indicating that there *may be* some Californians who are not Americans. This shows that even if premises 1 and 2 are both true the possibility that the conclusion is false is still open. In other words, the inference is not valid.

You may still wonder *why* this is an invalid inference. This may be because of your awareness that California is one of the United States of America. So you may be thinking, it's not possible to be a Californian without also being an American. But it *is* possible to be a Californian without being an American. Someone can be a legal, taxpaying, permanent resident of the state of California without being an American citizen. Suppose an American woman who resides in California marries a Frenchman and the couple chooses to reside in California but the husband retains his French citizenship. One can even be a *native-born* legal, taxpaying, permanent resident of the state of California without being an American citizen. The main point here, however, is that these possibilities don't conflict with either of the premises of the inference. In other words, it's possible for the premises both to be true and the conclusion still to be false, which again, is what the Venn diagram shows.

We've now diagrammed two syllogisms involving universal categorical statements. Try a couple of examples involving particular categorical statements as well.

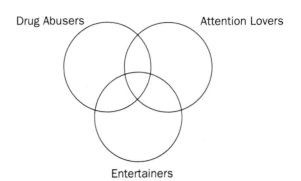

FIGURE 6.23 Drug Abusers, Attention Lovers, and Entertainers I

(1)   All entertainers love attention.

(2)   Some drug abusers are entertainers.

∴ (3)   Some drug abusers love attention.

In Figure 6.23, let the circle on the left represent the category of drug abusers, the circle on the right represent the category of those who love attention, and the lower circle represent the middle category of entertainers.

To represent premise 1, we must shade the entire entertainers circle except where it intersects with the circle of attention lovers (Figure 6.24).

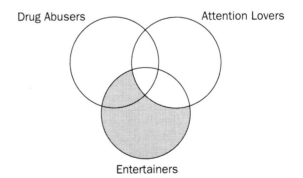

FIGURE 6.24 Drug Abusers, Attention Lovers, and Entertainers II

To represent premise 2, we must place an *X* somewhere in the intersection of the drug abusers and entertainers circles. But only half of that intersection remains open. Thus the *X* may appear only in the area where all three circles intersect (Figure 6.25).

Does Figure 6.25 represent the conclusion that some drug abusers love attention? Yes it does. An *X* already appears in the intersection of the circles representing drug abusers and those who love attention. This shows the inference to be valid.

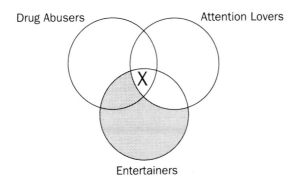

FIGURE 6.25 Drug Abusers, Attention Lovers, and Entertainers III

Compare this last example with the similar one we discussed earlier:

(1)   Some entertainers abuse drugs.

(2)   All comedians are entertainers.

∴ (3)   Some comedians are drug abusers.

In Figure 6.26, let the circle on the left represent the category of comedians, the circle on the right represent the category of drug abusers, and the lower circle represent the middle category of entertainers.

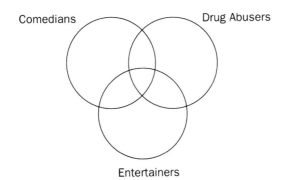

FIGURE 6.26 Comedians, Drug Abusers, and Entertainers I

This time start with premise 2, following the guideline to diagram a universal premise before a particular one. To represent premise 2, we shade the entire area in the comedians circle except where it intersects with the entertainers circle (Figure 6.27), indicating that there are no comedians who are not also entertainers.

To represent premise 1, we must place an *X* somewhere in the intersection of the drug abusers and entertainers circles. But do we place it inside or outside the circle of comedians? Nothing in the premises determines the answer to this question. Because we don't know, the *X* goes on the line (Figure 6.28).

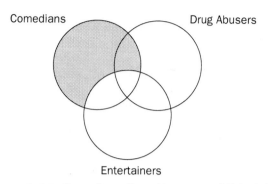

FIGURE 6.27 Comedians, Drug Abusers, and Entertainers II

Does Figure 6.28 represent the conclusion that some comedians are drug abusers? It would if the *X* appeared clearly within the intersection of the comedians and drug abusers circles. But it does not. It appears on the line, indicating that on the basis of the two premises it is not yet clear whether the conclusion is true, and thus that the inference is not valid.

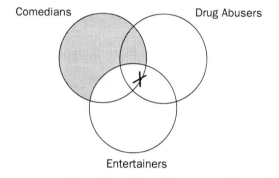

FIGURE 6.28 Comedians, Drug Abusers, and Entertainers III

REVIEW EXERCISE 6.11 | **Invalid Syllogisms II**

Here again are the syllogisms from Review Exercise 6.9. Use Venn diagrams to test for and demonstrate their validity or invalidity.

> All humans are mortals.
>
> All Americans are humans.
> _____
> ∴ All Americans are mortals.

> All men are human.
>
> All women are human.
> _____
> ∴ All women are men.

Some mysteries are entertaining.

Some books are mysteries.
_____
∴ Some books are entertaining.

Some mysteries are not entertaining.

Some books are not mysteries.
_____
∴ Some books are entertaining.

All mysteries are suspenseful.

Some books are not mysteries.
_____
∴ Some books are not suspenseful.

APPLICATION EXERCISE 6.1 | **Term Project**

Take any position on the issue you have been working with so far, and design an argument in support of that position, using any of the deductively valid argument forms discussed in this chapter. Then take an alternative or opposed position and design an argument in support of it using any of the deductively valid argument forms discussed in this chapter.

GLOSSARY

categorical statement   a statement about a relationship between categories

categorical syllogism   a deductive inference from two premises made up of statements about relationships between categories

contradiction   (in categorical logic) a form of opposition between categorical statements; two categorical statements that cannot both be true and cannot both be false are "contradictories"

contrariety   a form of opposition between categorical statements; two categorical statements that cannot both be true but that might both be false are "contraries"

deductive   reasoning designed and intended to secure its conclusion with certainty so that anyone who fully understands what the statements in the argument mean must recognize that the premises cannot both be true without the conclusion also being true

distributed   when the claim in which a term appears says something about every member of the category to which the term refers

fallacy   an unreliable inference

figure   the form of a syllogism as determined by the subject/predicate positions of the major, minor, and middle terms

formal fallacy   an inference that is unreliable because it follows an unreliable form or pattern

immediate inference   deductively valid inference proceeding directly from one categorical statement to another

inductive   reasoning designed and intended to make the conclusion reasonable, probable, or likely but not certain

inferential security   the degree to which an inference is safe against risk of error

invalidity   (in deductive argument) the absence of the essential formal characteristic of a successful deductive argument

major premise   the premise in a categorical syllogism in which the major term appears

major term   the term that appears in the predicate position in the conclusion of a categorical syllogism

middle term   the term in a categorical syllogism that does not appear in the conclusion

minor premise   the premise in a categorical syllogism in which the minor term appears

minor term   the term that appears in the subject position in the conclusion of a categorical syllogism

mood   any of the sixty-four possible combinations of the four categorical statement types in a syllogism

square of opposition   (in categorical logic) the array of relationships between the four statement forms, showing the immediate inferences that may be drawn on the basis of differences of quality and quantity

subalternation   (in categorical logic) the relationship between statements with the same subject and predicate terms that agree in quality (both affirmative or both negative) but differ in quality (not both universal)

subcontrariety   a form of opposition between categorical statements; two categorical statements that might both be true but that can't both be false are "subcontraries"

syllogism   a deductive inference from two premises

validity   the essential formal characteristic of a successful deductive argument: if the premises are taken to be true, then the conclusion must also be true

ADDITIONAL EXERCISES

REVIEW EXERCISE 6.12 IDENTIFYING REASONING TYPES   For each of the following passages, indicate whether it is a deductive argument, an inductive argument, or not an argument.

	Deductive	We can't lose. They have no offense and they have no one to stop our leading scorer. They've lost their last four games, and it'll be on our court.	Explain your answer:
	Inductive		
	Nonargumentative		

	Deductive	"In a democracy, the poor have more power than the rich, because there are more of them." —Aristotle	Explain your answer:
	Inductive		
	Nonargumentative		

		I've been eating corn on the cob for years, and I always count the number of rows. I have never found an ear of corn with an odd number of rows. I'm convinced that ears of corn always have even numbers of rows.	Explain your answer:
	Deductive		
	Inductive		
	Nonargumentative		

		Even God makes mistakes. In the Bible, God says, "It repenteth me that I have made man." Now either the Bible is not the word of God, or we must believe that God did say, "It repenteth me that I have made man." But then, if we are to believe the word of God, we must further conclude that He really did repent making man, in which case, either God made a mistake in making man or He made a mistake in repenting making man.	Explain your answer:
	Deductive		
	Inductive		
	Nonargumentative		

		"The theory of the unreality of evil now seems to me untenable. Supposing that it can be proved that all that we think evil was in reality good, the fact would still remain that we think it evil. This may be called a delusion or mistake. But a delusion or mistake is as real as anything else. The delusion that evil exists is therefore real. But then, to me at least, it seems certain that a delusion or an error which hid from us the goodness of the universe would itself be evil. And so there would be real evil after all." —J. M. E. McTaggart	Explain your answer:
	Deductive		
	Inductive		
	Nonargumentative		

		First, as the 18th-century Scottish philosopher David Hume pointed out, we never directly observe causal relationships. We have to infer them. Next, we can never infer them with deductive certainty. Because the evidence for a causal relationship is always indirect, there will always be some room for doubt when we infer a cause. In other words, we must reason inductively about them.	Explain your answer:
	Deductive		
	Inductive		
	Nonargumentative		

		In the entire history of the stock market, every bull market has been followed by a bear market, and vice versa. Therefore the stock market behaves cyclically.	Explain your answer:
	Deductive		
	Inductive		
	Nonargumentative		

Deductive	Grumble County has voted for the loser in every State Senate contest since 1876. Grumble County polls show incumbent Senator Press Fleshman running 27 points behind challenger Mary Kay Weedemout. But I'm tired of always voting for losers and lost causes. I'm going to vote for Fleshman, because it looks like he's going to win anyway.	Explain your answer:
Inductive		
Nonargumentative		

■ **REVIEW EXERCISE 6.13 STANDARD SYLLOGISTIC FORM** Translate each of the following arguments into standard syllogistic form.

All crooks deserve to be punished. But some politicians are not crooks. So some politicians do not deserve to be punished.	C = crooks D = deserve to be punished P = politicians	Standard form:

All artists are creative people. Some artists live in poverty. Therefore some creative people live in poverty.	A = artists C = creative people P = people who live in poverty	Standard form:

Some reference books are textbooks, because all textbooks are books intended for careful study and some reference books are intended for the same purpose.	R = reference books T = textbooks S = books intended for careful study	Standard form:

Because all birds eat worms and chickens are birds, chickens must eat worms.	B = birds W = eaters of worms C = chickens	Standard form:

Most poets drink to excess, and some poets are women. So some women drink to excess.	P = poets D = people who drink to excess W = women	Standard form:

Everyone who smokes marijuana goes on to try heroin. Everyone who tries heroin becomes a junkie. So everyone who smokes marijuana becomes a junkie.	M = marijuana smokers H = people who try heroin J = people who become junkies	Standard form:

This argument must be valid because its premises are true and its conclusion is true, and all arguments with true premises and conclusions are valid.	A = anything that is this argument V = things that are valid T = things with true premises and conclusions	Standard form:

This argument must be invalid because its premises are not true and all arguments with untrue premises are invalid.	A = anything that is this argument I = things that are invalid U = arguments with untrue premises	Standard form:

▨ **REVIEW EXERCISE 6.14 VALID DEDUCTIVE ARGUMENTS**   Using a combination of any two of the procedures discussed in this chapter (the intuitive test, the scenario method, Venn diagrams) determine which of the following are valid deductive arguments. For each invalid argument, compose a formally analogous argument that moves from obviously true premises to an obviously false conclusion.

	Valid	All crooks deserve to be punished. But some politicians are not crooks. So some politicians do not deserve to be punished.	Explain your answer:
	Invalid		

	Valid	All artists are creative people. Some artists live in poverty. Therefore some creative people live in poverty.	Explain your answer:
	Invalid		

	Valid	Some reference books are textbooks, because all textbooks are books intended for careful study and some reference books are intended for the same purpose.	Explain your answer:
	Invalid		

	Valid	Because all birds eat worms and chickens are birds, chickens must eat worms.	Explain your answer:
	Invalid		

	Valid	Most poets drink to excess, and some poets are women. So some women drink to excess.	Explain your answer:
	Invalid		

	Valid	Everyone who smokes marijuana goes on to try heroin. Everyone who tries heroin becomes a junkie. So everyone who smokes marijuana becomes a junkie.	Explain your answer:
	Invalid		

	Valid	This argument must be valid because its premises are true and its conclusion is true, and all arguments with true premises and conclusions are valid.	Explain your answer:
	Invalid		

	Valid	This argument must be invalid because its premises are not true and all arguments with untrue premises are invalid.	Explain your answer:
	Invalid		

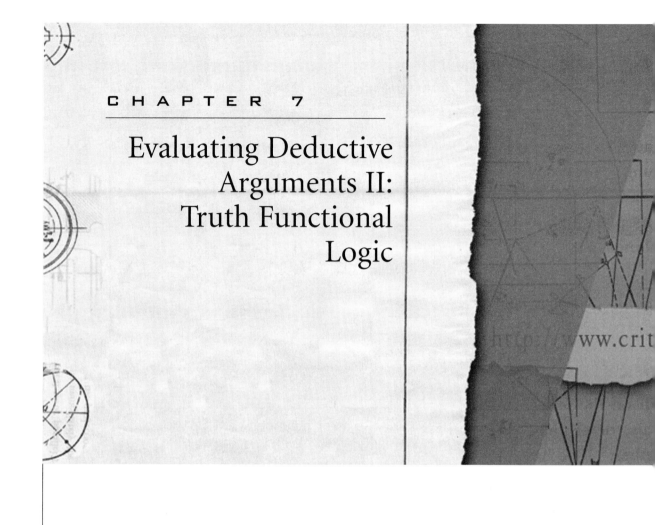

CHAPTER 7

Evaluating Deductive Arguments II: Truth Functional Logic

The argument forms we have been studying so far have been composed entirely out of categorical statements. But there are more kinds of claims in our language out of which arguments can be composed. Arguments often involve claims like these:

"Either we make a few sacrifices in the area of privacy, or we will continue to be vulnerable to terrorist attacks."

"If we allow our civil liberties to be destroyed in the name of greater security, then the terrorists will have won."

As powerful as Aristotle's system of categorical logic is, it is hopelessly awkward to try to translate claims like these into categorical statements. Because claims like these are so important in reasoning, logicians have developed a system known as **truth functional logic** (often called "symbolic logic") to deal with them. That is the subject of this chapter.

Farcus

by David Waisglass
Gordon Coulthart

WAISGLASS/COULTHART

© 1997 Farcus Cartoons

**"So, I say if it's not worth doing well,
it's not worth doing at all."**

TRUTH FUNCTIONAL ANALYSIS OF LOGICAL OPERATORS

The two examples in the opening have easily recognizable grammatical structures. The first example is a disjunction, which in terms of grammar means an "either . . . or . . ." statement. The second example is called a conditional, which in terms of grammar means an "if . . . then . . ." statement. However, in studying the role each plays in reasoning and argumentation, we need to understand not only their grammatical structure but also their *logical* structure. To do this, we need to introduce a bit more of the apparatus of modern logic: truth functional analysis of logical operators.

What in the world is a logical operator? As a first step, let us distinguish between simple and compound statements. A **simple statement** is one that does not contain another statement as a component part. A **compound statement** is one that contains at least one other statement as a component part. For example, "The weather is great" and "I wish you were here" are each simple statements, but "The weather is great, and I wish you were here" is a compound statement. Think of **logical operators** as devices for making compound statements out of simple ones. In the example, the word "and" is used to express the logical operator known as a **conjunction.**

NEGATIONS

Logical operators are defined and distinguished from each other according to how they affect the **truth values** of the compound sentences we make with them. And **truth functional analysis** is simply a way of keeping track of this. The simplest of the logical operators and the easiest for understanding truth functionally is **negation.** For example, the compound statement "The weather is not great" is 'not' produced by negating the component statement "The weather is great." In this example, the word "not" is used to express the logical operator negation. How does the logical operator negation affect the truth value of the statement "The weather is not great"? Well, if "The weather is great" is true, then "The weather is not great" is false, and if "The weather is great" is false, then "The weather is not great" is true. In other words, negation simply reverses the truth value of the component statement to which it is applied. Here is a simple graphic representation (Figure 7.1). Let the letter *P* represent any statement. The tilde (~) will be used to represent the logical operator negation. Thus ~P represents the negation of P.

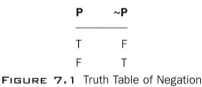

P	~P
T	F
F	T

FIGURE 7.1 Truth Table of Negation

This sort of graphic representation is called a **truth table.** We use it here to define the logical operator negation by showing what the truth value of the compound statement produced by negation would be for each of the possible truth values of its component statement.

CONJUNCTIONS

A truth table needs to have as many lines as there are possible combinations of truth value for the number of distinct components involved. Negation operates on a single component statement, P. Because P is either true or false (not true), the truth table for negation required only two lines. But most logical operators connect two component statements, each of which might be either true or false. So a truth table defining any such operator will require four lines to represent each of the four possible combinations of truth value for the components. To illustrate, we can use the example of conjunction mentioned earlier: "The weather is great, and I wish you were here." This again is composed of the two simple statements, "The weather is great" and "I wish you were here." The components of a conjunction are called **conjuncts.** Let the letter *P* stand for the first conjunct and the letter *Q* stand for the second. The ampersand (&) will be used to represent the logical operator conjunction. Thus "P & Q" represents the conjunction of P and Q. It is fairly easy to see intuitively that the conjunction "P & Q" is true only if both of its conjuncts are true. "The weather is great, and I wish you were here" is true only if the weather really is great and I really do wish you

P	Q	P & Q
T	T	T
T	F	F
F	T	F
F	F	F

FIGURE 7.2 Truth Table of Conjuction

were here. If either conjunct or both were not true, then the conjunction "P & Q" would also not be true, as indicated in the following truth table (Figure 7.2).

CONDITIONALS

We're now ready to examine the logical structure of conditionals. First, conditionals are compound statements. And what they assert is that a peculiar kind of relationship (a truth-dependency relationship) holds between their component parts. For example, the conditional

If love is blind, then fools rush in.

is composed of the two simple component statements, "Love is blind" and "Fools rush in." What it asserts is not that either of them *is* true but only that the truth of the second one *depends on* the truth of the first one. It asserts that the statement "Love is blind" *implies* the statement "Fools rush in." We call both this relationship and the logical operator involved in making conditionals **implication.**

Because this is not a reciprocal relationship—because it only goes in one direction—we'll need terms to keep track of which statement depends on which. In a conditional statement, the component introduced by the word "if" is called the **antecedent** and the component introduced by the word "then" is called the **consequent.** In this example, "Love is blind" is the antecedent and "Fools rush in" is the consequent.

Sometimes conditionals are used to say more than just that one statement implies another. For example, the statement

If abortion is homicide, then by definition it involves the killing of humans.

expresses also that the consequent *follows (by definition)* from the antecedent. For another example, the statement

If the economy does not improve, then the president will lose his bid for a second term.

expresses also that the antecedent is *causally* connected to the consequent. And the following statement

If the Congress overrides the president's last veto, then I'll eat my hat.

expresses also that the speaker is *committed* to do something on a certain condition. In each of these cases, however, the statement expresses at a minimum that the truth of the consequent depends on the truth of the antecedent. This is the

P	Q	P ⊃ Q
T	T	T
T	F	F
F	T	T
F	F	T

FIGURE 7.3 Truth Table of Implication

logical structure at the core of conditionals, represented in the truth table in Figure 7.3. Let the letter *P* represent the antecedent and the letter *Q* represent the consequent. A new symbol (⊃) will be used to represent the logical operator implication. Thus "P ⊃ Q" represents the conditional "If P, then Q" (Figure 7.3).

You may have noticed that according to this truth table the conditional "If P, then Q" comes out false *only* when the antecedent is true and the consequent is false. In all other cases, logic treats conditionals as true. It is intuitively reasonable to suppose a conditional with a true antecedent and a false consequent is false. Generally this is how conditionals are tested for truth. Take the following example:

If the economy does not improve, then the president will lose his bid for a second term.

We could be certain that this conditional is false only if the economy does not improve (that is, the antecedent is true) and the president nevertheless wins reelection (that is, the consequent is false). But you might wonder why we would want to call a conditional true whose antecedent and consequent are both false? Well, suppose you and your friend are scanning the radio dial for something new and you happen to tune into a station broadcasting the latest in avant-garde electronic music, which sounds to both of you something like the dishwasher full of bone china falling down a flight of stairs. And so your friend says:

If this is music, then I'm the king of Peru.

The point of such a statement is to assert the *falsity* of the antecedent, to claim that this isn't music. Here's how the conditional is being used to make this point: in effect, your friend is saying, "Because the consequent is obviously false (I'm not the king of Peru), if the antecedent *were* true the conditional itself would be false. But what I am saying is true, so the antecedent has to be false, too."

INTERPRETATION AND TRANSLATION

Because of the complexity and flexibility of language, there is quite a variety of ways of expressing a conditional relationship in English. For example, here is a conditional claim: "If I get an A in this class, then my GPA will be 3.8." And here are several other ways of expressing the same claim:

- My GPA will be 3.8 if I get an A in this class.
- My GPA will be 3.8, provided I get an A in this class.
- My GPA will be 3.8, on the condition that I get an A in this class.

TABLE 7.1   Translating Conditionals

P = I get an A in this class.	**Q = My GPA will be 3.8.**
If I get an A in this class, then my GPA will be 3.8.	P ⊃ Q
My GPA will be 3.8 *if* I get an A in this class.	P ⊃ Q
My GPA will be 3.8, *provided* I get an A in this class.	P ⊃ Q
My GPA will be 3.8, *on the condition that* I get an A in this class.	P ⊃ Q
My GPA will be 3.8 *only if* I get an A in this class. [0]	Q ⊃ P
Only if I get an A in this class will my GPA will be 3.8.	Q ⊃ P
Unless I get an A in this class, my GPA *won't* be 3.8.	~P ⊃ ~Q = Q ⊃ P
If I *don't* get an A in this class, my GPA *won't* be 3.8.	~P ⊃ ~Q = Q ⊃ P
To get my GPA up to 3.8, I *must* get an A in this class.	Q ⊃ P
If my GPA is 3.8, I will *have* received an A in this class. [0]	Q ⊃ P

By the same token, not every statement containing the word "if" is a conditional. "You're welcome to wait in the drawing room, if you like" would not ordinarily express a conditional relationship between two component statements. As in so many other situations, recognition of conditionals is an interpretive matter; we need to be aware of nuances of meaning in context.

One subtle but important difference to be aware of is the distinction between "if" and "only if." "My GPA will be 3.8 *only if* I get an A in this class," does not say the same thing as "My GPA will be 3.8 *if* I get an A in this class." It really says, "*Unless* I get an A in this class, my GPA *won't* be 3.8." This is the same as saying, "If I *don't* get an A in this class, my GPA *won't* be 3.8." In other words, "*To* get my GPA up to 3.8, I *must* get an A in this class." Finally, this means that "if my GPA is 3.8, I will *have* received an A in this class." Thus "only if" reverses the conditional relationship between the antecedent and the consequent (see Table 7.1).

DISJUNCTIONS 'OR'

Like conditionals, disjunctions assert a truth functional relationship between the two component statements of which they are made up. These component statements are called **disjuncts.** Logic distinguishes two truth functionally distinct forms of disjunction. In some cases what is meant is "either A or B (but not both)." This is called **exclusive disjunction.** For example, if someone asks you, "Was the woman who answered the phone your wife or your daughter?" this would be conventionally understood to imply an exclusive disjunction. The woman who answered the phone would presumably not be *both* your wife and your daughter. In other cases, what is meant is "either A or B (possibly both)." This is called **inclusive disjunction.** For example, if someone asks you, "Was your absence due to illness or a family emergency?" the answer might be "Both." The distinction between exclusive and inclusive disjunction is the same as the distinction between radio buttons and check boxes on Web forms. If your clickable options on a Web form are presented as radio buttons, only one option may be selected. If they are presented as check boxes, you can check all that apply. We can

P	Q	P v Q
T	T	F
T	F	T
F	T	T
F	F	F

FIGURE 7.4 Truth Table of Disjunction (Exclusive)

P	Q	P v Q
T	T	T
T	F	T
F	T	T
F	F	F

FIGURE 7.5 Truth Table of Disjunction (Inclusive)

represent these relationships and the logical operators used to make compound statements that assert them using truth tables (Figure 7.4). Let the letters *P* and *Q* represent the two disjuncts and a new symbol (v) represent the operator disjunction. Thus "P v Q" represents the statement "either P or Q." Notice how the truth tables for exclusive and inclusive disjunction differ from each other (Figures 7.4 and 7.5).

Inclusive disjunctions are false only when both disjuncts are false and are true in all other truth value combinations. Exclusive disjunctions are false when both disjuncts are false *and* when both disjuncts are true and are true only when just one disjunct is true. Modern truth functional logic generally treats disjunction as inclusive. For example, the statement

Either the battery is dead or there is a short in the ignition switch

asserts that *at least* one of the two statements, "the battery is dead" and "there is a short in the ignition switch," is true (possibly both).

REVIEW EXERCISE 7.1 | **Translating into Truth Functional Logical Format I**   ✳

Translate the following claims into truth functional logical format.

Either the governor will veto the bill or she won't be reelected.	*V* = The governor will veto the bill *R* = The governor will win reelection.	Truth functional format:

Judging from that getup, either he's the new Ronald McDonald or he thinks it's Halloween.	*R* = He's the new Ronald McDonald. *H* = He thinks it's Halloween.	Truth functional format:

We're going to be late and Grandma is not going to be happy.	*L* = We're going to be late. *H* = Grandma is going to be happy.	Truth functional format:

The weather is great, and I wish you were here.	*G* = The weather is great. *W* = I wish you were here.	Truth functional format:

If you're ever going to become a musician, you're going to have to practice.	*M* = You're going to become a musician. *P* = You're going to have to practice.	Truth functional format:

Paul will be graduating with honors if he keeps his GPA above 3.3 this semester.	*H* = Paul will be graduating with honors. *K* = Paul keeps his GPA above 3.3.	Truth functional format:

Paul will be graduating with honors only if he keeps his GPA above 3.3 this semester.	*H* = Paul will be graduating with honors. *K* = Paul keeps his GPA above 3.3.	Truth functional format:

Paul will not be graduating with honors unless he keeps his GPA above 3.3 this semester.	*H* = Paul will be graduating with honors. *K* = Paul keeps his GPA above 3.3.	Truth functional format:

ARGUMENT FORMS

MODUS PONENS

Because of their unique structure, conditionals are extremely powerful reasoning tools. So they play a crucial role in many arguments and argument forms. Suppose, for example, that an experimental space probe begins with the following conditional first premise:

(1) If there is life on Mars, then there is adequate life support on Mars.

Suppose the space probe establishes the following:

(2) There is life on Mars.

From this, as an additional premise with the first premise, we can conclude the following:

(3) There is adequate life support on Mars.

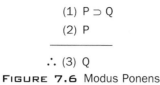

(1) P ⊃ Q

(2) P

_____

∴ (3) Q

FIGURE 7.6 Modus Ponens

Notice first that premise 2 is identical to the antecedent of the conditional premise 1 and that the conclusion is identical to its consequent. Notice also that it is impossible to assert premises 1 and 2 and deny conclusion 3 without contradicting yourself. Try it. Thus this is a deductively valid argument. It follows a form that can be represented schematically (Figure 7.6).

Logicians traditionally refer to this argument form by the Latin label **modus ponens,** which means affirmative mood. Because modus ponens is deductively valid, for any argument that follows the form of modus ponens, accepting the premises forces you to accept the conclusion. Try it. Make some up.

FALLACY OF AFFIRMING THE CONSEQUENT

Suppose the space probe turns up another kind of evidence. Suppose the space probe establishes the following:

(2a) There is adequate life support on Mars.

And suppose we drew the following conclusion from this, together with premise 1 (if there is life on Mars, then there is adequate life support on Mars):

(3a) There is life on Mars.

Perhaps conclusion 3a is correct. But do the two premises really guarantee it? No, they don't. It is possible to deny conclusion 3a without contradicting the assertion of either premise 1 or premise 2a. Try it (using the scenario method).

If you're having trouble with this, consider the following formally analogous argument:

(1) If a figure is square, then it has four sides.

(2a) This rhombus has four sides.

_____

∴ (3a) This rhombus is square.

This argument is not deductively valid. And the form it follows, which can be schematically represented as shown in Figure 7.7, is unreliable, or formally fallacious.

(1) P ⊃ Q

(2a) Q

_____

∴ (3a) P

FIGURE 7.7 Fallacy of Affirming the Consequent

Logicians traditionally refer to this form as the **fallacy of affirming the consequent,** because that's what the second premise does. It asserts the consequent of the conditional first premise.

MODUS TOLLENS

Suppose the space probe turns up yet another kind of evidence. Suppose the space probe establishes the following:

(2b) There is no adequate life support on Mars.

From this, with the first premise (if there is life on Mars, then there is adequate life support on Mars), it is possible to conclude the following:

(3b) There is no life on Mars.

Notice here that premise 2b is the denial of the consequent of premise 1, whereas conclusion 3b is the denial of its antecedent. And notice that here, again, it is impossible to assert premises 1 and 2b and deny conclusion 3b without contradicting yourself. Try it. Thus this inference is deductively valid. It follows a pattern that can be represented schematically (Figure 7.8).

$$(1)\ P \supset Q$$
$$(2b)\ \sim Q$$

$$\therefore\ (3c)\ \sim Q$$

FIGURE 7.8 Modus Tollens

Logicians traditionally refer to this argument form by the Latin label **modus tollens,** which means denying mood. Because modus tollens, like modus ponens, is deductively valid, for any argument that follows the form of modus tollens, accepting the premises forces you to accept the conclusion. Try it. Make some up.

FALLACY OF DENYING THE ANTECEDENT

Next, suppose the space probe establishes the following:

(2c) There is no life on Mars.

Suppose we drew from this and the first premise (if there is life on Mars, then there is adequate life support on Mars) the following conclusion:

(3c) There isn't adequate life support on Mars.

Again, perhaps conclusion 3c is correct, but do premises 1 and 2c guarantee it? No they don't. It is possible to assert both premise 1 and premise 2c and to deny conclusion 3c without contradicting yourself. Try it (again using the scenario method).

Recall the earlier example. You can demonstrate the invalidity of this inference using a formally analogous argument, thus:

(1) If a figure is square, then it has four sides.

(2c) This figure (a rhombus) is not a square.

∴ (3c) This figure (a rhombus) does not have four sides.

This argument is not deductively valid. And the form it follows, which can be represented schematically, is unreliable, or formally fallacious (Figure 7.9).

$$(1)\ P \supset Q$$
$$(2c)\ \sim P$$

$$\therefore (3c)\ \sim Q$$

FIGURE 7.9 Fallacy of Denying the Antecedent

Logicians traditionally refer to this form as the **fallacy of denying the antecedent,** because that's what the second premise does. It denies the antecedent of the conditional first premise.

REVIEW EXERCISE 7.2 | Formal Fallacy Demonstration

Demonstrate the fallacious status of affirming the consequent and denying the antecedent by composing arguments of each form that move from intuitively acceptable or obviously true premises to intuitively unacceptable or obviously false conclusions.

TABLE 7.2   summarizes what we've said about these four conditional forms

	Valid		Invalid	
Modus Ponens	$(1)\ P \supset Q$ $(2)\ P$ $\therefore (3)\ Q$		Affirming the Consequent	$(1)\ P \supset Q$ $(2a)\ Q$ $\therefore (3a)\ P$
Modus Tollens	$(1)\ P \supset Q$ $(2b)\ \sim Q$ $\therefore (3b)\ \sim P$		Denying the Antecedent	$(1)\ P \supset Q$ $(2c)\ \sim P$ $\therefore (3c)\ \sim Q$

REVIEW EXERCISE 7.3 | Valid and Invalid Forms

Analyze and evaluate the following three arguments:

1. If astrology is correct, then all people born at the same time would have the same sort of personalities, experiences, and opportunities, yet this is not the case.

   • What is the thesis of this argument?
   • The argument is an example of which argument form?
   • Is the argument deductively valid or not?

2. If astrology has been refuted, then we should not depend on the predictions in the horoscope. But because astrology has not been refuted, we should depend on them.
   - What is the thesis of this argument?
   - The argument is an example of which argument form?
   - Is the argument deductively valid or not?

3. If drugs make people well, then those who take the most should be the healthiest, but this simply isn't the case.[1]
   - What is the thesis of this argument?
   - The argument is an example of which argument form?
   - Is the argument deductively valid or not?

HYPOTHETICAL SYLLOGISM

Another commonly used and important argument form involves two conditional premises. Suppose, again, that an experimental space probe begins with the following conditional first premise:

(1) If there is life on Mars, then there is adequate life support on Mars.

This time, however, let's add a second conditional premise:

(2d) If there is adequate life support on Mars, then a manned mission to Mars is feasible.

From this, with premise 1, it is possible to conclude the following:

(3d) If there is life on Mars, then a manned mission to Mars is feasible.

Notice here that premise 2d is a conditional whose antecedent is identical to the consequent of premise 1, whereas the conclusion, 3d, is another conditional, whose antecedent is identical to the antecedent of premise 1 and whose consequent is identical to the consequent of premise 2d. And notice that here, again, it is impossible to assert premises 1 and 2d and deny conclusion 3d without contradicting yourself. Try it. Thus this inference is deductively valid. It follows a pattern that can be represented schematically (Figure 7.10).

$$(1) \ P \supset Q$$
$$(2d) \ Q \supset R$$
$$\therefore (3d) \ P \supset R$$

FIGURE 7.10 Hypothetical Syllogism

Logicians traditionally refer to this argument form as **hypothetical syllogism.** Because hypothetical syllogism, like modus ponens and modus tollens, is deductively valid, for any argument that follows the form of hypothetical syllogism, accepting the premises forces you to accept the conclusion. Try it. Make some up.

But compare the last example with this one:

(1) If there is life on Mars, then there is adequate life support on Mars.

(2e) A manned mission to Mars is feasible *only if* there is adequate life support on Mars.

∴ (3d) If there is life on Mars, then a manned mission to Mars is feasible.

This inference is not deductively valid. Remember that "only if" (as in premise 2e) reverses the positions of antecedent and consequent (see Table 7.1). You can also see the invalidity using the following scenario: Suppose it's true that the existence of life on Mars presupposes adequate life support on Mars (premise 1). Suppose also that a manned mission to Mars is feasible *only if* there is adequate life support on Mars (premise 2e). Also suppose there is indeed life on Mars and, therefore, adequate life support on Mars. Yet intuitively it's clear that the feasibility of a manned mission to Mars is still an open question. So the conclusion (3d) does not follow logically from these two premises.

DISJUNCTIVE SYLLOGISM

Like conditional statements, disjunctions are extremely powerful reasoning tools, so they play a crucial role in a great many arguments and argument forms. Suppose, for example, that we've been trying to diagnose a mechanical problem with the car and we have eliminated all possible problems but two: the battery and the ignition switch. So we now have good reason to believe the following:

(1) Either the battery is dead or there is a short in the ignition switch.

Suppose we check the battery and find that it's fully charged and functioning properly. We now know the following:

(2) The battery is not dead.

From this, with the first premise, it is possible to conclude the following:

(3) There is a short in the ignition switch.

Notice here that premise 2 is the denial of one of the disjuncts of premise 1, whereas conclusion 3 is identical with the other disjunct. And notice that here, again, it is impossible to assert premises 1 and 2 and deny conclusion 3 without contradicting yourself. Try it. Thus this inference is deductively valid. It follows a pattern that can be represented schematically (Figure 7.11).

(1) P v Q

(2b) ~P

∴ (3b) ~Q

FIGURE 7.11 Disjunctive Syllogism

Logicians traditionally refer to this argument form as **disjunctive syllogism**.

FALLACY OF ILLICIT DISJUNCTIVE SYLLOGISM

Just as with modus ponens and modus tollens, it is worth noting that there are unreliable inferences that closely resemble the valid form of disjunctive syllogism. To illustrate, continue with the same example. Suppose we're trying to troubleshoot the car and we've narrowed the possible causes down to two: the battery and the ignition switch. So we have good reason to believe the following:

(1) Either there is a short in the ignition switch or the battery is dead.

Suppose we find a short in the ignition switch. We now know the following:

(2a) There is a short in the ignition switch.

Suppose we conclude the following from this, with the first premise:

(3a) The battery is not dead.

Notice here that premise 2a affirms one of the disjuncts of premise 1, whereas conclusion 3a negates or denies the other disjunct. But does conclusion 3a follow from premise 1 plus premise 2a? No it does not, because even if premises 1 and 2a are both true, the battery might still be dead. This illustrates what some logicians refer to as the **fallacy of illicit disjunctive syllogism.** It can be explained as resulting from failure to distinguish between inclusive and exclusive disjunction as defined earlier. It follows a pattern that can be represented schematically (Figure 7.12).

(1) P v Q
(2) P
———
∴ (3) ~Q

FIGURE 7.12 Fallacy of Illicit Disjunctive Syllogism

DILEMMA

One of the oldest and most powerful argumentative strategies combines conditional and disjunctive premises. The strategy aims to prove its point by showing that it is implied by each of two alternatives, at least one of which must be true. The strategy and the argument form that embodies it are called **dilemma.** For example, suppose that during the Monday Night Football pregame commentary you hear John Madden say,

If the Saints beat the Rams tonight, then the Forty-niners are in the playoffs as division champs.
But if the Rams beat the Saints, then the 'Niners are in the playoffs as a wild card.

APPLICATION EXERCISE 7.1 | Argument Reconstruction I

This is an incompletely stated argument. Using the tools presented in chapter 4, see if you can reconstruct it before reading any further.

> If the Saints beat the Rams tonight, then the Forty-niners are in the playoffs as division champs. But if the Rams beat the Saints, then the 'Niners are in the playoffs as a wild card.

The argument as presented consists of two claims, both conditionals, neither of which seems to support the other. What is the point? Apparently that the 'Niners are in the playoffs (regardless of the outcome of tonight's game). Thus the implied conclusion of the argument would be "The 'Niners are in the play-offs." But the argument also depends on a third premise, which is unstated because it is so obvious—namely, that either the Saints will beat the Rams or the Rams will beat the Saints. When these elements are filled in, the argument is as shown in Figure 7.13.

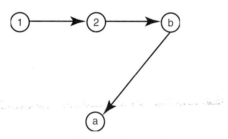

FIGURE 7.13 Diagramming an Argument

(1) If the Saints beat the Rams tonight, then the Forty-niners are in the playoffs *as division champs.*

(2) If the Rams beat the Saints, then the 'Niners are in the playoffs *as a wild card.*

(b) Either the Saints will beat the Rams or the Rams will beat the Saints.

∴ (a) The 'Niners are in the playoffs.

Notice here that the antecedent of claim 1 is one of the disjuncts of the implied premise (b) and that the antecedent of claim 2 is the other disjunct. The consequent of each conditional claim is the argument's implied conclusion. And notice that here, again, it is impossible to assert the three premises and deny the conclusion without contradicting yourself. Try it. Thus this inference is deductively valid. It follows a pattern that can be represented schematically (Figure 7.14).

(1) P ⊃ R

(2) Q ⊃ R

(b) P v Q

_____

∴ (a) R

FIGURE 7.14 Dilemma

Somewhat more sophisticated argument forms follow essentially the same reasoning strategy. For example, we may argue that one or the other of two options is implied by each of two alternatives, at least one of which must be true. A rather famous example comes from the legendary physicist Richard Feynman. Among his more famous exploits is having figured out the cause of the space shuttle *Challenger* disaster in 1986, to the deep embarrassment of NASA administrators. Speaking about the experience 2 years later, Feynman said:

> It struck me that there were several fishinesses associated with the big cheeses at NASA. Every time we talked to higher level managers, they kept saying they didn't know anything about the problems below them. We're getting this kind of thing again in the Iran-contra hearings, but at that time, this kind of situation was new to me: either the guys at the top didn't know, in which case they should have known, or they did know, in which case they're lying to us.[2]

APPLICATION EXERCISE 7.2 | **Argument Reconstruction II**

The last sentence in the preceding quotation from Richard Feynman presents an argument in compressed and abbreviated form—an excellent example on which to test your argument analysis skills. Here it is again. See if you can reconstruct it more completely before reading any further.

> Either the guys at the top didn't know, in which case they should have known, or they did know, in which case they're lying to us.

Let's compare notes. One of the premises is the disjunction "either the guys at the top didn't know . . . or they did know." Two additional premises express what is implied by each of these alternatives. First, if the guys at the top didn't know, then they should have known (that is, they were negligent). Second, if they did know, then they are being dishonest. The conclusion that follows from this is that the guys at the top were either negligent or are being dishonest. It doesn't matter to the validity of this argument in which order we list these premises. Following the order established earlier for dilemma, with the disjunction coming after the two hypothetical premises, the formal structure looks as shown in Figure 7.15.

$$(1) \ P \supset R$$
$$(2) \ Q \supset S$$
$$(3) \ P \lor Q$$

$$\therefore (4) \ R \lor S$$

FIGURE 7.15 Constructive Dilemma

You can perhaps begin to appreciate the beauty of formal logic as a system if you think about how the formal structure of constructive dilemma relates to modus ponens. It can be understood as two modus ponens arguments, whose minor premises are disjoined (Figure 7.16).

$$P \supset R \qquad Q \supset S$$
$$P \qquad \lor \qquad Q$$

$$R \qquad \lor \qquad S$$

FIGURE 7.16 Constructive Dilemma as Disjunction of Modus Ponens Arguments

A slightly more sophisticated combination results from a similar disjunction of two modus tollens arguments (Figure 7.17).

$$P \supset R \qquad Q \supset S$$
$$\sim R \qquad \lor \qquad \sim S$$

$$\sim P \qquad \lor \qquad \sim R$$

FIGURE 7.17 Disjunction of Modus Tollens Arguments

For example, suppose you're a juror in a murder trial. Expert testimony has established that the time of death was at midnight and that it is a 25-minute drive from the scene of the crime to the house where the defendant, who is blind and cannot drive, was arrested at 12:30 a.m. The defense attorney argues as follows: "If my client was present at the scene of the crime when it took place, then he must have had transportation home. But if he were alone with the victim at the crime scene, he would have had to walk and could not have been arrested. Therefore either my client was not at the scene of the crime at the time of the murder or there was someone else there, too." Here we have two premises each in the form of a hypothetical statement. The facts of the case establish a further (implied) premise that the consequents of the two hypothetical premises cannot both be true. One of them, at least, must be false. It follows logically that the antecedents of the two hypothetical premises cannot both be true. At least one of them must be false. Logicians refer to this argument form as **destructive dilemma** and represent it formally as shown in Figure 7.18.

(1) P ⊃ R
(2) Q ⊃ S
(3) ~R v ~S
———————
∴ (4) ~P v ~R

FIGURE 7.18 Destructive Dilemma

REVIEW EXERCISE 7.4 │ **Identifying Logical Structure**   ✳

Identify the logical structure of each of the following examples.

	Modus ponens	If Paul keeps his GPA above 3.3 this semester, then he will be graduating with honors. And his GPA is 3.7. So he's going to be graduating with honors.
	Affirming consequent	
	Modus tollens	
	Denying antecedent	
	Hypothetical syllogism	
	Disjunctive syllogism	
	Dilemma	

	Modus ponens	Unless Paul keeps his GPA above 3.3 this semester he won't be graduating with honors. But his GPA is 3.7. So he's going to be graduating with honors.
	Affirming consequent	
	Modus tollens	
	Denying antecedent	
	Hypothetical syllogism	
	Disjunctive syllogism	
	Dilemma	

	Modus ponens	Unless Paul keeps his GPA above 3.3 this semester he won't be graduating with honors. And his GPA is 2.7. So he's not going to be graduating with honors.
	Affirming consequent	
	Modus tollens	
	Denying antecedent	
	Hypothetical syllogism	
	Disjunctive syllogism	
	Dilemma	

Modus ponens	Paul will be graduating with honors only if he keeps his GPA above 3.3 this semester. He will keep his GPA above 3.3 only if he studies an extra 20 hours per week. So Paul will be graduating with honors only if he studies an extra 20 hours per week.
Affirming consequent	
Modus tollens	
Denying antecedent	
Hypothetical syllogism	
Disjunctive syllogism	
Dilemma	

Modus ponens	We're not going to get to sleep unless the dog stops barking. The dog won't stop barking until the porch light is turned off. So we'll get to sleep only if the porch light is turned off.
Affirming consequent	
Modus tollens	
Denying antecedent	
Hypothetical syllogism	
Disjunctive syllogism	
Dilemma	

Modus ponens	Either we turn the porch light off, or that dog will keep on barking. We're not going to get any sleep until the dog stops barking. So we'd better go turn that porch light off.
Affirming consequent	
Modus tollens	
Denying antecedent	
Hypothetical syllogism	
Disjunctive syllogism	
Dilemma	

Modus ponens	"Every time we talked to higher level managers, they kept saying they didn't know anything about the problems below them. . . . Either the group at the top didn't know, in which case they should have known, or they did know, in which case they're lying to us."[3]
Affirming consequent	
Modus tollens	
Denying antecedent	
Hypothetical syllogism	
Disjunctive syllogism	
Dilemma	

APPLICATION EXERCISE 7.3 | **Argument Reconstruction III**

At the beginning of this chapter is a Farcus cartoon. Using the tools of truth functional logic, can you explain the point of the cartoon? Hint: What argument form or forms do you see?

TESTING FOR VALIDITY WITH TRUTH TABLES

In Chapter 6 we found the system of Venn diagrams useful as a graphic means of testing the validity of categorical syllogisms. Venn diagrams poorly accommodate the kind of argument forms we've just been considering. But we can use truth tables for this purpose. We conclude this chapter by demonstrating this feature of truth tables. Thus far we have used truth tables to define and explain logical operators. A truth table will list all possible combinations of truth value for all components of a truth functional compound statement in the left columns, with the corresponding truth value of the compound statement in the far right column, as, for example, in the truth table for implication (Figure 7.19).

P	Q	P ⊃ Q
T	T	T
T	F	F
F	T	T
F	F	T

FIGURE 7.19 Truth Table for Implication

MODUS PONENS

It so happens that the truth table also represents all possible truth value combinations of the premises and conclusion of the argument form modus ponens. The column on the right corresponds to premise 1, the column on the left corresponds to premise 2, and the column in the middle corresponds to the conclusion. So we should also be able to tell from the truth table whether or not it's possible for both premises to be true while the conclusion is false. As always, if so, the argument form is not deductively valid, but if not, the argument form is deductively valid. There is only one line (line 1) of the truth table on which both premises are true (the shaded line in Figure 7.20), and on that line the conclusion is also true (as indicated by the circled ⓣ in the truth table). So the argument form is a valid one.

P	Q	P ⊃ Q
T	Ⓣ	T
T	F	F
F	T	T
F	F	T

FIGURE 7.20 Truth Table for Modus Ponens

FALLACY OF AFFIRMING THE CONSEQUENT

It turns out also that the truth table for implication represents all possible truth value combinations of the premises and conclusion of the fallacy of affirming the consequent. In this case, the column on the right corresponds to premise 1, the column in the middle corresponds to premise 2, and the column on the left corresponds to the conclusion. So again we should be able to tell from the truth table whether or not it's possible for both premises to be true while the conclusion is false. This time, there are two lines (lines 1 and 3) of the truth table on which both premises are true (Figure 7.21). On line 3 the conclusion is false. In other words, the truth table shows that it is possible for an argument of this form to have true premises and a false·conclusion; therefore, the argument is not valid.

P	Q	P ⊃ Q
T	T	T
T	F	F
Ⓕ	T	T
F	F	T

FIGURE 7.21 Truth Table for Fallacy of Affirming the Consequent

MODUS TOLLENS

To test the validity of modus tollens and the fallacy of denying the antecedent is only slightly more complicated. This is because none of the truth tables we have generated so far represents all possible truth value combinations for the premises and conclusions of either of these two argument forms. However, we need merely add a couple of columns to the truth table for implication to accomplish this (Figure 7.22). These two columns are to represent the truth values of ~P and ~Q, which, according to the truth table for negation, are simply the reverse of the truth values for P and Q, respectively.

P	Q	P ⊃ Q	~P	~Q
T	T	T	F	F
T	F	F	F	T
F	T	T	T	F
F	F	T	Ⓣ	T

FIGURE 7.22 Truth Table for Modus Tollens

To test the validity of modus tollens, we simply need to locate the columns representing the premises and conclusion and check to see whether or not it's possible for both of the premises to be true while the conclusion is false. In the preceding truth table, the third column now represents premise 1, the column on the far right represents premise 2, and the column between them represents the conclusion. There is only one line (line 4) on which both premises are true. Because the conclusion is also true on this line, the argument form is a valid one.

FALLACY OF DENYING THE ANTECEDENT

Similarly, to test the fallacy of denying the antecedent, we simply need to locate the columns representing the premises and conclusion and check to see whether or not it's possible for both premises to be true while the conclusion is false. In the truth table, the third column now represents premise 1, the column immediately to the right of it represents premise 2, and the column on the far right represents the conclusion (Figure 7.23). But this time, there are two lines (lines 3 and 4) of the truth table on which both premises are true. On line 3 the conclusion is false. In other words, the truth table shows that it is possible for an argument of this form to have true premises and a false conclusion; therefore, the argument is not valid.

P	Q	P ⊃ Q	~P	~Q
T	T	T	F	F
T	F	F	F	T
F	T	T	T	(F)
F	F	T	T	T

FIGURE 7.23 Truth Table for Fallacy of Denying the Antecedent

DILEMMA

To test the validity of constructive dilemma, we follow the same procedure using a truth table. This time we are dealing with three distinct components: P, Q, and R. So the truth table (Figure 7.24) will need eight lines to represent all possible combinations of truth value for the number of distinct components involved.

P	Q	R	P ⊃ R	Q ⊃ R	P v Q
T	T	(T)	T	T	T
T	T	F	F	F	T
T	F	(T)	T	T	T
T	F	F	F	T	T
F	T	(T)	T	T	T
F	T	F	T	F	T
F	F	T	T	T	F
F	F	F	T	T	F

FIGURE 7.24 Eight-Line Truth Table for Constructive Dilemma

This time, there are three lines (lines 1, 3, and 5) of the truth table on which all of the premises are true. Because the conclusion is also true on each of these lines, the argument form is a valid one.

APPLICATION EXERCISE 7.4 | **Hypothetical Syllogism Validity Demonstration**

Demonstrate the validity of the argument form hypothetical syllogism using the truth table here. Highlight the rows in which the truth values of both premises are true. Then determine whether the argument form is valid as illustrated earlier.

P	Q	R	P ⊃ R	Q ⊃ R	P ⊃ R
T	T	T	T	T	T
T	T	F	T	F	F
T	F	T	F	T	T
T	F	F	F	T	F
F	T	T	T	T	T
F	T	F	T	F	T
F	F	T	T	T	T
F	F	F	T	T	T

APPLICATION EXERCISE 7.5 | **Disjunctive Syllogism Validity Demonstration**

Demonstrate the validity of the argument form disjunctive syllogism using the truth table here. Highlight the rows in which the truth values of both premises are true. Then determine whether the argument form is valid as illustrated earlier.

P	Q	P v Q	~P
T	T	T	F
T	F	T	F
F	T	T	T
F	F	F	T

APPLICATION EXERCISE 7.6 | Invalidity Demonstration

Demonstrate the invalidity of the argument form illicit disjunctive syllogism using the truth table here. Highlight the rows in which the truth values of both premises are true. Then determine whether the argument form is valid as illustrated earlier.

P	Q	P v Q	~P
T	T	T	F
T	F	T	T
F	T	T	F
F	F	F	T

APPLICATION EXERCISE 7.7 | Term Project

Take any position on the issue you have been working with so far and design an argument in support of that position, using any of the deductively valid argument forms discussed in this chapter. Then take an alternative or opposed position and design an argument in support of it, using any of the deductively valid argument forms discussed in this chapter.

GLOSSARY

antecedent in a hypothetical statement, the component introduced by the word "if"

compound statement any statement that contains a simple(r) statement as a truth functional component

conjunct a component of a conjunction

conjunction a compound statement that is true only when both of its components are true; the logical operator "and" is used to make such a statement

consequent in a hypothetical statement, the component introduced by the word "then"

destructive dilemma a variation of the dilemma form in which the disjunction is between two alternatives, at least one of which must be false

dilemma an argument form or strategy combining hypothetical and disjunctive premises that seeks to prove its point by showing it is implied by each of two alternatives, at least one of which must be true

disjunct a component of a disjunction

disjunction, exclusive a compound statement that is true when either one or the other of its components is true but not both

disjunction, inclusive a compound statement that is true when either one or both of its components are true; the logical operator "or" is used to make such a statement

disjunctive syllogism   a deductively valid argument form based on a disjunction and the denial of one of its disjuncts

fallacy of affirming the consequent   a deductively invalid argument form based on a hypothetical statement and the affirmation of its consequent

fallacy of denying the antecedent   a deductively invalid argument form based on a hypothetical statement and the denial of its antecedent

fallacy of illicit disjunctive syllogism   a deductively invalid argument form based on a disjunction and the affirmation of one of its disjuncts, leading to the denial of its other disjunct

hypothetical syllogism   a deductively valid argument form based on two hypothetical statements as premises, where the consequent of the first is the antecedent of the second

implication   the truth dependency relationship asserted by a truth functional conditional statement, or the logical operator used in making a truth functional conditional statement

logical operator   (in truth functional logic) a device for making a compound statement out of simpler ones

modus ponens   a deductively valid argument form based on a hypothetical statement and the affirmation of its antecedent

modus tollens   a deductively valid argument form based on a hypothetical statement and the denial of its consequent

negation   the logical operator that reverses the truth value of the component statement to which it is applied; a statement formed by applying this logical operator

simple statement   any statement that does not contain a simple(r) statement as a truth functional component

truth functional analysis   a system for keeping track of how logical operators affect the truth values of compound sentences made with them

truth functional logic   a system of logic based on truth functional analysis

truth table   a chart used in truth functional logic for listing variable truth values

truth value   the truth of falsity of a statement

ADDITIONAL EXERCISES

▨ REVIEW EXERCISE 7.5 TRANSLATING INTO TRUTH FUNCTIONAL LOGICAL
FORMAT II   Translate the following claims into truth functional logical format.

If a government harbors terrorists, we will hold that government responsible.	G = A government harbors terrorists. H = We will hold that government responsible.	Truth functional format:

If a government harbors terrorists, we will not hesitate to use military force.	G = A government harbors terrorists. H = We will hesitate to use military force.	Truth functional format:

Either the FBI memo was lost, or CIA analysts misunderstood the memo's implications.	F = The FBI memo was lost. C = CIA analysts misunderstood the memo's implications.	Truth functional format:

Either the FBI memo was lost, or CIA analysts did not understand the memo's implications.	F = The FBI memo was lost. C = CIA analysts understood the memo's implications.	Truth functional format:

The FBI memo was lost, and CIA analysts did not understand its implications.	F = The FBI memo was lost. C = CIA analysts understood the memo's implications.	Truth functional format:

Unless interagency communication is improved, national security will continue to be at risk.	I = Interagency communication is improved. N = National security will continue to be at risk.	Truth functional format:

■ **REVIEW EXERCISE 7.6 FROM TRUTH FUNCTIONAL LOGICAL FORMAT TO TRUTH TABLE**   Translate each of the following arguments into standard form using the scheme of abbreviation provided. Then set up and complete a truth table for each argument and determine each argument's validity status.

If Paul keeps his GPA above 3.3 this semester, then he will be graduating with honors. And his GPA is 3.7. So he's going to be graduating with honors.	H = Paul will be graduating with honors. K = Paul keeps his GPA above 3.3. S = Paul studies an extra 20 hours per week.	

H	K	S	Premise 1	Premise 2	Conclusion	Valid	Invalid
T	T	T					
T	T	F					
T	F	T					
T	F	F					
F	T	T					
F	T	F					
F	F	T					
F	F	F					

| Unless Paul keeps his GPA above 3.3 this semester, he won't be graduating with honors. But his GPA is 3.7. So he's going to be graduating with honors. | H = Paul will be graduating with honors. K = Paul keeps his GPA above 3.3. S = Paul studies an extra 20 hours per week. | |

			Premise 1	Premise 2	Conclusion	Valid	Invalid
H	**K**	**S**					
T	T	T					
T	T	F					
T	F	T					
T	F	F					
F	T	T					
F	T	F					
F	F	T					
F	F	F					

| Unless Paul keeps his GPA above 3.3 this semester he won't be graduating with honors. And his GPA is 2.7. So he's not going to be graduating with honors. | H = Paul will be graduating with honors. K = Paul keeps his GPA above 3.3. S = Paul studies an extra 20 hours per week. | |

			Premise 1	Premise 2	Conclusion	Valid	Invalid
H	**K**	**S**					
T	T	T					
T	T	F					
T	F	T					
T	F	F					
F	T	T					
F	T	F					
F	F	T					
F	F	F					

| Paul will be graduating with honors only if he keeps his GPA above 3.3 this semester. He will keep his GPA above 3.3 only if he studies an extra 20 hours per week. So Paul will be graduating with honors only if he studies an extra 20 hours per week. | H = Paul will be graduating with honors. K = Paul keeps his GPA above 3.3. S = Paul studies an extra 20 hours per week. | |

H	K	S	Premise 1	Premise 2	Conclusion	Valid	Invalid
T	T	T					
T	T	F					
T	F	T					
T	F	F					
F	T	T					
F	T	F					
F	F	T					
F	F	F					

We're not going to get to sleep unless the dog stops barking. The dog won't stop barking until the porch light is turned off. So we'll get to sleep only if the porch light is turned off.	W = We are going to get to sleep. D = The dog will stop barking. P = The porch light is turned off.	

H	K	S	Premise 1	Premise 2	Conclusion	Valid	Invalid
T	T	T					
T	T	F					
T	F	T					
T	F	F					
F	T	T					
F	T	F					
F	F	T					
F	F	F					

NOTES

[1] This statement is from a chiropractor's ad.

[2] Richard P. Feynman, "Afterthoughts", *"What Do You Care What Other People Think?"*:
Further Adventures of a Curious Character, (New York: W. W. Norton, 1988) pp. 212–213.

[3] Ibid.

Inductive Reasoning

Inductive reasoning
  Generalizing, polling, probability, statistics
    Reasoning by analogy
      Causality and hypothetical reasoning

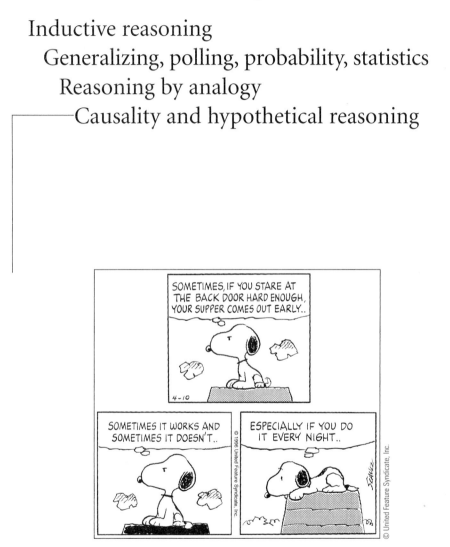

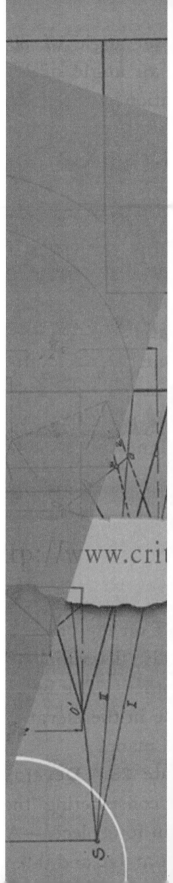

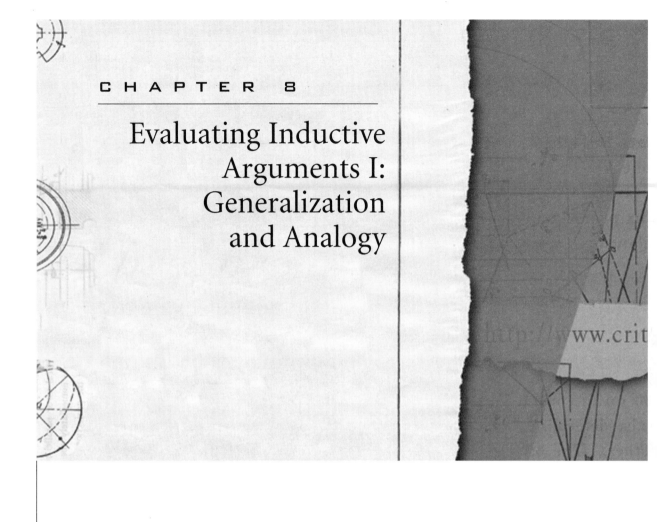

CHAPTER 8

Evaluating Inductive Arguments I: Generalization and Analogy

As we have seen in the previous two chapters, deductively valid arguments guarantee their conclusions. If the truth of the premises of a deductively valid argument has been established, there is no more room for doubt about the argument's conclusion. But many arguments that do not provide this "absolute" level of inferential security nevertheless provide substantial support for their conclusions and are therefore not to be dismissed simply on the grounds that they are not *deductively* valid. There are some arguments whose premises, although they do not guarantee the conclusion, nevertheless make the conclusion more reasonable or probable or likely. Here is an example of such an argument:

[Professor Jones has never missed a class ①]. So chances are [she'll be in class today ②].

If the premise (claim 1) is accepted as true, then it would be reasonable to accept the argument's conclusion (claim 2). Of course, even if the premise is true,

THE NORM Michael Jantze

WOMEN ARE SO DIFFERENT FROM MEN.

WHAT? LIKE I HAVE TO PROVE IT?

the conclusion may prove to be false: Professor Jones may not show up for class. Perhaps she's ill, has had an accident, has been arrested, or has an important conflicting appointment. Nevertheless, the premise provides reasonable support for the conclusion. Here is another example:

> [It's highly unlikely that any female will play football in the National Football League in the near future (1)], because [none has so far (2)].

Again, if the premise (claim 2) is accepted as true, it provides good—although not deductively valid—grounds for accepting the conclusion (claim 1). These are examples of *inductive* inferences. As we explained in chapter 6, the essential difference between deductive and inductive reasoning is that deductive inferences are designed to achieve absolute inferential security, whereas inductive inferences are designed to manage risk of error when absolute inferential security is unattainable.

ASSESSING INDUCTIVE STRENGTH

A deductive argument is either valid or not valid. But inductive strength is **relative,** which means it admits of degrees. Some valid inductive arguments are stronger than others. In the absence of *absolute* security of inferences—that is, when the premises, even if true, leave room for doubt about the conclusion—the essential question becomes, "How much room for doubt?" To evaluate inductive reasoning, we must estimate the *relative* security of inferences.

THOUGHT EXPERIMENT 8.1 | **Inductive Strength I**

Which is the "stronger" of the following two arguments?

1. The last three cars I owned were Chrysler products, and they've all been great! So I'm not the least bit worried about the new Dodge. You can't argue with firsthand experience.

2. In Consumers' Union nationwide studies of new cars purchased over the last 10 years, Chrysler had a 30% lower frequency of repair than the other manufacturers. So it's probably safe to assume that a new Dodge will be reliable.

In each argument, the premise provides some reason for accepting the conclusion. But even if the first argument is worded more emphatically, the second argument is the stronger of the two. Why? There's more room for doubt in the first argument than there is in the second. And why is this? The second argument is based on more and better evidence than the first one.

If inductive strength is a matter of degree—and the essential question for assessing inductive strength is, "How much room for doubt is there left here?"—the answer to this question is, "It depends." Inductive strength depends on a number of variables, according to the type of inductive reasoning involved.

INDUCTIVE GENERALIZATIONS

We will begin with the simplest and most common of inductive reasoning types, called **inductive generalization.** This type of inductive reasoning is a systematic approach to drawing general conclusions based on particular observed instances. We want to stress the word "systematic" because (if you'll pardon an unsystematic generalization) a lot of generalizations seem to just circulate around and people seem to believe them without much systematic rational support. We speculate (someone should test this hypothesis) that this *may* have something to do with an innate human tendency to want to know things. And so we like to generalize, because when we believe a generalization, the generality amplifies our sense of knowing something. To know a general truth is to know a lot of particular truths. But, again speaking generally, general claims are *not easy* to establish as true, so we ought to look more deeply into inductive reasoning.

THOUGHT EXPERIMENT 8.2 | Generalizations

Here's a list of generalizations. Check the ones you think are true, and then consider what basis you have for thinking they are true. Did you arrive at any of these generalizations by using systematic experimentation? If you did not arrive at a given generalization by using a systematic experiment, how did you arrive at it?

☐ Everything happens for a reason.

☐ Honesty is the best policy.

☐ You can't change what you don't acknowledge.

☐ Smoking causes cancer.

☐ Regular exercise reduces the risk of a heart attack.

☐ Everybody lies about sex.

☐ Everybody needs food and water to live.

☐ Money can't buy happiness.

☐ Everybody has a price.

☐ You can't predict the weather.

☐ You can't predict the future.

☐ You can't change the past.

☐ It's always now.

☐ Human nature is basically good.

☐ Human nature is basically evil.

☐ Human nature is an ongoing struggle between good and evil.

Suppose you work with computers and you have just opened a new shipment of floppy disks. It will make things easier if we imagine that floppy disks are delivered in shipments of 100. The first disk you try is defective. So you try a second one; it's defective, too. You try a third disk. Also defective. At some point, you begin to wonder whether the whole shipment might be defective. So far you've only tried three disks. They've all been defective, but you can't be sure that the entire shipment is defective. At this point, you merely suspect that the entire shipment might be defective. That's because you've barely sampled the shipment. Suppose you keep going. You try a fourth disk and a fifth disk. Both defective. This confirms your suspicion. The more disks you try (assuming each one is defective), the more certain you become that the entire shipment is defective. By the time you test the 35th disk (assuming each one is defective), you're going to be more certain—although still not absolutely certain—that the entire shipment is defective. This highlights two of the variables that affect the strength of an inductive generalization. From now on, we'll refer to the number of disks you've tried as the **sample** and the entire shipment (the general class you're wondering about) as the **population.** The **sample size** and the population size each affect the strength of the inductive inference. *As the size of the sample increases relative to the population, so does the strength of the induction.*

CRITICAL THINKING TIP 8.1 | **Sample Size**

As the Size of the Sample Increases Relative to the Population, so Does the Strength of the Induction.

There are other variables that affect inductive strength. If the only variables affecting inductive strength were the size of the sample and the size of the population, then the only way to increase inductive strength—or reduce doubt—would be to keep plodding along—testing the disks one by one until the sample coincides with the population. But you don't need to test every disk to be reasonably certain about the entire population. A common sense shortcut would be, after the first three or so disks have been identified as defective, to dig deeper into the shipment and try a disk from the middle and another one from near the bottom. If they, too, turn out to be defective, you can be more certain—although still not absolutely certain—that the entire shipment is defective. But notice that if you followed this procedure and obtained these results you would be more certain than if you had just tried the *next two* disks. Why? Because, it is more unlikely that by sampling in this random way you would end up picking just those disks that are defective. This highlights another of the variables that affect the strength of an inductive inference: the degree to which the sample is representative of the population. *The more representative the sample is of the population, the stronger the induction.*

CRITICAL THINKING TIP 8.2 | Randomness

The More Representative the Sample Is of the Population, the Stronger the Induction.

How do we determine the degree to which the sample is representative of the population? This is a matter of variety. In this example, the "expanded for variety" sample is equal in size to the "keep on plodding along" sample, but it covers more variables (see Figure 8.1).

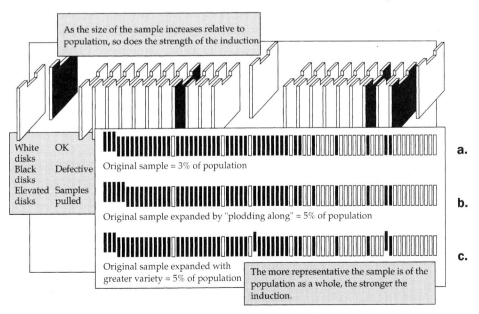

As the size of the sample increases relative to population, so does the strength of the induction

White disks — OK
Black disks — Defective
Elevated disks — Samples pulled

Original sample = 3% of population   **a.**

Original sample expanded by "plodding along" = 5% of population   **b.**

Original sample expanded with greater variety = 5% of population   **c.**

The more representative the sample is of the population as a whole, the stronger the induction.

FIGURE 8.1 Defective Disks

Suppose the disks are packed in the order that they came off the assembly line and you began by sampling them in (reverse) order. In sampling the middle and both ends of the shipment, rather than just sampling the beginning, you're adding to the variety of the sample by including within it particular examples representing the entire population, whether packed first, middle, or last. You've added to the variety of the sample in the dimension of "numerical order within the shipment." This is significant because numerical order within the shipment—numerical position in the packing order—could have something to do with whether a given disk is defective. Maybe there was a short run of 30 consecutive defective disks. By varying the sample through the dimension of numerical order, you have a way of ruling this out as a possible source of error—a way to reduce the risk of error. Because numerical order within the shipment might have something to do with whether a disk is defective or not, numerical order within the shipment is a relevant dimension here. *Generally, you should try to vary the sample as widely and in as many different relevant dimensions as you can think of.* In science, this is called "controlling the variables." These two factors—sample size relative to population size and representativeness of the sample—help explain why the first of the two examples of induction was weaker than the second. A nationwide comparative study of frequency of repair involving not just Chrysler products but also those of other manufacturers constitutes both a larger and a more representative sample than the tiny and highly selective "last three cars I owned" sample.

APPLICATION EXERCISE 8.1 | Inductive Strength II

Rank the following inductive arguments in order of decreasing strength (strongest to weakest). Be prepared to explain your ranking.

1. Contrary to current media claims, our schools appear to be doing a superb job of teaching our children to read. A leading news magazine recently tabulated the results of the thousands of responses it received to the survey it published in its May issue. Readers from every state in the union responded. Ninety percent of the respondents believed that their school-age children's reading skills were good to excellent. Eight percent more believed that their children's reading skills were at least adequate. Less that 1% felt that their children were developing less than adequate reading skills. (1% of the respondents failed to answer this question.)

2. In all studies that have been done over the past 30 years concerning the relationship between standardized test performance and success in school, involving several hundred thousand school-age subjects from a variety of ethnic, regional, and socioeconomic backgrounds, intelligent quotient (IQ) tests have been shown to be the single most reliable predictor of success in school. Therefore, if someone scores highly on IQ tests, he or she will probably perform well in school.

3. An hour in a hot tub will probably impair a man's fertility for up to 6 weeks. According to one study, three men who sat in a hot tub with water heated to 102.4°F (most health clubs heat theirs to 104°F) showed reductions in the number and penetrating capacity of their sperm cells. In samples taken 36 hours later, the damage was present, but the most dramatic effects did not show up until 4 weeks later. This indicated that even immature sperm cells had been harmed by the high heat. (It takes about 7 weeks for a newly created sperm cell to mature and pass through a system of storage ducts.) Seven weeks after their dip in the hot tub, their sperm returned to normal.

STATISTICAL GENERALIZATIONS

In the example of the defective computer disks, notice that *all* members of the sample turned out to be one way: defective. Life is rarely as simple as that. More often, some members of the sample will be one way and some another. So a variation on simple inductive generalization involves projecting trends or percentages observed in the sample onto other instances or onto the population. This is commonly called **statistical generalization.** For instance, suppose we're interested in how likely college students with different majors are to gain admission to law school. We might survey law school admissions for a certain period. Suppose the survey shows that 20% more of those applicants with philosophy majors than of those with the next most successful major were admitted. We might then project inductively that philosophy majors are 20% more likely to gain admission to law school than other college students.

The same principles used to evaluate the strength of simple inductive generalizations apply in evaluating the strength of statistical generalizations. In both, the strength of the inference increases with the size of the sample relative to the population and with the degree to which the sample is representative of the population. Suppose the survey of law school admissions was only 1 year long or was confined to the state of California. Then we might be overlooking variables that might otherwise show up in a 10-year nationwide survey. Perhaps in a particular year more students with law school aptitude happened to elect philosophy as a major. Perhaps California has particularly strong instructional programs in philosophy. In any case, the smaller and more selective the sample, the weaker the induction.

MARGIN OF ERROR

Another variable that affects the strength of statistical generalizations is the degree of precision and certainty attached to the conclusion relative to the evidence contained in the premises. A statistical generalization can usually be strengthened by hedging the conclusion with appropriate qualifications, essentially by toning down the language with which the conclusion is presented. This is one reason statistical arguments often sound so wishy-washy despite all the numbers in them. Similarly, the degree of precision with which the figures in the conclusion are stated can affect the strength of a statistical generalization. We may lack sufficient evidence to conclude with certainty that precisely 73.86% of the electorate favors the president's new economic program. However, the same data might be sufficient to conclude with a higher degree of certainty that *more than two-thirds* or *most* of the electorate favors it. To handle this variable in a systematic way, statisticians use a conceptual tool known as **margin of error,** as in the following:

> The exit polling predicts that Proposition X will pass by a 62% majority, with a 3% margin of error.

Margin of error is an estimate of the likelihood of error in the conclusion of an inductive inference. You may wonder how it would be possible to estimate such a thing so precisely—especially given the size of the sample relative to the population in most public opinion polling. To give a detailed and systematic answer to this reasonable question would require a course in statistics. Statistics is the branch of mathematics having to do with collecting and interpreting numerical data. Nevertheless, here's a way to begin to think about the problem conceptually: margin of error is an estimate of how well you think the research has controlled the variables. Notice how closely this is relates to both the degree of precision and the certainty with which the results of the polling are presented and understood.

DISCUSSION TOPIC 8.1 | Inductive Strength III

Identify two distinct ways in which each of the following inferences might be strengthened. Be prepared to explain your answer in terms of how each of the ways you suggest would lower the margin of error.

- The last three cars I owned were Chrysler products, and they've all been great! So I'm not the least bit worried about the new Dodge. You can't argue with firsthand experience.
- In Consumers' Union nationwide studies of new cars purchased over the last 10 years, Chrysler had a 30% lower frequency of repair than the other manufacturers. So it's probably safe to assume that a new Dodge will be reliable.
- My English teacher has recommended three novels, and they've all been wonderful. I think I'm going to enjoy this book of poetry because she just recommended it, too.

REASONING BY ANALOGY

An **analogy** is a kind of comparison—one of the most useful and powerful reasoning tools there is. Why is this? Comparison essentially involves focusing attention on similarity. Similarity is an indispensable guide to the environment of any intelligent and sentient being. And there's a lot of similarity in the world to pay attention to.

THOUGHT EXPERIMENT 8.3 | Nothing in Common

Try to think of two things—any two things—that are so different from each other that they have *nothing* in common. Then see if you can't find some similarity between them.

Reasoning with analogies involves the application of three of the most basic intellectual concepts: similarity, difference, and relevance. The connection between analogy and similarity is obvious to the point of being overwhelming. The words "analogous" and "similar" are listed in many places as synonymous.

What is less obvious, although no less important, is that comparison always implies its inseparable opposite, its flip side—contrast, which essentially involves focusing attention on difference. Difference, too, is an indispensable guide to the environment of any intelligent and sentient being. And there's a lot of difference in the world to pay attention to.

THOUGHT EXPERIMENT 8.4 | No Difference

Try to think of two things—any two things—that are so identical to each other that they cannot be told apart in *any way.* Then see if you can't find some difference between them.

Analogies are comparisons applied to some specific intellectual purpose. There are many such purposes. For example, trumpet virtuoso Wynton Marsalis uses an analogy to explain the usefulness of analogies in explaining some of the fascinating dimensions of music:

> As we explore the world of music, we'll be looking for similarities. It's kind of like when you try to begin a conversation with someone you don't know. It's better to talk about what you have in common, rather than be stifled by your obvious differences.[1]

Analogies can be used effectively to explain new and unfamiliar or abstract and intangible things by comparing them to more familiar and tangible ones. Analogies can be used simply to give a vivid description or to spice up a narrative. Imagine a recent divorcée telling her sister the story of how she fended off unwanted advances at the office, adding, "and I need a date like a fish needs a bicycle." An analogy can be used as the basis for a joke. Comedian Lily Tomlin did this when she pointed out that we get olive oil by squeezing olives, corn oil by squeezing kernels of corn, sesame oil by pressing sesame seeds, and peanut oil by mashing peanuts and then wondered how we get baby oil.

AND SPEAKING OF: | Analogies—Remember This?

"Underlining, highlighting, mapping, casting—these are all merely means to that end [a fair, accurate, and detailed understanding of the argument]. As useful as these tools may be in many cases, they are to full-fledged argument analysis what training wheels are to riding a bike" (Chapter 5).

DISCUSSION TOPIC 8.2 | How Many Analogies?

How many analogies can you find in the following passage? What is the author trying to accomplish using each of the analogies you notice?

> In a *Scientific American* column on innumeracy, the computer scientist Douglas Hofstadter cites the case of the Ideal Toy Company, which stated on the package of the original Rubik's cube that there

were more than 3 billion possible states the cube could attain. Calculations show that there are more than 4×10^{19} possible states, 4 with 19 zeroes after it. What the package says isn't wrong; there are more than 3 billion possible states. The understatement, however, is symptomatic of a pervasive innumeracy which ill suits a technologically based society. It's analogous to a sign at the entrance to the Lincoln Tunnel stating: New York, population more than 6; or McDonald's proudly announces that they have sold more than 120 hamburgers.[2]

There are two prominent analogies in the preceding passage: one involving an imagined sign at the entrance to the Lincoln Tunnel in New York City and one involving McDonald's proud announcement of hamburger sales. The point of each of these analogies is to give an easier way to grasp the magnitude of an understatement that most of us would otherwise find incomprehensible. Innumeracy itself is quite possibly an unfamiliar concept, coined by mathematician John Allen Paulos using an analogy with the more familiar concept of illiteracy. This analogy is compressed into his book's title, *Innumeracy: Mathematical Illiteracy and Its Consequences.* Implied in this analogy is also an argument about the importance of overcoming the handicap of innumeracy.

ARGUMENT BY ANALOGY

Analogies can also be used inferentially or argumentatively, that is, to infer conclusions and to support or defend controversial positions. We call this reasoning by analogy or argument by analogy. Here is an example in which the 18th-century Scottish philosopher Thomas Reid argues for the probability of extraterrestrial organic life in our solar system:

> We may observe a very great similitude between this earth that we inhabit, and the other planets, Saturn, Jupiter, Mars, Venus and Mercury. They all revolve round the sun, as the earth does, although at different distances and in different periods. They borrow all their light from the sun, as the earth does. Several of them are known to revolve round their axis like the earth, and by that means, must have a like succession of day and night. Some of them have moons, that serve to give them light in the absence of the sun, as our moon does to us. They are all, in their motions, subject to the same law of gravitation, as the earth is. From all this similitude, it is not unreasonable to think that those planets may, like our earth, be the habitation of various orders of living creatures. There is some probability in this conclusion from analogy.[3]

Notice that Reid recognized that the inference is not deductively valid, in other words, that this is a form of inductive inference in which there is room for doubt and error. Nevertheless, he expressed cautious confidence in it as an inference. At some points in history, for instance, in the middle of the 20th century, it may have appeared that the conclusion Reid was cautiously drawing was not true, although the question remains an open one to this day. But he was not essentially misguided in placing confidence in the argument. He was following a familiar and generally reliable line of reasoning, which many of our everyday inferences follow. If you try to enroll in Professor Smith's section of the upper-division poetry course because you have taken three of her lower-division courses and found her to be a knowledgeable and stimulating instructor, you are following the same reasoning strategy Reid was following. In effect, you are reasoning as follows:

1. I have observed several items, a, b, and c, each of which has important characteristic 1 in common with target item d. (*I have taken three courses taught by the instructor of the course I'm contemplating.*)

2. The observed items a, b, and c also have characteristics 2 and 3. (*The three courses I've taken were stimulating and imparted knowledge.*)

3. Therefore it is likely that target item d will have characteristics 2 and 3 as well. (*The course I'm contemplating is likely to be stimulating and to impart knowledge.*)

The basic inferential strategy of an argument by analogy, as illustrated in these examples, is to infer that if things are similar in some way or ways they are probably similar in other ways as well.

In the process of analysis and evaluation of arguments by analogy, it is useful to distinguish the items compared by the roles they play in the comparison. For this purpose, we will call any item used as the basis of the comparison an **analogue** and we will refer to any item about which conclusions are drawn or explanations are offered as a **target**. So, for example, in Thomas Reid's argument about extraterrestrial life, the planet Earth is the analogue and the other planets in our solar system are the targets. In the example about Professor Smith's poetry class, the three lower-division courses you have taken are the analogues and the target is her upper-division class.

REVIEW EXERCISE 8.1 | Analogue and Target

Identify the analogues and targets in each of the following analogies. Which analogies are used inferentially or argumentatively (arg), which are used for explanatory purposes (exp), and which are used for something else, like narrative enhancement or entertainment (other)?

1. "Suppose that someone tells me that he has had a tooth extracted without an anaesthetic, and I express my sympathy, and suppose that I am then asked, 'How do you know that it hurt him?' I might reasonably reply, 'Well, I know that it would hurt me. I have been to the dentist and know how painful it is to have a tooth stopped [filled] without an anaesthetic, let alone taken out. And he has the same sort of nervous system as I have. I infer, therefore, that in these conditions he felt considerable pain, just as I should have.'"[4]

analogue	target	arg	exp	other

2. "Social Security has given a bunch of money to old people. That's not terrible. But Social Security is a pyramid scheme. People who get in early make out like bandits. People who get in late are screwed. And

Social Security is a very sophisticated pyramid scheme. The people who are going to get screwed weren't even born when Social Security was set up. But they have been now. And they're you."[5]

analogue	target	arg	exp	other

3. "When Dubya [U.S. President George W. Bush] wants to sound presidential, he'll try to construct a sentence that suggests some sense of mission, what his father [former U.S. President George H. W. Bush] used to call 'the vision thing.' But it's like someone assembling a barbecue—when the sentence is finished there are always a half-dozen parts left over."[6]

analogue	target	arg	exp	other

4. "Perhaps the most startling discovery made in astronomy this century is that the universe is populated by billions of galaxies and that they are systematically receding from one another, like raisins in an expanding pudding."[7]

analogue	target	arg	exp	other

5. "What grounds have we for attributing suffering to other animals[?] It is best to begin by asking what grounds any individual human has for supposing that other humans feel pain. Since pain is a state of consciousness, a 'mental event,' it can never be directly observed. No observations, whether behavioral signs such as writhing or screaming or physiological or neurological recordings, are observations of pain itself. Pain is something one feels, and one can only infer that others are feeling it from various external indications. The fact that only philosophers are ever skeptical about whether other humans feels pain shows that we regard such inference is justifiable in the case of humans. Is there any reason why the same inference should be unjustifiable for other animals? Nearly all the external signs which lead us to infer pain in other humans can be seen in other species, especially 'higher' animals such as mammals and birds. Behavioral signs—writhing, yelping, or other forms of calling, attempts to avoid the source of pain, and many others—are present. We know, too, that these animals are biologically similar in the relevant respects, having nervous systems like ours which can be observed to function as ours do. So the grounds for inferring that these animals can feel pain are nearly as good as the grounds for inferring other humans do."[8]

analogue	target	arg	exp	other

6. "If we were to repeat the same note without accents, it would be like our pulse. But what happens if we accent the first of every four beats—*one,* two, three, four, *one,* two, three, four? Accenting that first note sets up a rhythm we can count. Each note becomes part of a four-beat rhythm, and every four beats is one unit. This could get confusing if we didn't have a way to organize these units. But other things are that way, too. For example, if I ask you how far from home to school, you might say 5 blocks, but you wouldn't say 6,737 steps. Or you might say 10 minutes, not 600 seconds. You divide the distance or organize the time into convenient units."[9]

analogue	target	arg	exp	other

7. "The larger problem with seeing global warming as a harbinger of better beach weather is that it assumes that the climate is a steady, balanced system. And it has been—recently. For most of history, however, the climate has been wildly unstable. . . . 'You might think of the climate as a drunk,' writes Richard Alley, a paleoclimatologist at Pennsylvania State University. 'When left alone, it sits; when forced to move, it staggers.' Every ton of carbon dioxide we dump into the atmosphere is another kick in the drunk's ass."[10]

analogue	target	arg	exp	other

EVALUATING REASONING BY ANALOGY

The variables that affect the strength of inductive inferences generally also pertain in evaluating reasoning by analogy. The number of analogues relative to the number of targets affects the strength of an argument by analogy just as the size of the sample relative to the size of the population affects the strength of an inductive generalization. An argument based on a large series of analogous cases will tend to be stronger than one based on a single analogue, just as an inductive generalization based on many instances will be stronger than one based on a tiny sample. Similarly, the number of observed similarities between analogue and target affects the strength of the analogy just as the representativeness of the sample relative to the population affects the strength of an inductive generalization. This is intuitively fairly obvious. In general, the more similar things are *observed to be,* the more likely they are to be similar in additional ways.

Another variable that affects the strength of both inductive inferences generally and arguments by analogy is the strength of the conclusion relative to the evidence contained in the premises. An argument by analogy can be strengthened by hedging the conclusion with appropriate qualifications, as Thomas Reid did in the example about extraterrestrial life. Had he expressed the conclusion with greater certainty than he did, his argument would have been weaker than it was. These same general considerations apply to differences, too, only in reverse. The more differences there are between analogue and target, the weaker the analogy tends to be.

But there is another factor to consider in the evaluation of arguments by analogy, a factor that affects both similarities and differences and that is more important than either similarities or differences by themselves. This is the factor of **relevance.** In the earlier example of the defective computer disks, we noted that numerical order within the shipment might have something to do with whether a disk is defective or not. Thus numerical order within the shipment is a relevant variable. Similarly, in evaluating arguments or inferences by analogy, we are most interested in similarities and differences that might reasonably be thought to have something to do with the point of the comparison—the conclusion being inferred about the target. In general, the more relevant the observed similarities between analogue and target are to the conclusion being inferred, the stronger the analogy. By the same token, the more relevant the differences between analogue and target are to the conclusion being inferred, the weaker the analogy.

Suppose you are shopping for a new car. You decide that the new Honda Accord is likely to be a reliable, low-maintenance vehicle because Hondas you have owned in the past have been reliable and required minimal maintenance. Your inference is based on a relevant similarity, the identity of the manufacturer. Why? On the other hand, suppose you drew the same conclusion about a car because it was blue and the blue cars you owned in the past had been reliable and required minimal maintenance. This inference would be based on an irrelevant similarity. Why? There are good reasons for thinking that, in general, cars made by the same manufacturer will meet similar standards of reliability, but there are no similarly good reasons to suppose that the color of a car makes a difference in its reliability. There is a plausible explanatory basis for linking the identity of the manufacturer to quality control in the production process. There is no plausible explanatory link between color and reliability.

Thus to evaluate an argument or inference by analogy, we must add up the relevant similarities and differences. This can be accomplished in a systematic way using a simple form (Figure 8.2).

For purposes of illustration we will use examples from Review Exercise 8.1, starting with Alfred Jules Ayer's inference (argument 4) to the conclusion that another person besides himself feels pain. Ayer uses himself as the analogue. The

	Analogue	Target	Degree of Similarity or/ Difference	Relevance
Basic points of similarity used as premises				
Conclusion				
Differences				

FIGURE 8.2 Form for Evaluating an Argument by Analogy

Ayer's Argument	Analogue: Ayer	Target: Other Humans	Degree of Similarity or/ Difference	Relevance
Basic points of similarity used as premises	Central nervous system basic to physiology of sensory experience of pain	Central nervous system basic to physiology of sensory experience of pain		
Conclusion	Ayer experiences pain when undergoing dental work w/o anaesthetic	**Other people experience pain when undergoing dental work w/o anaesthetic**		
Differences				

FIGURE 8.3 Evaluating Ayer's Argument by Analogy I

target is some other person. There is one basic similarity used as a premise: similar nervous system. And the conclusion is that the other person would have the same sort of pain that Ayer would (Figure 8.3).

To evaluate this as an argument by analogy, we would first want to know whether the similarity Ayer asserts is true. Do people really have similar neurophysiology? They do. We should also note that the human central nervous system is a highly complex mechanism with a high degree of similarity both physically and functionally from person to person. Thus although there is only one similarity claimed here, that similarity is of a high degree.

Next, we want to determine whether this similarity is *relevant* to the conclusion Ayer is trying to draw. It is. We have good theoretical grounds and empirical evidence to suppose that a body's neurophysiology is the central mechanism involved in the person's sensory experience. So we might add assessments under the "Degree of Similarity" and "Relevance" headings (Figure 8.4).

At this point, we would want to determine whether there are significant relevant differences between the analogue and the target. In this particular argument, because the analogy is between Ayer and *any* other human, the differences would have to relate to characteristics that are unique to Ayer and that would distinguish him from any other human. There are many such characteristics, as there are with all human individuals. For example, Ayer was the author of an important work of philosophy published in 1936 entitled *Language, Truth and Logic*. This is true of no other human. But we can't think of any such differences that would be relevant to Ayer's conclusion. So we complete the evaluation as shown in Figure 8.5.

Ayer's Argument	Analogue: Ayer	Target: Other Humans	Degree of Similarity or/ Difference	Relevance
Basic points of similarity used as premises	Central nervous system basic to physiology of sensory experience of pain	Central nervous system basic to physiology of sensory experience of pain	High degree of similarity	Highly relevant to conclusion
Conclusion	Ayer experiences pain when undergoing dental work w/o anaesthetic	**Other people experience pain when undergoing dental work w/o anaesthetic**		
Differences				

FIGURE 8.4 Evaluating Ayer's Argument by Analogy II

Ayer's Argument	Analogue: Ayer	Target: Other Humans	Degree of Similarity or/ Difference	Relevance
Basic points of similarity used as premises	Central nervous system basic to physiology of sensory experience of pain	Central nervous system basic to physiology of sensory experience of pain	High degree of similarity	Highly relevant to conclusion
Conclusion	Ayer experiences pain when undergoing dental work w/o anaesthetic	**Other people experience pain when undergoing dental work w/o anaesthetic**		
Differences	Ayer was the author of *Language, Truth and Logic,* published in 1936	No other human being was the author of *Language, Truth and Logic,* published in 1936	True	Irrelevant

FIGURE 8.5 Evaluating Ayer's Argument by Analogy III

So Ayer's argument appears to be quite strong, despite its basis on a lone similarity.

APPLICATION EXERCISE 8.2 | **Evaluating an Argument by Analogy I**

Look at Peter Singer's analogous argument about nonhuman animals (argument 5 in Review Exercise 8.1). Using the previous example as a model, set up the form for evaluating Singer's argument by identifying the analogue, the target, the basic points of similarity, and the conclusion.

Singer's Argument	Analogue	Target	Degree of Similarity or Difference	Relevance
Basic points of similarity used as premises				
Conclusion				
Differences				

In this case, the analogue is humans and the target is nonhuman animals. The conclusion is that nonhuman animals have experiences of pain similar to those of humans. This inference rests on two basic points of similarity: similarity of neurophysiology and similarity in behavioral responses to stimuli.

APPLICATION EXERCISE 8.3 | **Evaluating an Argument by Analogy II**

Complete the evaluation of Singer's argument by assessing the degree and relevance of similarity in the premises and the degree and relevance of differences you can identify to Singer's conclusion.

Singer's Argument	Analogue: Humans	Target: Nonhuman Animals	Degree of Similarity or Difference	Relevance
Basic points of similarity used as premises	Central nervous system basic to physiology of sensory experience of pain	Central nervous system basic to physiology of sensory experience of pain		
	Expressive behavioral responses to sensory stimuli	Expressive behavioral responses to sensory stimuli		
Conclusion	Humans enjoy pleasure and suffer pain	**Nonhuman animals enjoy pleasure and suffer pain**		
Differences				

Here are our findings: To evaluate Singer's argument as an argument by analogy, we would first want to know whether the similarities Singer asserts are true. Do humans and nonhuman animals really have similar neurophysiology? It turns out that they do. How similar are human and nonhuman animals in terms of neurophysiology? In some cases, that is, with so-called higher animals, the similarity is extremely high in complex and sophisticated detail both physically and functionally. Next, do humans and nonhuman animals exhibit similar behavioral responses to stimuli? Again, the answer is "yes, to a remarkably high and complex degree of similarity in many cases." Next, we want to determine whether these similarities are relevant to the conclusion Singer is trying to draw. It seems that they are, because we have good theoretical grounds and empirical evidence to suppose that a body's neurophysiology is the central mechanism involved in an organism's sensory experience and similarly good theoretical and evidentiary grounds to connect behavioral manifestations to inner experience. So we would make the preliminary assessment in Figure 8.6.

At this point, we would want to determine whether there are significant relevant differences between the analogue and the target. And there are many differences between humans and other species. There are several, perhaps, that people might think relevant to Singer's conclusion. For example, Singer goes on in the essay from which the example was taken to consider the issue of language. There may be some controversy over whether humans are the only species of animal with the capacity to develop and use languages. But for illustration suppose that this difference genuinely holds true. The question is whether this is a relevant difference.

Singer's Argument	Analogue	Target	Degree of Similarity or/ Difference	Relevance
Basic points of similarity used as premises	Central nervous system basic to physiology of sensory experience of pain	Central nervous system basic to physiology of sensory experience of pain	High degree of similarity	Highly relevant to conclusion
	Expressive behavioral responses to sensory stimuli	Expressive behavioral responses to sensory stimuli	High degree of similarity	Highly relevant to conclusion
Conclusion	Humans enjoy pleasure and suffer pain	**Nonhuman animals enjoy pleasure and suffer pain**		
Differences				

FIGURE 8.6 Evaluating Singer's Argument by Analogy I

Singer argues that it is not relevant because we do not attribute pain to humans on the basis of linguistic behavior but rather on the basis of the sorts of behavior exhibited by other species of animal. So, on this basis, we judge Singer's argument to be, like Ayer's, quite strong (Figure 8.7).

REFUTATION BY ANALOGY

One use of analogy that deserves special mention is the refutation of arguments by comparison. In this strategy, the target is usually an argument (occasionally the thesis of an argument) and the goal is to discredit the target by showing that it is analogous to some other argument (or thesis) that is obviously weak or objectionable. In the following passage from *Alice in Wonderland*, Alice is refuted by the Mad Hatter and the March Hare. The Mad Hatter has told Alice, who has just said something illogical, that she should "say what she means."

> "I do," Alice hastily replied; "at least—at least I mean what I say—that's the same thing, you know."
>
> "Not the same thing a bit!" said the Hatter. "Why, you might just as well say that 'I see what I eat' is the same thing as 'I eat what I see'!"
>
> "You might just as well say," added the March Hare, "that 'I like what I get' is the same thing as 'I get what I like'!"[11]

Singer's Argument	Analogue	Target	Degree of Similarity or/ Difference	Relevance
Basic points of similarity used as premises	Central nervous system basic to physiology of sensory experience of pain	Central nervous system basic to physiology of sensory experience of pain	High degree of similarity	Highly relevant to conclusion
	Expressive behavioral responses to sensory stimuli	Expressive behavioral responses to sensory stimuli	High degree of similarity	Highly relevant to conclusion
Conclusion	Humans enjoy pleasure and suffer pain	**Nonhuman animals enjoy pleasure and suffer pain**		
Differences	Human beings have linguistic capacity	Nonhuman animals do not have linguistic capacity	Plausible, though open to question	Irrelevant to conclusion

FIGURE 8.7 Evaluating Singer's Argument by Analogy II

In Chapter 6 we used an example of refutation by logical analogy in presenting and explaining the concept of a formal fallacy when we compared the two arguments that follow:

(1) All Americans are humans.   (1) All men are human.

(2) All Californians are humans.   (2) All women are human.

∴ (3) All Californians are Americans.   ∴ (3) All women are men.

And we presented a strategy for demonstrating an argument to be formally fallacious by constructing a formally analogous argument, that is, one that follows an identical formal pattern but has obviously true premises and an obviously false conclusion.

APPLICATION EXERCISE 8.4 | **Term Project: Generalizations and Statistics**

Within the context of the issue you have been working on, identify areas where generalizations or statistics would be relevant. Identify reliable sources for such information. Pick one such application of inductive reasoning and design the sort of research program or experiment that would be likely to yield reliable results.

APPLICATION EXERCISE 8.5 | Term Project: Analogies

Take any position on the issue you have been working on and design an argument in support of that position based on an analogy. Then take an alternative or opposed position and design an argument in support of it based on an analogy.

GLOSSARY

analogue   an item used as a basis of comparison in an explanation or argument by analogy

analogy   a comparison

inductive generalization   a variety of inductive reasoning in which general conclusions are projected from a number of particular instances

margin of error   an estimate of the likelihood of error in the conclusion of an inductive inference

population   the set of instances about which general conclusions are projected in an inductive or statistical generalization

relative   admits of degrees, as applied to inferential security

relevance   in inductive reasoning, factors that might reasonably be thought to have something to do with the conclusion being inferred

sample   particular observed instances used in inductive or statistical generalizations

sample size   a measure of the number of particular observed instances relative to the population in an inductive or statistical generalization

statistical generalization   a variety of inductive reasoning in which trends or percentages observed in the sample are projected onto other instances or onto the population

target   an item about which conclusions are drawn or explanations are offered by analogy

ADDITIONAL EXERCISES

REVIEW EXERCISE 8.2 EVALUATING THE SAMPLE   Suppose we were to evaluate the sample in each of the following inductive generalizations. Check those among the listed dimensions that would in your opinion be relevant to the generalization and would need to be controlled to make the sample more representative. Compare your answers with those of your classmates. Try to resolve any points of disagreement rationally by explaining your answers to one another.

1. In Consumers' Union nationwide studies of new cars purchased over the last 10 years, Chrysler had a 30% lower frequency of repair than the other

manufacturers. So it's probably safe to assume that a new Dodge will be reliable.

- ☐ The color of the car
- ☐ The age of the principle driver of the car
- ☐ The price paid for the car
- ☐ The number of miles driven annually
- ☐ The size of the car
- ☐ The size of the owner's family
- ☐ The trim package
- ☐ The brand of gasoline used in the car

2. "Look! The first 10 people to come out of the theater are all smiling and laughing. I guess this is going to be a good show."

- ☐ The ages of the people
- ☐ The gender identities of the people
- ☐ The racial identities of the people
- ☐ The ethnic identities of the people
- ☐ The religious affiliations of the people
- ☐ The economic status of the people
- ☐ The political affiliations of the people
- ☐ The class status of the people

REVIEW EXERCISE 8.3 IDENTIFYING AND EXPLAINING ANALOGIES Identify and explain as many analogies as you can find in each of the following passages. For each analogy, specify the analogue and the target, as well as the purpose (argumentative, explanatory, entertaining, and so on), of the comparison.

1. "Well, thish-yer Smiley had rat-tarriers, and chicken cocks, and tom-cats, and all them kind of things, till you couldn't rest, and you couldn't fetch nothing for him to bet on but he'd match you. He ketched a frog one day, and took him home, and said he calculated to educate him; and so he never done nothing for three months but set in his back yard and learn that frog to jump. And you bet he did learn him, too. He'd give him a little punch behind, and the next minute you'd see that frog whirling in the air like a doughnut."[12]

2. "So we need a bit of theory to support, to guide, and to explain our evaluative intuitions. For theoretical purposes, we'll make a basic distinction between the structural features of an argument and the materials used in its construction. One way to understand this distinction is to think of an argument as a building. Suppose we are evaluating buildings; for example, suppose we're buying a house. Some houses are obviously and intuitively better built than others. We can tell intuitively that the White House is a stronger building than the outhouse. But we need a more systematic set of criteria to make reasonable decisions when houses are

more closely matched. Buildings are complicated, so there are many criteria relevant to evaluating buildings. That's why we would want to make the set of criteria systematic. The system gives us organization. One way to organize is to divide. And with buildings, a reasonable and powerful first distinction for purposes of evaluation would be between which materials are used and how those materials are put together—the design and the execution of the design. So in evaluating arguments we could look at design factors and materials factors. In this comparison (or analogy) the 'materials' are the premises of the argument and the 'design' is the plan according to which the premises are assembled in support of the conclusion."[13]

3. "Up to this point we've talked about accents and rests of the same length. But what do musicians like to do most with rhythms? Well, we like to do what everybody likes to do. We like to play. That's right. In basketball, when we first learned how to dribble, it was an achievement just to bounce the ball in a steady motion. You know, you could spend a long time just learning to bounce the ball in one unchanging rhythm. It might take two weeks to learn how to do that comfortably, or a month. But in order to to have fun playing, we have to vary the bounces with accents and rests. In a game you would want to fake out an opponent. You wouldn't dribble only at one speed, or in the same predictable rhythm. Sometimes you would go fast, sometimes a little slower, and then maybe real quick between your legs or behind your back. And then sometimes you'd stop dribbling and pass the ball. In a basketball game we dribble the ball to go from one point on the court to another, we hope closer to the basket, and of course we always want to dribble with imagination and style. If you're not going to have imagination and some type of style, it doesn't make sense to play. In music we play with rhythms from tiny fast ones to long slow ones, just like dribbling the ball."[14]

4. "When someone writes a piece of music, what he or she puts on the paper is roughly the equivalent of a recipe—in the sense that the recipe is not the food, only instructions for the preparation of the food. Unless you are very weird, you don't eat the recipe. If I write something on a piece of paper, I can't actually 'hear' it. I can conjure up visions of what the symbols on the page mean, and imagine a piece of music as it might sound in performance, but that sensation is nontransferable; it can't be shared or transmitted. It doesn't become a 'musical experience' in normal terms until 'the recipe' has been converted into wiggling air molecules. Music, in performance, is a type of sculpture. The air in the performance space is sculpted into something. This 'molecule-sculpture-over-time' is then 'looked at' by the ears of the listeners—or a microphone."[15]

5. "'We shall make no distinction,' the President proclaimed, 'between terrorists and countries that harbor terrorists.' So now we are bombing Afghanistan and

inevitably killing innocent people because it is in the nature of bombing (and I say this as a former Air Force bombardier) to be indiscriminate, to 'make no distinction.' We are committing terrorism in order to 'send a message' to terrorists. . . . War is terrorism, magnified a hundred times. Yes, let's find the perpetrators of the awful acts of September 11. We must find the guilty parties and prosecute them. But we shouldn't engage in indiscriminate retaliation. When a crime is committed by someone in a certain neighborhood, you don't destroy the neighborhood."[16]

6. "When we identify an argument as an enthymeme—when we determine, in other words, that its conclusion doesn't follow from its explicitly stated premises alone—we in effect sense a gap or hole in it. But we can be more specific than this. The hole has a shape that we can discern, to some extent at least, by paying close attention to what surrounds it—to the argument's conclusion and explicit premise or premises. Think of this as similar to searching for a missing piece in a jigsaw puzzle. You study closely the shapes and colors of the pieces that surround the one you're searching for. This helps you find the missing piece. When the puzzle is an incompletely stated argument and what you're searching for is a missing premise, you can guide yourself by paying close attention to what the conclusion and explicit premise or premises of the argument are about. This helps you gain a better sense of the shape of the hole or gap you're trying to fill, and so of the missing premise that can fill it."[17]

7. "In the past two decades, Ireland has gone from being one of the most economically backward countries in Western Europe to being one of the strongest: its growth rate has been roughly double that of the rest of Europe. There is no shortage of conventional explanations. But, as the Harvard economists David Bloom and David Canning suggest in their study 'Celtic Tiger,' of greater importance may have been a singular demographic fact. In 1979, restrictions on contraception that had been in place since Ireland's founding were lifted, and the birth rate began to fall. In 1970, the average Irishwoman had 3.9 children. By the mid-nineteen-nineties, that number was less than two. As a result, when the Irish children born in the nineteen-sixties hit the workforce, there weren't a lot of children in the generation just behind them. Ireland was suddenly free of the enormous social cost of supporting and educating and caring for a large dependent population. It was like a family of four in which, all of a sudden, the elder child is old enough to take care of her little brother and the mother can rejoin the workforce. Overnight, that family doubles its number of breadwinners and becomes much better off."[18]

■ **REVIEW EXERCISE 8.4 EVALUATING ARGUMENTS**   Evaluate each of the following analogy-based arguments using the tools and procedures outlined in this chapter.

1. Putting up a traffic light after last week's deadly accident is like locking the barn door after the horse has been stolen.

	Analogue	Target	Comment
Basic Points of Similarity Used as Premises			
Conclusion			
Differences			

2. "Last spring, when Arsenio Hall's new sitcom was yanked from the lineup after a handful of showings, the comic appeared on *The Late Show With Tom Snyder* and told the host that the show was being 'retooled.' This did not mean that Arsenio had been cancelled, he insisted, but only sent back to the shop for more work. Hall ingeniously explained that a flawed sitcom was like an aircraft, which was much easier to repair while parked on the ground than in mid-flight."[19]

	Analogue	Target	Comment
Basic Points of Similarity Used as Premises			
Conclusion			
Differences			

3. One of the most well-known instances of argument by analogy is the famous teleological argument for the existence of God. As formulated by the 18th-century theologian William Paley, the argument goes something like this:

Suppose we happened to find a watch lying on the ground in the woods, or on the moon. How could we explain it? Unlike a rock, which we could easily imagine to have just been lying there indefinitely, a watch, we would be forced to conclude, was the product of some intelligent designer, because no other explanation would be adequate to account for the marvelous degree to which the parts and features of the watch seem to be designed, adapted and coordinated for the purpose of telling time. But compare the watch to the natural universe or to organic phenomena in the natural universe such as the human eye. The human eye, like the watch, is a complex organ whose parts, like the parts of a watch, seems marvelously well adapted and coordinated for the purpose of enabling visual experience. So it is reasonable to suppose that the human eye, and other similar phenomena in nature, and indeed the entire natural universe, are the products of an intelligent designer: God.

	Analogue	Target	Comment
Basic Points of Similarity Used as Premises			
Conclusion			
Differences			

4. "Now if we survey the universe, so far as it falls under our knowledge, it bears a great resemblance to an animal or organized body, and seems actuated with a like principle of life and motion. A continual circulation of matter in it produces no disorder; a continual waste in every part is incessantly repaired; the closest sympathy is perceived throughout the entire system; and each part or member, in performing its proper offices, operates both to its own preservation and to that of the whole. The world, therefore, I infer, is an animal, and the Deity is the soul of the world, actuating it, and actuated by it"[20]

	Analogue	Target	Comment
Basic Points of Similarity Used as Premises			
Conclusion			
Differences			

RESEARCH ASSIGNMENT 8.1 FROM ANALOGY TO DISCOVERY   Although analogies never prove anything, they often suggest a possibility, a line of investigation, a hypothesis that might otherwise be overlooked. When Benjamin Franklin drew an analogy between electric sparks and lightning based on a number of observed similarities, he didn't thereby *prove* that lightning was a form of electricity. Only an experiment could establish that. But the analogy did lead to his famous kite-and-key experiment. Research the following important discoveries: What were the analogies that led to the following:

1. Archimedes' discovery that a body immersed in fluid loses in weight an amount equal to the weight of the fluid it displaces

2. Copernicus' theory of a sun-centered universe

3. Fleming's discovery of penicillin

NOTES

[1] Wynton Marsalis, *Marsalis on Music* (New York: Norton, 1995), p. 20.

[2] John Allen Paulos, *Innumeracy: Mathematical Illiteracy and Its Consequences* (New York: Hill and Wang, 1988), pp. 9–10.

[3] Thomas Reid, *Essays on the Intellectual Powers of Man,* essay 1, chapter 4.

[4] Alfred J. Ayer, "One's Knowledge of Other Minds," *Theoria* 19 (1953).

[5] P. J. O'Rourke, "Why I Believe What I Believe" *Rolling Stone* (July 13–27, 1995).

[6] Geoffrey Nunberg, *The Way We Talk Now* (Boston: Houghton Mifflin, 2001), p. 130.

[7] Martin J. Rees and Joseph Silk, "The Origin of Galaxies," *Scientific American* (August 1969), p. 81.

[8] Peter Singer, "Animal Liberation," *New York Review of Books,* April 5, 1973.

[9] Marsalis, *Marsalis on Music,* p. 26.

[10] Jeff Goodell, "Was It Global Warming? As the Planet Heats Up and Storms Grow Stronger, Katrina Could Be a Sign of the Coming Destruction," *Rolling Stone* 984 (October 6, 2005), p. 132.

[11] Lewis Carroll, *Alice's Adventures in Wonderland,* in *The Complete Works of Lewis Carroll* (New York: Random House, 1936), chapter 7.

[12] Mark Twain, "The Celebrated Jumping Frog of Calaveras County."

[13] Joel Rudinow and Vincent Barry, *Invitation to Critical Thinking,* 6th edition (Belmont, CA: Wadsworth, 2007), p. 159–160.

[14] Marsalis, *Marsalis on Music,* pp. 26–27.

[15] Frank Zappa, "All About Music," in *The Real Frank Zappa Book* (New York: Poseidon, 1989), p. 161.

[16] Howard Zinn, "The Odd Way of Thinking," *The Progressive,* November 2001, p. 8.

[17] Rudinow and Barry, *Invitation to Critical Thinking,* p. 122.

[18] Malcolm Gladwell, "The Risk Pool: What's Behind Ireland's Economic Miracle—and G.M.'s Financial Crisis?" *The New Yorker,* August 28, 2006, p. 31.

[19] Joe Queenan, "The Retooling Channel," *TV Guide* (July 26–August 1, 1997).

[20] David Hume, *Dialogues Concerning Natural Religion,* I. A. Selby-Bigge (ed.) (Oxford, UK: Clarendon Press, 1850), p. 103.

CHAPTER 9

Evaluating Inductive Arguments II: Hypothetical Reasoning and Burden of Proof

> When you believe in things that you don't understand, then you suffer. . . . Superstition ain't the way. —STEVIE WONDER

As we explained in Chapter 8, the evaluation of inductive inferences is based on assessing their relative security, which depends on a number of variables according to the *type* of inductive reasoning involved. In this chapter we explore two more important and common categories or types of inductive reasoning: hypothetical reasoning and burden of proof arguments.

PRESUMPTION AND THE BURDEN OF PROOF

Burden of proof reasoning is a kind of inductive reasoning useful in resolving disputes that cannot be compromised or reconciled on a win–win basis—in other words, it is used to resolve disputes between two parties or sides in which a winner must be declared. There are many situations like this, often arising in legal contexts. One of the most obvious and familiar examples of burden of

"Let me tell you, folks—I've been around long enough to develop an instinct for these things, and my client is innocent or I'm very much mistaken."

proof reasoning is the **presumption of innocence.** In many of the world's legal systems, for example, in the American system of jurisprudence, the accused is presumed innocent unless and until the prosecution meets its burden of proof. The party (or side) with the burden of proof is the party that has to produce the argument. It is convenient to think of this as a procedural rule in a structured contest according to which one side is assigned the role or position of offense and the other side plays defense. If the side that bears the burden of proof fails to meet its obligation, the issue is decided in favor of the other side. Thus in American criminal law, the prosecution bears the burden of proof and has to make its case beyond a reasonable doubt. Meanwhile, the defense need not make any argument of its own beyond simply attacking the argument of the prosecution and enjoying the benefit of the doubt.

In most real-life situations, we find that the procedural rules are already established and we just need to be competently informed of what they are. Thus as jurors, we are instructed by the judge as to what the rules are and how to weigh the evidence and arguments presented to us in court as we deliberate to a verdict. As plaintiffs and defendants, we will ordinarily be advised by our attorneys what our best argumentative strategy may be. But thinking of the burden of proof in this way (as a procedural rule) raises the question of how we decide where—on which side of any given issue—the burden of proof properly belongs. How is the presumption of innocence or any other procedural rule of this kind justified? Why, for example, does the prosecution have the burden of proof in American criminal law? Why not the defense? Why shouldn't the accused have to prove his or her innocence? A similar question concerns the size or weight of that burden. For example, the burden of proof is heavier in a criminal trial than in a civil trial. In a criminal trial, the prosecution must prove guilt beyond a reasonable doubt (a deliberately vague but nevertheless high standard of proof). In a civil trial, the plaintiff (the one bringing the lawsuit or making the complaint) has only the obligation of making a *prima facie* case, which then shifts the burden of proof onto the defense. We can imagine many alternatives to such arrangements— many ways of formulating the procedural rules.

Approach these questions at the general theoretical level. For example, if someone suggested that you invest a small sum of money in a mutual fund, you might want some evidence that the fund is well and profitably managed but you'd want *more* evidence of the security of your investment if it represented your entire life savings. In general, the greater the risk of error—and the higher the cost associated with being wrong—the heavier the burden of proof. Thus the burden of proof is placed and the standard of proof is set where they "reasonably belong," which is to say where reasonable explanation and argument will support. Thus the placement and apportionment of the burden of proof, like many of the concepts you have already encountered in this study, is governed by a number of general rules of thumb. One such rule is based on the concept of plausibility (as introduced in Chapter 4). The less plausible the arguer's position, the heavier the burden of proof. Another general rule, derived from the discipline and traditions of rhetoric, has to do with the distinction between the affirmative and the negative positions in a debate. The affirmative side in a debate has the burden of proof. This is because it is generally so much harder to prove the negative. For example, if people believe in the healing power of the mind, the therapeutic efficacy of marijuana, or the existence of intelligent extraterrestrial life, they are expected to produce the evidence. All the affirmative side would need to do to prove conclusively that extraterrestrial intelligent life exists would be to bring forward one specimen. You can see how much harder it would be to prove *conclusively* that extraterrestrial intelligent life does not exist. So in fairness, the general rule is to place the burden of proof on the affirmative position in a dispute. Fairness is also behind the placement of the burden of proof on the prosecution in American criminal and civil law. In civil law, it seems fair to place the burden of proof initially on the party making the complaint but then to have it shift to the other party if there's enough evidence to support reasonable suspicion. In criminal law, the accused is (usually) an individual, whereas the prosecution is the "people" acting collectively through the agency of the government. The stakes are almost always some form of punishment. Fairness seems to call for the prosecution to produce conclusive proof of guilt. There is another rationale for placing the burden of proof on the prosecution. Consider the question of how justice could be miscarried. It seems that there are only two kinds of miscarriage of justice: where a guilty party gets off without penalty and where an innocent party is penalized. Which of these two kinds of miscarriage of justice is worse? Some legal traditions, the American system, for example, are based on the idea that it's worse to punish an innocent person than to let a guilty person go unpunished.

DISCUSSION TOPIC 9.1 | **Burden of Proof**

Not everyone agrees with this idea. Is it worse to punish an innocent person than to let a guilty person go unpunished? Or is it the other way around? Or are the two equally bad? An interesting exercise would be to consider the arguments that might be made on all sides.

REASONING HYPOTHETICALLY

A subtle and complex but crucial variety of inductive reasoning consists of reasoning from facts or observations to explanatory hypotheses. An **explanation** is an idea or set of ideas that succeeds in reducing or eliminating puzzlement. An "explanatory hypothesis" is an idea or set of ideas put forward for that purpose. The word **hypothesis** means supposition or conjecture. It comes originally from the Greek word *thesis,* which means an idea proposed or laid down for consideration, and the Greek root *hypo-,* which means under. Here the "under" is meant to indicate that the proposed idea is under investigation.

As the terms suggest, this variety of inductive reasoning, called **hypothetical reasoning,** is used primarily in trying to better understand the many puzzling things there are in life—the many things that prompt the question, "Why?" Why is the water salty in the Pacific Ocean but not in Lake Tahoe? Why do so many incumbents continue to win reelection despite overwhelming anti-incumbent sentiment in the polls? Why does the Dow Jones index continue rising when fundamental economic indicators such as the unemployment rate indicate a recession? Why does the sound of an approaching train whistle appear to drop in pitch as the train passes? We draw inferences to explanations constantly in all sorts of situations. When we do, just as when we generalize, we risk error—that is, we reason inductively.

A simple example can illustrate the general structure of inferences to explanatory hypotheses. A customs inspector is examining the contents of a crate. In it she finds several plastic bags of white powder. What is it? Heroin? Cocaine? Flour? She tests it by tasting it and finds that it is sweet, identifying it as powdered sugar. We might represent her reasoning in the form of the argument or inference:

This tastes sweet.
—————————————
∴ This is sugar.

In identifying the powder as sugar, the customs inspector has not reasoned deductively. The conclusion does not follow deductively from the premise. But the inference from the taste of the substance to its classification is a reasonable induction. Although there remains room for doubt about the truth of the conclusion, the premise makes it reasonable to suppose that the conclusion is true. What makes the inference reasonable is the idea that *if the conclusion were true, it would explain the truth of the premise, and if the conclusion were not true, it would make the premise more puzzling.* In other words, the observed fact that the substance tastes sweet can be best explained by assuming the substance is sugar. This is the general structure of inferences to explanatory hypotheses, or hypothetical reasoning.

The importance of hypothetical reasoning lies in its capacity to extend or expand our knowledge of the world. Because hypothetical reasoning always takes us beyond what we already know, it always involves the risk of error. Just as with inductive generalizations, the strength of an inference to an explanatory hypothesis is essentially a matter of how well the risk of error is managed or controlled. There is no way to manage the risk of error in hypothetical reasoning on an inference-by-inference basis. To manage the risk of error in hypothetical reasoning, we must increasingly engage in it—in effect, using hypothetical reasoning to evaluate hypothetical reasoning. More precisely, the risk of error is measured and managed in terms of the relative plausibility of competing explanatory hypotheses, their relative explanatory power, and the degree to which a given hypothesis can be supported by experimental evidence.

PLAUSIBILITY

In Chapter 4 we introduced the idea of plausibility as a measure of how well we think an idea is likely to survive critical scrutiny. How well would the idea hold up if we were to devise strenuous tests designed to expose any falsity in the idea? A plausible idea is one that we think would hold up well. An implausible idea is one that we think would not hold up well. Neither plausibility nor implausibility is absolute. They both admit of degrees. Some claims are more plausible than others. A good place to look for examples to illustrate this point (implausible as this may sound) is in tabloids like the *National Enquirer.* In these publications you will find a steady diet of highly implausible claims, like "Confederate Flag Sighted on Bottom of UFO" and "Elvis Presley Planning Return to United States from Seclusion in Brazil to Expose His Death as Hoax," and many claims that are somewhat less implausible, like "Hypnosis Cures Urge to Smoke." You'll see these alongside a few claims that might be quite a bit more plausible, like "Madonna Has New Love Interest" or "Royal Family Locked in Power Struggle over Engagement of Prince William." Moreover, our estimates of a claim's plausibility or implausibility are not static. Rather, they are subject to adjustment in accordance with new incoming information. What may appear initially to be a plausible idea may, on further investigation, seem more and more or less and less plausible. And plausibility is only loosely correlated with truth. A plausible idea may well turn out to be false. And there are many cases throughout history of initially implausible ideas that have nonetheless been confirmed as true. *In general, the more plausible the explanatory hypothesis, the stronger the inference.* Here we are interested in *relative* plausibility. We need to know how the explanatory hypothesis under investigation compares with others. Is there another hypothesis that is just as or even more likely to survive critical scrutiny? If not, that strengthens the inference.

CRITICAL THINKING TIP 9.1 | **Plausibility I**

The More Plausible the Explanatory Hypothesis, the Stronger the Inference

---

For example, remember the customs inspector. As soon as she tastes the powder, she can consider the explanatory hypothesis that the powder is sugar. This is not the only hypothesis that might account for the observed fact that the powder tastes sweet. It could be a new derivative of coca, genetically engineered to have a taste indistinguishable from powdered sugar so as to escape detection as a variety of cocaine. This hypothesis, if true, would account for the observed fact that the powder tastes sweet, and it is certainly within the realm of the possible, but it is much less plausible than the simple powdered-sugar hypothesis.

Here's another hypothesis that might account for the observed fact that the powder tastes sweet. Perhaps the powder is cocaine and the customs inspector has suddenly developed "taste blindness" so that cocaine and powdered sugar taste identical to her. Again, this hypothesis, if true, would account for the observed fact that the powder tastes sweet. This hypothesis, too, is within the realm of the possible. But like the sweet cocaine hypothesis, it is less plausible than the simple powdered-sugar hypothesis.

An interesting theoretical problem arises when you compare the taste blindness hypothesis and the sweet cocaine hypothesis against each other. Is one of them more plausible than the other? If so, which one? Or are they equally implausible? How do we tell? In this case, it doesn't matter a lot because there's a more plausible option available in the simple powdered-sugar hypothesis. But what if we had to choose between competing hypotheses that seemed equally plausible—or equally implausible? Or what if we couldn't agree which of several competing hypotheses was the most plausible—or the least plausible? Fortunately, plausibility is not the only standard we have to appeal to.

DISCUSSION TOPIC 9.2 | **Plausibility II**

In July 2004, the official findings of the National Commission of Terrorist Attacks on the United States (the 9/11 Commission) were published. A year later, a growing 9/11 truth movement is challenging these official findings, alleging crucial omissions, inconsistencies, and distortions in the official report. Assuming (for the sake of the exercise) that there are indeed crucial omissions and inconsistencies in the official report, rank the following claims in descending order of plausibility. Compare your rankings with those of your classmates. Try to resolve any points of disagreement by explaining your answers to one another.

	A false account of events leading up to and including the 9/11 attacks was officially commissioned by the U.S. government.
	A false account of events leading up to and including the 9/11 attacks was officially accepted as true by the U.S. government.
	The official account covers up for the fact that officials and agencies of the government were expecting the 9/11 attacks but did nothing to stop them.
	The official account covers up for the fact that officials and agencies of the government were expecting something like the 9/11 attacks but did nothing to stop them.
	The official account covers up for the fact that the Bush White House was involved in the planning of the 9/11 attacks.
	The official account covers up for the fact that officials and agencies of the government were involved in planning the 9/11 attacks.
	The official account covers up for the fact that the Bush White House was expecting the 9/11 attacks but did nothing to stop them.
	The official account covers up for the fact that the Bush White House was expecting something like the 9/11 attacks but did nothing to stop them.

EXPLANATORY POWER

Remember that an explanatory hypothesis is an idea or set of ideas put forward to reduce or eliminate puzzlement. And a good explanation is one that succeeds in reducing or eliminating puzzlement. The **explanatory power** of a given hypothesis is the capacity it has to reduce or eliminate puzzlement. *In general, the greater the explanatory power of a given hypothesis, the stronger the inference.* Here, as with plausibility, we are interested in *relative* explanatory power. We need to know how the explanatory hypothesis under investigation compares with others. Is there another hypothesis that would explain the observed fact or facts in the premise or premises equally well or better? If not, that strengthens the inference. Are there other observed facts besides the ones in the premises that the hypothesis explains better than competing hypotheses? If so, that too strengthens the inference.

CRITICAL THINKING TIP 9.2 | **Explanatory Power I**

The Greater the Explanatory Power of a Given Hypothesis, the Stronger the Inference

For example, consider the following case: Neighbors have discovered the body of a well-known but reclusive novelist. The homicide inspector arrives at the scene. The body of the deceased is slumped over the typewriter in which there is a sheet of paper with what appears to be an unfinished suicide note. Beside the body is a hypodermic syringe. Traces of white powder are recovered from the table beside the typewriter. The autopsy establishes the cause of death as heroin overdose and fixes the time of death around 3 a.m. A psychiatric history of the deceased reveals several bouts of depression over a 10-year period and two previous suicide attempts. One plausible hypothesis, the obvious one, is that the novelist committed suicide by injecting himself with heroin and lost consciousness while at the typewriter composing the suicide note. Still, the inspector is puzzled. She cannot account for the fact that the typewriter, an IBM Selectric, is switched off. Nor can she account for the fact that neither the reading lamp nor the overhead light was on in the room at the time the body was discovered. If the novelist died at 3 a.m. while typing, how did he turn off the typewriter and all of the lights?

What the inspector needs now is an explanatory hypothesis with greater explanatory power. Perhaps the novelist was murdered by someone who tried to make the murder look like a suicide. Perhaps the murderer was surprised at the scene of the crime by approaching footsteps and, to discourage the approaching party from intruding upon the scene and discovering the crime, turned out the lights and the typewriter. This hypothesis, although not nearly as plausible as the suicide hypothesis, nevertheless has greater explanatory power, because it accounts for everything the suicide hypothesis accounts for plus the typewriter and lights being switched off.

DISCUSSION TOPIC 9.3 | Explanatory Power II

One of the strongest arguments that can be made in support of Newtonian mechanics as a general description of the physical universe is the awesome explanatory power that Newton's laws of motion appear to have as hypotheses. They can be used to successfully explain such a variety of phenomena—from the motion of the tides to the gathering of dust on horizontal surfaces, the falling of leaves, the behavior of billiard balls, and the motion of the planets. A similarly strong argument is made by those who believe that everything in the world is animated by spirits. Yet scientists are more fully persuaded of Newtonian physics than they are of spiritual animism. Can you explain why?

AND SPEAKING OF: | Explanatory Power

"According to the official account, the Twin Towers collapsed due to the impact of the airliners plus the intense heat of the resulting fires. . . . [However,] the facts about the fire seem to rule out any version of the official account according to which each tower had hot, widespread, long-lasting fires. . . . Another count against the fire theory is the likelihood that, even if the Twin Towers had been engulfed in raging fires, they would not have collapsed. . . . Third, [the official account does not] do justice to the fact that the towers collapsed 'within ten seconds' . . . almost free-fall speed. . . . Still another fact about the collapse of the towers that counts against the fire theory is the fact that the South Tower collapsed first. . . . Although the South Tower was struck 17 minutes later than the North Tower, it collapsed 29 minutes earlier. . . . This surprising fact would perhaps not create a problem if the fire in the South Tower had been much bigger. . . . However, the fire in the South Tower was actually much smaller. Upon hearing that one tower took almost twice as long [to collapse] as the other one; therefore, one would assume that that was the South Tower. And yet the opposite was the case. This complete reversal of expectations suggests that the collapse of these buildings was caused by something other than the fires. And that is, of course, what the critics maintain. Their alternative explanation is that the collapse was an example of a controlled demolition, based on explosives that had been placed throughout the building. This theory, point out its advocates, can explain all the facts discussed thus far. . . . There are, furthermore, some additional facts about the collapse of the Twin Towers that seem explainable only by the demolition theory. One of these is the fact that each collapse produced a lot of fine dust or powder, which upon analysis proved to consist primarily of gypsum and concrete."[1]

DISCUSSION TOPIC 9.4 | Explanatory Power III

Here again are the theories mentioned in Discussion Topic 9.2. This time, rank the theories in descending order of explanatory power. Compare your rankings with those of your classmates. Try to resolve any points of disagreement by explaining your answers to one another.

	A false account of events leading up to and including the 9/11 attacks was officially commissioned by the U.S. government.
	A false account of events leading up to and including the 9/11 attacks was officially accepted as true by the U.S. government.
	The official account covers up for the fact that officials and agencies of the government were expecting the 9/11 attacks but did nothing to stop them.
	The official account covers up for the fact that officials and agencies of the government were expecting something like the 9/11 attacks but did nothing to stop them.
	The official account covers up for the fact that the Bush White House was involved in the planning of the 9/11 attacks.
	The official account covers up for the fact that officials and agencies of the government were involved in planning the 9/11 attacks.
	The official account covers up for the fact that the Bush White House was expecting the 9/11 attacks but did nothing to stop them.
	The official account covers up for the fact that the Bush White House was expecting something like the 9/11 attacks but did nothing to stop them.

INFERENCE TO THE BEST EXPLANATION

In some cases of hypothetical reasoning both criteria, plausibility and explanatory power, decisively weigh in favor of the same hypothesis. In such cases, it is reasonable to think that the hypothesis is correct. We call this **inductive inference to the best explanation.**

AND SPEAKING OF: | **The Best Explanation**

In the past two decades, Ireland has gone from being one of the most economically backward countries in Western Europe to being one of the strongest: its growth rate has been roughly double that of the rest of Europe. There is no shortage of conventional explanations. But, as the Harvard economists David Bloom and David Canning suggest in their study "Celtic Tiger," of greater importance may have been a singular demographic fact. In 1979, restrictions on contraception that had been in place since Ireland's founding were lifted, and the birth rate began to fall. In 1970, the average Irishwoman had 3.9 children. By the mid-nineteen-nineties, that number was less than two. As a result, when the Irish children born in the nineteen-sixties hit the workforce, there weren't a lot of children in the generation just behind them. Ireland was suddenly free of the enormous social cost of supporting and educating and caring for a large dependent population. It was like a family of four in which, all of a sudden, the elder child is old enough to take care of her little brother and the mother can rejoin the workforce. Overnight, that family doubles its number of breadwinners and becomes much better off.[2]

However, just as with plausibility, a theoretical problem arises in connection with explanatory power when we have to compare competing hypotheses that seem equally powerful or when we can't agree which of several competing hypotheses is the most powerful. Just as with the earlier problem, we can appeal to the plausibility standard when the explanatory power standard is not decisive. But we're left with the problem of what to do when competing hypotheses seem to measure up equally in both areas. And there is another theoretical problem. In the deceased novelist example, the murder hypothesis is less plausible but more powerful as an explanatory hypothesis. This raises questions: How do we determine the strength of a hypothetical inference when our standards conflict? Does explanatory power outweigh plausibility? Or is it the other way around? Or does it depend? Maybe explanatory power outweighs plausibility when the explanatory power gap is bigger than the plausibility gap, and vice versa. It would be nice if there were good answers to these questions that were both simple and straightforward. But as far as we know, the best approach to resolving any of these problems is just to test hypotheses experimentally.

TESTING HYPOTHESES

The word "hypothesis" means an idea (or set of ideas) under investigation. To investigate hypotheses is to search for experimental evidence relevant to their truth or falsity. And the scientific method for doing this boils down to first using the hypothesis under investigation to predict things and then seeing whether or not the predictions turn out to be true. *If what the hypothesis predicts turns out to be true, it counts in favor of, or confirms, the hypothesis. If what the hypothesis predicts turns out not to be true, it counts against, or disconfirms, the hypothesis.*

AND SPEAKING OF: | **Testing Hypotheses**

Do you remember the example of the defective computer disks we used in this Chapter 8 to illustrate inductive generalization? Well, a funny thing happened when we were writing that particular section of the book. You may find this hard to believe, but just as we were putting the finishing touches on that section, the computer froze and the message "Disk Error #10" came up in the dialog box. We tried saving the document. No way. About a month's worth of work was gone, or so it seemed. It took the next week or so and a data recovery expert to return us to where we had been before Disk Error #10 zapped us. As you can probably imagine, quite a few thoughts flashed through our minds under the circumstances, one of which was this: "That's one heck of a coincidence! Never before have we been zapped by 'Disk Error #10,' or any other disk error for that matter, and for it to happen at this particular moment, when what's going on the disk is a discussion of defective disks! I wonder if the computer is playing a conscious joke on us?" Has your computer ever behaved in such a way that you thought it might be doing so consciously and deliberately? What kind of experiments can you think of to try to confirm or disconfirm such an idea?

For example, go back to the customs inspector's first hypothesis, that the white powder is sugar. What else do we know about sugar, besides its sweetness, that we could use to test this hypothesis? We know that sugar is soluble in water. So using the hypothesis, along with this knowledge, we might predict that the powder will dissolve in water. Now if we place the powder in water and it does dissolve, this counts as evidence confirming the hypothesis that the powder is indeed sugar. If we place the powder in water and it does not dissolve, this counts as evidence disconfirming the hypothesis that the powder is sugar. **Confirming evidence** and **disconfirming evidence** vary in strength according to the strength of the prediction involved. *The more certain the prediction, the stronger the evidence. In testing hypotheses, we should search for both confirming and disconfirming evidence.*

In quite a few cases we may expect to find evidence of both kinds. For example, in the case of the deceased novelist there is some evidence that confirms the suicide hypothesis and some evidence that disconfirms it. Naturally, we would be interested in the relative weight of the evidence for and against a given hypothesis. At first there seems to be more evidence in favor of the suicide hypothesis than there is against it. But when the disconfirming evidence first emerges, the homicide inspector quite correctly becomes suspicious. She not only begins to consider other hypotheses but also begins to focus her investigation specifically on searching for more evidence disconfirming the suicide hypothesis. Why does she proceed in this way instead of simply concluding that the suicide hypothesis is correct because there is more confirming evidence than disconfirming evidence? The homicide inspector is following the general principle that *disconfirming evidence weighs more heavily than confirming evidence.*

CRITICAL THINKING TIP 9.3 | Confirming and Disconfirming Evidence

Disconfirming Evidence Weighs More Heavily Than Confirming Evidence

---

Why does disconfirming evidence outweigh confirming evidence? Again, consider the customs inspector and the white powder. To test the sugar hypothesis, we derived the prediction that the powder will dissolve in water. So if it does, we have confirming evidence; otherwise, we have disconfirming evidence. Confirming evidence does not completely verify the hypothesis. But notice that disconfirming evidence completely refutes it. Here's why. The prediction that the powder will dissolve takes the form of the hypothetical statement:

> If the hypothesis that the powder is sugar is correct, then the powder will dissolve in water.

When the test confirms the hypothesis, what we observe is, in effect, the consequent of this hypothetical statement coming true:

> The powder dissolves in water.

You'll remember that from these two statements we cannot validly deduce the conclusion that the powder is sugar. If we simply inferred this as a conclusion we would be committing the fallacy of affirming the consequent. This makes sense when you consider that there may be other white, powdered substances (like artificial sweeteners) that taste sweet and dissolve in water. Nevertheless, the combination of the two statements does, in this sort of situation, provide relevant although not conclusive evidence in support of the hypothesis under investigation. On the other hand, when the test disconfirms the hypothesis, what we observe is, in effect, the negation of the consequent coming true:

> The powder does not dissolve in water.

You'll remember that from the preceding statement and the hypothesis we can validly deduce the conclusion that the powder is not sugar by modus tollens. This is why disconfirming evidence is stronger than confirming evidence and why this inferential method is often referred to as the **hypothetical deductive method.**

An interesting application of the principle that disconfirming evidence outweighs confirming evidence generates an additional form of confirming evidence. If we search thoroughly for disconfirming evidence and find none, that in itself constitutes a kind of confirming evidence. This is sometimes referred to as **indirect confirmation.** Every *unsuccessful* attempt to falsify a hypothesis strengthens it.

This is why scientists try so hard to disprove their hypotheses. Every time they fail, the hypothesis succeeds. And if they succeed, they learn something.

I love unexpected results in medical research because they are always the opening chapter of an interesting story. The absolute best ones are when we uncover our own ignorance. — DR. MICHAEL CARLSTON

APPLICATION EXERCISE 9.1 | Science and Foreign Policy

Are sound principles of scientific reasoning applicable in planning foreign policy? Here is a strategic prediction made by Undersecretary of Defense Paul Wolfowitz, followed by a relevant data published by the Associated Press 3 years later. In your own words, state the predictions made by Wolfowitz and compare these predictions with the evidence cited in the Associated Press story.

Undersecretary of Defense Paul Wolfowitz, March 27, 2003:

> There's a lot of money to pay for this that doesn't have to be U.S. taxpayer money, and it starts with the assets of the Iraqi people . . . and on a rough recollection, the oil revenues of that country could bring between $50 and $100 billion over the course of the next two or three years. . . . We're dealing with a country that can really finance its own reconstruction, and relatively soon.

Associated Press, August 17, 2006:

> Iraq has doubled the money allocated for importing oil products in August and September to tackle the country's worst fuel shortage since Saddam Hussein's 2003 ouster, a senior Iraqi official said Thursday. Even though Iraq has the world's third-largest proven oil reserves, it is forced to depend on imports because of an acute shortage of refined products such as gasoline, kerosene and cooking gas.

WRITING ASSIGNMENT 9.1 | Testing Hypotheses

The following is an argument from businessman (and former presidential candidate) H. Ross Perot. Write a short essay in which you explain Perot's argument using the concepts discussed earlier. What hypotheses is Perot considering? What evidence does he present? Explain how the evidence is being used by Perot to confirm or disconfirm the hypotheses he's considering.

> We have unfairly blamed the American worker for the poor quality of our products. The unsatisfactory quality is the result of poor design and engineering—not poor assembly. If you take a car made in Japan by Japanese workers and place it alongside a Japanese car made in a U.S. plant by U.S. workers (led by Japanese executives) there is no difference in quality. The Honda cars made in this country by U.S. workers are of such high quality that Honda intends to export them. Obviously the American worker is not the problem. The problem is failure of leadership.

CAUSAL REASONING

One of the most widespread and important applications of hypothetical inductive reasoning has to do with figuring out how things work—determining the causes and effects of things. Why is the left channel of the stereo intermittently fuzzy and distorted? What is causing that little clicking noise at 40 miles per hour? What will the environmental, psychological, and social consequences of the development of virtual reality technology be? These are typical of the kind of causal reasoning problems we encounter so often in so many aspects of our lives. But reasoning about causes and effects is tricky. First, as the 18th-century Scottish philosopher David Hume pointed out, we never directly observe causal relationships. We have to infer them. Next, we can never infer them with deductive certainty. Because the evidence for a causal relationship is always indirect, there will always be some room for doubt when we infer a cause. In other words, we must reason inductively about them. Finally, reasoning about causes using simple inductive generalization turns out to be unreliable because inductive generalization by itself provides no basis for distinguishing between a causal relationship and a mere coincidence.

MILL'S METHOD OF AGREEMENT

The 19th-century English philosopher John Stuart Mill, best known for his work in moral and political philosophy, also made significant contributions to inductive logic, particularly in its applications to causal reasoning. Mill spelled out a number of guidelines—extensions of the preceding evaluative principles for inductive generalization—designed to make reasoning about causes and effects more reliable. These guidelines, often referred to as **Mill's methods,** are widely respected and followed as part of what we now call the scientific method. Mill's **method of agreement** is a variation of simple inductive generalization. It consists of seeking out some common antecedent condition in all cases of the effect whose cause we are trying to determine. It is based on the (reasonable) assumption that *the cause will be present in every instance in which the effect occurs.* Thus if we can identify some common antecedent condition, it is a likely candidate for the cause. For example, suppose that certain people start showing a strange new set of debilitating symptoms in several major cities around the same time. Symptoms include severe intestinal cramps, diarrhea, vomiting, respiratory congestion, severe headaches, and sudden loss of vision. What is the cause of the strange new disease? Right away we would want to know what these people have in common that might account for their symptoms. We know they live in different parts of the world. Suppose that no two individuals live within 500 miles of each other, that they range in age from 5 to 75 years old, that some of them are male and some are female, and that they have no common occupation. Now if we were to discover that all of the people

Instance	Antecedent Conditions							Effect
1	A	B		D	E	F		s
2	A		C		E	F	G	s
3		B		D	E	F	G	s
4			C	D	E	F		s
5	A	B				F		s
6				D		F	G	s
7						F		s
8	A	B	C	D	E	F	G	s
9	A	B				F		s
10			C			F	G	s

FIGURE 9.1 Mill's Method of Agreement

suffering from these symptoms had traveled during the month of June to a particular vacation spot (call it Fantasy Island), then we might suppose that the cause of the symptoms is related in some way to vacationing on Fantasy Island in June. Figure 9.1 illustrates the method of agreement. Let the 10 instances represent the 10 individual cases under investigation, the letter s represent the effect of suffering from the symptoms, and the letters A, B, C, D, E, F, and G represent a range of antecedent conditions, with F representing having vacationed on Fantasy Island in June.

That all symptom sufferers vacationed on Fantasy Island in June does not prove (deductively) a causal connection. But it does make it reasonable to suppose that such a causal relationship exists, and that is all we can expect from an inductive inference. If having vacationed on Fantasy Island were the only common factor we could find among all symptom sufferers, we could be even more confident of a causal connection. In general, the more isolated the common antecedent condition, the more likely it is to be causally related to the effect.

CRITICAL THINKING TIP 9.4 | Mill's Method of Agreement

In General, the More Isolated the Common Antecedent Condition, the More Likely It Is to Be Causally Related to the Effect

MILL'S METHOD OF DIFFERENCE

Any collection of individuals will have not one but many different antecedent conditions in common, most of which will turn out not to have any causal connection with the effect we are seeking to understand. In this example, having been on Fantasy Island in June means having not just one but many things in common: exposure to common sources of food and water; exposure to the full range of substances and organisms present in the environment, including the other vacationers; and so on. So we need a way of narrowing the field—eliminating some of the many candidates we're likely to identify using the method of agreement.

For this purpose, Mill formulated the **method of difference.** This method is based on the reasonable assumption that *the cause will be absent from every instance in which the effect does not occur.* To continue with the example, suppose that we obtain a list of all of the people who traveled to Fantasy Island in June. It turns out that some of them have not suffered any of the symptoms we're investigating. So we would want to know what differences there are between these people and the symptom sufferers. Now suppose we discover that the Fantasy Island vacationers who did not become sick also did not go swimming. This would suggest that the cause of the symptoms has something to do with swimming.

Figure 9.2 illustrates the method of difference. Let the 12 instances represent the 12 individuals who vacationed on Fantasy Island in June, the letter *s* represent the effect of suffering from the symptoms, and the letters *L, M, N, O, P, R,* and *S* represent a range of activities—attending the luau, beach volleyball, cycling, drinking rum, and so on—with *S* representing swimming.

Instance	Antecedent Conditions							Effect
1	L	M	N	O	P	R	S	s
2	L		N	O	P		S	s
3	L	M	N	O	P		S	s
4		M		O	P	R	S	s
5	L	M	N		P	R	S	s
6	L	M	N	O	P	R	S	s
7	L	M		O		R	S	s
8			N	O	P		S	s
9	L		N	O	P	R	S	s
10	L	M		O	P	R	S	s
11	L	M	N	O	P	R	—	—
12	L	M	N	O	P		—	—

FIGURE 9.2 Mill's Method of Difference

Like the method of agreement, the method of difference is a variation of simple inductive generalization. Instead of looking for a correlation between instances of the effect and some common antecedent condition, here we are looking for a correlation between the *absence* of the effect and the *absence* of an antecedent condition. Like the method of agreement, the method of difference is not conclusive. The discovery of such a correlation—in this example, between not having gone swimming and not suffering the symptoms—does not prove (deductively) that the symptoms and swimming are causally related, but it does make it reasonable to suppose that they are. If having gone swimming were the only difference we could find between the symptom sufferers and the vacationers who did not become sick, we could be even more confident of a causal connection. In general, the more isolated the difference, the more likely it is to be causally related to the effect.

CRITICAL THINKING TIP 9.5 | **Mill's Method of Difference**

In General, the More Isolated the Difference, the More Likely It Is to Be Causally Related to the Effect

---

Because the method of agreement and the method of difference each enhance the reliability of inductive inferences about causal relationships when used separately, it is reasonable to suppose that using them in the same investigation (as in the example) would further strengthen the inductive inference to a causal relationship. In other words, if some antecedent condition is common to all instances of the effect whose cause is under investigation *and* absent from instances in which the effect is also absent, that makes a causal connection more likely.

MILL'S METHOD OF RESIDUES

All of Mill's methods discussed so far have been applications of the process of elimination. What can we do experimentally in complex situations in which it is difficult to eliminate an effect or a suspected cause from the picture? One option, the **method of residues,** is based on using what we already know about the causal picture and "subtracting" it from the equation (like determining the weight of the payload by driving the loaded truck onto the scales and then subtracting the weight of the unloaded truck). Or imagine you wanted to weigh the fish in your aquarium (without taking them out of the water).

APPLICATION EXERCISE 9.2 | **Weighing the Fish**

So how would you do it (weigh the fish without taking them out of the water)?

Continue with the Fantasy Island example. Again, Fantasy Island syndrome is a complex of symptoms: severe intestinal cramps, diarrhea, vomiting, respiratory congestion, severe headaches, and sudden loss of vision. The **joint method of agreement and difference** has isolated swimming as a causal factor. But water is complex, too. There are many possible causes in the water. Suppose an analysis of the water in the ocean at Fantasy Island finds a rare algae bloom. The algae contain a toxin that in experimental trials produces some of the symptoms we're investigating. Suppose it accounts for the headaches and loss of vision. Subtracting this cause and these effects from the equation leaves a residual array of symptoms to account for (the intestinal and respiratory symptoms). Now suppose that further analysis of the water samples shows the presence in high concentration of a bacterium that feeds on the rare algae. It would be reasonable on the basis of the method of residues to suspect this as a probable cause of at least some of the residual symptoms.

MILL'S METHOD OF CONCOMITANT VARIATION

We demonstrated earlier how the method of agreement is limited because any collection of individuals will share not just one but many common antecedent conditions, most of which will have no causal connection with the effect we are seeking to understand. Therefore the method of agreement, by itself, is rarely adequate to identify the cause of any phenomenon. And we saw how the method of difference helps identify the cause by a process of elimination. But the method of difference has a limitation of its own, which in turn limits the joint method of agreement and difference. The method of difference—and therefore the joint method of agreement and difference—depend upon being able to observe instances from which a suspected cause is *absent*. Furthermore, all methods discussed thus far depend on the ability to eliminate either the effect or the suspected cause. The method of residues depends on being able to weigh the truck empty (even if we can't weigh the payload without the truck to carry it). Similarly, establishing the algae as the cause of its particular range of symptoms would depend upon cultivation of and exposure to the algae in isolation from other possible causes. Thus to use any of the preceding methods, we need to find, or experimentally bring about, an instance in which some effects, antecedent conditions, or both are out of the picture. And this is not always easy to do. Sometimes it's impossible. Mill's example of isolating the cause of tides shows this. When it was suspected that one of the many antecedent conditions that accompanies the ebb and flow of the tides—the position of the moon—was the actual cause of tidal motion, it was nevertheless impossible to confirm this suspicion by the method of difference or the method of residues. As Mill said, "We cannot try an experiment in the absence of the moon, so as to observe what terrestrial phenomena her annihilation would put an end to."[3] To overcome this limitation, Mill formulated the **method of concomitant variation.** When it is difficult or impossible to eliminate a suspected cause, it may nevertheless be possible to *vary* it, or to observe its natural variations, and see whether these variations are accompanied by corresponding variations in the effect under investigation. In the case of the moon and the tides, the closer the moon is to a particular coastal region, the higher the tide. And the further the moon is from a particular coastal region, the lower the tide. This makes it reasonable to suppose that there is a causal connection.

Figure 9.3 illustrates the joint method of agreement and difference supplemented by the method of concomitant variation for three instances of some effect, *s*. The letters *L, M, N, O, P, R,* and *S* represent a range of antecedent conditions. By the method of agreement, we determine that five of these conditions—*L, N, O, P,* and *S*—are present in all cases where *s* is observed. So these are the causal candidates. But there are no cases in which any of these conditions, or the effect *s*, is absent. So we cannot isolate a cause by the method of difference. But each of the antecedent conditions varies in degree (represented by the plus and minus signs). And only one of them varies in a way that corresponds to variations in the effect. So that condition, *O*, is most likely to be causally connected to *s*.

Instance	Antecedent Conditions							Effect
1	L+	M	N−	O	P−	R	S+	s
2	L		N+	O+	P		S−	s+
3	L−	M	N	O−	P+		S	s−

FIGURE 9.3 Mill's Joint Method of Agreement and Difference
with Concomitant Variation

The method of concomitant variation is a widely used experimental strategy in the sciences. For example, in pharmacology researchers routinely study the efficacy of experimental drugs by varying the dosage. If the observed effects on the alleviation of symptoms vary with the dosage, going up when the dosage is increased and going down when the dosage is decreased, that counts as confirmation of the causal efficacy of the drug. If the alleviation of symptoms does not vary with the dosage—if, for example, the symptoms are alleviated slightly with small doses and slightly more with slightly larger doses but not at all with large doses—that would raise doubts about the causal efficacy of the drug (see Figure 9.4).

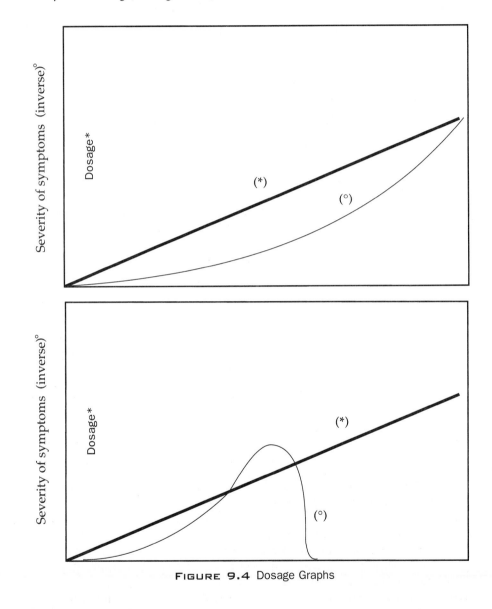

FIGURE 9.4 Dosage Graphs

DISCUSSION TOPIC 9.5 | Causal Reasoning I

Continue the Fantasy Island example. We've used Mill's methods thus far to isolate a marine algae and parasitic bacterium as the likely cause of Fantasy Island syndrome.

1. Suppose we turn up a Fantasy Island vacationer who went swimming but didn't become sick. What, if anything, must we reconsider? What further experiment should we consider, and why?

2. Suppose we turn up a Fantasy Island vacationer who became sick but didn't go swimming. What, if anything, must we reconsider? What further experiment should we consider, and why?

DISCUSSION TOPIC 9.6 | Causal Reasoning II

1. Think of the different areas of common routine human interest and concern within which causal reasoning plays a crucial role. Brainstorm a list of such areas.

2. As a group, pick some phenomenon of common interest or concern to you, whose cause or causes are not yet known.

3. Develop a list of reasonable causal hypotheses.

4. Discuss the design of experiments to test these hypotheses.

APPLICATION EXERCISE 9.3 | Term Project

Identify areas within the context of the issue you have been working on where causal or hypothetical reasoning would be relevant. Formulate causal, interpretive, or other appropriate hypotheses. Evaluate these for plausibility and explanatory power. On this basis, select a leading hypothesis. Finally, design an experiment to test the leading hypothesis.

GLOSSARY

burden of proof   obligation to produce the argument in a dispute over an issue; failure to meet the burden of proof settles the issue in favor of the other side

confirming evidence   data consistent with what a hypothesis predicts

disconfirming evidence   data inconsistent with what a hypothesis predicts

explanation   idea(s) intended or used to reduce or eliminate puzzlement

explanatory power   an idea's capacity to reduce or eliminate puzzlement

hypothesis   an idea or set of ideas under investigation

hypothetical deductive method   a method of scientific investigation involving both hypothetical inductive reasoning and deductive reasoning

hypothetical reasoning   reasoning toward improved understanding using ideas still under investigation

indirect confirmation   confirmation by thorough but unsuccessful attempt at disconfirmation

inductive inference to the best explanation   inductive inference based on both the superior plausibility and the superior explanatory power of a given explanatory hypothesis

joint method of agreement and difference   a principle of causal reasoning that combines the method of agreement with the method of difference

method of agreement   a principle of causal reasoning that consists of seeking out some common antecedent condition in all cases of the effect whose cause one is trying to determine

method of concomitant variation   a principle of causal reasoning that consists of varying a suspected cause and checking for corresponding variations in the effect, useful for situations in which it is difficult or impossible to eliminate a suspected cause

method of difference   a principle of causal reasoning that consists of looking for a correlation between the *absence* of the effect and the *absence* of an antecedent condition

method of residues   a principle of causal reasoning in which established causes and effects are subtracted, leaving residual causes and effects to be identified

Mill's methods   guidelines for reliable causal reasoning formulated by philosopher John Stuart Mill

presumption of innocence   principle that places the burden of proof on the prosecution in criminal law

---

ADDITIONAL EXERCISES

REVIEW EXERCISE 9.1 PLAUSIBILITY OF THEORIES I   Several theories have arisen since the assassination of President John F. Kennedy, which remains shrouded in mystery and controversy more than 30 years after the fact. Rank the following theories in descending order of plausibility. Compare your rankings with those of your classmates. Try to resolve any points of disagreement by explaining your answers to one another.

	Lee Harvey Oswald, acting alone, assassinated the president.
	The assassination was planned and executed by the mafia.
	The assassination was planned and executed by officials of the U.S. government.
	The assassination was planned and executed by officials of the U.S. government in collaboration with the mafia.
	The assassination was planned and executed by officials of a foreign government.
	The assassination was planned and executed by officials of a foreign government in collaboration with officials of the U.S. government.
	The assassination was carried out by aliens from outer space.

▓ **REVIEW EXERCISE 9.2 PLAUSIBILITY OF THEORIES II**   Here again are the theories listed in Review Exercise 9.1. This time, rank the theories in descending order of explanatory power. Compare your rankings with those of your classmates. Try to resolve any points of disagreement by explaining your answers to one another.

	Lee Harvey Oswald, acting alone, assassinated the president.
	The assassination was planned and executed by the mafia.
	The assassination was planned and executed by officials of the U.S. government.
	The assassination was planned and executed by officials of the U.S. government in collaboration with the mafia.
	The assassination was planned and executed by officials of a foreign government.
	The assassination was planned and executed by officials of a foreign government in collaboration with officials of the U.S. government.
	The assassination was carried out by aliens from outer space.

▓ **REVIEW EXERCISE 9.3 APPLYING MILL'S METHODS**   Using the concepts and terminology of Mill's methods, explain how, in the following story from the history of medicine, the 19th-century medical researcher Ignaz Semmelweis discovered and demonstrated the importance of physician hygiene in patient care.

Between 1844 and 1846, the death rate from a mysterious disease termed "childbed fever" in the First Maternity Division of the Vienna General Hospital averaged an alarming 10%. But the rate in the Second Division, where midwives rather than doctors attended the mothers, was only about 2%. For some time no one could explain why. Then one day a colleague accidentally cut himself on the finger with a student's scalpel while performing an autopsy. Although the cut seemed harmless enough, the man died shortly thereafter, exhibiting symptoms identical to those of childbed fever. Semmelweis formed the hypothesis that doctors and medical students, who spent their mornings doing autopsies before making their divisional rounds, were unwittingly transmitting to the women something they picked up from the cadavers. Semmelweis tested this hypothesis by requiring the doctors and students to clean their hands before examining patients. Doctors and students were forbidden to examine patients without first washing their hands in a solution of chlorinated lime. The death rate in the First Division fell to less than 2%.[4]

▓ **APPLICATION EXERCISE 9.4 NOT SO FAITHFUL**   According to Paul and Nathalie Silver, of the Carnegie Institute, California's Old Faithful geyser can predict large earthquakes within a radius of 150 miles. They argue for this conclusion on the basis of a 20-year record of geyser eruptions. Ordinarily the geyser erupts at regular intervals (which is why it came to be known as Old Faithful, like geysers in Wyoming and New Zealand that also erupt regularly). On the day before the Oroville earthquake of August 1, 1975, the interval between geyser eruptions suddenly changed from 50 minutes to 120 minutes. In 1984, the geyser was erupting every 40 minutes. But the day before the April 24 Morgan Hill tremor, the pattern became irregular, fluctuating among 25-, 40-, and 50-minute intervals. A change was also noted before the 1989 Loma Prieta quake in the San Francisco area. Two and a half days before the quake, eruption intervals at the geyser suddenly shifted from 90 minutes to 150 minutes. The researchers noted that a number of things, including rainfall, can affect the regularity of eruptions in geysers. However, an analysis of rainfall amounts in the Calistoga area rules this out as an explanation of the abrupt pattern changes preceding each of these earthquakes. Evaluate the evidence and the reasoning involved here. What strengths can you identify? What weaknesses? What kinds of further evidence would confirm the hypothesis that Old Faithful is an effective earthquake predictor? What kinds of further evidence would disconfirm the hypothesis? What kinds of experiments can you think of to discover such evidence?

▓ **APPLICATION EXERCISE 9.5 HYPOTHETICAL REASONING**   Using the terminology and concepts of hypothetical reasoning covered in this chapter, evaluate the research and discussion presented in the following news story.

Teenagers whose MP3 players are full of music with raunchy, sexual lyrics start having sex sooner than those who prefer other songs, a study found.

According to the study, teens who said they listened to lots of music with degrading sexual messages were almost twice as likely to start having intercourse or other sexual activities within the following two years as were teens who listened to little or no sexually-charged music.

Songs depicting men as "sex-driven studs," women as sex objects and with explicit references to sex acts are also more likely to trigger early sexual behaviour than those where sexual references are more veiled and relationships appear more committed, the study found.

Among heavy listeners, 51 per cent started having sex within two years, versus 29 per cent of those who said they listened to little or no sexually-degrading music.

Exposure to lots of sexually-charged music "gives them a specific message about sex," said lead author Steven Martino, a researcher for Rand Corp.

Boys learn they should be relentless in pursuit of women and girls learn to view themselves as sex objects, he said.

"We think that really lowers kids' inhibitions and makes them less thoughtful about sexual decisions and may influence them to make decisions they'd regret," he added.

The study, based on telephone interviews with 1,461 participants aged 12 to 17, appears in the August issue of *Pediatrics,* being released Monday.

Miss Natasha Ramsey, a 17-year-old from New Brunswick, New Jersey, agreed with the study, saying that listening to the sexually-charged lyrics could send the wrong message to teens.

"A lot of teens think that's the way they're supposed to be, they think that's the cool thing to do. Because it's so common, it's accepted," said Miss Ramsey, a teen editor for Sexetc.Org, a teen sexual health Web site produced at Rutgers University.

"Teens will try to deny it, they'll say 'No, it's not the music,' but it is the music. That has one of the biggest impacts on our lives."

However, New York-based sex researcher and author Yvonne Fulbright said factors including peer pressure, self-esteem and home environment are probably more influential than the research suggests.

"It's a little dangerous to just pinpoint one thing," she said. "When somebody has a healthy sense of themselves, they don't take these lyrics too seriously."[5]

NOTES

[1] David Ray Griffin, *The New Pearl Harbor: Disturbing Questions About the Bush Administration and 9/11* (Northampton, MA: Olive Branch Press, 2004), pp. 12–23.

[2] Malcolm Gladwell, "The Risk Pool: What's Behind Ireland's Economic Miracle—and G.M.'s Financial Crisis?" *The New Yorker,* August 28, 2006, p. 31.

[3] John Stuart Mill, *A System of Logic,* Book III, Chapter 8, Section 6.

[4] G.B. Risse, Ignaz Philipp Semelweis, *Dictionary of Specific Biography,* C.C. Gilespie (ed.). New York: Charles Scribner's Sons, 1971–1980.

[5] S.C. Martino, R.L. Collins, M.N. Elliott, A. Strachman, D.E. Kanouse, and S.H. Berry, "Exposure to Degrading Versus Nondegrading Music Lyrics and Sexual Behavior Among Youth." *Pediatrics,* 118, no. 2 (Aug 2006): e430–e431.

UNIT 5

Evaluating Whole Arguments

Evaluating whole arguments
Informal fallacy criticism
Argument design and composition

"I shall now punch a huge hole in your argument."

CHAPTER 10

Evaluating Premises: Self-Evidence, Consistency, and Indirect Proof

Belief in an external world is more compelling than belief in any philosophical theory which purports to disprove it. With [some moral disasters], any ethical theory which either justifies them or can give no help in avoiding them is inadequate. Auschwitz . . . is more compelling than any abstract ethical principle. . . . If persuaded that an otherwise convincing ethical theory could justify the Nazi genocide, I should without hesitation give up the theory.[1]

—JONATHAN GLOVER

In Chapter 6, we distinguished between the structural features of arguments and the materials out of which they are constructed. In Chapters 6 and 7, you learned how to evaluate deductive arguments structurally for validity. In Chapters 8 and 9, you learned how to assess the strength of inductive arguments. Now that you have studied the structural features of arguments in both of these two main argument design categories, it's time to look at the standards and practices of evaluating premises. You'll be happy (we imagine) to know that there's not much new for you to learn at this stage about evaluating the premises of an argument. Because the premises of any argument are themselves each conclusions of subarguments—or potential

conclusions of potential subarguments—evaluating the premises of an argument turns out to be a matter of applying what you've already learned about issues and arguments. If there is support for a particular premise offered in the text of the argument itself, then in effect there is a subargument whose conclusion is the premise we're interested in evaluating, so we can evaluate the subargument. But eventually you will run into premises that aren't supported in the text of the argument itself. All arguments have to start somewhere, and this means that every argument will have unsupported premises in it.

In designing and constructing an argument, common sense would suggest that we establish as firm a foundation as possible. So experienced arguers generally try to use as their most "basic" premises, claims that are as uncontroversial, as easy to accept, and as hard to challenge or refute as possible. For example, when Thomas Jefferson wrote in the Declaration of Independence "We hold these truths to be self-evident," he meant, "Here are some basic premises we don't think we *need* to argue for." These are claims (for example, that basic human rights belong equally to every human) that can and should be accepted at face value by any rational human.

DISCUSSION TOPIC 10.1 | Arguing for Self-Evident Truths

Even if you agree with Jefferson that a claim as basic as "All people are equal when it comes to basic human rights" doesn't (or shouldn't) need to be argued for, it's still an interesting question: Why not? Do you think it's true that basic human rights belong equally to every human? Suppose someone challenged this claim. How would you support a claim as basic as this?

Again, all arguments have to start somewhere. But is there anywhere for an argument to start where it can move forward without having to back up? The problem critical thinking faces at this point is how to avoid an infinite regress of argument evaluation. **Infinite regress** refers to a bottomless pit of premises supported by more premises, supported by more premises, and so on, to infinity—so that it becomes logically impossible to complete the evaluation of any argument.

DISCUSSION TOPIC 10.2 | Zeno's Paradox

One version of one of Zeno's famous paradoxes of motion goes like this: Try to go from wherever you are (point A) to anywhere else (point B). First you have to go half the distance from point A to point B. But before you can go half the distance from point A to point B, you have to go half *that* distance. But before you can go half of half the distance from point A to point B, you have to go half of *that* distance, and so on, to infinity. So not only can you never go from point A to point B but you can't even start! Now, everybody knows from experience that motion is possible, so something must be wrong with the reasoning in Zeno's paradox. What can it be?

Philosophers, and other theorists generally, tend to run from infinite regresses as they would from the plague. There is a general theoretical rule of thumb in many disciplines to the effect that if some hypothesis can be shown to lead to an infinite regress, then that hypothesis is untenable (must be considered incorrect). We can easily understand the urge to apply such a rule of thumb in critical thinking. If there are no "first premises"—if the demand for deeper support can be made repeatedly at increasing levels of depth *ad infinitum*—then no resolution to any issue could ever be achieved. And that's not reasonable. Consequently, some way of avoiding an infinite regress of argument evaluation must be found. So it is worth inquiring whether there are self-evident truths beneath which the inquiry cannot or need not go. First, are there any claims that are beyond question or dispute?

NECESSARY TRUTHS

Are there any claims available for use as premises that don't require their own additional support?

THOUGHT EXPERIMENT 10.1 | Tautology

Try to deny the following claim: "Either the president knew of the arms-for-hostages deal before it was negotiated or he didn't."

What do you notice when you attempt to deny this claim?

TAUTOLOGIES

Some people consider certain claims to be **necessarily true,** meaning that these claims can't be denied in a coherent way. For example, when you try to deny the claim in Thought Experiment 10.1, a contradiction arises. To deny this claim would be in effect to say that the president both knew of the deal in advance and did not know of the deal in advance, which is **logically impossible.** "Logically impossible" means the impossibility can be traced to the logical form of the claim itself. Thus *any* statement whose formal structure is "either P or not P" must be necessarily true,

P	~P	P v ~P	~(P v ~P)
T	F	T	(F)
F	T	T	(F)

FIGURE 10.1 Truth Table

because the negation of any statement of the form "either P or not P" is self-contra-dictory (and therefore necessarily false). A claim that you can't deny without for-mally contradicting yourself is called a **tautology** and considered necessarily true. This can be demonstrated by the truth table in Figure 10.1.

But even though tautologies always carry the value "true," they don't convey much information. The claim that either the president knew in advance or he didn't doesn't by itself tell us much, does it? Therefore tautologies are often referred to as *trivially* true.

AND SPEAKING OF: | **Trivially True**

When Tim Russert, host of *Meet the Press,* said that "there were a lot of misjudgments made" regarding Iraq, his guest Condoleezza Rice pointed out, "There are also some misjudgments that were not made."

Nevertheless, tautologies can occasionally play a crucial role in an argument. For example:

1. Either the president knew of the arms-for-hostages deal before it was negotiated or he didn't.
2. If he did know of the arms-for-hostages deal in advance, then he's involved in the cover-up and is therefore unworthy of his office.
3. If he didn't know of the arms-for-hostages deal in advance, then he's not in control of his own administration and is therefore unworthy of his office.
4. Therefore, either way, he's unworthy of his office.

REVIEW EXERCISE 10.1 | **Find the Tautology**

1. What is the formal structure of the preceding argument?
2. Which premise is a tautology?

THOUGHT EXPERIMENT 10.2 | **Trivially True?**

Do you think that Jefferson's claim that all men are created equal is a tautology? Do you think it is trivially true? Can you deny it without contradicting yourself?

TRUISMS BY DEFINITION

Are there any other kinds of statement that are necessarily true—that cannot coherently be denied? Perhaps there are. For example, consider the following statements: "Murder is a form of homicide," "All bachelors are unmarried," and "'phonetic' isn't." It seems impossible to deny any of these statements without contradicting yourself, although this would be not so much because of the formal structures of the statements as because of the meanings of the terms in them. Murder is, by definition, a subset of the larger category homicide; "unmarried" is part of the meaning of "bachelor"; and the word "phonetic" means spelled the way it sounds. Thus to deny any of these statements would be a contradiction *in terms*. So we would expect anyone who understands the meanings of the terms involved to immediately recognize any such statement as true. Such statements might be called truisms by definition.

DISCUSSION TOPIC 10.3 | **True by Definition?**

Do you think that Jefferson's claim that all men are created equal is a truism by definition? Do you think it would be a contradiction in terms to deny it?

REVIEW EXERCISE 10.2 | **Necessary Truths**

Sort the following statements into the following categories: (1) tautologies, (2) true by definition, (3) formal contradictions, (4) contradictions in terms, and (5) statements that are neither necessarily true nor self-contradictory. Compare your results with those of your classmates. Be prepared to explain your answers.

	Tautology	Tautology by Definition	Formal Contradiction	Contradiction in Terms	Neither
A rectangle has four sides.					
This rectangle has only three sides.					
Either she's married or she's not married.					
She is both married and unmarried.					
She is either married or engaged.					
She is neither married nor engaged.					
Abortion is murder.					
Murder is wrong.					
White is a shape.					
No statement that contradicts itself is true.					
The White House is white.					
This sentence has seven words in it.					
This sentence has eight words in it.					

	All men are created equal.					
	Wherever you go, there you are.					
	All arguments have to start somewhere.					

CONTINGENT CLAIMS

Most claims are neither self-contradictory nor necessarily true. Claims that are neither self-contradictory nor necessarily true are called **contingent,** meaning that their truth or falsity depends on something outside of themselves, something beyond their formal structures or the meanings of their terms. Return to Jefferson's self-evident truth that all men are created equal. Is it a tautology? If someone were to deny it, would that result in a formal contradiction? We think not. There is no formal inconsistency in the claim "Not all men are created equal" or the logically equivalent claim "Some men are created unequal." Nor is Jefferson's claim that all men are created equal trivially true, as we would expect a tautology to be. It seems to say something important. Is it true by definition? Would its denial constitute a contradiction in terms? Again, apparently not. So by "self-evident" Jefferson evidently means something other than "necessarily true." Therefore suppose that Jefferson's self-evident truth that all men are created equal is a contingent claim. That would mean that its truth value depends on something outside its formal structure and the meanings of its terms. What does its truth value depend on?

Suppose someone were to deny the claim that all men are created equal. The first question to ask, when we come to the evaluation of a contingent claim that has been used as an unsupported premise, is, What *kind* of claim is being made here? This means asking, Does the premise make a factual claim? An evaluative claim? Does it offer an interpretation? This is like asking, if someone were to challenge this claim, what sort of issue would that raise? A factual issue, an evaluative issue, an interpretive issue, a complex issue involving more than one of these categories? Thinking about these questions helps determine what sorts of additional support may be needed to establish a given contingent claim as a premise in an argument.

REVIEW EXERCISE 10.3 | Issue Analysis

We highly recommend at this point that you review the section in Chapter 1 on issues and issue analysis. It's especially relevant at this point, and it may make more sense now than it did at the beginning.

FACTUAL CLAIMS

As we pointed out in Chapter 1, most issues are complex and involve elements from all three issue categories. Factual issues often give rise to both evaluative and interpretive issues as well. Thus establishing a particular premise as a matter of fact can turn out to be a tall and complicated order. For example, suppose we're trying to determine as a matter of fact what caused the stock market to suddenly lose 500 points. Right away we are deep into the realm of hypothetical reasoning with all of its nuances and complexities as described in Chapter 9—and a long way from anything that might be considered self-evident. But there are many factual claims that are simpler and more directly linked to firsthand experience. Thus, for example, in law, eyewitness testimony carries great weight in any fact-finding process. The statement "I was there; I saw the crime being committed with my own eyes," sworn under oath and subject to the penalty for perjury, is hard to overcome as evidence at trial. Even here, however, there are ways to occasionally undermine the force of eyewitness testimony. A witness's memory, reliability as an observer, or sanity may be impeached, or there may be contradictory eyewitness testimony. So even eyewitness testimony, as probative and as fundamentally unassailable as it may be generally, can be doubted and overturned and therefore probably should not be considered self-evident. Still perhaps there are some factual claims so basic that they might be considered self-evident. Suppose you were to say,

My best friend is more than 5 feet tall.

The claim made here is a contingent statement of fact. Its truth value depends upon the height of your best friend, something out there in the world, which can be tested empirically, that is, by reference to sense experience or to what scientists call observations. Whenever scientists weigh, measure, or take the temperature of something, they are making observations. Then when they record or report these observations, they are making observation claims. Suppose someone now challenges your claim that your best friend is more than 5 feet tall. How do you respond? Well, suppose you say, "I'm 5'2" and my best friend is taller than I am, so my best friend is more than 5 feet tall." Now suppose you are challenged to defend these two claims. How do you know you are 5'2"? The truth of this sort of observation claim in general would depend on the conditions under which the measurements had been made, and so on. In this rather simple instance, it would be more than sufficient to know that you had been measured, when standing erect, using an accurate standard instrument of measurement, by someone who knew how to use it, in circumstances that didn't impair the user's performance. So how do you know you were standing erect when your height was being measured? And how do you know your best friend is taller than you are? At some point, you wind up saying something like, "Look. There isn't anything *more basic* for me to appeal to here in support of this claim. We stand next to each other, and I look up and he looks down. That's all there is to it! It's a basic observation! It's self-evident!" Notice that if you say something like this, you're also admitting that there are indeed further claims that you could appeal to in support of the observation that your best friend is taller than you are. You've even specified a little empirical experiment, (standing next to each other), whose results support the claim. "Self-evident" in this context seems to mean something like this: the supporting claims are no more basic or evident than what they support. This may be close to what Jefferson meant when he called the claim that all men are created equal "self-evident," but it is also clearly evident that he was neither reporting a basic observation nor making any *factual* claim.

EVALUATIVE CLAIMS

Probably the best short answer to the question "what sort of claim does 'all men are created equal' express?" is a basic moral principle, which would put it in the category of evaluative claims. And if the principle were challenged, the issue that would arise would be an evaluative issue. So on what rational foundation are evaluative issues to be resolved? On what rational foundation are evaluative claims to be established as true? There is a widely held position (which we will call **values relativism**) that it can't be done because of the essential difference and an unbridgeable gap between facts and values. Facts are objective, values are relative or even subjective. The best argument we can think of in support of values relativism goes something like this:

1. Factual claims can be rationally supported empirically.

2. This means they are established as true on the basis of verifiable observations.

3. Evaluative claims cannot be rationally supported empirically, nor can they be derived from factual claims alone.

4. There is no other basis besides empirical observations on which issues may be rationally resolved or claims may be rationally established as true.

5. Therefore, there is neither rational basis for the resolution of evaluative issues nor rational foundation for the establishment of evaluative claims as true.

What we have to say about this view is an extension of what we said about relativism in Chapter 1.

REVIEW EXERCISE 10.4 | Relativism

We highly recommend at this point that you review the section in Chapter 1 on relativism and limited relativism, under the "Obstacles to Critical Thinking" section, pp. 16–18.

Values relativism is a specific version of what we referred to in Chapter 1 as "limited relativism." As such, it is inherently more reasonable and understandable than relativism in general and even more reasonable still because evaluative issues—which cannot be resolved by doing science or looking things up—generally are harder to resolve than factual issues. Still, even though evaluative claims can't be established *empirically,* ' it does not follow that they can't be established at all. The weakness in the preceding argument for values relativism is in the last premise, which claims that there is no basis other than empirical observation on which issues may be rationally resolved or claims rationally established as true. We deny this claim. There is another rational basis for resolving issues and establishing claims as true: *by considering and evaluating the best available arguments on all sides of the issue (like we're doing here).*

We'll go a step further and argue that there are certain evaluative claims already *more firmly established as true* than certain factual claims are or can hope to be.

DISCUSSION TOPIC 10.4 | Fact vs. Value I

Of the following two claims, which one is evaluative? Which one is factual? Which one do you think is more firmly established as true? Why?

1. Ghandi's political leadership of his people was morally superior to Hitler's political leadership of his people.
2. There is intelligent extraterrestrial organic life in our galaxy.

We think claim 1 clearly expresses a value judgment. Yet we think it is also much more firmly established as true than (the clearly factual) claim 2 is now or will likely be in the foreseeable future. How can this be? It isn't *certain* that Ghandi's leadership of his people was morally superior to Hitler's. But even though this claim expresses a value judgment and even though it may yet be open to challenge and debate, we consider it to be quite firmly established as true. How so?

THOUGHT EXPERIMENT 10.3 | Fact vs. Value II

The following pair of arguments adds up in our opinion to a powerful and persuasive case, even though it is full of evaluative claims. First read the pair of arguments, and then consider the questions that follow.

> Ghandi led his people out of the bondage of colonial rule. He also guided that struggle away from violence. To do this required great courage and wisdom, saved many human lives, and provided a model to the world of an effective and humane way to engage in political struggle. Human life is precious. Freedom is better than colonial bondage as a way of life. Therefore Ghandi was a great leader.
>
> By contrast, Hitler led his people into World War II. He directed his people to invade and forcibly occupy the territory of neighboring sovereign states. He directed his people to exterminate several million civilian noncombatants. He led his country eventually to ruinous defeat. He led the world to develop nuclear and other weapons of mass destruction. Human life is precious. Peace is precious. Therefore Hitler was a terrible leader.

1. How many evaluative claims can you count? Highlight all the evaluative claims you can find.
2. How many factual claims? Underline all the factual claims you can find.
3. Now, can you think of any counterarguments?
4. How do the best counterarguments you can find—or think of—compare? Are they as powerful? Anywhere close?

The reasoning in Thought Experiment 10.3 illustrates how evaluative issues generally are resolved and evaluative claims established as true. The best rational way to resolve evaluative issues or to establish the truth of an evaluative claim is *by considering and evaluating the best available arguments on all sides of the issue (like we're doing here).*

This brings us back to the problem posed at the beginning of this chapter—how to avoid an infinite regress of argument evaluation. To evaluate an argument, we have to evaluate the premises. But to do that we have to evaluate arguments. Do we ever reach the end of this? Perhaps not. But once you learn how to swim, you stop worrying about sinking to the bottom.

Do not forget, either, that the infinite regress problem arose also about contingent statements of fact. Yet this does not prevent us from determining matters of fact. At some point, we encounter observation claims so basic that, even though we could continue to support them by appeal to further observations, these would be no more basic or evident than what they support. So unless there is good reason for doubting them, such claims may be taken as self-evident. Similarly, with value judgments, at some point, you get down to an evaluative claim so basic that, even if you could continue to support it with further arguments based on further claims, these arguments and claims would be no more convincing than the claims they support. So even if we can't reach the absolute bottom of the theoretical heap of premises supported by other premises, supported by other premises, supported by other premises, perhaps we do eventually reach a level where the burden of proof shifts decisively in favor of some basic claim.

DISCUSSION TOPIC 10.5 | Arguing in the Domain of Values

Pick any of the following evaluative claims and compose (a) the best argument you can in support of it and (b) the best argument you can against it.

1. Human life is precious.

2. Peace is precious.

3. Freedom is better than colonial bondage as a way of life.

4. Basic human rights belong equally to every human.

Take a claim like "Human life is precious." If all arguments have to start somewhere, this would be the sort of claim we would want to start with. It's not that we couldn't argue in support of such a claim, but what would the argument add to the strength of the claim itself? Moreover, what sort of argument can be made against such a claim? The burden of proof clearly falls on the challenger here. And for at least some such claims the burden of proof seems so substantial that intuitively it is hard to imagine how someone might overturn it.

DISCUSSION TOPIC 10.6 | Self-Evidence Again

Here is an argument in support of the claim that basic human rights belong equally to every human. Compare the argument to the claim that it supports. Which do you find more convincing: the argument or the conclusion itself?

1. Morality presumes consistency.
2. In other words, in the absence of a justification for differential treatment, all moral rules and considerations apply equally to all parties.
3. This includes basic human rights.
4. There is apparently no justification for differential treatment among individual humans with respect to basic human rights.
5. Therefore, basic human rights belong equally to every human.

Here is what we would say. The first two premises of the preceding argument *appear* to reach higher levels of generality and abstraction than the conclusion does, but that doesn't make them more convincing than the conclusion itself. Premise 4 makes this a burden of proof argument and as such inherently inconclusive. The conclusion itself is more convincing on its face than *any* burden of proof argument. This is what we think Jefferson had in mind when he called his first premises self-evident truths: not that they can't be argued for but an argument has to start somewhere and these claims seem as good as any candidates for the office of first premise.

BEYOND SELF-EVIDENCE

By far, most claims you will find as premises in the arguments you encounter will be neither necessarily true nor self-evident. For example, we doubt that the question of self-evidence arises in connection with interpretive claims. To recognize a given claim as an interpretation is to recognize the possibility of other interpretations and therefore the presence of an interpretive issue. And this puts the claim beyond consideration as self-evident. An interpretation, in other words, is a claim we can always legitimately be challenged to argue for. Nor is there a single simple procedure for resolving interpretive issues. So there is no single simple procedure for establishing interpretive claims as premises in an argument. Rather it is, as with evaluative claims and indeed with contingent claims generally, a matter of considering the best arguments that can be made for and against them and weighing the arguments and the evidence on all sides. Again, don't worry too much about getting to the bottom of this process of rational evaluation of arguments in support of premises in arguments. Just do it.

Here are some additional techniques and strategies, using concepts we've already discussed. Following these procedures can streamline the process and significantly improve results.

CONSISTENCY

One of the most powerful tools for both formal and informal argument evaluation is the concept of consistency. Two statements are **consistent** if they could both be true. Two statements are **inconsistent** if there are no possible circumstances in which they could both be true. A group of statements is inconsistent if any two statements in the group are inconsistent. Not only is the concept of consistency crucial to our understanding of deductive validity but, because inconsistency is always a sign that something is wrong somewhere, the concept can also be applied to the evaluation of premises in several useful ways. We used it earlier to explain the concept of a tautology as necessarily true. Similarly, just as a self-contradiction must necessarily be false, and hence its denial or negation necessarily true, a good rule of thumb is to check an argument's entire set of claims *as a group* for consistency. If a given set of claims is internally inconsistent, then although you may not know which of the premises is false, you know they can't all be true.

CRITICAL THINKING TIP 10.1 | Consistency

Check for Consistency; If an Argument's Premises Are Not Internally Consistent as a Group, They Can't All Be True

AND SPEAKING OF: | (In)consistency

Many Democratic lawmakers criticized Iraqi Prime Minister Nouri al-Maliki for criticizing Israel. Howard Dean, for example, said: "We don't need to spend $200 and $300 and $500 billion bringing democracy to Iraq to turn it over to people who believe that Israel doesn't have a right to defend itself and who refuse to condemn Hezbollah." The *Washington Post*'s Howard Kurtz caught the inconsistency of Dean's remark: "But that raises an interesting dilemma. If this bloody and costly war was about making democracy possible in the Middle East, as President Bush contends, then doesn't Iraq get to pick its own leaders? And if that's the case, how can we use their positions, however abhorrent, as an argument against the war? If al-Maliki suddenly took a pro-Israel stance, wouldn't much of his country view him as an American puppet?"[2]

IMPLICATIONS

Although the truth value of a claim remains to be determined, one effective strategy is to treat it hypothetically. That is, assume that the claim is true and trace out its further implications. What follows logically from the claim? What further claims does it logically entail or strongly support inductively? The **implications** of a claim are those additional claims that either follow from it by logic (are required for consistency) or are strongly supported by it inductively. If a claim leads by implication to any further claim that is self-contradictory, or known to be false or otherwise absurd, then there is good reason to doubt the claim. In this way, it is often possible to refute a claim indirectly. This strategy has traditionally been known by its Latin name **reductio ad absurdum** (which means to reduce to absurdity). For example, return to the scenario we used in Chapter 7 to illustrate the logic of the argument form destructive dilemma. Suppose you're a juror in a murder trial. Expert testimony has established that the time of death was at midnight and that it is a 25-minute drive from the scene of the crime to the house where the defendant, who is blind and cannot drive, was arrested at 12:30 a.m. The defense attorney argues as follows: "Suppose my client was alone with the victim at the scene and time of the crime. That would imply that he made his own way home, covering more than 20 miles in less than a half-hour, which is impossible. So he can't possibly have been alone with the victim at the scene and time of the crime."

The strategy can also be inverted to use in defense of a position. This is sometimes referred to as the **method of indirect proof.** In this strategy, we assume that the thesis we want to argue for is *false*. We then trace the implications of that assumption, hoping to find that it leads to some absurd or contradictory conclusion. This then constitutes a good reason to reject the original assumption, which leaves our thesis standing. One of the most famous and enduring examples of this strategy is Euclid's demonstration that prime numbers continue infinitely. He started by assuming that there is a finite set of prime numbers. Then through a long and complex series of deductively valid logical steps, he reached a contradiction. If each step in this demonstration is deductively valid, and a contradiction is necessarily false, then the only thing left to do is reject the initial assumption. Thus Euclid demonstrated that we are forced by logic to the conclusion that there are infinitely many prime numbers.

AND SPEAKING OF: | Indirect Proof

Do you remember this? "If there are no 'first premises'—if the demand for deeper support can be made repeatedly at increasing levels of depth *ad infinitum*—then no resolution to any issue could ever be achieved. And that's not reasonable. Consequently, some way of avoiding an infinite regress of argument evaluation must be found."

DISCUSSION TOPIC 10.7 | *Tracing the Implications*

The following passage makes a host of interesting claims, each with its own set of implications. Trace the implications to highlight any apparent inconsistencies.

Most therapies are dualistic. They try to do what seems good and to correct or avoid what seems bad. If they confuse good and bad, as they are sometimes bound to do, their attempt to do good will compound problems and make them harder to resolve. Non-dualistic therapy makes no value judgment about possible alternatives. It looks at the facts, does experiments, and views the results with an open mind. In this way, it is like science, while dualistic therapy is like moralism. Paradoxes should not disturb us. Awareness, if there is enough of it, can always reach the underlying unity of life and merge apparent opposites.[3]

WRITING ASSIGNMENT 10.1 | Term Project

All of the work you have invested so far in this series of exercises should now be paying off. By carefully stating and researching the issue you have been studying, by finding and analyzing opposed arguments, and by exploring various argument design options, you naturally are better informed about the issue than when you started. Now it is time to make some decisions. Answer the following question for yourself in 100 words or less: "Where do I stand on this issue?"

GLOSSARY

consistent   two statements that could both be true

contingent   dependent on something outside itself

implications   additional claims that either follow logically from or are strongly supported inductively by a given claim

inconsistent   two statements that under no circumstances could both be true; a group of statements is inconsistent if any two statements in the group are inconsistent

infinite regress   a bottomless pit of premises supported by more premises, supported by more premises, and so on, to infinity—so that it becomes logically impossible to complete the evaluation of any argument

logically impossible   impossibility traceable to the logical form of a claim (a self-contradiction)

method of indirect proof   method of proof by assuming the negation of one's thesis, then deriving an absurd or self-contradictory result from that assumption

necessarily true   impossible to deny in a coherent way

reductio ad absurdium   method of proof by assuming the negation of one's thesis, then deriving an absurd or self-contradictory result from that assumption

tautology   a claim that is necessarily true because to deny it would be self-contradictory

values relativism   the view that the truth about matters of value is "relative" and varies

ADDITIONAL EXERCISES

■ **APPLICATION EXERCISE 10.1 BASIC PREMISES**   What are the most basic premises of each of the following arguments? Include in your analysis any hidden inferential assumptions. If these premises were challenged, how might they be defended?

1. "According to modern physics, radio is our only hope of picking up an intelligent signal from space. Sending an interstellar probe would take too long—roughly 50 years even for nearby Alpha Centauri—even if we had the

technology and funds to accomplish it. But radio is too slow for much dialogue. The most we can hope from it is to establish the existence (or, more accurately, the former existence) of another civilization."[4]

2. How important are professional athletes to society? Not very. They're mere entertainers. They often present bad role models for children—for every Dave Dravecky there's a Pete Rose, a Steve Garvey, or a Jose Canseco; for every Michael Jordan or Grant Hill there's a Dennis Rodman. And, given the attention they receive, they tend to distract us from serious social concerns. At the least, then, the salaries of these prima donnas should be drastically reduced to reflect their social insignificance.

3. "If a being suffers, there can be no moral justification for refusing to take that suffering into consideration, and, indeed, to count it equally with the like suffering (if rough comparisons can be made) of another being. So the only question is: Do animals other than man suffer? Most people agree unhesitatingly that animals like cats and dogs can and do suffer, and this seems also to be assumed by those laws that prohibit wanton cruelty to such animals."[5]

4. "Proposition 215 will allow seriously and terminally ill patients to legally use marijuana, if, and only if, they have the approval of a licensed physician. We are physicians and nurses who have witnessed firsthand the medical benefits of marijuana. Yet today in California, medical use of marijuana is illegal. Doctors cannot prescribe marijuana, and terminally ill patients must break the law to use it. Marijuana is not a cure, but it can help cancer patients. Most have severe reactions to the disease and chemotherapy—commonly severe nausea and vomiting. One in three patients discontinues treatment despite a 50% chance of improvement. When standard anti-nausea drugs fail, marijuana often eases patients' nausea and permits continued treatment. . . . University doctors and researchers have found that marijuana is also effective in: lowering internal eye pressure associated with glaucoma, slowing the onset of blindness; reducing the pain of AIDS patients, and stimulating the appetites of those suffering malnutrition because of AIDS 'wasting syndrome'; and alleviating muscle spasticity and chronic pain due to multiple sclerosis, epilepsy, and spinal cord injuries. When one in five Americans will have cancer, and 20 million may develop glaucoma, shouldn't our government let physicians prescribe any medicine capable of relieving suffering? . . . Today, physicians are allowed to prescribe powerful drugs like morphine and codeine. It doesn't make sense that they cannot prescribe marijuana, too."[6]

5. "There are an estimated 2 billion children (people under age 18) in the world. Because Santa Claus is apparently not responsible for visiting the Muslim, Hindu, Jewish, and Buddhist children, that reduces his workload to 15% of the total, or 378 million children, according to the Population Reference Bureau. Assuming an average of 3.5 children per household, that means 91.8 million homes (assuming at least one good child per household). Assuming Santa travels from east to west, and factoring in the Earth's rotation and the different time zones, Santa has 31 hours of Christmas to work with. This works out to 823 visits per second, which means that Santa has a little more

than 1/1000th of a second to park, climb out of the sleigh, slide down the chimney, fill stockings, distribute presents under the tree, eat the snacks left for him, rise back up the chimney, climb into the sleigh, and fly to the next house. Assuming the 91.8 million stops are evenly distributed geographically, each stop would be 0.78 miles apart, which means that Santa's sleigh will be traveling at 650 miles per second, thousands of times the speed of sound. Assuming that each child receives nothing more than a medium-sized Lego set (approximately 2 pounds), the payload of the sleigh, not counting Santa, would be 321,300 tons. On land, conventional reindeer can pull about 300 pounds. Assuming even that "flying reindeer" could pull 10 times that amount, the team required to pull Santa's payload would be 214,200 reindeer, which increases the weight of the loaded sleigh and team to 353,430 tons (four times the weight of the *Queen Elizabeth*). An object weighing 350,000 tons traveling at 650 miles per second creates enormous air resistance, with resultant friction and heat, enough to vaporize a reindeer in about 4/1000ths of a second. In conclusion, if Santa ever did deliver presents on Christmas Eve, he's dead now.[7]

■ **WRITING ASSIGNMENT 10.2 VALUE JUDGMENTS I**   One of the principles on which the American system of criminal justice is theoretically based is that it's worse to punish innocent people than to let guilty people escape punishment. This principle can be understood to express a value judgment. Do you agree with this principle and the value judgment it expresses? If so, formulate three distinct justifications for them. If not, construct three distinct justifications for rejecting them. Write a short essay in which you explain your position.

■ **APPLICATION EXERCISE 10.3 VALUE JUDGMENTS II**   Here are several justifications for the principle mentioned in Writing Assignment 10.1. What are the most basic premises of each of these arguments? If these premises were challenged, how might they be defended? Which of the following arguments—1, 2, or 3—do you find the most deeply persuasive? Explain why.

1. When a society punishes an innocent person, it inevitably increases the unwarranted suffering in the world. It is always wrong to increase the unwarranted suffering in the world.

2. When you punish an innocent person, you turn that person against society, and this leads to an increase in antisocial behavior.

3. Punishing the innocent is inherently wrong because they've done nothing to deserve punishment. Letting the guilty escape punishment is inherently wrong because they don't get what they deserve. But punishing the innocent is always worse because when you punish an innocent person for a crime they didn't commit, you are also letting the person guilty of that crime escape punishment.

■ **APPLICATION EXERCISE 10.2 APPEAL TO CONSISTENCY**   The following passage involves an appeal to consistency. Highlight the portion of the passage where the appeal to consistency is explicitly made. Then explain that appeal in your own words. What are the further implications of this appeal to consistency?

Suppose that the businesses in a certain industry are trying to earn a government contract. The government, however, has had difficulties with other corporations breaking the rules of other contracts. As a result it has lost large sums of money. To prevent this in the present case it says that it is going to set up devices to monitor the reactions of board members and managers when a questionnaire is sent to them which they must answer. A business, of course, need not agree to this procedure but if it does then it will be noted in their file regarding this and future government contracts. The questionnaire will include questions about the corporation's past fulfillment of contracts, competency to fulfill the present contract, loopholes used in past contract, collusion with other companies, etc. The reactions of the managers and board members, as they respond to these questions, will be monitored and a decision on the worthiness of that corporation to receive the contract will be made in part on this basis.

There can be little doubt, I think, that the management and directors of the affected corporations would object to the proposed process even though the right of the government to defend itself from the violation of its contracts and serious financial losses is at stake. It would be said to be an unjustified violation of the privacy of decision-making processes in a business, and an illegitimate encroachment of the government on free enterprise. But surely if this is the legitimate response for the corporate job applicant, the same kind of response would be legitimate in the case of the individual job applicant.[8]

APPLICATION EXERCISE 10.3 MAKING ASSUMPTIONS In medical ethics, there is a distinction that many people make between active and passive euthanasia, sometimes expressed as the distinction between killing and letting die. Furthermore, many people assume as intuitively obvious that it would be harder to justify active euthanasia (killing someone) than to justify passive euthanasia (letting someone die). Using the concepts and terminology discussed in this chapter, explain how the following argument refutes this assumption.

To begin with a familiar type of situation, a patient who is dying of incurable cancer of the throat is in terrible pain, which can no longer be satisfactorily alleviated. He is certain to die within a few days, even if present treatment is continued, but he does not want to go on living for those days because the pain is unbearable. So he asks the doctor for an end to it, and his family joins in his request. Suppose the doctor agrees to withhold treatment (passive euthanasia), as the conventional doctrine says he may. The justification for his doing so is that the patient is in terrible agony, and because he is going to die anyway, it would be wrong to prolong his suffering needlessly. But now notice this. If one simply withholds treatment, it may take the patient longer to die, and so he may suffer more than he would if more direct action were taken and lethal injection given. This fact provides strong reasons for thinking that, once the initial decision not to prolong his agony has been made, active euthanasia is actually preferable to passive euthanasia, rather than the reverse. To say otherwise is to endorse the option that leads to more suffering rather than less, and is contrary to the humanitarian impulse that prompts the decision not to prolong life in the first place.[9]

NOTES

[1] Jonathan Glover, *Humanity: A Moral History of the Twentieth Century* (New Haven, CT: Yale University Press, 1999), p. 406.

[2] Howard Kurtz, "Al-Maliki's Rhetoric," *Washington Post,* July 28, 2006, online ed.

[3] Ishvara, *Oneness in Living: Kundalini Yoga, the Spiritual Path, and Intentional Community* (Berkeley, CA: North Atlantic Books, 2002).

[4] Patrick Moore, "Speaking English in Space: Stars," *Omni*, November 1979, p. 26.

[5] Peter Singer, "Animal Liberation," in James Rachels (ed.), *Moral Problems,* 2nd Edition (New York: Harper & Row, 1975), p. 166.

[6] Excerpt from the "Argument in Favor of Proposition 215," in *State of California Voter Manual,* 1996.

[7] Richard Waller, "Is There a Santa Claus?" *Spy,* January 1990.

[8] George Brenkert, "Privacy, Polygraphs and Work," *Journal of Business and Professional Ethics,* vol. 1, no. 1 (Fall 1981).

[9] J. Rachels, "Active and Passive Euthanasia," *New England Journal of Medicine*, 292, pp. 78–80.

CHAPTER 11

Informal Fallacies I: Assumptions, Language, Relevance, and Authority

Hence it is that any class of men who have an interest in the rise or continuance of any system of abuse no matter how flagrant will, with few or no exceptions, support such a system of abuse with any means they deem necessary, even at the cost of probity and sincerity. . . . But it is one of the characteristics of abuse, that it can only be defended by fallacy. It is therefore, to the interests of all the confederates of abuse to give the most extensive currency to fallacies. . . . It is of the utmost importance to such persons to keep the human mind in such a state of imbecility that shall render it incapable of distinguishing truth from error.[1] —JEREMY BENTHAM

In Chapter 6 we introduced the concept of a fallacy as an unreliable inference—an important concept for argument criticism. Why so important? First, because fallacies are inferences, they tend to *appear* as reasonable. Second, their unreliability tends not to be apparent on the surface. They even can be persuasive. Because of their persuasive power, they're quite widespread and prevalent in all sorts of everyday discourse, both public and private. And this leads to a lot of confusion and mistakes. So understanding how fallacies work and knowing how to spot them are useful to the critical thinker. We started with formal fallacies, because within the framework of formal logic it is possible to demonstrate clearly that a fallacy is unreliable and

FIGURE 11.1

it is relatively easy to show the formal structure of the fallacy and thus how the fallacy works. There are other aspects of reasoning besides the formal structure of inferences that can undermine reliability. Thus an **informal fallacy** is an unreliable inference whose unreliability is caused by something other than its formal structure.

The informal fallacies constitute a large and mixed bag. The author of one critical thinking textbook estimates that if you were to consult a random selection of informal logic texts you would likely find several hundred informal fallacy categories listed. One such text distinguishes more than 90. This proliferation of categories and terminology makes the study of the informal fallacies bewildering and intimidating for many students. And it leads many students of critical thinking, and even quite a few instructors, to approach the informal fallacies as essentially a memory challenge—a long list of labels to memorize. This is a terrible way to approach the informal fallacies. Try hard not to fall into this trap. We must be honest here and tell you that one reason there are so many categories is that there is no common classification system for the informal fallacies. This is a good reason *not* to try memorizing a list of fallacy labels.

Here is a better approach. Think of the informal fallacy terminology as part of a toolkit for doing a certain kind of work. Just as a carpenter has carpentry tools, you are assembling a set of tools for critiquing arguments. Your goal should be to attain mastery in their employment, and the best way to pursue this goal is by working with the tools. The tools are mind tools, rather than hand tools—concepts rather than hardware. You already have the tools. They are concepts you've studied. In this chapter, we demonstrate a few applications of the tools. Occasionally, we also give you a few tips about using the tools. Like this:

CRITICAL THINKING TIP 11.1 | **The Work of the Critical Thinker**

The Work of the Carpenter Is to Construct Things out of Wood. The Mastery of the Carpenter Shows in the Product. The Work of the Critical Thinker Is to Produce a Form of Understanding.

FALLACIOUS ASSUMPTIONS

In Chapter 1 we discussed the role of assumptions in reasoning and proposed the first of our series of critical thinking tips: Be *aware* of assumptions. Assumptions become more "dangerous" to reasoning to the extent that they remain hidden. Thus we should be generally on the alert for hidden assumptions wherever inferences are being made from one or more claims to another and for hidden assumptions underlying any claims explicitly being made. In general, this sort of vigilance and awareness constitutes a tool of informal fallacy criticism. Whenever we become aware of the presence of a hidden assumption in an argument and that assumption is questionable or dubious, we may say that the argument commits the informal fallacy of questionable assumptions.

FALSE DILEMMA

The label is not what is most important. What is most important is the *critical activity* of carefully pointing out where the assumption is hidden and calling that assumption into question, making clear precisely what is questionable about it. Here is an example. Suppose someone presents an argument to us in the form of a logical dilemma. Dilemma is the logical strategy of proving a point by showing that it is implied by each of two alternatives, at least one of which must be true (see Chapter 7). Essentially, the argument says: Here are the choices. Either A or B, and both A and B lead to C. Therefore C. The logic is unassailable. We can *feel* the force of the logic. And we might not even notice that the argument depends on the assumption that there aren't any *other* alternatives (besides A and B). Only when we notice this assumption are we in a position to determine whether it's true or not. If this assumption should turn out to be false or doubtful, we may say that the argument commits the informal fallacy of **false dilemma**—one of the most powerfully persuasive of the common informal fallacies. The best strategy for exposing instances of this fallacy is to identify a specific alternative left out of consideration in the premises. If the argument is fully explicated in the form of a dilemma, in effect you are challenging the premise that expresses the disjunction. You are saying that the premise "either A or B" is false. In many cases, this premise is left implied. The persuasive power of the fallacy comes partly from the force of its logic. But it also gets a powerful psychological boost from our natural tendency to prefer simplicity. Issues are just easier to deal with when they can be reduced to a pair of mutually exclusive alternatives—when we can see them "in black and white." A common variation of this fallacy is based on the logical form of disjunctive syllogism (see Chapter 7). Have you ever heard people argue in favor of some course of action by saying something like, "Well, we've gotta do *something*, don't we?" The unstated inferential assumption being made here is that either we follow the proposed course of action or we don't do anything. Again, if you can think of one reasonable alternative beyond those two options, the argument is fallacious.

COMPLEX QUESTION

The rhetorical strategy of the **complex question** is an old debater's trick based on exploiting the language of assumptions. The question is carefully worded to pre-suppose something that you don't want to agree to. The classic example is the question, "Have you stopped cheating on your spouse?" See how that works? Yes or no! Either answer presupposes that you have been cheating on your spouse. Nasty trick, isn't it?

INNUENDO

Innuendo is Latin for *by hinting*. The informal fallacy of innuendo consists of implying a judgment, usually derogatory, by hinting. No argument is offered. Instead, the audience is invited by suggestion, by a nod and a wink, to make the assumption. Someone asks, "Where is Jones? Did he get fired or something?" Someone answers, "Not yet." By innuendo, the response numbers Jones's days. The political candidate who distributes a brochure promising to restore honesty and integrity to an office has suggested, without presenting any argument, that the incumbent is crooked.

CIRCULAR REASONING

Three thieves have stolen seven bags of gold. The thief in the middle hands two bags of gold to the thief on the left and two bags of gold to the thief on the right and says, "I'm keeping three for myself." The thief on the left asks, "Why do you get to keep three, when we each only get two?" The thief in the middle says, "because I'm the leader of this outfit." The thief on the right asks, "What makes you the leader?" to which the thief in the middle responds, "I've got the most gold."[2]

THOUGHT EXPERIMENT 11.1 | Question Begging

Perhaps the moral of the little fable presented earlier is that there's no honor among thieves. In any case, it should be readily apparent that the thief in the middle is engaging in a bit of "sleight of mouth" with his two "partners in crime." Can you explain the trickery?

The informal fallacy of **begging the question** or **circular reasoning** occurs when the conclusion of the argument is presupposed, either directly or indirectly, as a premise. What makes this fallacy particularly tricky to deal with is that arguers are rarely so clumsy as to appeal to a premise that is obviously identical to the conclusion. More often, the question-begging premise is a subtle rewording of the conclusion or is presupposed by some other claim in the argument. The strategy we often need to pursue to effectively diagnose and expose this fallacy therefore involves sensitive use of paraphrase. If the premise and the conclusion can be paraphrased into each other without significant loss of meaning, then we have a plausible case of begging the question.

REVIEW EXERCISE 11.1 | Fallacious Assumptions

Each of the following examples contains (or points out) at least one major fallacy involving unwarranted assumptions. In each example, check all fallacy categories that apply. Most important, explain each fallacy you identify.

1. "By the time you have wisely purchased this tome (book, for those of you in Rio Linda, California) most critics will have undoubtedly savaged it. In many cases, their reviews will have been written before the book was published. How do I know this? Because I do."[3]

False dilemma	Explain your answer:
Complex question	
Innuendo	
Begging the question	

2. "We must believe in the existence of God because it is written in the Holy scriptures, and conversely we must believe in the Holy scriptures because they come from God."[4]

False dilemma	Explain your answer:
Complex question	
Innuendo	
Begging the question	

3. "Captain L had a first mate who was at times addicted to the use of strong drink, and occasionally, as the slang has it, "got full." The ship was lying in port in China, and the mate had been on shore and had there indulged rather freely in some of the vile compounds common in Chinese ports. He came on board, "drunk as a lord," and thought he had a mortgage on the whole world. The captain, who rarely ever touched liquor himself, was greatly disturbed by the disgraceful conduct of his officer, particularly as the crew had all observed his condition. One of the duties of the first mate is to write up the log each day, but as that worthy was not able to do it, the captain made the proper entry, but added: "The mate was drunk all day." The ship left port the next day and the mate got "sobered off." He attended to his writing at the proper time, but was appalled when he saw what the captain had done. He went back on deck,

and soon after the following colloquy took place:

"Cap'n, why did you write in the log yesterday that I was drunk all day?"

"It was true, wasn't it?"

"Yes, but what will the ship owners say if they see it? It will hurt me with them."

But the mate could get nothing more from the Captain than, "It was true, wasn't it?"

The next day, when the Captain was examining the book, he found at the bottom of the mate's entry of observation, course, winds, and tides: "The captain was sober all day."[5]

	False dilemma	Explain your answer:
	Complex question	
	Innuendo	
	Begging the question	

FALLACIES OF LANGUAGE

> This notion that the United States is getting ready to attack Iran is simply ridiculous. And having said that, all options are on the table.
>
> —GEORGE W. BUSH, FEBRUARY 2005

AMBIGUITY

If a genie came out of a lamp and offered you the gift of everlasting perfect happiness, would you accept? And now suppose the same genie came back a second time and said, "I'll trade you what I gave you last time for this ratty old bowl of leftover party mix." Would you accept the offer? In Chapter 2, the concept of ambiguity was presented as a flexibility feature of language that enables it to handle multiple meanings at once. Although this kind of flexibility is essential to effective communication, here we will focus on the downside of ambiguity—the ways in which ambiguity can undermine the reliability of a piece of reasoning.

Suppose the genie offered you the following argument:

> Look, nothing is better than everlasting perfect happiness, but this ratty old bowl of leftover party mix is better than nothing, so you'd really be better off accepting my generous offer.

APPLICATION EXERCISE 11.1 | Ambiguity

What is wrong with the genie's argument? Can you explain the trick?

There's something wrong with this argument. But what can it be? It *looks* so logical. Here's a hint. Go back and highlight the terms that appear in both premises of the argument. Does each term carry the same meaning consistently from premise 1 through premise 2, or do the meanings change? And if so how?

APPLICATION EXERCISE 11.2 | Equivocation I

Highlight the terms that appear in both premises of the argument:

> Nothing is better than everlasting perfect happiness, but this ratty old bowl of leftover party mix is better than nothing, so the party mix is better than everlasting perfect happiness.

The trick here is that the word "nothing," on which the apparently logical comparison hinges, changes meaning from the first premise to the second. The first premise can be paraphrased as follows:

> Everlasting perfect happiness is better than *anything else.*

And the second premise can be paraphrased as follows:

> *Having* this ratty old bowl of leftover party mix is better than *not having anything.*

When the premises have been paraphrased in this way, we're no longer tempted to think that everlasting perfect happiness and this ratty old bowl of leftover party mix are both being compared to the same thing. Thus the apparent logic of the argument falls away. When an argument depends on switching the meanings of an ambiguous crucial term or expression, as in this example, the argument commits the informal fallacy of equivocation. The conceptual tool we are using in diagnosing this fallacy is the concept of ambiguity. In critiquing an argument as an instance of this fallacy, we should be able to identify each term or expression being used ambiguously and demonstrate the ambiguity by making clear at least two distinct meanings for each ambiguous item. The best way to do this is to paraphrase the claims in which it is used, as we did here.

APPLICATION EXERCISE 11.3 | Equivocation II

OK, now you try it. Use the cartoon in Figure 11.1.

VARIETIES OF AMBIGUITY

A good basic understanding of language—for example, the distinction between syntax and semantics—is obviously helpful in diagnosing and explaining informal fallacies of ambiguity. Some ambiguity arises at the verbal level as a result of the capacity of individual words or idiomatic expressions to support more than one interpretation. Such ambiguity is called **semantic.** Thus the example used earlier, which we called **equivocation,** results from semantic ambiguity—a matter of semantics. Ambiguity can also arise at the grammatical level as a result of grammatical structure or word order.

APPLICATION EXERCISE 11.4 | Amphibole I

Can you explain the how the ambiguity arises in the following example?

The loot and the car were listed as stolen by the Los Angeles Police Department.

In the preceding example, there is an ambiguity of reference. Which of the two verbs in the sentence is modified by the prepositional phrase? The expression is presumably intended to indicate that the police *listed* the loot and car as stolen, not that they *stole* it. This would be an example of syntactical ambiguity—a matter of syntax. The technical term for an expression whose ambiguity is caused by its grammatical structure or word order is amphibole. The same sort of thing is going on in the cartoon in Figure 11.2.

An argument that exploits or depends on this sort of ambiguity commits the informal fallacy of amphibole. Such fallacies are almost always deliberate and sometimes verge on fraud.

Lance couldn't understand why they had to be licensed, but he brought his plates in anyway.

FIGURE 11.2 Amphibole

APPLICATION EXERCISE 11.5 | Amphibole II

We found this example in a direct mail sales offer. Can you figure out the trick?

> We're convinced that you will love your new Acme widget even more than you could begin to imagine. In fact, we're so confident, we're making the following guarantee now IN WRITING! If for ANY REASON you are the least bit dissatisfied, just send it back. We'll give you a prompt and a full refund.

Does this mean that you will receive a full refund promptly? Suppose you apply for the refund. And 2 weeks later you receive a check for half of the purchase price, along with a statement of "service charges, restocking fees, plus shipping and handling." Apparently this is not what the guarantor had in mind—even if it *is* what the guarantor expects you to think. Should you insist upon a full refund, you may expect to wage an indefinitely long and unpleasant battle.

ADVANCED APPLICATIONS

The genie's argument, which we used earlier to illustrate the fallacy of equivocation, is, shall we say, bogus on its face. In other words, there's clearly a trick in it—even if the trick is hard to identify. But fallacies can be more seductive and difficult to spot.

APPLICATION EXERCISE 11.6 | False Implication

Here is an example of a widely used ad strategy: We spotted on a candy bar wrapper the words "BIGGEST EVER!" imprinted in bright orange 64-point type. Guess the trick.

The preceding strategy, known as **false implication,** consists of *stating* something true, while *implying* something else that's not true. It's the implied falsehood that motivates the consumer. The implication in this case is that the candy bar is bigger now than it was before—that it has been increased in size. The literal truth is that the candy bar is as big as it has ever been (as BIG AS EVER!)—and as small as it has ever been—because it's the same size as it has always been. This maneuver is standard procedure in writing advertising copy. It explains the conventional advertising industry usage of superlative adjectives, especially in promoting so-called parity products. A **parity product** is one that is practically the same regardless of brand name. Aspirin is a good example of a parity product. Aspirin is aspirin is aspirin. It doesn't matter whether you buy it in the bottle that says "Bayer," in the bottle with the regional brand name, or in the bottle with the generic label. You receive the same number of milligrams of the same chemical formula per

Table 11.1   Superlatives and Comparisons

Superlative:	Best	Strongest	Sweetest	Biggest	Fastest
Comparative:	Better	Stronger	Sweeter	Bigger	Faster
Descriptive:	Good	Strong	Sweet	Big	Fast

tablet. Understandably, producers of parity products work hard in their ads to promote name recognition and brand loyalty, and they often use superlatives such as "best," "strongest," and "most powerful" to describe their products. "How can this be?" you may ask. "If all of the products are identical, they must all be equally good, equally strong, equally powerful, and so on." Quite right. If you have this doubt, it's probably because you recognize that normally a superlative implies a comparison. For example, consider the sets of adjectives in Table 11.1.

Normally, as you read down the list, each adjective implies the one below it. If something is better than something else, this implies that it is good. If something is the best, this implies that it is better than the rest. But as employed in advertising, the superlative "best" is taken to mean "there is none better"; the superlative "strongest" is taken to mean "there is none stronger"; and so on. The literal truth is that the pain reliever is "just as strong as any of the other over-the-counter pain relievers." You are simply receiving the maximum dosage legally dispensable without a doctor's prescription, as with all other over-the-counter pain pills.

FURTHER APPLICATIONS

Another kind of ambiguity arises out of referential uses of the language—when we use language to refer to or point to things. It is not always clear whether things are being referred to individually or collectively. This can result in one of two common informal fallacies. The informal fallacy of **composition** consists of incorrectly inferring characteristics of the group from characteristics of its individual parts or members. For example, a man observes that every member of the local country club is wealthy and therefore infers that the country club must be financially sound. Not necessarily. Often, the "whole" is different from simply the sum or combination of its parts. Even when the whole *is* the sum of its parts, what is true of a part (even of all parts) need not be true of the whole. For example, a program of short pieces of music can be a long program. A team of highly efficient workers may nonetheless be hopelessly inefficient as a team.

It is sometimes true that a whole has the characteristics of its individual members. It may be the case, for example, that a series of good lectures is a good series of lectures. But there is no generally reliable equation here.

By the same token, the informal fallacy of **division** works in the opposite direction, incorrectly inferring characteristics of the individual parts or members of a group from characteristics of the group as a whole. Observing that a club is well connected politically, a man infers that each club member or that a particular member must be well connected politically. But just as a property of the part need not imply a property of the whole, so a property of the whole need not imply a property of the part. That a book is a masterpiece doesn't mean that each chapter is one; that an orchestra is outstanding doesn't imply that each member is an outstanding musician. Again, it is sometimes the case that the individual parts or members have some characteristics of the group, but this is not always the case. A million-dollar inventory, for example, might be made up of a many 5- and 10-cent items.

VAGUENESS

In Chapter 2, the concept of vagueness was presented as a feature of language in which questions of definition are left open. Like ambiguity, vagueness is useful. We often need the flexibility to use discretion in applying familiar terms, concepts, rules, and procedures in new and unforeseeable situations. However, for the same reason, vagueness is also prone to certain forms of abuse. Because vague terms and expression are essentially undefined, they lend themselves rather easily and naturally to evasive and manipulative applications. To criticize a piece of reasoning as a case of the abuse of vagueness depends on identifying an instance of vagueness and arguing that it needs to be used more precisely to avoid falling into error.

AND SPEAKING OF: | Vagueness

Highlight the terms and concepts you find used in the following passages in vague ways. Then compare and contrast: where is the vagueness warranted and reasonable; where is it unwarranted or problematic?

Excerpt from President George W. Bush's address to the nation on October 7, 2001, announcing the military campaign against the Taliban government of Afghanistan:

> This military action is a part of our campaign against terrorism, another front in a war that has already been joined through diplomacy, intelligence, the freezing of financial assets and the arrests of known terrorists by law enforcement agents in 38 countries. Given the nature and reach of our enemies, we will win this conflict by the patient accumulation of successes, by meeting a series of challenges with determination and will and purpose. Today we focus on Afghanistan, but the battle is broader. Every nation has a choice to make. In this conflict, there is no neutral ground. If any government sponsors the outlaws and killers of innocents, they have become outlaws and murderers, themselves. And they will take that lonely path at their own peril.

Excerpt from President George W. Bush's radio address to the nation on April 20, 2002, reporting on Secretary of State Colin Powell's diplomatic mission to the Middle East during a period of intensified violence in Israel and the occupied territories of Palestine:

The time is now for all of us to make the choice for peace. America will continue to work toward this vision of peace in the Middle East, and America continues to press forward in our war against global terror. We will use every available tool to tighten the noose around the terrorists and their supporters. And when it comes to the threat of terror, the only path to safety is the path of action.

In the days just after September the 11th, I told the American people our war against terrorism would be a different war, fought on many fronts. And we are making progress on many fronts. Yesterday the United States and the world's other leading industrialized nations blocked the financial assets of another 10 terrorists and terrorist organizations. This joint action among close allies is an important step in choking off the financial pipeline that pays for terrorist training and attacks.

A total of 161 nations around the world have joined together to block more than $100 million of suspected terrorist assets. The United States also continues to work with our friends and allies around the world to round up individual terrorists, such as Abu Zubaydah, a top al Qaeda leader captured in Pakistan. From Spain to Singapore, our partners are breaking up terrorist cells and disrupting their plans. Altogether, more than 1,600 terrorists and their supporters have been arrested or detained in 95 foreign nations.

In Afghanistan, the United States and its partners are pressing forward with a military campaign against al Qaeda and the Taliban. More than a dozen of our NATO allies are contributing forces to this fight. Right now, hundreds of Royal Marines from Great Britain are leading an operation to clear and seal off regions where our enemies are trying to regroup to commit murder and mayhem, and to undermine Afghanistan's efforts to build a lasting peace.

And we're working with nations such as Yemen, the Philippines and Georgia that seek our help in training and equipping their military forces to fight terror in some of the world's distant corners.

We're making progress. Yet nothing about this war will be quick or easy. We face dangers and sacrifices ahead. America is ready; the morale of our military is high; the will of our people is strong. We are determined, we are steadfast, and we will continue for as long as it takes, until the mission is done.

No doubt you can see that there is considerable room here for discussion. There are, first, quite a few terms and concepts in play in each of the preceding passages, many of which are used in ways that could be defined more precisely and are thus arguably vague. For purposes of illustration, we focus only on three central ones: "peace," "war," and "terrorism." So now the question arises as to the precise definitions of these terms. In what ways are these terms left open to interpretation?

The concept of peace is not defined, but it is reasonable to assume that it means at least the absence of war. Among the ways the concept of war is left open to interpretation are the specific goals, objectives, and means to be used. At the outset, the goals and objectives are defined simply in the phrase "campaign against terrorism." But suppose we want to know more specifics: How long will this war go on? How far will this war extend geographically? What precisely is our mission? How will we know when we have completed it? The means of achieving these goals are also unspecified. However, it is clear that they are not confined to the use of conventional military force, because they include the use of diplomatic, law enforcement, surveillance, and intelligence procedures.

This raises a question as to what additional, perhaps covert, means of achieving the goals and objectives may be under consideration. How are we to know whether we are "at war" or not?

The concept of terrorism is given what sounds like a definitive statement in the context of an ultimatum delivered to all nations in stark black-and-white terms. There is no gray area. Either you support "the outlaws and killers of innocents" or not. But acting and speaking as though there are no gray areas does not eliminate gray areas. Questions may arise as to precisely *who* the outlaws and killers of innocents are in many cases, including the aftermath of September 11, 2001. So how precise can we make the definition of terrorism?

REVIEW EXERCISE 11.2 | Essential Definitions I

Look back at Thought Experiment 2.5 (Chapter 2, p. 62). Then read the "official" U.S. government definition of terrorism:

> An act of terrorism means any activity that [A] involves a violent act or an act dangerous to human life that is a violation of the criminal laws of the United States or any State, or that would be a criminal violation if committed within the jurisdiction of the United States or of any State; and [B] appears to be intended (i) to intimidate or coerce a civilian population; (ii) to influence the policy of a government by intimidation or coercion; or (iii) to affect the conduct of a government by assassination or kidnapping.[6]

Now consider the following questions:

1. Does the U.S. government or any of its allies ever engage in acts of violence and/or commit homicide against civilian populations for coercive political purposes?
2. Does the U.S. government or any of its allies ever take political hostages?
3. Does the U.S. government or any of its allies ever commit or issue contracts for political assassination?

The questions posed in the preceding exercise, whether the U.S. government or any of its allies (Israel, for example) ever engage in activities that would count as terrorism under its own official definition of that term, are questions the Bush administration would surely find troublesome and would therefore understandably prefer to avoid. Better to leave the concept of terrorism more loosely defined. There are also understandable reasons the Bush administration would prefer to keep military options both open and unspecified, even if they have been determined. But we can be sure that vagueness is being abused when the interpretations of the crucial concepts become so loose and broad as to be internally inconsistent (peace is war, war is peace, war is a means to peace, and so on).

VAGUENESS IN ADVERTISING

Puffery is advertising that praises with vague exaggerations. **Hyperbole,** or "hype" for short, is exaggeration or extravagance as a figure of speech. In advertising, such exaggerations and extravagances are there to create excitement, not to convey information. In his book *The Great American Blowup,* Ivan L. Preston gives a long list of examples, including, "When you say Budweiser, you've said it all"; "You can be sure if it's Westinghouse"; "Toshiba—in touch with tomorrow"; "Waterford—the ultimate gift"; and "Diamonds are forever!" The general strategy these advertisers pursue is to raise the level of enthusiasm and excitement without making substantive claims.

APPLICATION EXERCISE 11.7 | Hype and Puffery

Here is an excerpt from an unsolicited direct mail brochure we received while working on this chapter. How many instances of hype and puffery can you find?

> This two-day weekend seminar will open you to the wonders of the contemporary experience of modern High-Tech Serendipity Meditation, as your seminar leader and originator of the High-Tech Serendipity Meditation Experience personally conducts this expansive program, demonstrating the power and potential of this contemporary meditative technology. The weekend includes four power-packed sessions of Holodynamic Serendipity material presented in such a way as to enable each participant to personally experience the contemporary ease and the full potential of High-Tech Meditation.

The pitch in the preceding example sounds intriguing, beneficial, attractive, but what does it all mean? The terminology, although it *sounds* not only positive but technically precise, is hopelessly vague. That's the important thing to notice here. Because it is so vague, it invites the reader to project onto it whatever meanings are most closely connected with the reader's own fantasies and longings. If you want to find out in detail what High-Tech Holodynamic Serendipity Meditation is all about, you can sign up for the 2-day weekend seminar for a fee of $250. Assuming you can afford it, this might not be such a bad deal for 2 full days of whatever you want to believe you're hearing.

UNSPECIFIED COMPARISON

Already we have seen how ambiguity can be exploited to enable the advertiser to imply a claim that cannot truthfully be stated in an explicit and straightforward way by using that which arises when a comparison is left unfinished. In one famous ad we are told, "Ford LTD—700% quieter!" Compared to what? Viewers of this ad are understandably inclined to complete the comparison for themselves in one of several ways relevant to choosing a new car. For example, many viewers assume that the ad means that this year's model is 700% quieter than last year's model or that the Ford LTD is 700% quieter than the competitors in its price category. When the Federal Trade Commission challenged the claim, Ford admitted that the basis of the comparison was exterior noise. The inside of the car was 700% quieter than the outside.

WEASEL WORDS

The expression "weasel words" is derived from the egg-eating habits of weasels. A weasel will bite into the eggshell and suck out the contents, leaving what appears to the casual observer to be an intact egg. Similarly, a **weasel word** sucks out the substance of what appears on the surface to be a substantial claim. In effect, the weasel word makes the claim in which it is used a *vague* claim while at least partially concealing the vagueness. "Help" functions in advertising as a weasel. "Help" means literally aid or assist and nothing more. Yet as one author has observed, "'help' is the one single word which, in all the annals of advertising, has done the most to say something that couldn't be said."[7] Once "help" is used to qualify a claim, almost anything can be said after it. Accordingly, we are exposed to ads for products that "help keep us young," "help prevent cavities," and "help keep our houses germ free." Just think of how many times a day you hear or read pitches that say "helps stop," "helps prevent," "helps fight," "helps overcome," "helps you feel," and "helps you look." But don't think "help" is the only weasel in the advertiser's arsenal. "Like" (as in "makes your floor look like new"), "virtual" or "virtually" (as in "virtually no cavities"), "up to" (as in "provides relief for up to 8 hours"), "as much as" (as in "saves as much as one gallon of gas"), and other weasels say what cannot be said. Studies indicate that on hearing or reading a claim containing a weasel word, we tend to screen out the weasel word and just hear the claim. Thus on hearing that a medicine "can provide relief for up to 8 hours," we screen out the "can" and the "up to" and infer that the product will give us relief for 8 hours, because that's what we want—relief. According to a strict reading of the wording of the ad, the product may give no relief; and if it does give relief, the relief could vary in length from a moment or two to anywhere under 8 hours.

REVIEW EXERCISE 11.3 | Vagueness in Advertising Scavenger Hunt

1. Find an example of hype or puffery in a magazine ad.
2. Find two examples of unspecified comparison claims in print advertising.
3. Find three examples of weasel words in print advertising.

DENOTATION AND CONNOTATION

Many issues turn on how things are grouped in categories. In Chapter 2 we considered several examples, including what we classify as "terrorism" and whether a particular music video is in the category of "pornography." When an argument depends on a claim that either amounts to or presupposes a questionable classification, it is appropriate to challenge that classification. If a premise in an argument has been challenged in this way and this challenge is not met by a defensible essential definition, we may say that some informal fallacy of classification has occurred. All of this depends on the essential definition of the category in question. Thus making such a criticism will open the issue of defining the category. And this will, in many cases, be a formidable issue in its own right.

DISCUSSION TOPIC 11.1 | Essential Definitions II

Review the section on essential definitions and Thought Experiments 2.2–2.5 and Review Exercises 2.5 and 2.6 in Chapter 2, (pp. 60–69). Then consider the following example:

> Look around the neighborhood and count the houses and cars. Do you have any trouble deciding which is which? Not likely. But an interesting case in constitutional law called even this seemingly obvious classification into question. It seems that police officers had observed a certain vehicle parked for several days, during which time individuals and small groups of people were also observed coming and going to and from the vehicle. Suspecting possible drug activity, the police investigated further and indeed found the occupant of the vehicle had drugs in his possession. The occupant was arrested and brought to trial on drug charges. The hitch for the prosecution was that the police had not obtained a search warrant before moving to investigate the vehicle. Why would that be necessary? Police don't need a search warrant to inspect a motor vehicle. But it turned out that the occupant was *living in* the vehicle (a motor home), and it was argued that because the vehicle was the occupant's place of residence, it should be covered by the 4th Amendment provision which protects "the right of the people to be secure in their *houses* . . ." against unreasonable search and seizure.[8]

Does this argument commit an informal fallacy of classification?

In the heat of a passionate debate over an issue, it may be expected that people will use the most powerful language they can muster to make and present their case. So be aware of the connotations of the labels and descriptions used in an argument's text, bearing in mind Critical Thinking Tip 2.1 (p. 49). We may say that some informal fallacy of **loaded language** has occurred when the language distorts the issue under discussion or when the argument leans more heavily on the connotations of the language than on the reasoning.

EUPHEMISM

A good example of issue-distorting language is the common rhetorical device of **euphemism.** The term derives from the Greek for good speech or good word. It refers to a figure of speech in which things are labeled or described in overly positive terms or terms that understate the negative. The tendency to use and favor euphemisms is natural and understandable as a psychological defense mechanism in many situations. It is nice to be able to put things in a polite way that is respectful of people's feelings. But euphemisms can also be used to obscure, mislead, and confuse, as when a politician refers to a "tax" as a "revenue enhancement." Nor are euphemisms confined to the political sphere. Euphemism is a strategy of first resort throughout public relations, for instance, where "human resource managers" (that is, the boss) devise increasingly artful and evasive ways of saying "you're fired," like "your functions have been outsourced" (huh?), or "you've been made redundant." Or here's one from the wonderful world of customer service. It seems that Blockbuster Video has stopped charging a "late fee" for videos returned after they're due. Instead, it assesses "extended viewing fees." Sounds more agreeable, doesn't it? If we think of euphemism as exaggeration in the positive direction, an equally powerful strategy consists of exaggerating the negative. This strategy is particularly useful in "demonizing official enemies" of state and thereby motivating public support for aggressive and hostile foreign policy. Following the etymology of euphemism, we might call such negative exaggeration **dysphemism,** from the Greek for bad speech or bad word.

APPLICATION EXERCISE 11.8 | Euphemisms

Here is a collection of 20th-century military euphemisms. See if you can match the euphemism (left column) with the thing described (right column).

Euphemism	Means
1. A "pacification center"	☐ To spy
2. A "protective reaction strike"	☐ Retreat
3. "Incontinent ordnance"	☐ A bombing raid
4. "Friendly fire"	☐ Bombs
5. "Force packages"	☐ A concentration camp
6. "Strategic withdrawal"	☐ Bombing or shooting someone on your side
7. To "gather intelligence"	☐ Off-target bombs
8. To "terminate"	☐ To destroy by bombing
9. To "degrade" the target	☐ Kidnapping and torture
10. "Collateral damage"	☐ To kill
11. "Extraordinary rendition"	☐ Civilian casualties caused by our side

AND SPEAKING OF: | **Connotations**

"Just about everyone discerned an Orwellian note in the name of the Pentagon's "Total Information Awareness Project," which was aimed at mining a vast centralized database of personal information for patterns that might reveal terrorist activities. The name was ultimately changed to the Terrorist Information Awareness Project in an effort to reassure Americans who had nothing to hide."[9]

LANGUAGE FUNCTIONS

Just as loaded labels can distort an issue, so can inappropriate applications of rhetorical features and persuasive capacities of language. So focus attention on language functions, again bearing in mind Critical Thinking Tip 2.1 (p. 49). Be on the lookout for extreme quantifiers ("all," "every," and so on), extreme intensifiers ("absolutely," "totally," "completely," and the like), and other universalizing expressions. Heavy reliance on this sort of language often masks weakness in the reasoning. If an argument is strong, it shouldn't need exaggeration to make its point. Again, we may say that some informal fallacy of loaded language has occurred when the argument leans more heavily on the intensity of the language than it does on the reasoning.

RHETORICAL QUESTIONS

Sometimes language functions are exploited as negotiating tactics or as strategic means of eliciting agreement. For example, a question is a request or invitation to respond, ordinarily at the voluntary discretion of the respondent. But we sometimes run across questions—called **rhetorical questions**—worded in such a way that only one of the possible answers is invited because all other possible answers are discredited. In "polite" discourse this device can be quite useful for creating an air of understatement. (Don't you agree?) But rhetorical questions can also amplify and overstate the case. (How in the world could you imagine otherwise?) Rhetorical questions are often deployed in lieu of any better argument. When you see this happen, you may say that the informal fallacy of rhetorical question has been committed.

PHANTOM DISTINCTIONS

Another deceptive use of the language, often deployed as an evasive maneuver of last resort, is to speak as though there is some important distinction to be noticed even though you don't know what it is or how to explain it. Here's a magnificent example of a **phantom distinction,** as recounted by our favorite linguist, Geoffrey Nunberg:

Arnold Schwarzenegger may be a newcomer to California politics, but he has clearly been swatting up on the state's traditional rhetorical themes. He launched his campaign by pledging to become "the people's governor," vowing that he would accept no money from "the special interests who have a stranglehold on Sacramento." When it transpired that he had accepted contributions from developers and other wealthy individuals, he explained that those weren't special interests but merely "powerful interests who control things." What he had meant, he said, was only that he would refuse contributions from public employee unions or other groups he might have to negotiate with as governor. He apologized for the confusion about his fund-raising policy by saying, "I was not articulate enough to explain that."[10]

Who knows? Perhaps what Schwarzenegger really meant was that he would refuse contributions just from those with whom he might have to negotiate *publicly.* That would have made more sense, wouldn't it? (But that would be a politically stupid thing to admit! Maybe the moral of this story is that when you step in your own droppings you should go outside to clean your shoes.)

REVIEW EXERCISE 11.4 | Fallacies of Language

In each of the following examples, check all fallacy categories that apply. Most important, explain each fallacy you identify.

1. Airplanes are used for getting high. And airplanes are perfectly legal. Drugs are used for getting high. So they should be legal, too.

	Equivocation/amphibole	Explain your answer:
	Phantom distinction	
	Abuse of vagueness	
	Weasel words	
	Faulty classification	
	Loaded language	
	Euphemism/dysphemism	
	Rhetorical question	

2. Lewis Carroll wrote: "I passed nobody on the road. Therefore nobody is slower than I am."

	Equivocation/amphibole	Explain your answer:
	Complex question	
	Abuse of vagueness	
	Weasel words	
	Faulty classification	
	Loaded language	
	Euphemism/dysphemism	
	Rhetorical question	

3. U.S. Senator Ted Stevens explaining a congressional measure to increase the compensation of members of the U.S. Congress: "It's not a pay raise. It is a pay equalization concept."

		Explain your answer:
	Equivocation/amphibole	
	Phantom distinction	
	Abuse of vagueness	
	Weasel words	
	Faulty classification	
	Loaded language	
	Euphemism/dysphemism	
	Rhetorical question	

4. Look! The notice on his office door says "Back Soon." But I've been waiting here for over an hour and a half!

		Explain your answer:
	Equivocation/amphibole	
	Phantom distinction	
	Abuse of vagueness	
	Weasel words	
	Faulty classification	
	Loaded language	
	Euphemism/dysphemism	
	Rhetorical question	

5. God is love. Love is blind. Therefore God is blind.

		Explain your answer:
	Equivocation/amphibole	
	Phantom distinction	
	Abuse of vagueness	
	Weasel words	
	Faulty classification	
	Loaded language	
	Euphemism/dysphemism	
	Rhetorical question	

6. News report: "High level FBI sources and Defense Department officials will neither confirm nor deny that a would-be terrorist suspect with possible links to al-Qaeda has been apprehended."

		Explain your answer:
	Equivocation/amphibole	
	Phantom distinction	
	Abuse of vagueness	
	Weasel words	
	Faulty classification	
	Loaded language	
	Euphemism/dysphemism	
	Rhetorical question	

7. "You couldn't have it if you did want it," the Queen said. "The rule is jam tomorrow and jam yesterday—but never jam today."

"It must sometimes come to jam today," Alice objected.

"No it can't," said the Queen. "It's jam every other day: today isn't any other day, you know."[11]

	Equivocation/amphibole	Explain your answer:
	Phantom distinction	
	Abuse of vagueness	
	Weasel words	
	Faulty classification	
	Loaded language	
	Euphemism/dysphemism	
	Rhetorical question	

FALLACIES OF RELEVANCE

Calvin and Hobbes   **by Bill Watterson**

FIGURE 11.3

IRRELEVANT REASONING

Suppose that someone came up to you and said, "Now that I know how to construct a deductively valid argument, I can finally settle the abortion issue once and for all! Here's my argument:

"If 'abortion' is an 8-letter word, then abortion should be against the law. 'Abortion' *is* an 8-letter word. Therefore, abortion should be against the law."

APPLICATION EXERCISE 11.9 | **"It Sounds So Logical!"**

Clearly something is wrong with the preceding argument. Can you explain what it is?

No reasonable person would be convinced by this argument, but what is wrong with the argument? Because the argument is in the form modus ponens, it can't be faulted formally. So what else might be wrong with it? Are the premises false? The second premise is true; count the letters. This leaves premise 1. Is premise 1 false? Before you answer this question, suppose that the conclusion of the argument is true. Now, is premise 1 false? Hard to tell, isn't it? You don't know yet whether the conclusion is true, but it might be, and in that case you can't be sure that premise 1 is false. (See the section in Chapter 6 on using truth tables to test for deductive validity.) So what *is* wrong with the argument? The problem here is that both premises are *irrelevant to the issue.* Why? Because the number of letters in the word "abortion" is irrelevant to the moral status of the act of abortion and therefore to the question of abortion law. Here you can see the concept of relevance in bold relief. An important informal consideration in evaluating arguments is whether the premises offered are relevant to what is at issue. If they are, so much the better for the argument. If not, some sort of informal fallacy of relevance, or irrelevant appeal, has been committed. The conceptual tools we use in detecting and diagnosing fallacies of relevance are the concept of relevance, as introduced and explained in Chapter 8, and the tools of issue analysis presented in Chapter 1. As we explained in Chapter 8, "relevance" means pertinent to the subject, related to the matter at hand, or on topic. Something is relevant only if it may reasonably be considered to count one way or another in a deliberation. In the preceding example, the *spelling* of the word "abortion" may not reasonably be considered to count for or against any position on the morality or legality of the procedure. And that's what we mean by irrelevant. The relevance problem in the argument in Application Exercise 11.9 is so glaring that the argument is clearly a fallacy. Other instances may be less obvious, although no less fallacious. Generally, the relevance of any premise of any argument to the issue in question may be challenged at any point. Bear in mind, however, that to challenge the relevance of a premise is not the same as establishing that it is irrelevant. Relevance is not always obvious. So it remains open to the arguer to meet the challenge by explaining how the premise bears on the conclusion or the issue at hand. But if a premise is relevant, the arguer should be able to explain the connection. Thus the most important thing to do is keep the issue or issues clearly in focus as you go and, where the relevance of some point to that issue is not readily apparent, challenge the relevance.

CRITICAL THINKING TIP 11.2 | **Maintain Issue Focus**

Keep the Issue or Issues in Focus.

DIVERSIONARY TACTICS

RED HERRING

A general label for diversionary tactics in argument is **red herring.** This colorful term derives from an old ruse used by prison escapees to throw dogs off their trails. (They would smear themselves with herring—which turns red when it spoils—to cover their scent.) Stuck for a good argument? Tell a story. Stuck for a good defense? Attack! No good answer? Evade the question—or give your canned answer to some *other* question. Can't prove your point? Change the subject. Got no point to make? Make a joke.

AND SPEAKING OF: | Red Herring

When it was first reported that the National Security Agency (NSA) was secretly engaged in domestic wire-tapping without search warrants, in violation of 1st and 4th Amendment civil liberties, the White House response was to denounce those who had "breached national security by leaking the information to the press" (and the press for publishing it).

STRAW PERSON

Sometimes when people are having trouble making a cogent argument in favor of a position, they distort the issue or address some alternative issue instead. For example, in opening arguments charging an executive with embezzlement, the prosecutor quotes harrowing statistics about white-collar crime. Although this statistical evidence may influence the jury, it is irrelevant to establishing the guilt of the defendant. Sometimes when people are having trouble making a cogent objection or argument against a position, they distort the position or set up some alternative position as a target for their objections. This distorted or alternative position is sometimes called a **straw person** because, like a person made out of straw, it is much easier to "knock down" than the real position or argument—or person. One of the nastier games played in electoral politics is distorting an opponent's voting record. Suppose an education appropriations bill is moving through the legislature. Now the party in power attaches a dozen or so budget-busting pork-barrel amendments to the bill. If your state assembly member votes against the bloated bill because of objections to the wasteful pork, a challenger in the next election can point to that voting record as evidence that the assembly member does not support education. Similarly, straw positions are often set up by out-of-context, selective quotation—a sneaky way to get your opponent to make your argument for you.

AND SPEAKING OF: | **Out-of-Context, Selective Quotation**

Op Ed

Peter Doran
Chicago Tribune

In the debate on global warming, the data on the climate of Antarctica has been distorted, at different times, by both sides. As a polar researcher caught in the middle, I'd like to set the record straight.

In January 2002, a research paper about Antarctic temperatures, of which I was the lead author, appeared in the journal *Nature*. At the time, the Antarctic Peninsula was warming, and many people assumed that meant the climate on the entire continent was heating up, as the Arctic was. But the Antarctic Peninsula represents only about 15 percent of the continent's land mass, so it could not tell the whole story of Antarctic climate. Our paper made the continental picture more clear.

My research colleagues and I found that from 1986 to 2000, one small, ice-free area of the Antarctic mainland had actually cooled. Our report also analyzed temperatures for the mainland in such a way as to remove the influence of the peninsula warming and found that, from 1966 to 2000, more of the continent had cooled than had warmed. Our summary statement pointed out how the cooling trend posed challenges to models of Antarctic climate and ecosystem change.

Newspaper and television reports focused on this part of the paper. And many news and opinion writers linked our study with another bit of polar research published that month, in *Science*, showing that part of Antarctica's ice sheet had been thickening—and erroneously concluded that the earth was not warming at all. "Scientific findings run counter to theory of global warming," said a headline on an editorial in the *San Diego Union-Tribune*. One conservative commentator wrote, "It's ironic that two studies suggesting that a new Ice Age may be under way may end the global warming debate."

In a rebuttal in the *Providence Journal*, in Rhode Island, the lead author of the *Science* paper and I explained that our studies offered no evidence that the earth was cooling. But the misinterpretation had already become legend, and in the four and half years since, it has only grown.

Our results have been misused as "evidence" against global warming by Michael Crichton in his novel *State of Fear* and by Ann Coulter in her latest book, *Godless: The Church of Liberalism.* Search my name on the Web, and you will find pages of links to everything from climate discussion groups to Senate policy committee documents—all citing my 2002 study as reason to doubt that the earth is warming. One recent Web column even put words in my mouth. I have never said that "the unexpected colder climate in Antarctica may possibly be signaling a lessening of the current global warming cycle." I have never thought such a thing either.

Our study did find that 58 percent of Antarctica cooled from 1966 to 2000. But during that period, the rest of the continent was warming. And climate models created since our paper was published have suggested a link between the lack of significant warming in Antarctica and the ozone hole over that continent. These models, conspicuously missing from the warming-skeptic literature, suggest that as the ozone hole heals—thanks to worldwide bans on ozone-destroying chemicals—all of Antarctica is likely to warm with the rest of the planet. An inconvenient truth?

Also missing from the skeptics' arguments is the debate over our conclusions. Another group of researchers who took a different approach found no clear cooling trend in Antarctica. We still stand by our results for the period we analyzed, but unbiased reporting would acknowledge differences of scientific opinion.

The disappointing thing is that we are even debating the direction of climate change on this globally important continent. And it may not end until we have more weather stations on Antarctica and longer-term data that demonstrate a clear trend.

In the meantime, I would like to remove my name from the list of scientists who dispute global warming. I know my coauthors would as well.[12]

TWO WRONGS (DON'T) MAKE A RIGHT

When blame is at issue, watch for an attempt to shift the blame. A police officer stops a speeding motorist. "Why stop me?" the driver asks. "Didn't you see that Jaguar fly by at 80 mph?" (This probably won't get the driver off the hook.) This kind of red herring is often referred to as the informal fallacy of **two wrongs,** which comes from the proverb "Two wrongs don't make a right." A variation of this move is spreading the blame. Caught using company stationery for personal use, an office worker says, "Everybody else does it." This kind of red herring is often referred to as the informal fallacy of **common practice.**

AND SPEAKING OF: | Two Wrongs

Rove Critical of Media's "Corrosive Role" in Politics
Associated Press

Presidential adviser Karl Rove said yesterday that journalists often criticize political strategists because they want to draw attention away from the "corrosive role" their own coverage plays in politics and government.

"Some decry the professional role of politics—they would like to see it disappear," Rove told graduating students at the George Washington University Graduate

School of Political Management. "Some argue political professionals are ruining American politics—trapping candidates in daily competition for the news cycle instead of long-term strategic thinking in the best interest of the country."

But Rove turned that criticism on journalists.

"It's odd to me that most of these critics are journalists and columnists," he said. "Perhaps they don't like sharing the field of play. Perhaps they want to draw attention away from the corrosive role their coverage has played focusing attention on process and not substance."[13]

REVIEW EXERCISE 11.5 | **Irrelevant Reasoning I**

1. Pushy father-in-law to new bride: "So, when are you kids planning to make us grandparents?"

		Explain your answer:
	Equivocation/amphibole	
	Phantom distinction	
	Abuse of vagueness	
	Weasel words	
	Faulty classification	
	Loaded language	
	Complex question	
	Rhetorical question	
	Straw person	
	Two wrongs/common practice	

2. The end of anything is its perfection. Therefore, because death is the end of life, death must be the perfection of life.

	Equivocation/amphibole	
	Phantom distinction	
	Abuse of vagueness	
	Weasel words	
	Faulty classification	
	Loaded language	
	Complex question	
	Rhetorical question	
	Straw person	
	Two wrongs/common practice	

3. Jump ahead and take a look at example 4 in Review Exercise 11.7 (p. 342). The example comes from a Philip Morris ad campaign. Then look at the following quote from the Philip Morris vice president for corporate affairs, Guy L. Smith: "[These ads were] an attempt to raise the level of awareness, but certainly not to scare anybody."

	Equivocation/amphibole	Explain your answer:
	Phantom distinction	
	Abuse of vagueness	
	Weasel words	
	Faulty classification	
	Loaded language	
	Complex question	
	Rhetorical question	
	Straw person	
	Two wrongs/common practice	

4. People object to sexism and racism on the ground that they involve "discrimination." But what is objectionable about discrimination? We discriminate all the time—in the cars we buy, the foods we eat, the books we read, the friends we choose. The fact is, there's nothing wrong with discrimination as such.

	Equivocation/amphibole	Explain your answer:
	Phantom distinction	
	Abuse of vagueness	
	Weasel words	
	Faulty classification	
	Loaded language	
	Complex question	
	Rhetorical question	
	Straw person	
	Two wrongs/common practice	

5. White House spokesperson Scott McClellan was asked by reporters to discuss the ethics of the administration's practice of presenting political propaganda to the public as though it were objective news. His response: "The informational news releases that you're referring to are something that have been in use for many years. It goes back to the early '90s."

	Equivocation/amphibole	Explain your answer:
	Phantom distinction	
	Abuse of vagueness	
	Weasel words	
	Faulty classification	
	Loaded language	
	Complex question	
	Rhetorical question	
	Straw person	
	Two wrongs/common practice	

6. The dean of a prestigious graduate school of business once objected to the inclusion of business ethics in his school's graduate program. "Much can be said about the moral and ethical nature of economic systems," he admitted, "but by the time students get to graduate schools, their moral and ethical standards have long been set. And I think it's quite presumptuous of us to tell them what is right and what is wrong."

		Explain your answer:
	Equivocation/amphibole	
	Phantom distinction	
	Abuse of vagueness	
	Weasel words	
	Faulty classification	
	Loaded language	
	Complex question	
	Rhetorical question	
	Straw person	
	Two wrongs/common practice	

DISCUSSION TOPIC 11.2 | Relevance

Political rivals Governor Hiram "Bull" Frogbottom and Senator G. Edgar Ragsdale are trading accusations and rejoinders in the press. On Monday, Ragsdale accuses Frogbottom of "taking money from special interests groups and having a political slush fund." Tuesday morning, Frogbottom holds a press conference. Consider the five "sound bites" that follow. With a classmate or study partner, take turns challenging and defending the relevance of Frogbottom's responses.

1. "Sen. Ragsdale evidently misunderstood my previous positions, so, let me clear the record."
2. "Special interest groups! Why, Ragsdale has been on the payroll of gambling interests for years!"
3. "What Sen. Ragadale terms a 'slush fund' is, in fact, a perfectly legal campaign account. Let me explain the campaign finance regulations to you."
4. "If Ragsdale didn't sense his own campaign was in trouble, he wouldn't be so desperate to smear me."
5. "Look, the whole process of political campaigning needs reform. And, if elected, I intend to get special interest money out of politics."

AD HOMINEM

One thing we find ourselves occasionally reminding our students is to depersonalize the discussion. Focus on the position and the reasoning, not the person. When we start talking about liberals and neocons, rather than liberal*ism* and neoconservat*ism*, we are already slipping into irrelevance. **Ad hominem** (Latin for to the man) refers to the rhetorical strategy of irrelevant personal attack. When people argue *ad hominem*, they argue against the person rather than the position or the reasoning. They argue that the person, not that person's reasoning or position, is defective or at fault. *Ad hominem*'s prevalence and remarkable rhetorical force both

PHILOSOPHICAL DIFFERENCES

probably stem from general psychological tendencies to personalize conflict and escalate hostility. As natural as it may be for us to turn attention to the personal weaknesses, flaws, and failures of others, these things—whether real or imagined—are, with only rare exceptions, irrelevant to whatever the issue is under discussion. A person may be a jerk, but that doesn't make his or her position incorrect.

ABUSIVE AD HOMINEM

The easiest to spot among the varieties of *ad hominem* is the flat-out gratuitous name-calling that has become the stock in trade of AM talk radio. The godfather of *ad hominem* in recent years has been right-wing radio talk-show host Rush Limbaugh. In a typical excerpt from the first of his several books, *The Way Things Ought to Be,* he writes,

> I have spoken extensively in this book about the various fringe movements and the spiritual tie that binds them: radical liberalism. Two groups that are particularly close, to the point of being nearly indistinguishable, are the environmentalists and the animal rights activists. Because I devoted a chapter to the environmentalists I thought it only fair to include one about animal rights activism. I certainly do not want to be accused of discrimination. Every wacko movement must have its day in my book. . . . The basic right to life of an animal—which is the source of energy for many animal rights wackos—must be inferred from the anticruelty laws humans have written, not from any divine source. Our laws do not prevent us from killing animals for food or sport, so the right to life of an animal is nonexistent.[14]

In this passage. Limbaugh begins by alluding to an opposing political or philosophical position that he calls "radical liberalism." But rather than develop a detailed criticism of the "radical liberal" position and its supporting arguments (assuming there is such a position and that anyone holds it), Limbaugh simply labels the people he wants to identify with it as "wackos." That's *ad hominem.* This sort of gratuitous name-calling we will refer to as **abusive ad hominem.**

AND SPEAKING OF: | **Abusive ad Hominem**

"The swing voters—I like to refer to them as the idiot voters because they don't have set philosophical principles. You're either a liberal or you're a conservative if you have an IQ above a toaster."[15]

It is deeply discouraging to behold the degree to which this sort of rhetoric has succeeded in building audiences, holding and entertaining audiences, and influencing the opinions of audiences. So many imitators now follow the Limbaugh formula that it has become the dominant form of public political discourse in the United States. Even some of the original targets of this strategy, political liberals, have adopted it, as intellectually disgraceful as it is.

CIRCUMSTANTIAL AD HOMINEM

A more sophisticated form of *ad hominem* consists of shifting attention from the issue in question and the position or the argument opposed to the person holding that position and his or her life circumstances. This is called **circumstantial ad hominem.** The way this is supposed to work is by making the suggestion (innuendo) that it's the person's life circumstances, rather than any reasoning, that lead him or her to that position on the issue. Thus we can dispense with (ignore) the reasoning. For example, someone is identified as a "liberal," and that by itself is taken as sufficient reason for dismissing his or her criticism of some particular policy. This is *ad hominem.* Similarly, if the political polarity is reversed, it is *ad hominem* to dismiss an argument simply on the basis of the "conservative" orientation of the person making the argument. Or suppose someone is identified as Jewish (or Palestinian) and this by itself is taken as sufficient reason for dismissing an argument about U.S. foreign policy in the Middle East, as though religious or ethnic affiliation, rather than reasoning, is what determines that person's views on the subject. Again this would be a case of circumstantial *ad hominem.*

GUILT BY ASSOCIATION

A special case of circumstantial *ad hominem,* in which the attack is based on the person's relationships with others, is often appropriately called the fallacy of **guilt by association.** In recent years, many "interest groups" have made names for themselves in mobilizing public opinion and lobbying in legislatures in support of their causes and agendas. The ACLU, the National Rifle Association (NRA), the National Organization for Women (NOW), Earth First, and other prominent advocacy groups have identified themselves with certain policy directions on a range of issues. This has given rise to a convenient shortcut for many people: Simply knowing which groups support or oppose a given policy position is enough for some people to make up their minds about the issue. Simply knowing a given person's current or prior affiliations is enough for some people to pass judgment on the substance of that person's argument or position in a debate. Strictly speaking, this would be a fallacious (unreliable) inference. A similar fallacy, often called **genetic appeal,** consists of evaluating something strictly in terms of its origin or sources (or genesis). For example, it has been argued by certain religious fundamentalists that dancing is evil and should be forbidden because it originated as a form of pagan worship. We used to hear conservative arguments against parent cooperative daycare programs based primarily on the grounds that the idea of cooperatives originated among socialists. Watch for *ad hominem* tactics like these wherever partisan lines are well known—wherever there's a well established "us" and "them."

POISONING THE WELL

A similar strategy—a sort of circumstantial *ad hominem* in advance—attempts to discredit a position before any argument for it has a chance to get a hearing. Don't listen to anything he says; he's nothing but a . . . This strategy is often called **poisoning the well.** The "well" is the reasoning. The "poison" is prejudice, which literally means "pre-judgment." A good critical thinker gives due and open-minded consideration to the reasoning before arriving at judgment. Anyone who tries to discourage this is committing the informal fallacy of poisoning the well.

WRITING ASSIGNMENT 11.1 | Genetic Appeal?

Some years ago in the state of California, the general election tested two competing measures concerning liquor taxation. Proposition 134, the "Nickel-a-Drink" measure, qualified for the ballot by a citizen petition drive organized by a coalition led by Mothers Against Drunk Driving (MADD). It was pitted against Proposition 126, which was lobbied onto the ballot through the state legislature by the liquor industry. Here you will find a portion of the argument used by the supporters of Proposition 134 against Proposition 126. Our question for you is this: Is this argument an instance of the fallacy of genetic appeal or not? Explain.

> Proposition 126 is sponsored by the liquor industry. The reason they say Proposition 126 is a better approach to taxing the liquor industry than Proposition 134, the "Nickel-a-Drink" proposal, is that Proposition 126 taxes them less.
>
> The only reason Proposition 126 is on the ballot is that the liquor industry spends $1,000,000 each year lobbying the Legislature and has contributed over $1,600,000 to politicians since 1988. What the liquor industry wants, the Legislature gives. That's why the Legislature has not changed the wine tax from 1 cent per gallon since 1937.
>
> The sole purpose of Proposition 126 is to defeat Proposition 134, the "Nickel-a-Drink" Alcohol Tax Initiative. When reading the argument in favor of Proposition 126, CONSIDER THE SOURCE—IT IS THE LIQUOR INDUSTRY!

REVIEW EXERCISE 11.6 | Irrelevant Reasoning II

In each of the following examples, check all fallacy categories that apply. Most important, explain each fallacy you identify.

1. No man can know anything about pregnancy and childbirth, because no man can ever go through the experience. So no man is qualified to render an opinion about abortion.

		Explain your answer:
	Abusive *ad hominem*	
	Circumstantial *ad hominem*	
	Guilt by association	
	Genetic appeal	
	Poisoning the well	

2. How can you believe anything that this bimbo has to say? Can't you see that she has everything to gain by implicating the president in this scandal? Look, she's sold her story to *Hard Copy!*

		Explain your answer:
	Abusive *ad hominem*	
	Circumstantial *ad hominem*	
	Guilt by association	
	Genetic appeal	
	Poisoning the well	

3. I was profoundly dismayed by the badgering of witnesses during the hearings by Senator D. "Mo" Cratic. Doesn't he realize that such criticism reflects badly on the president? If we can't expect the members of our own party to support the president in a time of crisis, just who can we turn to?

		Explain your answer:
	Abusive *ad hominem*	
	Circumstantial *ad hominem*	
	Guilt by association	
	Genetic appeal	
	Poisoning the well	

4. I can't vote for the man, because I remember some years ago in his law practice he defended that wacko Unabomber guy.

		Explain your answer:
	Abusive *ad hominem*	
	Circumstantial *ad hominem*	
	Guilt by association	
	Genetic appeal	
	Poisoning the well	

5. CNN journalist Wolf Blitzer interviewing neoconservative opinion-maker Richard Perle:

Blitzer: Let me read a quote from the *New Yorker* article [by Seymour Hersh], the March 17th issue, just out now. "There is no question that Perle believes that removing Saddam from power is the right thing to do. At the same time, he has set up a company that may gain from a war."

Perle: . . . Look, Sy Hersh is the closest thing American journalism has to a terrorist, frankly.[16]

	Abusive *ad hominem*	Explain your answer:
	Circumstantial *ad hominem*	
	Guilt by association	
	Genetic appeal	
	Poisoning the well	

PROVINCIALISM

Just as you should watch for *ad hominem* tactics wherever there's a well-established "us" and "them," you should be on the alert for language that appeals to considerations of group loyalty, patriotism, nationalism, and so on. Sometimes the group you're supposed to identify with is considerably smaller than a nation—a region, a city, or perhaps a professional, occupational, or religious group, or a school, or a team. Sometimes the group is even larger than a nation: a gender, for example. The general term for discourse that leans too heavily on irrelevant considerations of loyalty is **provincialism.** But, like *ad hominem,* the fallacy consists in shifting attention from the issues and from the substance of the reasoning to something else, in this case to emotionally potent aspects of identity and difference among people. We introduced this chapter with a quotation from the 18th-century British philosopher Jeremy Bentham. Please look at that quotation now. The fallacy of provincialism, whose quintessential employment is nationalism, patriotism, or both, has become a leading rhetorical strategy of the party in power in the United States in this century (so far). It has been used repeatedly by the Bush administration to deflect criticism, especially of its foreign policy, from any quarter. If any member of Congress questions the war in Iraq, for example, a spokesperson for the administration typically dismisses the question by associating the congressperson with "the enemy." In November 2005, a Pennsylvania member of the House of Representatives, John Murtha—a decorated Vietnam war veteran and one of the most consistent congressional supporters of the military—spoke in Congress against the administration's management of the Iraq war, calling it "a flawed policy wrapped in illusion." He went on to call for a withdrawal of American troops over a 6-month period, saying, "It's time to bring the troops home." The White House response was to accuse Murtha of "advocating surrender" and to associate him with antiwar filmmaker Michael Moore. Scott McClellan, White House press secretary at that time, said that it is "baffling that [Murtha] is endorsing the policy positions of Michael Moore and the extreme liberal wing of the Democratic party. . . . The eve of an historic democratic election in Iraq is not the time to surrender to the terrorists."[17] Murtha has so angered the Bush administration and its supporters that a "Boot Murtha" movement has arisen on the Internet, where the themes established by the White House press secretary have been picked up and amplified. In an "Open Letter to Congressman Murtha," dated June 24, 2006, one unidentified party writes, "You have become one of the key "useful idiots" that our enemy relies upon for assistance. You are now standing on the same moral and intellectual ground as Cindy Sheehan and that mountainous pile of anti-Americanism, Michael Moore. People see you now as 'Osama's Congressman.'" It is far too easy to be drawn into the kind of ugly battle over who's on whose "side" that this kind of rhetoric engenders, losing touch with the original issues.

AND SPEAKING OF: | PROVINCIALISM

What do you think of the name given to the piece of "homeland security" legislation rushed through Congress immediately following September 11, 2001: the "Uniting and Strengthening America by Providing Appropriate Tools Required to Intercept and Obstruct Terrorism" Act (USA PATRIOT Act)?

TRADITION AND NOVELTY

Provincialism is often coupled with an **appeal to tradition,** in which the argument rests heavily on whether something adheres to or departs from tradition. During the Watergate scandal in 1974, there were frequent appeals to tradition surrounding the attempt to impeach President Richard Nixon. Many insisted that Nixon should not be impeached simply because it had never been done before. But the fact that a president had never before been impeached was irrelevant to the issues of corruption and betrayal of public trust that undermined the Nixon presidency.

In contrast to the appeal to tradition but just as fallacious is the **appeal to novelty,** which consists of assuming or arguing that something is good or desirable just *because* it is new or different. Watch for this tactic around election time. Candidates who use slogans like "Leadership for a Change," or "It's Time for New Ideas" *may* have something new and different to offer, something that would advance the public interest, but the *claim* of novelty by itself is irrelevant.

POSITIONING

Whereas people sometimes attempt to discredit others through guilt by association, they can just as effectively promote themselves and others by **positioning—** by appropriating the reputation of a leader in a field to sell a product, candidate, or idea. In advertising, positioning is supposed to work by creating a link in the prospective buyer's mind between the upstart brand and its leading competitor. One of the most famous ad campaigns to rely on this strategy was 7Up's "The Un-Cola" campaign. But positioning is hardly confined to advertising. During presidential election years, many a congressional campaign is based almost entirely on party affiliation with the incumbent president or the front-runner. This is called "riding on the coattails." In politics, part of waging a successful campaign often means trading on the reputation of another well-known, popular political figure. Thus candidates of both parties are forever attempting to appropriate the mantle of a Lincoln or a Kennedy by invoking lines from their famous speeches and forging all sorts of tenuous connections. One of the most famous attempts at positioning was Dan Quayle's attempt to link himself with JFK in the

1988 vice presidential debate, saying that he was as seasoned and experienced a potential leader as Kennedy had been before his election as president. The attempt backfired when Democratic candidate Lloyd Bentson positioned himself even closer to Kennedy, saying "I served with Jack Kennedy in the Senate. Jack Kennedy was a friend of mine. Senator, you're no Jack Kennedy." Bentson's response to Quayle was and still is considered by many historians as the "knock out punch" of the entire campaign. Yet it was no less an instance of the informal fallacy of positioning than Quayle's.

WRITING ASSIGNMENT 11.2 | **Is Gender Relevant?**

Is gender relevant? Perhaps an even better question would be, "When is gender relevant?" Do you think Susie commits a fallacy of relevance in the Calvin and Hobbes cartoon earlier (Figure 11.3) p. 323 or not? Write a short essay in which you explain why. Are there any circumstances in which you think gender is relevant?

EMOTIONAL APPEALS

It may be that some of you, remembering his own case, will be annoyed that whereas he, in standing trial upon a less serious charge than this, made pitiful appeals to the jury with floods of tears, and had his infant children produced in court to excite the maximum of sympathy, I on the contrary intend to do nothing of the sort.[18] —SOCRATES, IN *THE APOLOGY* AT LINE 34C.

Emotions can exert a powerful influence over our thinking, but they are not always relevant to the issue at hand. In the examples used earlier to illustrate the fallacy of provincialism, it is easy to feel (indeed, difficult to miss) the emotional energy involved. Because emotional energy is such a forceful element in our thinking and relating to the world, there are widely used rhetorical strategies based on the evocation and expression of emotion. These are often intended to overwhelm or substitute for calm and dispassionate (Note: dis*passion*ate) rational deliberation. Probably the three leading emotional appeals are those to anger, pity, and fear.

CRITICAL THINKING TIP 11.3 | **Tune into Relevance**

Pay Attention to the Relevance (or Lack Thereof) of the Emotional Appeal. Relevance May Not Be Obvious on the Surface, but It Should Always Be Explainable.

APPEAL TO ANGER

One of the most powerful emotions is anger. Often anger is powerful enough to overwhelm reason and good common sense, as we recognize, for example, when we speak of crimes of passion and distinguish them from premeditated crimes.

Thus a powerful persuasive strategy consists of arousing and mobilizing anger in support of a position—a favorite of political campaign strategists, especially where the electorate is relatively poorly informed. When this strategy is pursued in place of reasoning, the informal fallacy of **appeal to anger** is being committed. To be sure, there is often good reason to be angry. And anger, when it's reasonably justified, is a powerful and appropriate motivator. But when little or no specific reason is presented for being angry, and instead a vague and rhetorical appeal to general frustration is used to arouse anger, watch out. This is the sort of urging that often leads people to "shoot themselves in the foot."

APPEAL TO PITY

A similar strategy consists of attempting to persuade people by making them feel sorrow, sympathy, or anguish, where such feelings, however understandable and genuine, are not relevant to the issue at stake. The informal fallacy of **appeal to pity** often is used in attempts to secure special dispensation or exemption from deadlines and penalties. For example, the student who deserves a "C" in history might try to persuade the teacher to raise the grade for a variety of lamentable reasons: it's the first grade below a "B" the student's ever received; it spoils a 3.85 GPA; the student needs a higher grade to qualify for law school and the family has taken a third mortgage to finance prelaw education. Pity is not *always* irrelevant. For example, when an attorney asks a judge to take into consideration the squalid upbringing of a client in determining a criminal sentence, this is probably not a fallacious appeal to pity. Although such an appeal would be irrelevant and fallacious in arguing for the person's innocence, it may be germane to the question of the severity of the sentence. Think of the German youth who in the summer of 1987 flew a small plane into the middle of Red Square in Moscow. That he may have been acting out of simple youthful exuberance rather than some motive more threatening to Soviet national security is irrelevant to whether he acted illegally, but it's not irrelevant to how severely he should be punished.

APPEAL TO FEAR

A similar strategy involves attempting to intimidate people into accepting a position. The informal fallacy of **appeal to fear** takes the basic form "Believe this (or do this), or else!" This, too, has become a favorite of the Bush administration in the wake of the September 11, 2001, attacks.

AND SPEAKING OF: | **Appealing to Fear**

Read through the following portion of the speech delivered October 7, 2002, by George W. Bush, urging Congress to authorize the invasion of Iraq. Count and highlight the references to terror, terrorism, weapons of mass destruction, threats, danger, and so on, that appeal to fear.

For Immediate Release
Office of the Press Secretary
October 7, 2002

President Bush Outlines Iraqi Threat

. . . Tonight I want to take a few minutes to discuss a grave threat to peace, and America's determination to lead the world in confronting that threat.

The threat comes from Iraq. It arises directly from the Iraqi regime's own actions—its history of aggression, and its drive toward an arsenal of terror. Eleven years ago, as a condition for ending the Persian Gulf War, the Iraqi regime was required to destroy its weapons of mass destruction, to cease all development of such weapons, and to stop all support for terrorist groups. The Iraqi regime has violated all of those obligations. It possesses and produces chemical and biological weapons. It is seeking nuclear weapons. It has given shelter and support to terrorism, and practices terror against its own people. The entire world has witnessed Iraq's eleven-year history of defiance, deception and bad faith.

We also must never forget the most vivid events of recent history. On September the 11th, 2001, America felt its vulnerability—even to threats that gather on the other side of the earth. We resolved then, and we are resolved today, to confront every threat, from any source, that could bring sudden terror and suffering to America.

Members of the Congress of both political parties, and members of the United Nations Security Council, agree that Saddam Hussein is a threat to peace and must disarm. We agree that the Iraqi dictator must not be permitted to threaten America and the world with horrible poisons and diseases and gases and atomic weapons. Since we all agree on this goal, the issue is: how can we best achieve it?

Many Americans have raised legitimate questions: about the nature of the threat; about the urgency of action—why be concerned now; about the link between Iraq developing weapons of terror, and the wider war on terror. These are all issues we've discussed broadly and fully within my administration. And tonight, I want to share those discussions with you.

First, some ask why Iraq is different from other countries or regimes that also have terrible weapons. While there are many dangers in the world, the threat from Iraq stands alone—because it gathers the most serious dangers of our age in one place. Iraq's weapons of mass destruction are controlled by a murderous tyrant who has already used chemical weapons to kill thousands of people. This same tyrant has tried to dominate the Middle East, has invaded and brutally occupied a small neighbor, has struck other nations without warning, and holds an unrelenting hostility toward the United States.

By its past and present actions, by its technological capabilities, by the merciless nature of its regime, Iraq is unique. As a former chief weapons inspector of the U.N. has said, "The fundamental problem with Iraq remains the nature of the regime, itself. Saddam Hussein is a homicidal dictator who is addicted to weapons of mass destruction."

Some ask how urgent this danger is to America and the world. The danger is already significant, and it only grows worse with time. If we know Saddam Hussein has dangerous weapons today—and we do—does it make any sense for the world to wait to confront him as he grows even stronger and develops even more dangerous weapons?

In 1995, after several years of deceit by the Iraqi regime, the head of Iraq's military industries defected. It was then that the regime was forced to admit that it had produced more than 30,000 liters of anthrax and other deadly biological agents. The inspectors, however, concluded that Iraq had likely produced two to four times that amount. This is a massive stockpile of biological weapons that has never been accounted for, and capable of killing millions.

We know that the regime has produced thousands of tons of chemical agents, including mustard gas, sarin nerve gas, VX nerve gas. Saddam Hussein also has experience in using chemical weapons. He has ordered chemical attacks on Iran, and on more than forty villages in his own country. These actions killed or injured at least 20,000 people, more than six times the number of people who died in the attacks of September the 11th.

And surveillance photos reveal that the regime is rebuilding facilities that it had used to produce chemical and biological weapons. Every chemical and biological weapon that Iraq has or makes is a direct violation of the truce that ended the Persian Gulf War in 1991. Yet, Saddam Hussein has chosen to build and keep these weapons despite international sanctions, U.N. demands, and isolation from the civilized world.

Iraq possesses ballistic missiles with a likely range of hundreds of miles—far enough to strike Saudi Arabia, Israel, Turkey, and other nations—in a region where more than 135,000 American civilians and service members live and work. We've also discovered through intelligence that Iraq has a growing fleet of manned and unmanned aerial vehicles that could be used to disperse chemical or biological weapons across broad areas. We're concerned that Iraq is exploring ways of using these UAVs for missions targeting the United States. And, of course, sophisticated delivery systems aren't required for a chemical or biological attack; all that might be required are a small container and one terrorist or Iraqi intelligence operative to deliver it.

And that is the source of our urgent concern about Saddam Hussein's links to international terrorist groups. Over the years, Iraq has provided safe haven to terrorists such as Abu Nidal, whose terror organization carried out more than 90 terrorist attacks in 20 countries that killed or injured nearly 900 people, including 12 Americans. Iraq has also provided safe haven to Abu Abbas, who was responsible for seizing the Achille Lauro and killing an American passenger. And we know that Iraq is continuing to finance terror and gives assistance to groups that use terrorism to undermine Middle East peace.

We know that Iraq and the al Qaeda terrorist network share a common enemy—the United States of America. We know that Iraq and al Qaeda have had high-level contacts that go back a decade. Some al Qaeda leaders who fled Afghanistan went to Iraq. These include one senior al Qaeda leader who received medical treatment in Baghdad this year, and who has been associated with planning for chemical and biological attacks. We've learned that Iraq has trained al Qaeda members in bomb-making and poisons and deadly gases. And we know that after September the 11th, Saddam Hussein's regime gleefully celebrated the terrorist attacks on America.

Iraq could decide on any given day to provide a biological or chemical weapon to a terrorist group or individual terrorists. Alliance with terrorists could allow the Iraqi regime to attack America without leaving any fingerprints. . . .

CRITICAL THINKING TIP 11.4 | Relevance and Maintaining Issue Focus

Remember That Issues Are Complex and That What Looks Like a Diversion May Occasionally Be Relevant. But If So, It Should Eventually Return to the Issue.

REVIEW EXERCISE 11.7 | Irrelevant Reasoning III

In each of the following examples, check all fallacy categories that apply. Most important, explain each fallacy you identify.

1. "And the Lord God commanded man, saying, 'You may eat freely of every tree of the garden; but the tree of the knowledge of good and evil you shall not eat, for in the day that you eat of it you shall die.'"[19]

		Explain your answer:
	Appeal to anger	
	Appeal to fear	
	Appeal to pity	
	Straw person	
	Two wrongs	
	Common practice	

2. "Precisely what is Nixon accused of doing that his predecessors didn't do many times over? The break in and wire-tapping at the Watergate? Just how different was that from the bugging of Barry Goldwater's apartment during the 1964 presidential campaign?"[20]

		Explain your answer:
	Appeal to anger	
	Appeal to fear	
	Appeal to pity	
	Straw person	
	Two wrongs	
	Common practice	

3. "[The fight for the Equal Rights Amendment in Iowa] is about a socialist, anti-family political movement that encourages women to leave their husbands, kill their children, practice witchcraft, destroy capitalism, and become lesbians."[21]

		Explain your answer:
	Appeal to anger	
	Appeal to fear	
	Appeal to pity	
	Straw person	
	Two wrongs	
	Common practice	

4. In the late 1980s, as the public policy issue over secondhand smoke swung further in the direction of segregating smokers and restricting them to designated smoking areas, the Philip Morris corporation placed the following full-page ad in major newspapers like the *New York Times*:

$1 trillion is too much financial power to ignore.

America's 55.8 million smokers are a powerful economic force. If their household income of $1 trillion were a Gross National Product, it would be the third largest in the world. The plain truth is that smokers are one of the most economically powerful groups in this country. They help fuel the engine of the largest economy on the globe. The American Smoker—an economic force.

		Explain your answer:
	Appeal to anger	
	Appeal to fear	
	Appeal to pity	
	Straw person	
	Two wrongs	
	Common practice	

5. "When confronted with evidence of errors or bias, Wikipedians invoke a favorite excuse: look how often the mainstream media, and the traditional encyclopedia are wrong!"[22]

		Explain your answer:
	Appeal to anger	
	Appeal to fear	
	Appeal to pity	
	Straw person	
	Two wrongs	
	Common practice	

FALLACIOUS APPEALS TO AUTHORITY

As we discussed in Chapter 1, reliance upon authority is appropriate and understandable in many circumstances. Most of what we learn comes from some authority. And because we never arrive at the stage of knowing everything or being expert in every field, we continue to rely on authority throughout our lives. But we also noted a risk inherent in reliance upon authority. The risk is that we might rely too heavily on authority or rely on authority when we shouldn't. To the extent that we rely upon unreliable authority, or upon authority whose reliability is open to serious question, we undermine the reliability of our reasoning and may be said to be committing some informal fallacy of **appeal to authority.** How do we know that the authority we are relying upon is reliable? How do we tell when we are relying too heavily on authority or relying on authority when we shouldn't? We now look more closely at these questions and develop some guidelines.

INVINCIBLE AUTHORITY

Begin with the example we used in Chapter 1 to illustrate the general risk of over-reliance upon authority. The Heaven's Gate mass suicide presents a particularly chilling example of overreliance on authority, but it is not the only such example. Vivid and scary accounts occasionally come to light of cults and groups such as Scientology, the Moonies, the Rajneeshees, Jonestown (where several hundred followers of Reverend Jim Jones were led to commit mass suicide), and David Koresh's Branch Davidians. All of these accounts illustrate the danger of allowing reality to be defined by appeal to the unassailable pronouncements of some "spiritual leader." When an appeal to authority wipes out all other considerations, it constitutes a fallacious appeal to authority. Such appeals to **invincible authority** have a notorious kind of currency within cults or groups whose organizational principles or doctrines depend upon subordinating all personal autonomy. But such appeals are not confined to the dark and sinister world of spiritual fascism. Such appeals to invincible authority can be found of all places in the history of science. Some of Galileo's colleagues refused to look into his telescope and see for themselves, because they were convinced that no evidence could contradict Aristotle's accounts of astronomy. This is no isolated aberration. Galileo himself makes a similar argument when he says, "But can you doubt that air has weight when you have the clear testimony of Aristotle affirming that all the elements have weight including air, and excepting only fire?"[23] This suggests that perhaps we should adopt a general rule that any authority worth relying on will remain open to question or challenge.

CRITICAL THINKING TIP 11.5 | **Reliable Authority**

Any Authority That Places Itself Beyond Question Is Unreliable. Any Authority Worth Relying on Remains Open to Question.

UNIDENTIFIED AUTHORITY

Think for a moment about Critical Thinking Tip 11.5. If we regard the reliability of any authority as depending on that authority's remaining open to question, it becomes obvious that any reliable authority must be identifiable. How can we question an authority if we don't know who the authority is? Despite this point, expert opinion is often merely alluded to or identified in such a vague and incomplete way as to make any verification of reliability impossible. This is a favorite device of tabloids such as the *National Enquirer,* which use phrases like "experts agree," "University studies show," and "a Russian scientist has discovered," to lend the weight of authority to all sorts of quackery. When an authority is left unspecified, we may say that an informal fallacy of appeal to **unidentified authority** has occurred.

IRRELEVANT AUTHORITY

These days, real expertise tends to be specialized. And although some remarkable individuals excel in more than one area of expertise, there is probably no such animal as an expert on everything. Accordingly, whenever an appeal to authority is introduced, it is wise to be aware of the area of expertise of any given authority— and to be mindful of the relevance of that particular area of expertise to the issue under discussion. When the appeal is to an authority whose expertise is in some field other than the one at issue, we may say that an informal fallacy of appeal to **irrelevant authority** has occurred. A common variety of appeal to irrelevant authority is the celebrity **testimonial** used throughout advertising for products ranging from aspirin to presidential candidates.

DIVISION OF EXPERT OPINION

Especially where controversial issues are involved, we may expect to find disagreement even among the experts. What then? We could simply quote the experts with whom we are in agreement, but the weakness of this as a reasoning strategy is easy to see. People who disagree with us can quote their own experts, and this leads to a standoff. Finding ourselves in agreement with one authority does not make this a more reliable authority than a competing authority with whom we are at odds. Simple appeal to congenial authority, where expert opinion is divided, can be dismissed as the informal fallacy of **division of expert opinion.** But it's not as though there is never a way to move beyond this sort of standoff. When expert opinion is divided, look into the credentials and affiliations of the experts. See if you can learn anything about their reputations. How are they regarded by their peers in their areas of expertise? This may be of some use in sifting through competing appeals to authority.

CONFLICT OF INTEREST

Sometimes claims are advanced by appeal to experts who have impressive and genuinely relevant credentials but whose testimony may legitimately be suspect because of a demonstrable **conflict of interest.** The reliability of any authority, even in his or her own area of specialized expertise, depends also on that person being impartial. An authority whose impartiality has been compromised is no longer reliable, regardless of the degree or relevance of his or her expertise. For example, if we find that some scientific study of the effects of secondhand tobacco smoke was underwritten by a research grant from the Tobacco Institute, we should at least look for other studies to compare this one with.

AND SPEAKING OF: | **Conflict of Interest**

Utilities Pay Scientist Ally on Warming

Associated Press

Coal-burning utilities are contributing money to one of the few remaining climate scientists openly critical of the broad consensus that fossil fuel emissions are intensifying global warming.

The critic, Patrick J. Michaels, is a professor of environmental sciences at the University of Virginia, a senior fellow at the libertarian Cato Institute and Virginia's state climatologist.

Dr. Michaels told Western business leaders last year that he was running out of money for his analyses of other scientists' global warming research. So a Colorado utility organized a collection campaign for him last week and has raised at least $150,000 in donations and pledges.

The utility, the Intermountain Rural Electric Association, based in Sedalia, Colo., has given Dr. Michaels $100,000 of its own, said Stanley R. Lewandowski Jr., its general manager. Mr. Lewandowski said that one company planned to give $50,000 and that a third planned to contribute to Dr. Michaels next year.

"We cannot allow the discussion to be monopolized by the alarmists," Mr. Lewandowski wrote in a July 17 letter to 50 other utilities. He also called on other electric cooperatives to undertake a counterattack on "alarmist" scientists and specifically Al Gore's movie *An Inconvenient Truth*, which lays much of the blame for global warming on heat-trapping gases like carbon dioxide.

Mr. Lewandowski and Dr. Michaels, who holds a Ph.D. in ecological climatology from the University of Wisconsin, have openly acknowledged the donations and say they see no problem. But some environmental advocates say the effort clearly poses a conflict of interest.

"This is a classic case of industry buying science to back up its anti-environmental agenda," said Frank O'Donnell, president of the Washington advocacy group Clean Air Watch.

Others, however, view it as the type of lobbying that goes along with many divisive issues. One environmental scientist, Donald Kennedy, former president of Stanford University and current editor in chief of the journal *Science,* said skeptics like Dr. Michaels were lobbyists more than researchers.

"I don't think it's unethical any more than most lobbying is unethical," Dr. Kennedy said.[24]

REVIEW EXERCISE 11.8 | **Fallacious Appeal to Authority**

In each of the following examples, check all fallacy categories that apply. Most important, explain each fallacy you identify.

1. "We are, quite bluntly, broke. We don't have the money to sustain the dreams and experiments of liberalism any longer. We have a $400 billion a year budget deficit and a $4 trillion debt. The economist Walter Williams points out that with the money we've spent on poverty programs since the 1960s we could have bought the entire assets of every Fortune 500 company and virtually every acre of U.S. farmland."[25]

		Explain your answer:
	Invincible authority	
	Unidentified authority	
	Irrelevant authority	
	Division of expert opinion	
	Conflict of interest	

2. "[Karl] Rove told the *Denver Post* that 'recent studies' show researchers 'have far more promise from adult stem cells than from embryonic stem cells.' The *Chicago Tribune* contacted top stem cell experts who all said Rove's claim was inaccurate and the White House 'could not provide the name of a stem cell researcher who shares Rove's views on the superior promise of adult stem cells.' Today (July 23, 2006) on *Meet the Press,* Tim Russert gave White House Chief of Staff Josh Bolten an opportunity to repudiate Rove's claims. Bolten refused, saying Rove 'knows a lot of stuff.'"[26]

		Explain your answer:
	Invincible authority	
	Unidentified authority	
	Irrelevant authority	
	Division of expert opinion	
	Conflict of interest	

APPLICATION EXERCISE 11.10 | Term Project

At the end of Chapter 10, you were challenged to take a position on your issue in a 100-word position statement (Writing Assignment 10.1). We bet that what you came up with is an argument. That is, it is a composition designed to be persuasive at a rational level, and it has a thesis or conclusion in it and other ideas and claims that support this thesis or conclusion. Suppose, then, it's a draft of an argument—in the "abstract." This means that it's short and could be developed more deeply and that it's still open to analysis and revision. OK? First, analyze your argument. Then ask, "Is my argument open to any of the kinds of criticisms (does it commit any of the fallacies) we have just studied?"

GLOSSARY

ad hominem   a fallacy consisting of irrelevant personal references or attacks
ad hominem, abusive   a fallacy consisting of baseless and irrelevant personal references or attacks
ad hominem, circumstantial   the fallacy of shifting attention from the issue and the position one opposes to the person holding that position and his or her life circumstances
amphibole   a grammatical ambiguity or a fallacy based on grammatical ambiguity

appeal to anger   the fallacious strategy of arousing irrelevant anger in support of a position

appeal to authority   the fallacious use of authority in support of a claim

appeal to fear   the fallacy of attempting to intimidate people into accepting a position

appeal to novelty   the fallacy of assuming or arguing that something is good or desirable simply because it is novel or new

appeal to pity   the fallacious strategy of arousing irrelevant pity in support of a position

appeal to tradition   the fallacy of assuming or arguing that something is good or desirable simply because it is old or traditional

begging the question   fallacy of presupposing one's thesis or conclusion (circular reasoning)

circular reasoning   fallacy of presupposing one's thesis or conclusion (begging the question)

common practice   a variety of the two wrongs fallacy in which one's own wrongdoing is excused by assimilation to widespread practice

complex question   a question presupposing a particular answer to some further question or a fallacy based upon such a presupposition

composition   the fallacy of inferring characteristics of the whole from characteristics of the parts

conflict of interest   any combination of interests that interferes with impartiality, hence a variety of fallacious appeal to authority where the authority cited has such a combination of interests

division   the fallacy of inferring characteristics of a part from characteristics of the whole

division of expert opinion   a variety of fallacious appeal to authority in which the authorities with relevant expertise are divided over the question at issue

dysphemism   negative exaggeration

equivocation   the inconsistent use of an ambiguous expression or a fallacy based on such usage

euphemism   positive exaggeration

false dilemma   argument in the form of a dilemma, but based on a false disjunctive premise

false implication   an advertising strategy in which important claims are strongly implied but remain literally unstated, often because they are known to be false

genetic appeal   the fallacy of assessment simply in terms of origin, sources, or genesis

guilt by association   the fallacy of supporting negative claims about people or their views or positions solely on the basis of their relationships with others

hyperbole   an advertising and public relations strategy in which exaggerated (hyperbolic) terminology is used to promote excitement

informal fallacy   an unreliable inference whose flaw or weakness is attributable to something other than its formal structure

innuendo   a public relations strategy in which important claims are strongly implied or suggested but left unstated, often because they cannot be proven

invincible authority   a variety of fallacious appeal to authority in which the authority is taken to outweigh any conflicting consideration

irrelevant authority   a variety of fallacious appeal to authority in which the authority cited lacks expertise relevant to the question at issue

loaded language   language that leans more heavily on connotation than reasoning

parity product   a product that is practically the same regardless of brand name

phantom distinction   the use of language to suggest a difference that doesn't exist

poisoning the well   the fallacious strategy of attempting to discredit a position, or its advocate, before the argument for the position can be considered

positioning   the fallacy of supporting positive claims about people or their views or positions solely on the basis of their relationships with others

provincialism   the fallacy of appealing to considerations of group loyalty in support of a claim

puffery   an advertising strategy in which vague terminology is used to promote enthusiasm

red herring   the fallacious argument strategy of diverting attention from the real issue to another one

rhetorical question   a question used to mask a claim or a fallacy based on such usage

straw person   the fallacious argument strategy of attacking a weak or distorted representation of an opponent's position

testimonial   an advertising and public relations strategy based on testimony of a celebrity; often an instance of the fallacy of irrelevant authority

two wrongs   the fallacy of excusing one's own wrong by comparing it to others' wrongs

unidentified authority   a variety of fallacious appeal to authority in which the authority is not identified sufficiently to make assessments of expertise, impartiality, or other relevant variables

weasel word   an advertising and public relations strategy based on the use of a vague word or expression to evade responsibility for an implied claim

ADDITIONAL EXERCISES

In our experience, the best way to study the material in this and the next chapter is in conversation with other people—in a facilitated discussion section, in a small autonomous study group, or with a study partner. Take turns critically examining examples, using the tools and terminology covered in this chapter. Listen to one another's critical assessments and rate them on their clarity, their explanatory power, and their fairness. To test the fairness of your study partner's or partners' criticisms, try to defend the argument against the proposed criticism. Points to remember throughout:

- The difference between a fallacy and a reasonable argument can be subtle and delicate.
- An argument can have more than one thing wrong with it.
- The label you put on the fallacy is not what matters most. What matters most is how you explain the example.

DISCUSSION TOPIC 11.3 INTELLIGENT INTELLIGENCE?   "We also have to work sort of the dark side if you will. We've got to spend time in the shadows in the intelligence world. A lot of what needs to be done here will have to be done quietly, without any discussion, using sources and methods that are available to our intelligence agencies, if we're going to be successful. That's the world these folks operate in, and so it's going to be vital for us to use any means at our disposal, basically, to achieve our objective."[27]

DISCUSSION TOPIC 11.4 CAN WE SLOW GROWTH?   "For three decades (60s, 70s, 80s) the environmentalists, Greens, tree huggers—choose any epithet that suits your fancy but mainly descriptions of those who've ranted and railed against growth—have managed to defeat every attempt to modernize Sonoma County transportation to handle the growing load. I would like to point out that sticking your head in the sand and saying you're against growth simply won't cut the mustard. You cannot pass a law (urban growth boundaries) against growth; stupid even to think of it. If you can manage to come up with an elixir that can be delivered in the water system a la Big Brother, which will prevent human sexuality, then you can slow growth."[28]

DISCUSSION TOPIC 11.5 NONACCIDENTAL SHOOTING   "As with all hunting accidents, it was an act of carelessness—no more, no less. Vice President Dick Cheney carelessly—but accidentally—wounded a companion in the face, neck and chest while quail hunting in Texas on Saturday. But if you really want to see people recklessly shooting mouths off, you need to turn on the TV, check out the blogosphere or—sigh—read the newspapers. The insinuation, of course, is that there might have been some attempt to hush things up. The tenets of good public relations argue for quick and full disclosure of bad news. Human nature runs to the contrary, however. Nothing could be more embarrassing for a hunter than to shoot someone, and it's doubtful that many things can be more traumatizing than shooting a friend. Why didn't the vice president immediately alert the press? Two words come to mind: chaos and humiliation. How would you react in that situation? Perhaps not unlike Cheney."[29]

DISCUSSION TOPIC 11.6 THE FIRST LADY   "Bill Clinton has ceased promising that the missus will play a key role in his White House. The reason is clear from [a recent] profile of Hillary in *American Spectator*. Since her Yale days, Hillary has been enthusiastically engaged with the radical Left. While she headed the New World Foundation, it gave grants to such leftist organizations as the fellow-traveling National Lawyers Guild and CISPES (the Committee in Support of the People of El Salvador)."[30]

DISCUSSION TOPIC 11.7 THE WHOLE AND THE PARTS I   "Should we not assume that just as the eye, the hand, the foot, and in general each part of the body clearly has its own proper function, so man too has some function over and above the function of his parts?"[31]

■ **DISCUSSION TOPIC 11.8 THE PRICE OF OBJECTIVITY**   "Many of my colleagues in the press are upset about the growing practice of paying newsmakers for news. The auction principle seems to them to strike somehow at the freedom of the press, or at least the freedom of the poor press to compete with the rich press. But I find their objections pious and, in an economy where everything and everybody has its price, absurd."[32]

■ **DISCUSSION TOPIC 11.9 PARTY LINES I**   Republican presidential candidate Jack Kemp in a 1988 televised presidential primary debate, attacking the eventual Republican nominee George H. W. Bush (who was supporting the ratification of the INF Treaty with the Soviet Union): "I can't believe I'm hearing a Republican say, 'Let's give peace a chance!'"

■ **DISCUSSION TOPIC 11.10 PARTY LINES II**   Lt. Colonel Oliver North campaigning in 1992 against Senator Barbara Boxer (Democrat from California): "[She's a] check-kiting, pay-raising, self-promoting, defense-cutting, tax-raising, free-spending permanent political potentate of pork. Who are Barbara Boxer's buddies? They are environmental radicals, people who believe in lifestyles we wouldn't even talk about, much less embrace. She believes spotted owls are higher on the food chain than we are, and that's not how I read Genesis."

■ **DISCUSSION TOPIC 11.11 PARTY LINES III**   President George H. W. Bush, losing to Bill Clinton and Al Gore: "My dog Millie knows more about foreign policy than these two Bozos (Democratic running mates Bill Clinton and Albert Gore)." In the same speech, this time about Gore in particular, "You know why I call him Ozone Man? This guy is so far out in the environmental extreme, we'll be up to our neck in owls and outta work for every American. He is way out, far out, man."

■ **DISCUSSION TOPIC 11.12 THE WHOLE AND THE PARTS II**   "Can the universe think about itself? We know that at least one part of it can: we ourselves. Is it not reasonable to conclude the whole can?"[33]

■ **DISCUSSION TOPIC 11.13 AGAINST ABORTION**   How can you deny that abortion is murder? A fetus is certainly alive, isn't it? And it certainly is human, isn't it? And it hasn't done anything wrong, has it? So you're talking about taking an innocent human life. I call that "murder." I can't imagine what you call it!

■ **DISCUSSION TOPIC 11.14 PHILOSOPHY OF PEACE**   "The Dalai Lama says that outer disarmament can only take place through inner disarmament. If the individual doesn't become more peaceful, a society that's the sum total of such individuals can never become more peaceful either."[34]

■ **DISCUSSION TOPIC 11.15 PEA SOUP**   "A term I use to describe the mess that surrounds most issues in the world today and prevents us from getting at what is really so about the world's problems is "pea soup." The pea soup is a mass of confusion, controversy, argument, conflict, and opinions. As long as you are asking what more can you do, what better solution have you got, what have you come up with that's different, you cannot see that the confusion, controversy, conflict, doubt, lack of trust, and opinions surrounding the problem of hunger and starvation result inevitably from any position you take. Once you are clear that you cannot take any position that will contribute in any way to the end of hunger and starvation, that any position you take will only contribute to the pea soup that engulfs the problem of hunger and starvation, then hope dies. And when hope dies, hopelessness dies with it: Without hope you can't have hopelessness. You are now close to the source of the problem of hunger and starvation on the planet. If you can see that the problem is without hope, you are no longer hopeless and frustrated. You are just there with whatever is so."[35]

■ **DISCUSSION TOPIC 11.16 PARTY LINES IV**   Below you will find a nicely matched pair of examples from the 1984 presidential campaign. The first is from the challenger, Democrat Walter Mondale. The second is from the incumbent, Republican President Ronald Reagan.

Walter Mondale: Our choice is between two futures, between a Reagan future and a better future. It is a choice between expediency and excellence. It is a choice between social Darwinism and social decency. It is a choice between salesmanship and leadership.

President Ronald Reagan: The truth is, Americans must choose between two drastically different points of view. One puts its faith in the pipe-dreamers and margin scribblers of Washington; the other believes in the collective wisdom of the American people. Our opponents believe the solutions to our nation's problems lie in the psychiatrist's notes or in a social worker's file or in a bureaucrat's budget. We believe in the working man's toil, the businessman's enterprise, and the clergyman's counsel.

■ **DISCUSSION TOPIC 11.17 A MATTER OF OPINION?**   "Repressive environmentalists and population and economic zero-growthers have requested President Reagan to oust James G. Watt as Secretary of the Interior. Those stop-all-progress destructionists have thick-skinned craniums. They lack the intelligence to realize that the United States of America is no longer a subsidiary of the baby-and-people hating and business-repressive do-gooders. President Reagan and Secretary Watt have done what should have been done long ago. Their critics can go to blazes on a one-way ticket."[36]

NOTES

[1] Jeremy Bentham, *The Handbook of Political Fallacies* (New York: Harper, 1962), Part 5, Chapter 2.

[2] Compare W. Fearnside and W. Holther, *Fallacy: the Counterfeit of Argument* (Englewood Cliffs, NJ: Prentice Hall, 1959), p. 167.

[3] Rush Limbaugh, *The Way Things Ought to Be* (New York: Simon and Schuster, 1992).

[4] Rene Descartes, "Letter of Dedication," *Meditations on First Philosophy. Discourse on Method and Meditations on First Philosophy* (Indianapolis, Hackett, 1999). p. 47.}

[5] Charles E. Trow, *The Old Shipmasters of Salem* (New York: Macmillan, 1905), pp. 14–15.

[6] 98th Congress, 2nd Session, October 19, 1984.

[7] Paul Stevens, "Weasel Words: God's Little Helpers," in Paul A. Eschol, Alfred A. Rosa, and Virginia P. Clark (eds.), *Language Awareness* (New York: St. Martins Press, 1974).

[8] In the early days of the automobile, the Supreme Court created an exception to the 4th Amendment's protection against unwarranted search for searches of vehicles, holding in *Carroll v. United States* that vehicles may be searched without warrants if the officer undertaking the search has probable cause to believe that the vehicle contains contraband. The Court explained that the mobility of vehicles would allow them to be quickly moved from the jurisdiction if time were taken to obtain a warrant. Later the Court developed a reduced privacy rationale to supplement the mobility rationale, explaining that "the configuration, use, and regulation of automobiles often may dilute the reasonable expectation of privacy that exists with respect to differently situated property. One has a lesser expectation of privacy in a motor vehicle because its function is transportation and it seldom serves as one's residence or as the repository of personal effects. . . . It travels public thoroughfares where both its occupants and its contents are in plain view." Although motor homes do serve as residences and as repositories for personal effects, and although their contents are often shielded from public view, in *California v. Carney,* 471 U.S. 386, 393 (1985), the Court extended the automobile exception to them as well, holding that there is a diminished expectation of privacy in a mobile home parked in a parking lot and licensed for vehicular travel, hence "readily mobile." See the FindLaw entry on the 4th Amendment at caselaw.lp.findlaw.com/data/constitution/amendment04.

[9] Geoffrey Nunberg, *Talking Right: How Conservatives Turned Liberalism into a Tax-Raising, Latte-Drinking, Sushi-Eating, Volvo-Driving, New York Times-Reading, Body-Piercing, Hollywood-Loving, Left-Wing Freak Show* (New York: Public Affairs, 2006) p. 22.

[10] Geoffrey Nunberg, "Week in Review," *The New York Times,* September 14, 2003.

[11] Lewis Carroll, *Through the Looking Glass,* in *The Complete Works of Lewis Carroll* (New York: Random House, 1936).

[12] Peter Doran, associate professor of earth and environmental sciences at the University of Illinois at Chicago, "Op Ed," *Chicago Tribune,* July 27, 2006.

[13] Associated Press, "Rove Critical of Media's 'Corrosive Role' in Politics," July 30, 2006,.

[14] Limbaugh, *The Way Things Ought to Be,* Chapter 10.

[15] Ann Coulter, "Beyond the News," *Fox News,* June 4, 2000.

[16] *CNN Late Edition with Wolf Blitzer,* March 9, 2003.

[17] "Democratic hawk: U.S. must leave Iraq," *CNN,* November 18, 2005.

[18] Plato, *The Apology,* in Edith Hamilton and Huntington Cairns (eds.) and Hugh Tredennick (tr.), *Plato: The Collected Dialogues* (Princeton, NJ: Princeton University Press, Bollingen Series, 1963), p. 20.

[19] Genesis 2: 16–17.

[20] Victor Lasky, "It Didn't Start With Watergate," *Book Digest* (November 1977), p. 47.

[21] Televangelist—and former candidate for president—Pat Robertson.

[22] Stacy Schiff, "Know It All: Can Wikipedia Conquer Expertise?" *The New Yorker,* July 31, 2006, p. 38.

[23] Galileo Galilei, *Dialogues Concerning Two New Sciences,* tr. Henry Crew and Alfonso de Salvio (Evanston, IL: Northwestern University Press, 1939).

[24] "Utilities Pay Scientist Ally on Warming", Associated Press, July 28, 2006.

[25] Limbaugh, *The Way Things Ought to Be,* p. xxx.

[26] "Bolten Defends Rove's False Claims on Stem Cells: Karl 'Knows a Lot of Stuff'," *ThinkProgress.org,* July 23, 2006.

[27] Dick Cheney, *Meet the Press,* September 16, 2001.

[28] Letter to the Editor, *Sonoma County Independent,* February 12, 1998.

[29] Editorial, *The Missoulian,* January 15, 2006.

[30] Editorial, *National Review,* August 1992.

[31] Aristotle, *Nicomachean Ethics,* Martin Ostwald (tr.) (Indianapolis, IN: Bobbs-Merrill, 1962), p. 16.

[32] Shana Alexander, "Loew"s Common Denominator," *Newsweek,* April 14, 1975, p. 96.

[33] Jose Silva, *The Silva Mind Control Method* (New York: Pocket Books, 1978), p. 116.

[34] Matthieu Ricard, *The Monk and the Philosopher* (New York: Schocken, 1998), p. 156.

[35] Werner Erhard, *The End of Starvation: Creating an Idea Whose Time Has Come* (San Francisco: The Hunger Project, 1982), pp. 10–11.

[36] Letter to the Editor, *Los Angeles Times,* July 24, 1981, part 2, p. 6.

CHAPTER 12

Informal Fallacies II: Inductive Reasoning

Will you forget about logic and give me the benefit of the doubt?!?[1]—WOODY ALLEN

POLLING, PROBABILITY, AND STATISTICS

In Chapters 8 and 9 we explained in a general way to evaluate inductive reasoning. Inductive strength is essentially a matter of degree—the degree to which the conclusion remains open to doubt assuming the premises are true. And this degree of doubtfulness depends on the *type* of inductive reasoning involved. Looking at the various types of inductive reasoning we discussed in Chapters 8 and 9, we can now highlight some of the more common informal fallacies of induction. These consist of overestimating the strength of a particular type of inductive inference.

IRREFUTABLE EVIDENCE

Fragments of UFO that crash-landed last week near Lambert's Corner, Saskatchewan

Soil taken from site

Some photos taken just prior to landing of craft

Enlarged photo (B.)

Drawings done by Mrs. Kitty Nederson, witness, while under hypnosis

Tape recording of nearby dog barking uncontrollably at time of visitation

R. Chast

SMALL SAMPLE

In Chapter 8 we explained that the strength of an inductive generalization depends most heavily on two factors: the size and the representativeness of the sample. This highlights two areas of possible overestimation of inductive strength. The informal fallacy of **small sample** consists of overestimating the statistical significance of evidence drawn from a small number of cases. Sometimes what appears to be a significant pattern in a small number of cases disappears when we investigate a larger number of cases. Suppose we are taking a poll to determine political preferences. Of the first 10 responses, 7 favor the challenger over the incumbent. But by the time we have interviewed 100 people, we may find the incumbent ahead 75 to 21 (with 4 undecided). But we must be careful in applying this as a criticism. The size of the sample relative to the target population is not the only factor involved in determining the reliability of the inductive inference. Even a relatively small sample can be used to reliably project trends on a massive scale if the study is carefully controlled and based on a representative sample. Thus it would be insufficient basis for criticism merely to point out, for example, that a national political preference poll had been conducted on the basis of 5,000 responses. A poll of just 1,500, adhering to all criteria of a scientifically respectable sample, can yield accurate information about the nation with a margin of error of only ±3%. And doubling the sample would only reduce the margin of error by about 1%.

UNREPRESENTATIVE SAMPLE

But suppose the aforementioned 5,000 responses were all taken from one geographical region. This regional bias would greatly increase liability to error. Fundamentally, the representativeness of a sample is more important than sample size, because what we are trying to do is to project conclusions affected by many variables. If we can control all relevant variables in a relatively small sample, so much the better for the economy of the study. The important thing is to control all variables. But this can be difficult to accomplish in an area such as political preference, because it is affected by such an assortment of variable factors. The problem is made greater because not all relevant variables may be known. The informal fallacy of **unrepresentative sample** consists of overestimating the statistical significance of evidence drawn from a sample of a particular kind. To see just how tricky this can be, consider the famous case of the 1936 *Reader's Digest* presidential preference poll, which incorrectly predicted that Alf Landon would defeat Franklin Delano Roosevelt. The poll was based on 2 million respondents randomly selected from phone books and motor vehicle registration lists. Random means that each member of the target population has a roughly equal chance of appearing among the sample. For example, if pollsters wish to find out what the American Catholic laity thinks about the sexual abuse scandal, they must ensure that every American lay Catholic is equally likely to be among those polled. Notice that this doesn't mean that every American lay Catholic needs to be polled—only that every American lay Catholic has an equal chance of *being asked*. If pollsters ask only California Catholics or New York Catholics, that's not random and therefore not representative. In its 1936 presidential preference poll, *Reader's Digest* randomly picked names from the phone book and the motor vehicle registration lists. What did they miss?

THOUGHT EXPERIMENT 12.1 | **What's Wrong with the Sample?**

In its 1936 presidential preference poll, *Reader's Digest* randomly picked names from the phone book and the motor vehicle registration lists. What did they miss? Can you guess?

The relevant variable the *Reader's Digest* poll overlooked was that in 1936 (during the Great Depression) a large part of the electorate couldn't afford a car or even a phone (and they tended to be angry about it). So even though the pollsters *tried* to take a random sample, the sample they used was far from random and failed spectacularly to reflect the political mood of the electorate.

BIASED METHODOLOGY

Besides the sample size and the degree to which the sample represents the target, other aspects of methodology can affect the strength of an inductive generalization. The reliability of inductive generalizations can partly depend on whether other informal fallacies, such as informal fallacies of language or fallacious assumptions, are involved. For example, if a public opinion poll has a **biased methodology**—that is, it is conducted using loaded or leading questions, questions that restrict the range of available responses, or questions that contain questionable presuppositions—the results are not to be trusted. If the data is generated or gathered in such a way that it might alter the data, then the methodology undermines the reliability of the result. Professor Smith, wishing to improve his teaching, decides to poll his physics class. He commissions a questionnaire from one of his colleagues in statistics that satisfies all criteria of a sound polling instrument. He calls each member of his class individually into his office and asks them to complete the questionnaire. What is wrong with his polling methods? They are less likely to result in candid responses than if the questionnaire were completed and submitted anonymously.

APPLICATION EXERCISE 12.1 | **Biased Methodology**

Critique the following hypothetical public opinion poll. Suppose that you live in a community where rapid growth has stretched the existing waste management resources to the breaking point, resulting in environmental pollution serious enough to have raised public concern. Now suppose the local newspaper conducts a readers' poll asking readers to rank the following three policy options:

1. A municipal bond issue to construct new sewage treatment facilities

2. A regional bond issue to construct a pipeline to transport excess sewage to the ocean

3. An increase in property tax to pay for improvement and expansion of existing facilities

Two weeks later, the newspaper reports that public opinion favors option 3 (a municipal bond measure to construct new sewage treatment facilities) at 48%, compared to 35% for the next most popular option.

AND SPEAKING OF: | **Pollution**

What do you think about this public opinion poll posted on Bill O'Reilly's website:

Question: Are we winning or losing the war on terror?

☐ Winning   ☐ Losing

SUPPRESSED EVIDENCE

So far we have focused on the way in which the inductive evidence is gathered and the generalizations are reached. We should also look critically at the way in which the results are presented and interpreted. Sometimes relevant evidence is deliberately kept from view because it conflicts with the arguer's intended interpretation of the evidence presented. This constitutes the informal fallacy of **suppressed evidence.** A common political foible and a particular favorite in the field of advertising, particularly where statistical data are used, this is a disreputable argumentative strategy. For example, advertisers are forever referring to "scientific" studies that "demonstrate" the superiority of their products but strategically neglecting to mention that they have commissioned the studies themselves, a crucial piece of information relevant to assessing the objectivity of the studies. It's worth noting that the fallacy of suppressed evidence is not confined to statistical generalizations. It occurs whenever significant information or evidence—information or evidence that makes a difference to the conclusion—is omitted. For example, in 1996 opponents of California's Proposition 215, the ballot initiative measure that made marijuana legally available as a prescription drug, argued correctly that marijuana's safety and effectiveness compared to the already legal synthetic substitute Marinol had not been scientifically established. What they conveniently neglected to mention was that this lack of scientific evidence was because the Food and Drug Administration had up to that point refused to investigate the matter.

AND SPEAKING OF: | **Suppressed Evidence**

"I don't think anybody anticipated the breach of the levees."
—George W. Bush, on *Good Morning America,* September 1, 2005

White House Got Early Warning on Katrina

By Joby Warrick

Washington Post Staff Writer

In the 48 hours before Hurricane Katrina hit, the White House received detailed warnings about the storm's likely impact, including eerily prescient predictions of breached levees, massive flooding, and major losses of life and property, documents show.

A 41-page assessment by the Department of Homeland Security's National Infrastructure Simulation and Analysis Center (NISAC), was delivered by e-mail to the White House's "situation room," the nerve center where crises are handled, at 1:47 a.m. on Aug. 29, the day the storm hit, according to an e-mail cover sheet accompanying the document.

The NISAC paper warned that a storm of Katrina's size would "likely lead to severe flooding and/or levee breaching" and specifically noted the potential for levee failures along Lake Pontchartrain. It predicted economic losses in the tens of billions of dollars, including damage to public utilities and industry that would take years to fully repair. Initial response and rescue operations would be hampered by disruption of telecommunications networks and the loss of power to fire, police and emergency workers, it said.

In a second document, also obtained by *The Washington Post,* a computer slide presentation by the Federal Emergency Management Agency, prepared for a 9 a.m. meeting on Aug. 27, two days before Katrina made landfall, compared Katrina's likely impact to that of "Hurricane Pam," a fictional Category 3 storm used in a series of FEMA disaster-preparedness exercises simulating the effects of a major hurricane striking New Orleans. But Katrina, the report warned, could be worse.

The hurricane's Category 4 storm surge "could greatly overtop levees and protective systems" and destroy nearly 90 percent of city structures, the FEMA report said. It further predicted "incredible search and rescue needs (60,000-plus)" and the displacement of more than a million residents.

The NISAC analysis accurately predicted the collapse of floodwalls along New Orleans's Lake Pontchartrain shoreline, an event that the report described as "the greatest concern." The breach of two canal floodwalls near the lake was the key failure that left much of central New Orleans underwater and accounted for the bulk of Louisiana's 1,100 Katrina-related deaths.[2]

BAD BASE LINE

Statistics often invite misinterpretation, particularly in the direction of overestimating the significance of some trend. One way that this can happen is by assuming an inappropriate basis of comparison. For example, suppose that that you live in a small town and the local weekly newspaper reports a 33% rise in the rate of car theft. This sounds rather alarming. But the alarm diminishes when we read past the headline and learn that the number of car thefts rose from three in the previous year to four. And now suppose that over the same period the town's population has doubled. In this case, the incidence of car theft *per capita* (relative to population) has significantly dropped. We may call this technique of distorting the implications of statistical data the informal fallacy of **bad base line.** Be on the lookout for this sort of misrepresentation in political speeches about trends in crime, unemployment, balance of trade, welfare dependency, and other social trends. For example, bear in mind that changing the eligibility requirements for unemployment insurance benefits can make it look statistically like the number of unemployed people is dropping.

AND SPEAKING OF: | **Statistical Misinterpretation**

I knew a guy who was so influenced by statistics, they pretty much ruled his entire life. One time he found out that more than 80% of all automobile accidents happen to people within 5 miles of where they live. So he moved!

GAMBLER'S FALLACY

The so-called **gambler's fallacy** consists of thinking that past outcomes of chance events influence the probability of future outcomes. For example, suppose we are gambling on coin flips and the last 10 flips have come up heads. Many people are tempted to think that tails are therefore *more* likely to come up than heads on the next flip. The problem here is failure to recognize that the chances of heads or tails coming up are the same for each flip (50:50), because each flip is an independent chance event. The chances of a run of 11 heads in a row are much lower than 50:50, but the odds against such a run have no bearing on the outcome of the next flip. Yet people persist in the belief to the contrary. Watch people play the slots in Nevada. You will repeatedly see people pumping coins into a machine that hasn't paid off for hours, thinking that this fact alone makes it more likely that the machine will pay off soon. Just as unreliable is people's inference to continue playing because they have been winning. The idea of riding a streak involves the same mistake as thinking that the odds against them eventually have to even out. If chance determines the outcome of the next play, past outcomes have no bearing. Gamblers also tend to be (sometimes pathologically) attracted to systems designed to beat the odds, most of which are fallacious products of wishful thinking and don't work. (The occasional exception, such as card-counting in blackjack, is quickly found out, and the counter is escorted from the premises of the gaming establishment.) One such system consists of doubling the bet. Suppose you put $2 on red at even money and lose. Following this system you would put $4 on red on the next play. If you win, you're up $2. If you lose, you're down $6, but you bet $8 on the next play. If you win, you're up $10. The idea is that eventually you win, and when you do, you're ahead of the game. The main trouble with this system is that the odds remain uniformly stacked against you throughout the game as you continue to raise your stake, which has the effect primarily of digging you more deeply and quickly into a hole. In other words, if you follow this "system," the only probability that you raise is the probability that you will run out of money before you win.

ANALOGY AND BURDEN OF PROOF

FAULTY ANALOGY

In Chapter 8 we gave a detailed explanation of the standards and procedures for the evaluation of arguments based on analogies. The examples we used to illustrate these standards and procedures are quite strong inductive arguments. Using these same standards, the identification and critique of a weak analogy is a matter of adding up relevant similarities and differences. If we find that the argument is based on similarities irrelevant to the conclusion, or that it glosses over relevant differences, then we may object that the argument is based on a questionable, false, or misleading analogy. This is a two-step process. First, we must establish that there is a difference between the items compared in the analogy. Second, and more important, the relevance of the difference to the point of the analogy needs to be established. Overlooking this second step will result in a misapplication of this criticism. We often hear, by way of objection, "Your argument is like comparing apples and oranges." Notice that this is also an analogy, the point of which is that the analogy being critiqued is misleading. Bear in mind that no two items in the universe are so different from each other that they cannot be compared in *some* useful way relevant to *some* purpose. Is a comparison between apples and oranges necessarily misleading? Not if you're trying to sort the fruit from the vegetables. So we must keep the point of the analogy we are critiquing clearly in mind as we look for differences. And we must show that the differences are relevant to that point. When we have done both of these

FIGURE 12.1 Faulty Analogy?

things, we may say that we have identified an instance of the informal fallacy of faulty analogy.

DISCUSSION TOPIC 12.1 | **Barnyard Logic**

Critique the argument in the cartoon in Figure 12.1. Do you think there's anything fallacious about the pig's argument? Explain any criticisms you would offer in detail. What about the fact that the cartoonist has put the argument into the mouth of a pig?

ARGUMENTUM AD IGNORANTIAM (ARGUING FROM IGNORANCE)

The informal fallacy of arguing **ad ignorantiam** (from Latin for arguing from ignorance) consists of treating the absence of evidence for (or against) a claim as proof of its falsity (or truth). The fallacy is a perversion of the concept of burden of proof and legitimate presumption discussed in Chapter 9. Essentially, it consists of misplacing the burden of proof. Understandably, many examples of this fallacy have to do with the unknown and the supernatural. For example, there is an argument for the existence of extraterrestrial intelligent life that goes like this: Because the universe is infinitely large, it is impossible to prove conclusively that the only intelligent life that exists is on the planet Earth, so we should assume that extraterrestrial intelligent life exists.

"I just think you're going to need a better rallying cry than 'Absence of evidence isn't evidence of absence.'"

FIGURE 12.2 Arguing from Ignorance

A more recent example arose in connection with the war in Iraq, rationalized by the Bush administration on grounds of claims about Saddam Hussein's vast stockpiles of weapons of mass destruction. During the occupation after the invasion, no evidence of such weapons was ever found. But although the official rationale for the invasion and occupation shifted many times, there were also many *ad ignorantiam* attempts to rehabilitate the original rationale.

DISCUSSION TOPIC 12.2 | Absence of Evidence

Notice in the cartoon in Figure 12.2 that the general's rallying cry "Absence of evidence isn't evidence of absence" is on its face a repudiation of the fallacy of arguing from ignorance. Why is it nevertheless reasonable to count it as an instance of that very fallacy?

INVINCIBLE IGNORANCE

A related fallacy, which we'll call arguing from **invincible ignorance,** consists of refusing to accept one's own burden of proof. For example, in the *Peanuts* episode in Figure 12.3, Snoopy commits this fallacy twice. In the first instance,

FIGURE 12.3 Invincible Ignorance

Snoopy dismisses Lucy's expression of doubt as ignorant; later, he dismisses the evidence of her research on the basis of the far-fetched assumption of a massive cover-up.

In each case there appears to be no reason for dismissing the information other than that it conflicts with the hypothesis Snoopy is initially and, as it seems, inflexibly committed to. In what might be called a definitive case of "sleeping dogmatism," Snoopy has simply closed his mind on this subject.

AND SPEAKING OF: | **Invincible Ignorance**

Did you know that there is no convincing astrological evidence that science is anything other than a primitive medieval superstition?

We'd like you to go back to Chapter 1 and review the passage on pages 26–28 about unexamined assumptions. As these words were written, we had just observed the fifth anniversary of September 11. Two years ago, in July 2004, the U.S. government's official account of what happened on September 11, 2001, was published in the form of *The 9/11 Commission Report: Final Report of the National Commission on Terrorist Attacks Upon the United States.* Since the publication of this report, well-documented challenges to a number of its crucial findings have been published in academic and scientific literature, giving rise to a "9/11 truth movement." The central thesis of the 9/11 truth movement is that there is enough forensic and documentary evidence to warrant an investigation into the possibility of high-level U.S. government complicity in the planning and execution of the 9/11 attacks. It is quite telling to observe some of the reactions to this suggestion.

AND SPEAKING OF: | **Invincible Ignorance (again)**

[Some right-wing and even middle-of-the-road commentators on political affairs]— including Jean Bethke Elshtain, a professor of social and political ethics—have declared that the accusation of official complicity is beyond the pale of reasonable debate, so that any arguments on its behalf can simply be ignored. Elshtain, calling the suggestion that American officials, including the president, were complicit in the attacks "preposterous," adds: "This sort of inflammatory madness exists outside the boundary of political debate" and therefore does not even "deserve a hearing." From this perspective it is not necessary to examine the evidence put forward by critics of the official account.[3]

DISCUSSION TOPIC 12.3 | **Invincible Ignorance?**

Snoopy *suspects* a sinister plot to cover up evidence of "dragonfly terrorism." We use this to illustrate the fallacy of invincible ignorance. Mainstream political commentators *refuse to consider* the possibility of a sinister U.S. government plot to commit and cover up terrorism. We use this to illustrate the same fallacy. Is this consistent or not? Explain.

DISCUSSION TOPIC 12.4 | **Arguing from Ignorance? Why Not?**

In frame 11 of the Peanuts episode used earlier (Figure 12.3) to illustrate the fallacy of invincible ignorance, Lucy refers to medical history. See if you can explain why her argument is *not* an instance of the fallacy of arguing *ad ignorantiam* (arguing from ignorance).

CAUSALITY

JUMPING FROM CORRELATION TO CAUSE

One of the most common kinds of evidence for a causal connection is a statistical correlation between two phenomena. For example, medical scientists knew for some time of a statistical correlation between cigarette smoking and lung cancer. The incidence of lung cancer in the smoking population was higher than in the nonsmoking population. Such a correlation is genuinely relevant inductive evidence for a causal connection between lung cancer and smoking. The problem is that by itself it is inconclusive. It suggests, but does not establish, the causal link. For several decades, the tobacco industry was successful in eluding the implications—and liabilities—of the causal connection between smoking and cancer on the basis of this distinction between statistical correlation and causality. That's how real and significant a distinction it is. Some people may find this hard to accept and may even be inclined to wonder why we should not, as a society, have been able to move earlier and more decisively against the tobacco industry to establish antismoking policies. Notice, however, that there is also a strong statistical correlation between the incidence of lung cancer and age. Yet it would be misleading to suggest that aging causes lung cancer or that lung cancer causes aging. So isolating the causal factor does indeed require further scientific evidence. The informal fallacy of jumping from correlation to cause occurs whenever an observed statistical **correlation** is interpreted as showing a causal connection without first having made a reasonable attempt to isolate the cause by controlling the relevant variables experimentally, as described in Chapter 9.

POST HOC ERGO PROPTER HOC

A similar fallacy consists of inferring a causal connection from temporal contiguity. In other words, it is a fallacy to infer that one thing is the cause of another simply because it is preceded by it in time. For example, someone observes that crime among youth has increased in the United States since the arrival of punk rock from England and concludes, therefore, that punk rock is causing an increase in juvenile crime. Or someone observes that every war in this century has followed the election of a Democratic president, concluding that the Democrats caused those wars. This kind of reasoning came to be known in Latin as **post hoc** *ergo propter hoc,* which means, literally, "after this, therefore because of this."

COMMON CAUSE

Two phenomena may be so closely connected that one of them seems to be the cause of the other, although both are really results of some additional, less obvious factor. Suppose a person suffers from both depression and alcoholism. Does the drinking cause the depression or the depression cause the drinking? Or could it be that the depression and the drinking sustain each other causally? Perhaps so. But we shouldn't overlook the further possibility that there is some additional underlying cause of both the depression and the drinking, for example, a biochemical imbalance or a profound emotional disturbance. The informal fallacy of overlooking a **common cause,** then, consists of failing to recognize that two seemingly related events may not be causally related but rather effects of a common cause.

CAUSAL OVERSIMPLIFICATION

The informal fallacy of **causal oversimplification** consists of assuming that what merely contributes causally to a phenomenon fully explains it. For example, intense debates are waged regularly over the wisdom of increased taxation as a means of balancing the federal budget. Opponents of such measures often point to the predictable negative effects that taxation will have on the vitality of the consumer economy, and proponents of such measures stress the effects on real disposable income of the increasing debt burden on the economy as a whole. It is likely that both sides have a point, but it is at least as likely that both sides are oversimplifying the economic equation in a number of ways. Clearly tax policy is not the only causal factor that affects the consumer economy. But neither is public indebtedness the only such causal factor. Both factors, and numerous others, are involved and influence one another in a many ways.

FALSE INFERENCE TO BEST EXPLANATION

As we explained in Chapter 9, there are at least some cases of hypothetical reasoning in which the criteria of plausibility and explanatory power decisively weigh in favor of the same hypothesis. In such cases, it is reasonable to think that the hypothesis is correct. But it is a fallacy to cling to an implausible hypothesis or one that fails to explain the available evidence simply because you can't think of any better explanation. We call this the fallacy of **false inference to best explanation.**

SLIPPERY SLOPE

A specific kind of causal fallacy consists of objecting to something on the grounds of the unwarranted assumption that it will inevitably lead to some evil consequence, which will lead to some even more evil consequence, which in turn will lead on down the slippery slope to some disastrous consequence. For example, it is commonly argued that marijuana is a dangerous drug that inevitably leads to experimentation with harder drugs and eventually to hard-drug abuse and addiction. Often, the alleged slippery slope is supported by further fallacious causal inferences such as pointing out that a high percentage of admitted heroin addicts testify to having tried marijuana early in their drug experience. But there is no slippery slope here, as can easily be established by pointing out that numerous people, who at one time or another have tried or used marijuana, have never experimented with harder drugs, much less become addicted to them, and have moderated or given up their use of marijuana. A variation on slippery slope reasoning takes the form of posing the rhetorical question, "Where do you draw the line?" This has the effect of suggesting that there is no location for the line to be drawn. For example, some people are moved by the arguments like this one:

> If you permit the withdrawal of life support from terminally ill patients, where do you draw the line between this form of mercy killing and the convenient disposal of one's sick and burdensome elders, or the euthanasia of the mentally or physically or racially "defective"?

This is **slippery slope** reasoning. Here, it is merely assumed that we can't clearly distinguish between cases of passive euthanasia (withholding extraordinary life-prolonging measures) and active euthanasia (taking steps to hasten death or bring about death) or between euthanasia done to alleviate pointless suffering of a terminal patient and euthanasia done for selfish reasons or with deliberate disregard for the interests of the patient. The argument makes these same distinctions, doesn't it? Otherwise, how are we to understand and appreciate the objection it wants to make? Now it is easy to see that such distinctions are possible, because they have just been made. It is not much harder to see that they are relevant distinctions. Indeed, the argument presumes the relevance of such distinctions; otherwise, why assume or suggest that they can't be made? Thus an effective strategy for exposing this sort of slippery slope reasoning is to simply draw the relevant distinctions and point them out. It is, however, important to recognize that in some contexts the question, "Where do you draw the line?" rhetorical though it is, makes a good point. These are contexts—and there are some important ones—in which some fundamental principle is at stake that would be irreparably compromised if a certain exception to it were allowed to pass.

REVIEW EXERCISE 12.1 | Causal Fallacies

In each of the following examples, check all fallacy categories that apply. Most important, explain each fallacy you identify.

1. Despite the objections of the Associated Students and the Faculty Senate, we are moving ahead to implement the new tuition fees recommended by the committee. We have to do something, and we have to do it immediately to restore our reputation as a leading undergraduate educational institution. No one has come forward with a better alternative.

	Ad ignorantiam	Explain your answer:
	Invincible ignorance	
	False inference to best explanation	
	Correlation to cause	
	Post hoc ergo propter hoc	
	Overlooking a common cause	
	Causal oversimplification	
	Slippery slope	
	Gamblers' fallacy	

2. My last three blind dates have been bombs. This one's bound to be better!

	Ad ignorantiam	Explain your answer:
	Invincible ignorance	
	False inference to best explanation	
	Correlation to cause	
	Post hoc ergo propter hoc	
	Overlooking a common cause	
	Causal oversimplification	
	Slippery slope	
	Gamblers' fallacy	

3. A real miracle is something that demonstrably does occur but that cannot be scientifically explained. We formed a prayer circle over Sister Sadie, and her T-cell count has returned to normal and she no longer tests positive for HIV. The doctors have confirmed what the lab work shows, but they can't seem to agree on an explanation. We believe God has sent the virus from her body.

	Ad ignorantiam	Explain your answer:
	Invincible ignorance	
	False inference to best explanation	
	Correlation to cause	
	Post hoc ergo propter hoc	
	Overlooking a common cause	
	Causal oversimplification	
	Slippery slope	
	Gamblers' fallacy	

4. "Everything in this book is right and you must be prepared to confront that reality. You can no longer be an honest liberal after reading this entire masterpiece. Throughout the book you will be challenged, because you will actually be persuaded to the conservative point of view. Whether you can admit this in the end will be a true test of your mettle as a human being."[4]

	Ad ignorantiam	Explain your answer:
	Invincible ignorance	
	False inference to best explanation	
	Correlation to cause	
	Post hoc ergo propter hoc	
	Overlooking a common cause	
	Causal oversimplification	
	Slippery slope	
	Gamblers' fallacy	

5. "I've always reckoned that looking at the new moon over your left shoulder is one of the carelessest and foolishest things a body can do. Old Hank Bunker done it once and bragged about it and in less than two years he got drunk and fell off of the shot-tower, and spread himself out so that he was just a kind of layer, as you may say; and they slid him edgeways between two barn doors for a coffin, and buried him so, so they say, but I didn't see it. Pap told me. But anyway it all come of looking at the moon that way like a fool."[5]

	Ad ignorantiam	Explain your answer:
	Invincible ignorance	
	False inference to best explanation	
	Correlation to cause	
	Post hoc ergo propter hoc	
	Overlooking a common cause	
	Causal oversimplification	
	Slippery slope	
	Gamblers' fallacy	

6. In 1997, the small town of Sulphur Springs experienced a 200% increase in felony auto theft, according to the *Sulphur Springs Weekly Standard*. (This report was based on the fact that three cars were stolen by joy-riding teenagers, compared to 1996 when only one car was stolen.)

	Ad ignorantiam	Explain your answer:
	Invincible ignorance	
	False inference to best explanation	
	Correlation to cause	
	Post hoc ergo propter hoc	
	Overlooking a common cause	
	Causal oversimplification	
	Slippery slope	
	Gamblers' fallacy	

A FINAL WORD OF CAUTION

By now it should be clear that evaluating arguments, particularly in informal terms, can be a messy business. You can expect to encounter a fair number of arguments that can clearly be faulted in one way or another, and occasionally you'll find an argument that is clearly impeccable. But many arguments are neither clearly fallacious nor clearly sound. In such cases, you should consider your criticisms to be essentially contestable; therefore you should also recognize the need to supply arguments in support of them, to deal with arguments against them, and perhaps to change your mind. In other words, assessing arguments, like verifying value judgments, takes you into areas where knowing how to construct and evaluate arguments becomes increasingly important.

AND SPEAKING OF: | **Care and Caution**

The Critical Thinking Hall of Shame

Few things are more embarrassing to a discipline like critical thinking than the kind of inept instruction that provoked the late Jack Smith to publish the following column.

Critique of an Ironic Writer's Critical Thought

By Jack Smith

Syndicated columnist

In writing these pieces, it never occurs to me that I am going to be accused of critical thinking, either good or bad.

However, I have received a letter from Howard Holter, professor of history at California State University Dominguez Hills, enclosing an analysis of my critical thinking by one of his students.

Holter explains, "I assigned my students the task of evaluating a piece of newspaper copy in terms of the formal evaluation of critical thinking. They were to use 'fallacies of critical thinking' listed in the textbook to apply to the piece in question."

A student named Melanie Martinez chose to evaluate one of my columns, and Holter says her paper was one of the best. I do not come off too well.

Her paper criticizes a column I wrote about transcendental meditation as taught at Maharishi International University, Fairfield, Iowa. These folks believe, as you may remember, that if enough people meditate together, achieving a state of pure consciousness and connecting with the Unified Field, the basis of all life, they can actually alter events—lowering crime rates, quelling riots, easing international tension and even causing the Dow Jones average to rise.

The theme of my essay was that I did not believe this. However, my tone was irony, which, as we have often seen, is a risky tone to effect.

Martinez aims right at the heart.

"This article," she begins, "contains many vague and ambiguous words and statements, as well as fallacies of presumption."

I am reeling already.

Pinpointing my first fallacy of presumption, she quotes a paragraph: "The meditators held a mass meditation . . . thereby raising the temperature and saving the Florida orange crop, lowering drunken driving arrests is Des Moines, influencing Fidel Castro to give up cigars, and causing the stock market to rally."

Obviously, I hope, I am being ironic. I do not for a moment believe that the meditation had any effect whatever on the events cited.

But Martinez comments:

"This is the fallacy of False Cause, or thinking that because someone did one thing, something else happened as a result. The meditators may have believed that they were the reason for the temperature rise in Florida, but were probably wrongly justified. . . ."

My thought exactly.

Later, Martinez observes, while I question the validity of the meditations, I claim that I was the one who meditated the success of Corazon Aquino in her bid for the presidency of the Philippines.

"Not only is this also a Fallacy of False Cause, but this is also a Fallacy of Special Pleading. After denouncing meditation, he does that exact thing."

Obviously, again, I was being ironic when I took credit for meditating Mrs. Aquino into the presidency. I was merely showing how easy it is for anyone to claim the Maharishi Effect for himself.

Martinez also accuses me of the Fallacy of Bifurcation. Bifurcation does not seem the sort of fallacy I might fall into, but let's see.

She quotes me: "I do believe that if we could get millions of people all around the world to sit down and meditate, instead of shooting and bombing one another, conditions would improve."

She says, "Here the author is saying, 'If we do one thing, this will happen.' Actually the opposite could happen: While the majority of people are meditating, a few of the people who aren't participating in the meditation could take advantage and cause destruction."

Alas, Martinez is all too close to the mark on that point. If we had thousands of people sitting around meditating, the barbarians might well say, "Hey, look at those crackpots meditating! Let's kill 'em!"

Or am I bifurcating?

She writes, "The author also included the phrase 'I am out on a limb,' which according to critical thinking, means either he is standing on someone's arm or leg, or he is standing on a tree branch. This is an ambiguous statement."

Nothing ambiguous about "out on a limb." It is an ancient metaphor, much honored in this use, which means, according to A Dictionary of American Idioms, "with your beliefs and opinions openly stated; in a dangerous position that can't be changed."

I am always out on a limb.

At the risk of redundancy, a few gentle reminders: The point of all of this activity is not to vanquish your opponent, not to humiliate anyone, not to experience the thrill of victory, not to score points. This is not an idle intellectual exercise—like some arcane variety of *Trivial Pursuit*. Fallacy labels have no intrinsic importance. Their value is entirely instrumental. The point of this activity is to *improve understanding*—to shed light, not generate heat. Above all, remember that a *fair and accurate understanding* of the argument is a prerequisite to a well-reasoned judgment of its merits. Make sure your criticisms are based on thorough and careful argument analysis.

APPLICATION EXERCISE 12.2 | Term Project

At the end of Chapter 11 (Application Exercise 11.11) you were challenged to write a critique of the argument in your original 100-word position statement (Writing Assignment 10.1). Has your position changed as a result of this process? If so, your argument will need revisions. When those have been accomplished, reanalyze your argument. Then ask: "Is my argument open to any of the kinds of criticisms (does it commit any of the fallacies) we have just studied in Chapter 12?"

GLOSSARY

ad ignorantiam   the fallacy of inferring a statement from the absence of evidence or lack of proof of its opposite

bad base line   the fallacy of statistical inference based on an inappropriate basis of comparison

biased methodology   any methodology, such as a loaded question, that distorts a statistical study

causal oversimplification   a variety of causal fallacy in which significant causal factors or variables are overlooked

common cause   a variety of causal fallacy in which one of two effects of some common cause is taken to cause the other

correlation   an observed or established statistical regularity, often fallaciously thought to establish a causal connection

false inference to best explanation   the fallacy of clinging to an implausible or failing explanatory hypothesis for want of a better alternative

gambler's fallacy   any of a variety of fallacies of inductive reasoning having to do with estimating or beating the odds, often based on the use of past outcomes to predict the future outcome of chance events

invincible ignorance   the fallacy of refusing to give due consideration to evidence that conflicts with what one is already committed to believing

post hoc   a variety of causal fallacy in which the order of events in time is taken to establish a cause-and-effect relationship

slippery slope   the fallacy of objecting to something on the grounds that it will lead, by dubious causal reasoning, to some unacceptable set of consequences

small sample   the fallacy of statistical inference, consisting of overestimating the statistical significance of evidence drawn from a small number of cases

suppressed evidence   the persuasive strategy of covering up available evidence that conflicts with an intended conclusion

unrepresentative sample   the fallacy of statistical inference in which the sample underrepresents the range of relevant variables in the population

ADDITIONAL EXERCISES

In our experience, the best way to study the material in this and the next chapter is in conversation with other people—in a facilitated discussion section, in a small autonomous study group, or with a study partner. Take turns critically examining examples using the tools and terminology covered in this chapter. Listen to everyone's critical assessments and rate their clarity, their explanatory power, and their fairness. To test fairness, try to defend each argument against the proposed criticism. Points to remember throughout:

- The difference between a fallacy and a reasonable argument can be subtle and delicate.
- An argument can have more than one thing wrong with it.
- The label you put on the fallacy is *not* what matters most. What matters most is how you explain the example.

DISCUSSION TOPIC 12.5 VALID OR INVALID ARGUMENT? "If drugs make people well, then those who take the most should be the healthiest, but this simply isn't the case."[6]

DISCUSSION TOPIC 12.6 JIHAD "The test of American willpower, Mr. Cheney and Mr. Bush have insisted, is in Baghdad, which explains why they stick to the language that it is the 'central front' in the war on terrorism and domino that America cannot let fall. Defeat there, they warn, would give the jihadists a victory and empower them to move on to the next country—maybe Pakistan, maybe Saudi Arabia, maybe Lebanon.'"[7]

DISCUSSION TOPIC 12.7 CORRUPTION "The Ayatollah Khomeini speaking in defense of state executions of those convicted of adultery, prostitution, or homosexuality: 'If your finger suffers from gangrene, what do you do? Let the whole hand and then the body become filled with gangrene, or cut the finger off? . . . Corruption, corruption. We have to eliminate corruption.'"[8]

DISCUSSION TOPIC 12.8 ONE STATISTIC, TWO CONCLUSIONS Suppose a survey shows that more than half of all college students with below-average grades smoke pot; by contrast, only 20% of nonsmokers have below-average grades. On the basis of these data, one person concludes that pot smoking causes students to receive lower grades. Another concludes that receiving lower grades causes students to smoke pot.

DISCUSSION TOPIC 12.9 TOBACCO TAXES I Argument against raising cigarette taxes: Taxing cigarettes encourages interstate traffickers in stolen cigarettes by opening up a whole new and very profitable market for them. A vote for this measure is a vote for increased crime. Vote 'NO.' Vote against the smugglers and traffickers and black marketeers.

DISCUSSION TOPIC 12.10 TOBACCO TAXES II Adding a health tax to tobacco products is unfair to the tobacco industry. We're like any other legitimate business in this country. We sell a legal product to willing buyers in a free market, and we pay a fair share into the public purse through various forms of taxation. If tax revenue is to be raised to support Medicare, let the burden be shared across the board.

◼ **DISCUSSION TOPIC 12.11 LUCKY CHARM** It's a bit mysterious, because Smith's numbers are less than spectacular. He scores fewer points than any of his teammates. We don't let him handle the ball, because he's sure to turn it over. And he's slow and clumsy on defense. But he's a starter and he plays the first few minutes of each game simply because, when he's in the starting lineup, we win 70% of our games. When he's not, we only win 50% of the time.

◼ **DISCUSSION TOPIC 12.12 HEART ATTACK** "Is adultery bad for your health? The chances of having a heart attack while making love are infinitesimal, but if you do have one, the chances are you'll have it with your mistress and not your wife. A study of 34 cardiac patients who died during intercourse revealed that 29 of the 34 were having an extramarital affair."[9]

◼ **DISCUSSION TOPIC 12.13 CHAIN LETTER** Whatever you do, DO NOT DESTROY THIS LETTER! Send it out to five of your friends. Mildred Wimplebush of Detroit destroyed her copy of this letter and a week later she died of a stroke. Henry Hinkleframp of El Segundo lost his copy of the letter and was fired within a month. Marlena Gorwangle of Missoula broke her ankle in a freak accident while tossing a salad only days after throwing her copy away.

◼ **DISCUSSION TOPIC 12.14 TACKLING GROWTH** "For three decades (60s, 70s, 80s) the environmentalists, Greens, tree huggers—choose any epithet that suits your fancy but mainly those who've ranted and railed against growth—have managed to defeat every attempt to modernize Sonoma County transportation to handle the growing load. I would like to point out that sticking your head in the sand and saying you're against growth simply won't cut the mustard. You cannot pass a law (urban growth boundaries) against growth; stupid even to think of it. If you can manage to come up with an elixir that can be delivered in the water system a la Big Brother, which will prevent human sexuality, then you can slow growth."[10]

◼ **DISCUSSION TOPIC 12.15 RUSH LIMBAUGH ON ABORTION** Rush Limbaugh on abortion: "Right to choose what? Can a woman choose to steal using her own body? Of course not. Can she choose to do drugs? No. Not according to the law. Can she legally choose to be a prostitute? Again, no, which establishes, as does the drug example, that there is precedent for society determining what a woman can and can't do with her body. Look at it in another, and admittedly provocative, way: What if a man claimed the right to rape using the same principle found in the theory that it is his body and he has the right to choose? Well it's nonsense, and it is nonsense for a woman, or any citizen to assert such a right as well."

◼ **WRITING ASSIGNMENT 12.1 FALLACIES IN ILLUSTRATION** At the beginning of this chapter there is a cartoon in which a bunch of dubious "irrefutable evidence" of a UFO landing is presented. Explain the particular fallacies illustrated in the cartoon.

■ **WRITING ASSIGNMENT 12.2 FAULTY METHODOLOGY**   A dissident student group has tried, so far without success, to push its viewpoints into the news and editorial pages of the school newspaper. Now they have conducted an opinion using the following methodology. A sample is taken in the cafeteria on a Tuesday between 8 a.m. and noon. Every fifth person who enters the cafeteria is asked his or her opinion. The results are being published all over campus by leaflet claiming that 72% of the students are highly critical of the newspaper. The student government is being petitioned, on the basis of these results, to revamp the editorial board. You're the editorial page editor of the school paper. Write your editorial.

■ **WRITING ASSIGNMENT 12.3 INFORMAL FALLACIES IN ADVERTISING**   Read the following report from the magazine *Consumer Reports,* in which the editors point out several distinct informal fallacies involved in a particular advertising campaign. Can you explain each of these fallacies, using the concepts and terminology presented in this chapter?

Dodge dealers in the New York City area recently aired a series of TV commercials boasting that more than 70% of the owners of Toyota Corollas, Honda Civics, Ford Escorts and Chevrolet Cavaliers actually preferred the new Dodge Shadow, according to "100 [people] surveyed." Because our own surveys of subscribers have shown that owners of Civics and Corollas are more satisfied with their cars than are owners of Dodge Shadows, the commercial piqued our interest. The reasons for the difference between our survey results and those reported in the Dodge commercial became clear after Chrysler described the survey's methodology to us.

A survey firm retained by Chrysler chose owners of 1988 to 1991 Civics, Corollas, Cavaliers, and Escorts to participate in an experiment. The willing respondents—about 25 for each competitor—were given an opportunity to inspect a '92 Dodge Shadow and a '92 version of the car they already owned. They were also allowed to take the Dodge—but not the other car—out for a spin. After the look-see, the 100 people were asked if they thought the Dodge was better or worse than their current car. 73% reportedly said the Dodge was better.

Does this mean that most Civic and Corolla owners would prefer a new Dodge Shadow to a new Civic or Corolla, as the commercial implied? Probably not. Here's why.

First, of course, since the respondents were allowed to test-drive only the Dodge, not a new version of the model they owned, they were actually comparing a new car with a used one. For balance, we would like to have seen what owners of an older Dodge Shadow thought of their car after driving a new Corolla, Civic, Escort, and Cavalier.

Second, combining the opinions of owners of four different cars hides any distinctions among them. Civic and Corolla owners, for example, might have preferred their own car to the Dodge Shadow, while Escort and Cavalier owners might have strongly opted for the Dodge. One can't know from the reported result.

Finally, it's hard to believe that the respondents couldn't have guessed what the test was all about (and perhaps have wanted to please the sponsor), since they'd been promised $60 apiece to do a test that involved driving just one manufacturer's car.

■ **WRITING ASSIGNMENT 12.4 PERSONAL VS. GLOBAL HEALTH?**   Evaluate the reasoning in the following op-ed piece.

The Case for Neglecting Global Warming

By Donald J. Boudreaux

Pittsburgh Tribune-Review

In the July 30 edition of the *New York Times,* Gina Kolata reports on recent research findings on the health of modern citizens of industrialized countries. You might expect that this
research reveals us denizens of early 21st-century capitalist economies to be staggeringly
unhealthy—our physiques so obese and flabby, our arteries so clogged with cholesterol,
our lungs so inundated with pollutants and our brains and spirits so burdened with stress
that we are aging faster and suffering more than ever before.

In fact, the opposite is true. The great majority of us today enjoy unprecedented good
health. According to the *Times:* "New research from around the world has begun to reveal
a picture of humans today that is so different from what it was in the past that scientists
say they are startled. Over the past 100 years, says one researcher, Robert W. Fogel of the
University of Chicago, humans in the industrialized world have undergone 'a form of evolution that is unique not only to humankind, but unique among the 7,000 or so generations
of humans who have ever inhabited the earth.'

"The difference does not involve changes in genes, as far as is known, but changes in
the human form. It shows up in several ways, from those that are well known and almost
taken for granted, like greater heights and longer lives, to ones that are emerging only from
comparisons of health records.

"The biggest surprise emerging from the new studies is that many chronic ailments like
heart disease, lung disease and arthritis are occurring an average of 10 to 25 years later
than they used to. There is also less disability among older people today."

The closest this long report comes to offering up bad news is to acknowledge that some
experts believe that today's childhood obesity will eventually negate, or seriously subtract
from, these remarkable health gains. But this prediction seems silly in light of the colos-
sal, documented health gains that people in the West have enjoyed over the past five or six
generations.

And although the *Times'* report avoids firmly answering the question "why?" the
reason for this much-improved health isn't hard to find given that these health gains have
been greatest in the industrialized world and that they started within the past two centuries.
The answer, in a word, is "capitalism."

Capitalism produces so much food that we are never malnourished; it produces ample
clothing and sturdy homes to protect us from the elements; it produces the soaps, sham-
poos, toothpastes and detergents that we use every day to cleanse our bodies and living
spaces of bacteria and other dirt. And by continually substituting machines for human
labor, capitalism progressively makes our work less backbreaking and less perilous.

These gains are significant and real. And they are continuing; no one knows where, or
even if, they will stop.

Those of us who recognize these important benefits of capitalism—those of us who
understand that capitalism's true greatness lies not (as many critics insinuate) in producing oceans of pointless trinkets and baubles but in making the lives of ordinary people
richer and fuller and longer—are reluctant to yield power to governments to tackle global
warming. We worry that this power will kill the goose that's laying this golden egg.

If you think that such a worry is exaggerated, recall the language Al Gore used in his
book *Earth in the Balance.* The former vice president asserted that we are suffering an
"environmental crisis" that can be avoided only if we "drastically change our civilization
and our way of thinking."

"Drastically change our civilization." Hmmm. This sounds like a call to significantly
scale back markets, trade and industrial activities to lessen humankind's "footprint" on the

Earth and its environment. We can, no doubt, make our environmental footprint smaller—but how great a benefit will this achievement be if it returns us to the ages-old condition of high mortality and morbidity?

Undoubtedly, most people who seek government action to fight global warming are "reasonable." They envision no drastic changes to our civilization. And I concede that, in principle, cost-effective steps to reduce global warming are possible. But I'm sure that it's also true that most of the "reasonable" people who demand action against global warming are unaware of the critical role that capitalism plays in improving the lives of ordinary men and women.

So given this fact along with the hysterical language used by the likes of Al Gore—who, after all, is not on society's fringes—it's a perfectly legitimate stance for truly reasonable people to conclude that the best policy regarding global warming is to neglect it—and let capitalism continue to make us healthier and wealthier.[11]

NOTES

[1] Woody Allen, *The Curse of the Jade Scorpion,* Allen's character, C. W. Briggs, protesting his innocence after being caught in possession of the stolen jewels.

[2] Joby Warrick, "White House Got Early Warning on Katrina," *The Washington Post,* January 24, 2006, p. A02.

[3] David Ray Griffin, *The New Pearl Harbor: Disturbing Questions about the Bush Administration and 9/11* (Northampton, MA: Olive Branch Press, 2004), p. xv.

[4] Rush Limbaugh, *The Way Things Ought to Be* (New York: Simon and Schuster, 1992).

[5] Mark Twain, *The Adventures of Huckleberry Finn.*

[6] This statement is from a chiropractor's ad.

[7] David E. Sanger, "Does Calling It Jihad Make It So?" *New York Times,* August 13, 2006.

[8] *Time* (October 22, 1979), p. 57.

[9] *Playboy* Magazine.

[10] Letter to the Editor, *Sonoma County Independent,* February 12, 1998.

[11] Donald J. Boudreaux, "The Case for Neglecting Global Warming," *Pittsburgh Tribune-Review,* August 13, 2006.

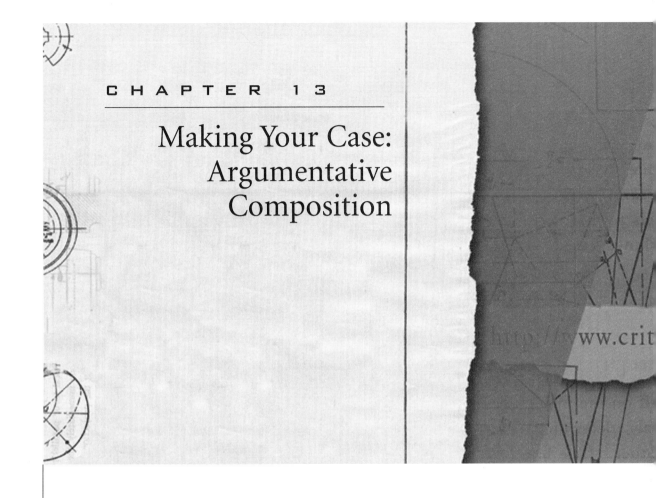

Making Your Case: Argumentative Composition

I write because I don't know what I think until I read what I say. —FLANNERY O'CONNOR

<hr>

At the beginning of this book, we discussed the importance of critical thinking in terms of both personal autonomy and democratic citizenship. At the culmination of our course of study in critical thinking, it is appropriate to reflect again on these crucial and connected ideas. Focus on the important connection between personal autonomy (the ability to use reasoning capacity to govern and regulate ourselves and the ability to make up our own minds rationally) and democratic citizenship. The well functioning—and hence the health and survival—of a democracy depends on an intellectually autonomous citizenry. If individual citizens are unprepared to make up their own minds on a rational basis, the collective decision-making processes of the society will be disabled and misguided as a consequence—and will therefore become vulnerable to corruption. The citizenry of a democratic society that loses its grounding in the "art of reasoning," as Thomas Jefferson worded it, may expect one day to find its democratic institutions (like the Congress) and processes (like elections) corrupted and no longer reliable or effective in serving the public interest.

"It's plotted out. I just have to write it."

In an earlier example, as is now a matter of public record, the citizens of the state of California had their treasury looted to the tune of $34 billion by the energy industry, after their own state legislature had deregulated the energy markets, according to plans *dictated* by energy industry. Energy deregulation was enacted into law in California by a nearly unanimous state legislature. Both political parties were on board, and both houses of the legislature signed off on the deal. It would be understandable if the citizenry of a democracy in such a state of corruption and decay started to feel angry yet powerless. And this might lead some citizens into apathy and others into committing acts of desperation and even violence. On January 16, 2001, during the first wave of "rolling blackouts" and while the State Assembly was in session, 37-year-old parolee Mike Bowers drove his 18-wheeler at 70 mph smack into the south façade of the state capitol building in Sacramento, where it burst into flames. No one knows what Bowers's motives were. He died in the fiery crash. Can you imagine how this news story would have played if it happened 8 months later (after 9/11)? Anyway, neither of these directions (apathy or violence) offers hope of improvement in the situation. Better to regain some command of the art of reasoning and get busy cleaning up the mess.

AWARENESS AND INVOLVEMENT

Suppose that you have taken this message to heart and you are now ready to engage as a citizen in the political processes of your community. Suppose you care enough about some local issue to go to a city council meeting and witness the process of public deliberation. Suppose there's a period for public comment. Now suppose you care enough about the issue that you would like to take a turn at the microphone and address the city council members and your fellow citizens. What are you prepared to say?

APPLICATION EXERCISE 13.1 | Field Trip

Move this out of the realm of the hypothetical. Pick some local organization or civic body that holds open public meetings in your community. It could be a city or town council, a local school board, a county board of supervisors, the board of trustees at your college or university, even a state legislature. Go to a meeting (or two). Witness the process of deliberation. Pay close attention to how decisions are made. How is discussion handled? Is there opportunity for direct public input into the discussion? What role is assigned to argumentation in the discussion? Find out what issues are coming up on the agenda. See if somewhere in your community you can find an issue that matters to you and is scheduled for discussion and deliberate resolution.

We try to encourage our students to think along these lines to help them understand and appreciate the value of what they are learning in critical thinking. In the context of democratic citizenship, what critical thinking provides can be understood and appreciated as follows: Suppose you are about to take your turn at the microphone at a public meeting where an issue that you care about is under discussion. Naturally, you want your contribution to the discussion to be attended to with respect by those present. Critical thinking is what makes it possible for you to make the kind of contribution *that commands the respectful attention of others* interested in the issue, whether or not they share your views. What kind of contribution will command respectful attention in an open and democratic discussion of an issue of common interest and concern? Answer: A good argument. An argument, as we defined it in Chapter 3 and understood it throughout this book, is a composition intended to persuade an audience by appeal to reason. A *good* argument, whether it is presented as a written composition, as a prepared speech, or extemporaneously,[1] will be one suited to the function of persuasion by appeal to reason. A good argument will be a composition that is well informed, well designed as an argument, and well presented.

As much as we might wish it to be otherwise, there are no reliable shortcuts here. A good argument is usually the result of a sustained investment of effort in which all general areas and many specific concepts and skills covered in this study of critical thinking can be usefully applied. Therefore, a standing assignment in our critical thinking classes is to carry out a sustained project focused on some significant issue. The work of the project involves research, argument identification, argument analysis, argument evaluation, argument design, and written composition. The finished product is an argumentative essay—or, to put it more plainly, a good argument presented in writing. In this final chapter, we discuss the composition of an argumentative essay in the context of the sort of project we assign in our critical thinking classes.

THE ISSUE STATEMENT

The project begins with the selection of an issue. In our classes, we as instructors sometimes select an issue as the common focus for the class; we sometimes allow the class to select the issue; and we sometimes allow each student in the class to select an issue. We try, in any case, to focus on issues that would score high in terms of both media visibility (how likely the issue is to come under public discussion in the media) and public importance (how much the issue does—or should—matter to the public).

Similarly, an argumentative essay will ordinarily begin with a statement of the issue to which it will be addressed. The introduction to an argumentative essay should orient the reader to and attract the reader's interest in the topic. At the end of Chapter 1 (Writing Wssignment 1.4), you were encouraged to draft a 1-page issue statement. Return to that assignment and process it more deeply.

REVIEW EXERCISE 13.1 | **The Issue Statement**

Review the section in Chapter 1 titled "Looking Ahead: Issues and Disputes," pp. 33–41.

We propose to evaluate issue statements according to three criteria: clarity, balance, and articulation. We will comment on each criterion in turn.

CLARITY

Clarity is in one sense the easiest of the three criteria to explain and understand. It refers to the overall mastery of the language used in the composition. Clarity applies as a criterion of evaluation not just to the issue statement but to the entire composition. When we evaluate a piece of writing for clarity, we ask, "Is the language being used effectively to get the ideas across without confusion?" To the extent that it is, the composition is clear. To the extent that it is not, the clarity can be improved. Grammar, vocabulary, idiom, and spelling all play a role in this. To check for clarity, we recommend having someone (preferably someone whose writing you respect or admire) read your draft. We will say a bit more about clarity shortly.

BALANCE

Because you're writing about an issue, a topic about which reasonable people may disagree, your initial statement of the issue should be **balanced.** This means it should not be not prejudiced either in favor of or against any of the positions that a reasonable person might be inclined to hold about the topic. You don't want to alienate any of your potential readers before they have a chance to consider your argument in its totality. One of the best ways to achieve this is to make a relatively clear distinction between your *issue* statement, in which you bring your topic into focus for your reader, and your **thesis** statement, in which you tell your reader where you stand on the issue. If you can present the issue in a balanced way, this tells your reader that you understand that there is room for reasonable disagreement on the matter and that you are capable of respectfully understanding positions that may differ from your own. This will encourage your reader to pay respectful attention to *your* argument.

ARTICULATION

Articulation relates to the inherent complexity of issues, as we explained in Chapter 1. For any given issue, there will be many different ways to frame, focus, and organize the inquiry. What do we mean by these terms? Let us say that **framing** the issue means situating it within a larger context and determining what will be considered within and what will be considered outside the scope of the discussion. **Focusing** the issue means determining what will be considered central and what will be considered peripheral within the scope of the discussion. And **organization** refers to the order within which things will be considered. When you enter into a complex area of controversy, you need to make decisions about all of these things to develop what we might call an orderly agenda of inquiry. This is what we mean by articulation. An articulate issue statement is one that has carefully considered how to frame, focus, and organize the discussion of the issue in its inherent complexity and has arrived at and clearly communicated an orderly agenda of inquiry. This is a challenging aspect of the process, but facing this challenge squarely at this early stage will greatly enhance your ability to maintain your bearings as you work your way through the complexity of the issue. And it will make your argument easier for your reader to follow.

WRITING ASSIGNMENT 13.1 | Term Project: Finalize the Issue Statement

Revise the issue statement you drafted in Writing Assignment 1.4, paying special attention to the clarity, balance, and articulation of the statement.

Drafting the issue statement is a good way to begin the kind of project we are discussing here, as well as a good way to begin the argumentative essay that comes out of the project as the final product. Before we return to a discussion of other elements in the argumentative essay, let us explore the second of the preliminary stages of the project: research. Remember that, in the end, a good argument will be a composition that is well informed. Thus even from the earliest stages of articulating the issue, one of the most important ingredients of a good argument will be the quality of the information that goes into it.

RESEARCH AND THE MEDIA

Once an appropriate issue has been selected, an early stage of the project involves research. Research essentially means finding out something we don't already know. In researching an issue, we need to gain access to reliable information relevant to our topic. Most important, because this topic is the subject of debate and disagreement among reasonable people, we need to gain access to arguments of a reasonably high standard representing the range of opinion on the topic. We live in what has come to be known as the age of information. Among the many meanings this label carries is reference to our unprecedented access to information. Individually and collectively, we can gather, collect, store, sort, process, transmit, and receive more information more quickly than at any previous time in human history. This is both a blessing and a curse for research. The availability of information is useful to research. But in an information-rich environment like ours, it's easy to become lost, distracted, and overwhelmed by the volume of information available—and equally or perhaps even more important, we need practical means of assessing the reliability of this information.

Over the last several decades, we have seen profound changes in the way research is conducted. A generation ago (when we, the authors of this book, were in college), to do research we went to the card catalogue in the college library. The information and the arguments were in books (or periodicals) in the library and listed in the card catalogue. We looked them up by subject, found them in the stacks, and took them home and read them. Today, the library is still the first and best place to do research. But now the information and the arguments are in all kinds of media, not just print, and all over the place, not necessarily housed in the library building. Today you can "go to the library" using the Internet. The age of information has made do-it-yourself research an easy undertaking, undoubtedly a good thing. Yet the age of information has raised some "quality control issues" for the do-it-yourself researcher. With so much information so readily available, how can we be sure that the information we're reviewing is reliable? How do we determine which of the many and often conflicting factual claims we may encounter in our research are accurate? How do we find among the arguments in circulation those that represent the broadest spectrum of opinion with the highest standard of reasoning? The best piece of general research advice we have to offer is to consult your college reference librarians. Make sure you have your issue well and clearly defined. Librarians are even more crucial as assistants to research today than they were a generation ago. They are the college's experts in using new and increasingly powerful information technologies (such as InfoTrac College Edition) to sift through the mountains of information available on most any issue. Beyond this piece of general advice, it may be worth saying a little about media, sources of information, reliability, and skepticism.

TELEVISION

In the woodcut *Selectovision,* by David Suter (Figure 13.1), a video cameraman is recording a man fleeing from an attacker with a knife but the identities of attacker and victim are reversed in the video image. Thus the artist makes the point that television is capable and often guilty of misrepresenting reality. This sort of skepticism of the medium of television is much deeper today and more commonplace than it has been throughout most of the medium's short history. It is worth considering the reasons for this sort of skepticism with respect not only to television but to other sources of information as well.

Although the technology was emerging in the 1920s, television really came into its own after World War II. During the 1950s, television quickly became a dominant communications medium in American society and throughout the industrialized world. Throughout much of this period, television was widely accepted as a generally reliable source of information. This may be partly attributable to the technology's ability to record and transmit audiovisual imagery of events taking place in real time. It may also be partly attributable to the "realism" of television programming. ("The camera does not lie.") Viewed as a technology and an information medium, television has always had immense functional potential for human society. It is a highly flexible medium, able to accommodate information in a range of forms—from spoken word, to music, to moving visual imagery, to graphic text—simultaneously in all manner of combinations. Once programmed, its messages engage the human perceiving subject simultaneously through multiple sense modalities, thus giving television unusually high power to attract and hold attention. With the enhancement of satellite transmission and reception technology, fiber optics, and cable, television makes possible the instantaneous transmission and reception of huge quantities of audiovisual information globally. Now an international audience of almost any size can witness a significant event—for example, the second hijacked airliner crashing into the North Tower of the World Trade Center—as it is occurring (as well as repeatedly after the fact).

However, even as television technology has become more elaborate and powerful, television audiences have become more sophisticated and are coming to understand television not only as a technology and an information medium but also as a business—indeed, an industry. Through this process of growth and maturation, television audiences have seen through certain naive illusions and become more skeptical and perhaps even cynical. For example, we've all heard the expression "brought to you through the courtesy of . . ." many times on television. Here, we are encouraged to understand television as a free entertainment and information service. Entertainment and information are delivered to the public free of charge, and this service is paid for by Dr. Pepper, or Nike, or ADM (Archer, Daniels, Midland—Supermarket to the World!). From the vantage point of the audience (the vantage point most of us occupy), this is no doubt a comfortable way to understand television's institutional role. But it misrepresents the economics of the industry. From within the television industry such a description makes no sense. Why would the makers of Dr. Pepper want to pour money into providing a free entertainment and information service for millions of people? What the makers of Dr. Pepper are paying for is public attention. What's going on is that *we* (the audience) are being brought to *them* (the sponsors) by CBS or another television station. Viewed in these terms, television's primary function in our culture has been as a tool for harvesting public attention for sale in the public attention market. The primary function of television programming is to round up an audience and hold that audience in place in a receptive attitude (what the industry calls a "buying mood") for the sponsor's message. This explains why television programming is nearly 100% entertainment and why the boundaries and distinctions between entertainment (showbiz) and public service programming (journalism) have become increasingly blurred. And television audiences are more acutely aware of this nowadays. When we see the major network news anchors Dan Rather, Tom Brokaw, and Peter Jennings making regular celebrity guest appearances on the late-night talk shows, after a while we start to realize that television news is as much a part of showbiz as *Wheel of Fortune*.

MASS MEDIA

During the 19th century, industrial expansion created so-called economies of scale in many areas of enterprise, including journalism. This meant that the capital costs of acquiring, maintaining, and operating a large industrialized printing press, and the associated need to reach an increasingly massive audience, rose by several orders of magnitude. In such a business climate, large businesses dominate and small businesses are eaten or die. As these trends progress, ownership and control grows increasingly concentrated and further removed from the community. Fewer ever-larger corporations come to control more of the flow of information, and small local independent voices are lost. These trends have been studied and documented by media scholar Ben Bagdikian, a Pulitzer Prize–winning journalist and former dean of the University of California Graduate School of Journalism, who writes:

A handful of mammoth private organizations have begun to dominate the world's mass media. Most of them confidently announce that by the 1990s they—five to ten corporate giants—will control most of the world's important newspapers, magazines, books, broadcast stations, movies, recordings and videocassettes. Moreover, each of these planetary corporations plans to gather under its control every step in the information process, from creation of "the product" to all the various means by which modern technology delivers media messages to the public. "The product" is news, information, ideas, entertainment and popular culture; the public is the whole world.[2]

The public is also increasingly aware that the major media, because they are big businesses, have interests to advance and protect that may interfere and conflict with the public interest in access to relevant and accurate information. This applies not just to television but to the major media generally. Professional journalists, who work in the industry, are aware of this potential for conflict of interest as an issue of professional ethics, and the best of them are capable of biting the hand that feeds them. But the public is still right to be skeptical.

Another factor contributing to growing public skepticism is an accumulating history of political and corporate scandal. Watergate, the Pentagon Papers, Iran-contra, pedophilia in the priesthood, the Enron–Anderson–WorldCom corporate accounting scandals, each with its own series of cover-ups and evasive press conferences, have had a cumulative effect of undermining public trust and confidence in many important social institutions, including the press. The public is now increasingly aware that presidential press conferences and Pentagon briefings are public relations events planned and orchestrated to manage public opinion. In short, we have good reason to be skeptical of information made available through the major media and to wonder what may be going on behind the scenes. However, there is a danger that we may become so cynical as to suspect the worst at all times and to never trust anyone. This is a form of intellectual paralysis and is something we should avoid. We should remember that at least some of these scandals (Watergate, the pedophile priests, and others) were brought to light through old-fashioned, hard-nosed investigative journalism. Instead of becoming cynical and refusing to trust or believe anything we hear or read, we should become skeptical consumers of information. This means actively seeking information (rather than passively receiving it) and questioning and challenging the information as it comes in to us (rather than simply accepting it as reliable).

INTERNET SEARCH TOOLS

The Internet provides an excellent environment within which to practice and develop good habits of active skepticism in research. One reason for this is the *importance* of active skepticism in researching the World Wide Web. When the first edition of this book was published in the 1980s, the Internet was little more than an obscure and geeky experiment and the World Wide Web didn't exist. Now we're talking about the world's largest and fastest growing computer and communications network, a development that has already brought big changes in information access generally and that promises more and perhaps bigger changes to come, especially in the practice of research and education. Once connected to the net, you gain access to information stored on computers literally all over the world. This is impressive technology. It literally opens up a world of information on any imaginable subject from astronomy to Zen. You can access the world's great libraries; you can dig through government files and databases; you can see detailed up-to-the-minute weather information, celebrity gossip, sports scores, and stock quotations from any part of the world; and on and on. So vast and dynamic is this information environment that it has spawned a hugely profitable new industry devoted to maintaining up-to-date Internet databases and constructing computer programs called search engines to assist people with Internet research. Type the words "global warming" into a search engine like Google, and in less the one-tenth of a second a list of more than 50 million references appears on your screen. This is no exaggeration. We just checked. You're not going to follow *all* of those references, and this immediately raises the question how to narrow the field. We'll be coming back to this question in a moment. Most people start at (or near) the top of the hit list.

APPLICATION EXERCISE 13.2 | Search Engine Optimization

Ever wonder how the search engine decides which references to list first? See if you can design a web search to find out.

If you're stumped on the preceding exercise, here's a hint: Anyone with a computer and an Internet connection can publish on the Internet. So look at the situation from that point of view. If you want to put your ideas out there, you could have a website. So you design a site. Now, how do you encourage people to visit your website? How do you help them find it? How do you make the search engine find *your* website and list it at or near the top of the list?

Many Internet enthusiasts point to the low barriers to publication and the resultant overabundance of information (as well as access to it) as evidence of the Internet's democratizing potential. By effectively eliminating barriers to publication, the Internet seems to enhance freedom of speech and expression and freedom of access to information. But these open conditions raise some of those quality control issues we mentioned earlier. If you find some information about the human genome project in the *New England Journal of Medicine* or the *Journal of the American Medical Association,* you can be confident in the reliability of the information. Why? Because reputable scientific and academic journals are careful about what they let into their pages, using rigorous peer review processes designed to maintain high standards of accuracy and integrity. There is no editorial board screening web pages. Anybody— including crackpots and hustlers—can put up a web page. They don't need any credentials. They don't have to know what they're talking about. They don't have to check their facts. And not only can they put up a web page, but it can *look* as "professional" as the official Harvard University web page. Indeed, this is exactly what members of the Heaven's Gate cult were doing to support themselves and raise money before they committed mass suicide—building web pages. So, Internet surfers need to beware: although the Internet is an abundant information resource, the garbage–to–good stuff ratio is higher on the Internet than in the Expanded Academic Index.

So we have to do the evaluation. Many institutional or organizational websites include statements about the type and source of information provided on their web pages, as well as the purpose of the organization. If this information is *not* offered, be especially careful about evaluating the data you find there. Here are a few common sense questions to ask:[3]

CRITICAL THINKING TIP 13.1 | **Active Skepticism in Research**

Be an Active Skeptic in Research and Ask Questions.

WHAT ARE THE SOURCES OF THE INFORMATION?

Where did the information originate? Who put it there?

WHERE TO LOOK   On a web page, look near the top of the page. Check the title, the section headings, and the opening paragraphs to see if some person or organization is named as the person or people responsible for the content of the web pages. Also look near the bottom of the page for this information. (Keep in mind that the webmaster or person who designed the web page is not necessarily the one responsible for the content of the page.)

You can sometimes learn something about the source of a web page by examining the page's URL. The URL often indicates what type of organization and what country a web page comes from.

If you can't find any information about the author or authors on the page you're looking at, try erasing the last part of the URL for that page in your web browser's location box. Delete from the end of the URL backward to the first slash mark (/), then press the RETURN or ENTER key on your keyboard. If you still don't see any information about the author or authors, back up one more directory or slash mark. Keep going until you come to a page that identifies the author or authors of these pages.

HOW AUTHORITATIVE IS THE SOURCE?

What qualifications does this person or organization have to talk on this topic? Does the author have a university degree in the discipline? Or is this person an amateur or a hobbyist or merely someone with an opinion to air? If an organization is responsible for the pages, is the organization widely recognized as a source of scholarly and reliable information? (For example, the American Cancer Society is a reliable source for information on cancer-related topics.) What other information can you find about the author or organization responsible for the content of this web page?

WHERE TO LOOK   On a web page, look near the top and the bottom of the page. Is there a link to more information about the person or organization?

For organizations, there's often a link called "About Us" or something similar that leads to a page explaining what the organization's mission is, when and how it was founded, and so forth. Read it for clues.

For a single person or author, there might be information about the person's educational background, research, or other qualifications for speaking on this topic. There might be a link to the author's faculty or professional web pages.

Look for links to articles and publications by the person or organization. Look for an address or a phone number you could use to contact the author or authors.

If you can't find any information about the author or authors on the page you're looking at, try erasing the last part of the URL for that page in your web browser's location box as described earlier. Keep going until you come to a page that has more information about the person or organization responsible for the pages. Remember that a URL that has a tilde (~) in it is almost always someone's personal home page as opposed to an organization's official page.

If you can't find any information about the author or authors anywhere on the web pages, try searching for the person's or organization's name using one of the Internet search engines to see if you can find web pages about them elsewhere. Check some library catalogues and magazine or newspaper databases to see if the person or organization has published books or articles in the field.

If you can find no information about the web page's author or authors, be wary. If you can't verify that the information is authoritative, don't use it in a class paper or project.

WHAT IS THE PURPOSE OF THE DOCUMENT?

Does the author claim this page to be factual? Is the author trying to persuade you of something? To whom is the author of this page talking? To scholars and experts? To students? To anyone who will listen? Is the author trying to sell you a product discussed on the page? Does the page include advertising? If so, can you tell clearly which parts are advertisement and which parts are informational content? Does the page remind you of a television infomercial—that is, does it look like an informational article even though it is an advertisement?

WHERE TO LOOK   If the author or organization has provided an "About Us" page, you can probably determine something about the web page's purpose by reading about the mission of the organization.

HOW STRAIGHTFORWARD IS THE SOURCE?

Does the author or the organization have an identifiable vested interest or an obvious bias concerning the topic? Does the author or the organization represent a particular point of view (the Catholic Church, the National Organization for Women, the R. J. Reynolds Tobacco Company, the Republican or Democratic Party, and so on)? If you don't know the answer to this question, be sure to read the "About Us" page. If the author does have a vested interest, or particular point of view, is this made clear or is there an attempt to obscure it?

WHERE TO LOOK   Does the page use inflammatory language, images or graphic styles (for example, huge red letters or lots of boldface type) to try and persuade you of the author's point of view?

Examine the URL to see where the web page comes from. Is it a commercial site (.com)? A nonprofit organization (.org)? An educational institution (.edu)? Think again about the person or organization's mission or charge as you read about it in the "About Us" link.

Try some of the same approaches you used to determine the authority of the information source, for example, look for the names of the authors using one of the web search engines to see if you can find other information about them. Is the organization an advocacy group; that is, does it advocate for a particular cause or point of view?

HOW CURRENT IS THE INFORMATION?

Can you tell when the web page was originally created? When it was last updated? Is this a topic on which it's important that you have up-to-date information (science, medicine, news, and so on) or one for which it is not as important that information be recent (history, literature, and so on)?

WHERE TO LOOK   Look near the top and the bottom of the page to see if any publication date, copyright date, or "date last modified" is indicated.

Look for other indications that the page is kept current. Is there a "What's New" section? If statistical data or charts are included, be especially careful to notice what dates are represented and when the data was collected or published.

A moment ago we mentioned that the refereed periodical literature in the sciences and humanities as a generally more reliable category of source material to consult in your research. Nowadays, most of this literature is also available or researchable and retrievable online. There are databases and search engines, like InfoTrac, dedicated to researching periodical literature. They function in like Internet search engines such as Google. Most college and university libraries subscribe to these databases. Check your school library's home page for directions. Even though as a whole it is more reliable, the academic periodical literature should be approached with the same good habits of active skepticism as you would apply on the Internet. We can ask similar questions to those supplied earlier about the authors and editors of these more old-fashioned sources of information. Who are they? What are their qualifications? Did the information they are presenting originate with them, or are they just passing it along? Are they acting with integrity in their capacity as authors and editors? Do they have an agenda? Do they have any general political orientation or bias? Are they open and forthright about any such agenda or orientation or bias, or do they try to hide it? Approaching all sources of information in this way will enable you to gather reliable information and to screen out the noise and misinformation more effectively.

THE THESIS STATEMENT

Return to the matter of composing an argumentative essay. By the time you reach this stage, you should have a good idea where you stand on the issue you have been considering. The introduction to your argumentative essay should accomplish two essential goals: (1) orienting and interesting your reader in your topic (your issue statement should accomplish this goal) and (2) letting your reader know where you stand. Your thesis statement should accomplish this second goal. The word "thesis" comes from Greek, where it means proposed idea. As used in the discipline of writing, the thesis is the main idea of an essay or longer composition, not necessarily just the conclusion of the argument, as described in Chapter 3. If the composition is an argumentative essay, the thesis will be in the position of the conclusion of the argument, supported by other ideas that you will present as premises. The essential difference between the thesis statement and the issue statement is that balance is no longer a relevant criterion of assessment. Your thesis statement should be clear and articulate, but it does not need to be balanced.

As we just said, by the time you write an argumentative essay, you should have a clear idea of where you stand. Ideally, your current convictions about the issue will have resulted from the work you have invested in researching the issue, finding the arguments both in favor of and against the various positions along the spectrum of opinion, and analyzing and evaluating those arguments. However, even after doing all this work, many people find formulating a thesis quite an intimidating challenge. This may be because people recognize the risks inherent in taking a position in an area of controversy. "People will disagree with me. I will be called upon to defend my position with an argument. I have no idea yet how I shall argue for my position. What if I'm wrong?" Do not let any of this paralyze you. Yes, people will disagree with you. Yes, you will be called upon to defend your position with an argument. But at this stage, even if you have no idea how that argument will go, you have time to figure it out. Remember that you are not required to opt for either one of the two "extreme" or "polar" positions along the spectrum of opinion on your issue (if that's how the public debate on the matter has been structured). Indeed, you are not restricted to choose among positions that have been formulated and articulated by others. You are free to be original and creative and to propose a new compromise position if you can think of one. Finally, if you *are* wrong, nothing prevents your changing your mind and correcting your position. So go ahead and be honest with yourself about where you stand on the subject. Write that down. This is a draft of your thesis statement.

WRITING ASSIGNMENT 13.2 | Term Project: Thesis Statement

At the end of Chapter 10 you were challenged to write a 100-word position statement (Writing Assignment 10.1)—which we expect will contain an argument. Through Chapters 11 and 12 you were prompted to analyze, critique, and revise that argument. Now, draft a thesis statement in 100 words or less. Make it just the thesis—just what you will go on to support with your argument.

ARGUMENT DESIGN

In general, good argument design flows from a clear and detailed understanding of both the thesis and the issue to which the thesis responds. Depending on the precise nature of the issue with which you are concerned, of the subissues involved in it, and of the claim you are defending as your thesis, different argument design strategies will be more or less viable and promising. The kind of argument you might need to design to effectively support and defend a value judgment may not work well to support and defend a causal hypothesis. One general principle for argument design, therefore, is simply to study your issue closely and analytically, letting your insights into its character and complexities guide you to a deeper awareness of the strengths and vulnerabilities of your position. Make your argument as logical as you can. If you can, build an argument that is deductively valid. If you can't find or devise valid deductive support for your thesis, perhaps one or more of the varieties of inductive reasoning will be applicable. In any case, make full use of what you have learned about argument analysis and argument evaluation in designing your argument. And be careful not to fall into any fallacious patterns or tendencies.

OUTLINING

As you build your case you will want to ensure that your argument hangs together and that your thesis is convincingly and legitimately supported. An excellent device for testing the web of logical relationships in your essay—as well as for guiding and controlling the work of composition—is an outline of your argument. Many student writers (and nonstudent writers, for that matter) fail to fully exploit the outline as an argument design tool. We've seen quite a few outlines that go no further than this:

  I. Introduction

   A. My issue statement

   B. My thesis statement

 II. Body

   A. Reasons in favor of my position

III. Conclusion

This is *not* what we mean by an outline of your argument. You can do better than this. To get the most out of your outline, you will want to go into greater depth and detail. Start with item II, and begin by breaking it down further. Concentrate on the *argument* you are building. What are the reasons in favor of your position? Be specific. And how are those reasons related to one another? What evidence supports those reasons? Then, what are the positions you oppose? What are your objections to those opposing positions? Be specific. And what objections do you anticipate coming from those opposing positions? How will you respond to such objections? Be specific. Make sure that you define key terms and concepts. Be conscious of the need to support your claims with facts and to illustrate your points with examples. All of this material needs to be placed in some order so that your reader can follow your train of thought through your composition. One the most basic functions of outlining is to allow you to think through these details of your argument and organize them—without having to work out all subtleties of wording and presentation that will eventually go into the finished composition. Outlining is a flexible tool. You can use it before *or* after you have written a draft—better yet, use outlining both before *and* after. Use outlining as a tool in revising what you've written.

APPRECIATING YOUR OPPONENT'S POSITION

Because your thesis responds to an issue, and because issues are by definition topics about which reasonable people may disagree, your thesis will tend to be relatively controversial. A second general principle for argument design flows from this. In addition, in arguing for your thesis, you are essentially trying to be persuasive, to win your audience over. Try to identify premises that are less controversial, less subject to debate, than your thesis. In other words, try to find common ground on which to base your argument for your thesis.

This second general principle of argument design suggests some further ideas about argument design and construction. The medieval philosopher and theologian Thomas Aquinas once remarked that when you want to convert someone to your view, you go over to where he is standing, take him by the hand (mentally speaking), and guide him to where you want him to go. You don't stand across the room and shout at him. You don't call him nasty names. You don't order him to come over to where you are. You start where he is and work from that position. To put it another way: When you think that someone is wrong and you disagree with her, you should first try to figure out in what way or ways she is right. This is not as paradoxical as it sounds. Suppose you're firmly convinced of some particular position on a complex and controversial subject like the death penalty. Are you certain that you're correct? Can you be certain that people who disagree with you are entirely wrong in everything they might have to say? Wouldn't it be wiser to thoughtfully consider what your opponents might have to say and to concede as much as you honestly can? Then when you go on to offer criticisms of your opponents' position, you can reasonably expect them to be given thoughtful consideration as well. After all, think about how you would react as a reader to a criticism of your position. If the criticism starts by identifying your position as out to lunch, you're not likely to be receptive, are you? You'd be more open to a criticism that began by stating your position in a way that you would yourself state it—recognizing its intuitive plausibility, its explanatory power, the weight of evidence in its favor, or whatever strengths it may have. If you are going to criticize others' argument or position, make sure you state it so that *they* know that you have fairly and accurately understood it.

OBJECTIONS AND REPLIES

Just as you should be aware of the possibility that your opponent's position may embody certain strengths, you should be aware of the possibility that your own position may have certain weaknesses—weaknesses that likely will be more apparent to your opponent than to you. Thus an additional strategic advantage for the writer of an argumentative essay flows from making a genuine attempt to appreciate the opponent's position. Your opponent's position affords you a better vantage point from which to troubleshoot your own position and argument—to make yourself aware of points at which you need additional support for your argument or qualifications and refinements of the thesis itself.

APPLICATION EXERCISE 13.3 | **Term Project: Outline**

Based on your issue statement as revised in Writing Assignment 13.1 and your thesis statement in Writing Assignment 13.2, outline your argument.

THE PRESENTATION

So much good advice is already available about writing and how to get better at it that for us to offer such advice here may seem redundant, arrogant, or both.[4] Do we have anything new and distinctive to add to what the many courses, tutorials, books, tapes, websites, and consultants on becoming a better writer have to offer? Probably not. But we're not going to let that stop us. We will, however, try to keep this brief and to the point. In Chapter 1 we made a quick comparison, almost in passing, between thinking and writing (p. 14). We were talking about discipline. Our point there was that even though learning a discipline (like writing, critical thinking, or music—our other example) involves the mastery of rules and regularities through extensive practice, there is still room for you to develop a distinctive individual style. This is important because writing is a means of self-expression. It would be disappointing if to learn how to express ourselves effectively in words we each had to sound exactly like everybody else. At the same time, just as you can keep developing and refining your thinking throughout your life by disciplined study, so too can you continue to improve your writing—with disciplined practice—as you develop your individual style. (So it's good that there is so much advice out there for the developing writer.)

In Chapter 2 we began an exploration of language by remarking on its amazing flexibility and power as a toolkit for communication. There are *so many* things we can accomplish, so many tasks we can undertake through the use of language. There are, accordingly, many kinds of writing. And what makes for a good piece of writing of one kind (poetry or a sermon) may not serve the purposes of some other kind of writing (say, a software user manual). We do better as writers generally when we are guided by an understanding of the specific goals of the kind of writing we are working on. Composing an argumentative essay is a rather specialized application of writing. It requires and also helps build language skills of certain kinds in special ways. Some of these should come as no surprise because they have occupied center stage throughout this course of study. They all derive from the function of an argument: to persuade by appeal to reason.

RELEVANCE

We have a friend who tells endless stream-of-consciousness stories. She might start by saying, "Do you remember Sally so and so from junior high school? Well I ran into her the other day in the parking lot outside the supermarket, and she had just been to the deli. You know they have this new deli in the supermarket and they make the greatest pasta salad. They use pine nuts. That's the secret ingredient. And smoothies! You know, because they started making smoothies, I seem to have to go in there every single day! Smoothies have changed my life! But you know I think they've started using less frozen yogurt and more ice. Don't you just hate when they do that? Take some good thing, and just when people start to catch on, raise the price or something. Like my cell phone company . . ." and on and on she goes. We began taking bets as to whether the story will ever wander back around to the initial topic, such as Sally so and so from junior high school. Try not to write like this. This kind of improvised discourse is OK for around the campfire, although even there it can be exasperating. But it is not appropriate when you are composing an argumentative essay. Know where you are headed, and go there. Don't wander. Don't interrupt yourself. Don't go off on tangents. If something suddenly occurs to you as an important point that should not be left out, try to find the place in the argument where it is most relevant and insert it there so that the orderly flow of the reasoning is preserved. This is one of the most important applications of outlining. You don't want to leave anything important out, but you do want to present it all in good order.

CARE AND PRECISION IN CHOOSING AND DEFINING TERMS

This applies throughout the entire composition. Suppose your issue is about terrorism. Naturally, you will want to define the term "terrorism." But it is not enough to define the word if in so doing you don't *choose the terms in the definition with great care and precision.* Many students seem unaware of this, or at least that's how it looks when we read their essays and notice the general carelessness with which words and phrases are thrown around. If you don't know the difference in meaning between the word "credible" and the word "credulous," you shouldn't use either one. If you don't know the difference between "affect" and "effect" or between "principal" and "principle," don't just fake it by alternating between them. If you aren't certain what the word you're thinking of using means, *look it up.* Otherwise, how can you know if you have made a good vocabulary choice? How can you know if the word is going to work the way you need it to work in its context? How will you improve your vocabulary? The same goes for idiomatic phrases. People often seem to be shuffling these together like some kind of refrigerator-door-poetry kit, ending up with accidental comedy like, "We need to grab the bull by the tail and look the facts squarely in the eye." This is not the effect you want to have on your reader.

CRITICAL THINKING TIP 13.2 | **How to Use Your "Spell Checker"**

Instead of tinkering with Spelling until Highlighting or Underlining Disappears from a Word, Go to the Dictionary and Look the Word Up.

ECONOMY OF EXPRESSION

Don't waste words. Don't pad your paper. Don't embellish. Many writing instructors advise their students to avoid repetitive use of the same terminology throughout a single composition. You may have received such advice. The idea is to spice up the composition by using a variety of synonymous or roughly synonymous terms instead of consistently using the same ones. This may be good advice if what you are writing is a short story, a travelogue, or a biographical essay for a scholarship competition. But when you are writing an argumentative essay, you're trying to enlighten, not entertain. So, you should be more concerned about confusing than about boring your reader. Also, avoid affectation. Don't try to sound like you think an academic scholar should sound. Academic scholarship, you might as well know, often presents a model of how *not* to write. Here, for example, is the winner of last year's "Bad Writing Contest," sponsored by the academic journal *Philosophy & Literature:*

> Indeed dialectical critical realism may be seen under the aspect of Foucauldian strategic reversal—of the unholy trinity of Parmenidean/Platonic/Aristotelean provenance; of the Cartesian-Lockean-Humean-Kantian paradigm, of foundationalisms (in practice, fideistic foundationalisms) and irrationalisms (in practice, capricious exercises of the will-to-power or some other ideologically and/or psycho-somatically buried source) new and old alike; of the primordial failing of western philosophy, ontological monovalence, and its close ally, the epistemic fallacy with its ontic dual; of the analytic problematic laid down by Plato,

which Hegel served only to replicate in his actualist monovalent analytic reinstatement in transfigurative reconciling dialectical connection, while in his hubristic claims for absolute idealism he inaugurated the Comtean, Kierkegaardian and Nietzschean eclipses of reason, replicating the fundaments of positivism through its transmutation route to the superidealism of a Baudrillard.[5]

Is this what you want to sound like? God help us! Keep it simple. Be direct. Get straight to your point.

CRITICAL THINKING TIP 13.3 | **Concision**

As You Write, and Especially as You Revise, Ask Yourself, "What Is My Point in This Sentence (or Paragraph)?" Then Ask Yourself, "Can I Make My Point Clear in Half the Words?" Cut Anything That Is Not Necessary to Making the Point Clear.

RHETORIC

Rhetoric is the classical discipline devoted to the general study of expressive discourse. Indeed, the word "rhetoric" derives from the Greek expression for "I say." Classical rhetoric classifies all kinds of writing into four categories: narrative (storytelling); descriptive (using words to create mental imagery); expository (the presentation or explication of information); and finally, persuasive (using words to change other people's minds). Arguments and argumentative essays fall into this last category, which has received the most attention among the four categories. The main traditional concern of rhetoric as an academic discipline has been the development and systematic refinement of skills, techniques, and strategies of persuasion—strategies like rhythmic repetition, alliteration, presenting ideas and examples in groups of three, and so on. Historically, rhetoric's traditional emphasis on persuasion arose in ancient Greece. In the developing political context of the city-states, citizens found it increasingly important to learn how to make effective and persuasive presentations in the assemblies and law courts, the principal institutions of self-government, where the laws were made and interpreted. So there is a deep historical connection between rhetoric and argument. Argument design is part of rhetoric understood as the general art of persuasion. And argumentative essays—although they may employ narrative, descriptive, and expository discourse—fall into the persuasive category. However, rhetoric is broader than argument and encompasses more than argument design, because persuasion is a broader category than *rational* persuasion. There are other ways to be persuasive than by appeal to reason. So the question arises when you come to the presentation of the argument, "Should I (and if so *how* should I) use persuasive strategies and rhetorical devices other than the argument itself in my composition?" Answer: By all means sweeten the presentation as best you can. But remember that the main persuasive tool in the composition should be the argument. Don't let the rhetorical sweeteners be a substitute for a good argument. In the absence of a good argument, all rhetoric is "empty."

EXAMPLES

Well-placed and well-chosen examples will do more to enhance your presentation and strengthen your argument than just about anything else we can think of. Examples assist the reader to grasp difficult and unfamiliar material. Examples also lend support to points that the reader may be inclined to question. In addition, many of the ingredients of a good argument—for example, precisely defined terms and concepts, and rigorous logic—tend to make the argument "abstract." Examples help keep it "real." Examples can also be colorful, juicy, spicy, and entertaining. They provide an excellent opportunity to liven up a composition. So, make good use of examples, but just as with the rhetorical sweeteners, make sure the examples serve—rather than distract from—the argument.

REVISIONS

Real writers revise, and revise, and revise again. Real writers are constantly reviewing and revising—taking the composition apart and reorganizing it, inserting and deleting, making small improvements here and there—because they *care* how the composition comes out. Some of us can't even stop revising after we're finished. So take a cue from the best writers and revise your work. Start early so that you have time to revise. Writing is at least as much a process of *discovering what you think* as it is a matter of composing the results of prior thinking. The essay is not merely a format for the presentation of the results of your deliberations, a sort of literary Jell-O mold into which you pour your thoughts when they're finished and ready to go to market. The activity of organizing and composing the essay is—or can and should be—an integral part of those deliberations—an integral part of the process of rationally making up your mind.[6] Sometimes in the course of outlining (or drafting or revising) you may find your argument taking you in unplanned and unanticipated directions, suggesting maybe a different approach or even a different thesis than the one you originally undertook to defend. If this happens, it is not necessary to resist. Perhaps what is happening is that you are discovering things about the argument and the issue that are important. Let your reasoning take you where it wants to go. There's nothing wrong with adjusting your thesis in accordance with the best reasoning you find yourself able to develop. Use the insights you gain through this process of working out your argument to revise your thesis statement. We recommend working with a partner or in a small study group. Have someone else read your draft and offer criticisms. Have that person read your draft aloud to you. This may help you to detach from your draft enough to hear areas where there may be room or a need for improvement.

   We could go on, but what is most essential to your learning now is practice. So we think it is time to wish you the best of luck and let you get to work.

WRITING ASSIGNMENT 13.3 | Term Project: First Draft

Based on your issue statement as revised in Writing Assignment 13.1, your thesis statement from Writing Assignment 13.2, and your outline from Application Exercise 13.3, now draft an argumentative essay. Try to make your case in 1,500 words (5–6 pages).

GLOSSARY

articulation   as applied to the analysis of complex issues, framing, focusing, and organizing the inquiry

balance   as applied to an issue statement, not prejudiced either in favor of or against any positions a reasonable person might be inclined to hold about the issue

clarity   as applied to an issue statement, the ability to get ideas across without confusion

framing   as applied to the analysis of complex issues, determining what will be considered within and outside the scope of discussion

focusing   as applied to the analysis of complex issues, determining what will be considered central, peripheral, or both within the scope of discussion

organization   as applied to an issue statement, the order in which things will be considered

rhetoric   a classical discipline devoted to the general study of expressive discourse; currently, the art or science of persuasion by stylistic and expressive means

thesis   from Greek, proposed idea; in the discipline of writing, the main idea of an essay or longer composition

ADDITIONAL EXERCISES

■ **WRITING ASSIGNMENT 13.4 TERM PROJECT: LETTER TO THE EDITOR**   When you have worked out your position and your argument for it at the length prescribed in Writing Assignment 13.3 or by your instructor, try condensing it. Try to compose it as a Letter to the Editor. Consult the opinion pages of your local newspaper for guidance as to length and format.

■ **WRITING ASSIGNMENT 13.5 TERM PROJECT: ORAL PRESENTATION**   When you have worked out your position and your argument for it at the length prescribed in Writing Assignment 13.3 or by your instructor, try condensing it for oral presentation. Reduce it to a set of notes from which to speak publicly. Try your speech before a mirror or, better yet, a video camera.

NOTES

[1] It is most impressive to see someone present a good argument without any apparent "script" to follow. But we should be clear that in nearly every case, this ability to think critically "on your feet," so to speak, results from the same sort of sustained investment of effort that goes into a well-developed argumentative essay.

[2] Ben Bagdikian, "Lords of the Global Village," *The Nation,* June 12, 1989.

[3] This list is derived from a web page developed by reference librarians at Santa Rosa Junior College.

[4] We recommend Michael Harvey's *The Nuts and Bolts of College Writing* (Chicago: Hackett Publishing, 2003), and the associated website at www.nutsandboltsguide.com.

[5] From Roy Bhaskar, *Plato etc.: The Problems of Philosophy and Their Resolution* (London: Verso, 1994).

[6] See V. A. Howard and J. H. Barton, *Thinking on Paper* (New York: William Morrow, 1986).

A P P E N D I X

ANSWERS & HINTS
FOR SELECTED
EXERCISES

THOUGHT EXPERIMENT 1.6: A CRITICAL THINKING KOAN

We'd keep it. Why? Well, suppose that all *other* false or dubious beliefs have been weeded out. Wouldn't that make it *false* that some of my beliefs are not true? OK. Suppose it does. But then that would mean that I still have one belief which is not true, namely *this one*, which would make it **true**. Nice safe belief.

REVIEW EXERCISE 1.6: ISSUE ANALYSIS III

1. What is "hate speech?" 2. Should the service provider or the government be responsible for the enforcement of regulations prohibiting hate speech over the Internet? 3. Should there be a law against hate speech on the Internet? 4. What kinds of penalties should be imposed on people who post hate speech on the Internet?

REVIEW EXERCISE 2.2: FUNCTIONS OF LANGUAGE

1. Informative; 2. Directive; 3. Persuasive; 4. Expressive; 5. Directive; Expressive; Directive; 7. Persuasive; 8. Informative; 9. Informative and Persuasive.

REVIEW EXERCISE 2.5: ESSENTIAL DEFINITIONS V

1. Too broad; 2. Too narrow; 3. Unclear/figurative; 4. Circular; 5. Too broad; 6. Circular; 7. Both too broad and too narrow; 8. Correct; 9. Humorous (figurative)

REVIEW EXERCISE 3.1: ARGUMENT IDENTIFICATION

1. Explanation (why Leonard Cohen became a poet); 2. Other (a joke); 3. Other (a simple unsupported claim); 4. A long descriptive list containing an explanation; 5. Argument; 6. Argument; 7. Other (a joke); 8. Argument.

REVIEW EXERCISE 3.6: ARGUMENT ANALYSIS/UNSTATED CONCLUSIONS

1. You may not stay in the country; 2. God is benevolent; 3. The battery in the remote control is dead; 4. Orangutans suckle their young; 5. Software contains mistakes; 6. Internet censorship legislation is useless.

REVIEW EXERCISE 3.7: ARGUMENT ANALYSIS/HIDDEN INFERENTIAL ASSUMPTIONS

1. Fox network news is propaganda; 2. UCLA will be Pac 10 champion; 3. The Internet has commercial potential; 4. All fads fade.

REVIEW EXERCISE 4.5: DOES IT FOLLOW?

1. Does not follow; 2. Does not follow; 3. Does not follow; 4. Does not follow; 5. Follows; 6. Follows; 7. Does not follow; 8. Does not follow; 9. Does not follow; 10. Follows; 11. Does not follow; 12. Does not follow.

REVIEW EXERCISE 4.6: COMPLETING THE ARGUMENT

1. God has all the virtues. And *benevolence* is one of the *virtues*. So God must have benevolence; 2. Abortion involves the taking of a human life. And that's *homicide*, and you would *never* encourage homicide, would you?. So, abortion should not ever be encouraged; 3. Prisons do not rehabilitate anyone. No criminal penalty that *fails* to rehabilitate can be *effective*. That's *why* prisons are ineffective as punishment for criminal behavior; 4. The United States must become energy-independent. *Unless* we develop solar energy on a widespread basis, our survival *depends* on increasingly scarce petrochemical energy. That's why the United States should *develop* solar energy on a widespread basis.

REVIEW EXERCISE 4.8: RECONSTRUCTING MISSING PREMISES

1. The Internet has commercial potential; 2. All golfers carry clubs; 3. Any bill that originates unconstitutionally should not be made law; 4. An increase in the rate of crime following the abolition of a punishment is evidence that the punishment is a deterrent; 5. Morals enter only into the real world; 6. Adding something to a great Canadian whisky would dilute it; 7. Your computer program has more than ten lines; 8. If astrology were a reliable predictive system, people born at exactly the same time would not have vastly different life histories and personalities; 9. No irreversible penalty is acceptable as a form of punishment in a fallible system of justice.

REVIEW EXERCISE 6.1: DEDUCTIVE/INDUCTIVE

1. Deductive; 2. Inductive; 3. Inductive; 4. Inductive.

REVIEW EXERCISE 6.2: DEDUCTIVE VALIDITY

1. True; 2. True; 3. False; 4. True; 5. False.

REVIEW EXERCISE 6.3: TESTING FOR DEDUCTIVE VALIDITY

1. Valid (unstated premise, true by definition: Anything that is perfect is good); 2. Invalid; 3. Invalid; 4. Valid; 5. Valid; 6. Invalid.

REVIEW EXERCISE 6.6: TRANSLATING CATEGORICAL STATEMENTS INTO STANDARD FORM

1. All C are S; 2. Some B are F; 3. All M are C; 4. Some M are R; 5. All D are R; 6. Some A are N; 7. Some A are L; 8. All S are C; 9. All F are G; 10. All D are L.

REVIEW EXERCISE 6.7: IMMEDIATE INFERENCES

1. Some U.S. Treasury bonds are safe investments; 2. Some U.S. Treasury bonds are not safe investments; 3. No valid immediate inference; 4. No valid immediate inference.

REVIEW EXERCISE 6.8: STANDARD FORM

1. All humans are mortals; all Americans are humans; therefore, all Americans are mortals; 2. All men are human; all women are human; therefore all women are men; 3. Some mysteries are entertaining; some books are mysteries; therefore some books are entertaining.

REVIEW EXERCISE 6.10: INVALID SYLLOGISMS I

1. Undistributed middle term; 2 Undistributed middle term; 3. Two negative premises, and an affirmative conclusion.

REVIEW EXERCISE 7.1: TRANSLATING INTO TRUTH FUNCTIONAL LOGICAL FORMAT

1. V v ~R; 2. R v H; 3. L & ~H; 4. G & W; 5. M ⊃ P; 6. K ⊃ H; 7. H ⊃ K; 8. ~K ⊃ ~H.

REVIEW EXERCISE 7.4: IDENTIFYING LOGICAL STRUCTURE

1. Modus ponens; 2. Modus tollens; 3. Modus ponens; 4. Hypothetical syllogism; 5. Hypothetical syllogism; 6. Disjunctive syllogism; 7. Dilemma.

REVIEW EXERCISE 10.1: FIND THE TAUTOLOGY

1. Constructive dilemma; 2. Premise #1 is a tautology.

REVIEW EXERCISE 10.2: NECESSARY TRUTHS

1. True by definition; 2. Contradiction in terms; 3. Tautology; 4. Formal contradiction; 5. Contingent; 6. Contingent; 7. Contingent; 8. True by definition; 9. Contradiction in terms; 10. True by definition; 11. Contingent; 12. Contingent (but self-referentially tautologous); 13. Contingent (but self-referentially contradictory); the last 3 make interesting discussion topics for you to talk over amongst yourselves!

APPLICATION EXERCISE 11.8: EUPHEMISMS

A "pacification center" = a concentration camp; A "protective reaction strike" = a bombing raid; "Incontinent ordnance" = off-target bombs; "Friendly fire" = bombing or shooting someone on your side; "Force packages" = bombs; "Strategic withdrawal" = retreat; "To gather intelligence" = to spy; "Terminate" = kill; "Degrade the target" = destroy by bombing; "Collateral damage" = civilian casualties caused by our side; "Extraordinary rendition" = kidnapping and torture.

APPLICATION EXERCISE 13.2: SEARCH ENGINE OPTIMIZATION

Hint: Try searching under "Search Engine Optimization."

INDEX

Absurdity, refutation by reducing to, 296–297
Abuse of vagueness, 313–317
Ad hominem, informal fallacy of, 331–332
Ad ignorantiam, informal fallacy of, 362–363
Advertising, 311–312, 315–317, 376
  vagueness in, 315–317
Affirming the consequent, fallacy of, 207–208, 219
Agreement, Mill's method of, 270–271
Allen, Woody, 355, 378n
Ambiguity, 34, 56, 308–313
  fallacies of, 308–313
  in language, 56
  semantic, 139, 310
  signal words and, 92, 162
  syntactic, 310–311
Amphibole, 139, 310–311
Analogy, 160, 169–173, 236–248, 361–362
  argument by, 238–248, 361–362
  evaluating arguments by, 239, 241–248, 319
  faulty, informal fallacy of, 361–362
  formal, 169–173, 248
  questionable, informal fallacy of, 361–362
  refutation by, 247–248
Analysis
  argument, 86, 88, 90–98, 105–130
  issue, 34–40, 383
Anger, informal fallacy of appeal to, 338
Appeals, emotional, 337–340
  irrelevant, 324–340
Aquinas, Thomas, 89, 394
Archimedes, 255
Argument, 17, 27, 85–98, 105–130, 140–148, 159–160, 163–165, 206–216, 361–362, 393–395

by analogy, 238–248, 361–362
analysis, 86, 88, 90–98, 105–130, 159
casting, 111–116
defined, 85–86
design, 85, 393–395
evaluation, 85, 88, 105–106, 117, 159–160
form, 163–165, 206–216
good, 381, 383
identification, 85, 87–89, 106, 159
paraphrasing, 107, 140–148
premises, 90, 94, 108–110
Aristotle, 81n, 173, 194, 343
Artificial intelligence, 140
Ashcroft, John, 143–146
Assumption, 6, 16, 21, 26–29, 40, 117, 123, 305–307, 358
  defined, 27
  fallacious, 305–307, 358
  hidden, 28, 135n
  inferential, 29, 97–98, 135n, 306
  unexamined, 26–28, 117, 123
Astrology, 364
Authority, 22–23, 342–345
  defined, 22
  fallacious appeals to, 342–345
  intimidation by, 22
  invincible, 343
  irrelevant, 344
  unidentified, 343–344
  reliability of, 23
Ayer, Alfred J., 242–245, 255n

Bagdikian, Ben, 386–387, 401n
Base line, bad, informal fallacy of, 360
Begging the question, informal fallacy of, 306–307
Belief, 6, 17, 19–23, 50
Bentham, Jeremy, 303, 352n
bin Laden, Osama, 26
Bloom, Benjamin, 70

Page numbers followed by "n" indicate a citation in the "Notes" section at the end of a chapter.